In Her Mother's House

CRITICAL PERSPECTIVES
ON ASIAN PACIFIC AMERICANS SERIES

Critical Perspectives on Asian Pacific Americans aims to educate and inform readers regarding the Asian Pacific American experience and critically examines key social, economic, psychological, cultural, and political issues facing Asian Pacific Americans. The series presents books that are theoretically engaging, comparative, and multidisciplinary, and works that reflect the contemporary concerns that are of critical importance to understanding and empowering Asian Pacific Americans.

Series Titles Include:

Submission Guidelines

Prospective authors of single or co-authored books and editors of anthologies should submit a letter of introduction, the manuscript or a four to ten page proposal, a book outline, and a curriculum vitae. Please send your book manuscript/proposal packet to:

Critical Perspectives on Asian Pacific Americans Series
AltaMira Press
1630 North Main Street, Suite 367
Walnut Creek, CA 94596
(925) 938-7243

In Her Mother's House

The Politics of Asian American Mother-Daughter Writing

WENDY HO

ALTAMIRA
PRESS

A Division of Rowman & Littlefield Publishers, Inc.

Walnut Creek • Oxford

For information address:

AltaMira Press
A Division of Rowman & Littlefield Publishers, Inc.
1630 North Main Street, Suite 367
Walnut Creek, California 94596
www.altamirapress.com

Rowman & Littlefield Publishers, Inc.
12 Hid's Copse Road
Cumnor Hill
Oxford OX2 9JJ England

Printed in the United States of America

Library of Congress Cataloging-in-Publication Data
Ho, Wendy.
In her mother's house: the politics of Asian American mother-daughter writing / by Wendy Ho.
p. cm.— (Critical perspectives on Asian Pacific Americans series) Includes index.
  ISBN 0-7425-0336-4 (cloth:alk paper)   ISBN 0-7425-0337-2 (pbk:alk. paper)
1. American literature—Asian American authors—History and criticism. 2. Politics and literature—United States—History—20th century. 3. American literature—Women authors—History and criticism. 4. Women and literature—United States—History—20th century. 5. Ng, Fae Myenne, 1956—Criticism and interpretation. 6. Kingston, Maxine Hong—Criticism and interpretation. 7. Tan, Amy—Criticism and interpretation. 8. Mothers and daughters in literature. 9. Asian American women in literature. 10. Asian Americans in literature. I. Title. II. Series.

PS153.A84 H6   1999   99-6245
813'.54099287—dc21   CIP

The paper used in this publication meets the minimum requirements of American National Standard for Information Sciences–Permanence of Paper for Printed Library Materials, ANSI/NISO z39.48-1992

_____

Permissions

Yamada, Mitsuye, *Camp Notes and Other Writings*, copyright 1976, 1980, 1986, 1988, 1992 by Mitsuye Yamada. Reprinted by permission of Rutgers University Press.

Excerpt from "Little Gidding" in *Four Quartets* by T. S. Eliot, copyright 1943 by T. S. Eliot and renewed 1971 by Esme Valerie Eliot, reprinted by Harcourt, Inc.

Excerpt from "Four Quartets" in *Collected Poems 1909–1962* by T. S. Eliot, copyright 1963, reprinted by Faber and Faber Ltd.

_____

Production and Editorial Services: Pattie Rechtman
Cover Design: Raymond Cogan   Cover Photo: Jeffrey Ho

In deepest gratitude to my loving family,
especially to Popo and my Mother

. . . and for the newest branch of our fierce tree of life,
Julia Marguerite Sanchez Ho

CONTENTS

7

ACKNOWLEDGMENTS

A heartfelt debt to my parents, brothers (Greg, Jeff, Brian, and Terry), and sister (Marianne) for their graceful and empowering practices of love and generosity. I thank my friends of longstanding who have sustained me through the roller-coaster stages of writing this book: Peggy Choy, Christine Hacskaylo, Becky and Joe Hogan, Mimi Kim, May King, Jan Miyasaki, Andrea Musher, Sharon Nichols, J. Winston Nunes, James Riggs, Michael Thornton, Alice Thurau, and Peter Weiss. I am fortunate to have a community of colleagues, students, and staff, especially those affiliated with Asian American Studies and Women and Gender Studies, at the University of California, Davis; they continue to provide me a warm social space and intellectual community in which to grow as an activist scholar, teacher, and person. To Judith Newton, gentle needlewoman, and Suad Joseph, much gratitude for your patience, advice, and care. I thank Angela Cheer, Angie Chabram-Dernersesian, Susan Kaiser, Beatriz Pesquera, Betsy Draine, Amy Ling, Stanley Sue, Roy Doi, Peter and Eileen Leung, Keith Osajima, Vicki Ruiz, and Valerie Matsumoto for their strong and continued support of my work. To Jeff Escoffier, Wendy Winslow, and Ronald Cotterel, thank you for your wise care in specific times of need. Much gratitude to my colleague Kent Ono, who has made life in academia a lot more hopeful through many hours of conversation, friendship, and shared struggle. To John H. Stanfield II, a friend and companion of the intellect, heart and spirit, much gratitude and love.

I wish to acknowledge the Davis Humanities Institute for a fellowship, which gave me quiet time to work on this book in its earlier stages. I thank David Peck and John Maitino as well as the Association for Asian American Studies for providing me opportunities to articulate ideas in writing and at conferences that were fruitful in the making of this book. I also thank my former graduate researcher Laura Konigsberg for her fine work in organizing bilbiographic materials and the library staff at Shields Library for research assistance. Finally, much appreciation to my publisher Mitch Allen, editor Jennifer Collier, copyeditor Pattie Rechtman, and the friendly and efficient staff at AltaMira for believing in my ideas and vision for this book.

I

Beneath the Pirie Mango Tree: The Self Talking-Story about Mothers and Daughters

> My child
> Write this
> There take your pen
> There write it
> Say that I am not going back
> I am staying here
> Mitsuye Yamada, "I Learned to Sew" from
> Desert Run: Poems and Stories

> Family exists only because somebody has a story,
> and knowing the story connects us to a history.
> Leila Fu, from Fae Myenne Ng, Bone

The Thoughts of the Heart

I imagine myself sitting outside under the dark leafy canopy of the Pirie mango tree in the backyard of my family home in Honolulu, O'ahu. This was my custom as a child, especially when I wanted to be alone to ramble quietly through my own private girl-world. In the early evenings, just before dinner, I would sit in its branches and scan the glittering lights of the city below and the vast sandy shoreline of the salty Pacific—all of it illuminated by the breathtaking expanse of purple-orange skies. In these memories, the world seems radiant with possibility. The mango tree is my mother's favorite—a gift, she says, from a woman friend whom she has known since girlhood. With the passing of time, this strongly rooted tree has become more than a tree to my mother and me; her memories speak of female friendships and loves that have weathered the seasons of sun, wind, and rain. I can see the snaking feeder roots below, intertwining red earth and ancient tree. The creamy mango blossoms flutter high above the rooftop, near my mother's bedroom window, fragile and fragrant—refreshing—in the warm evening air.

On very windy days of summer, the garden grass is littered with tiny green mangoes, reminders of desire and regret in what-could-have-been. The surviving mangoes ripen slowly and sparingly; they tease us with delicious anticipation throughout the tropical season. When they are ready to be eaten, they are a rose-freckled yellow and full of the taste and smell of rarest perfume—not like the stringy common green mangoes that grow wild along the mountainsides and highways. I see Mom, Popo and myself—three young Amazon girls—hunting for the ripe treasures peeking among the green-ribbed leaves with our makeshift bamboo pole pickers. When they plop! heavy into the canvas pouch at the end of the flexing bamboo pole, there is deep contentment in the sweet fruit of our harvest. Even the juicy yellow-orange pulp that clings fiercely to the fleshy heart of the mango will be savored after the evening meal. In truth, we enjoy each other's company in all the variable seasons of our backyard garden of fruit—fig, dragon eye, lychee, tangerine, guava, and lime.

The Making of a Women's Talk-story Culture: Homeplaces

My Popo is in her early 90s—almost a century of living daily changes; most of her dearest friends—those she knew in China and those whom she befriended in Honolulu in the early hardscrabble days—are dead. This passing of a way of life has taken a serious toll on her heart and spirit. Now older myself, I think more often about the richness of this early social-historical legacy, especially in the sensual embrace of this talk-story culture that constitutes my first world, the ground on which I stand and which shapes my life.[1]

The African American writer bell hooks discusses the excitement of listening to women's voices in her own childhood: "I can remember watching fascinated as our mother talked with her mother, sisters, and women friends. The intimacy and intensity of their speech—the satisfaction they received from talking to one another, the pleasure, the joy. It was in this world of woman speech, loud talk, angry tongues quick and sharp, tender sweet tongues, touching our world with their words, that I made speech my birthright—and the right to voice, to authorship, a privilege I would not be denied" (hooks 1989, 6).

In a revelatory moment at a reading by Ntozake Shange, Cherríe Moraga re-discovers an earlier language of the heart and emotions in the long-denied and marginalized voice of her "brown mother," a voice she had learned to deny within herself as well in order to pass for an Anglo in mainstream society. "Sitting in the auditorium chair was the first time I had realized to the core of me that for years I had disowned the language I knew best—ignored the words and rhythms that were the closest to me. The sounds of my mother and aunts gossiping—half in English, half in Spanish—while drinking cerveza in the kitchen" (Moraga 1981, 31). Though coming from Chinese American talk-story traditions, I can relate to the social, gendered spaces of women's talk and culture. On my return home, it is no wonder I look forward to the precious remnants of this community in the nightly talk-story jam sessions with my mother and Popo. They continue the vibrant tradition of talk-story in all its imaginative and critical transformations within the dynamics of a community in flux.

Mom, I, and Popo spend hours conversing, like a talking caravan winding its way through the house—in the kitchen preparing meals for the family, in the dining room eating with everyone, in the upstairs bedrooms resting together, in the living room sorting laundry and watching the news, on the lanai caring for Popo, or in the downstairs rooms feeding my sister. The language of our talk-story varies, sometimes in Cantonese; or in a more obscure village dialect that my mother and Popo use to speak to each other more privately (the meanings of which I can guess at); or in the local pidgin English creole of Hawai'i; or in a standard English. It is an eclectic feast of living language, culture, memory, and affiliations that brings us to a more intimate knowledge of each other and our many identities in the diverse communities and daily locations we inhabit.

We catch up on our latest personal and domestic cliffhangers and news about extended family and friends who are dispersed throughout the United States and the world. It is not surprising to hear these stories about people—some of whom I have never met—in Hong Kong, China, Macao, Thailand, Australia, the Philippines, England, and Canada. Sometimes, there is a momentary pause in this animated flow of talk-story to refuel the body and mind with a dim sum lunch at China House at the Ala Moana Shopping Center or Hee Hing's in Kapahulu; or a platter of fried cake noodles and choi sum at Lee Ho Fook restaurant in Chinatown, on River Street at the Chinese Cultural Plaza, where elderly Chinatown men hang out with old friends for a game of cards, mah jong, food, and talk.

On certain light-hearted evenings, when Popo would sew in the basement sewing room or in the bedroom, there would be time for a new cycle of stories—not just stories about families and friends. Amid homemade paper dress patterns, recycled tea and biscuit tins of buttons and multicolored thread, red tomato cushions of needles and pins, scissors, and silver thimbles, Popo's voice would talk-story above the droning buzz of the black Singer sewing machine, keeping us enraptured with children's rhymes and stories about Chinese male and female heroes. Woven in with her seamstress work were retellings of old Hawaiian, Japanese, and Chinese "chickenskin" stories about ghostly white-haired women spotted in the bathroom of the local drive-in (built over a former cemetery no less) or on a dark, winding mountain road over the Pali—Pele the volcano goddess or the Japanese obake or the white snake woman of Chinese legend, all prowling for the company of a distracted or lost human soul. Popo contributed to the text and texture of my young imagination in fashioning not only her stories but also her gorgeous cheongsams. Maxine Hong Kingston reminds us that Fa Mu Lan, the hero, was a weaver of stories and material: "The chant begins with the sound of her shuttle and loom: 'jik jik jik' 'Weave weave weave.' I love it that *texture* and *text* come from the same root" (Lim 1991, 25). Fae Myenne Ng also remembers that the discipline of sewing helped her learn to write (Hunnewell 1993, 9). The prickly language of the sewing world, the "homework" of the garment sweatshops, is intimately stitched into the telling of her mother-daughter stories. It is, in many ways, the bone structure of her cultural text, the "underneath thread of [her] heart" (B 81).[2]

Popo transformed the bleakness of her sewing-woman life with dresses tucked and fitted to the soft curves of a woman's body in the rich textures of satin, silk, damask, velvet, brocade—sometimes hand-embroidered or beaded with intricate flowers or chimerical phoenixes, a royal and public symbol of female power. She was an artist of the Chinese dress. Her silk-satin frog buttons were a final signature of her delicate and attentive creativity. For her artwork, she was often paid a pittance. With the remnants of the beautiful materials, as well as with the homely cottons of her own dresses, she would make fabulous patchwork quilts for all of her grandchildren so that we would sleep and dream in the practical, imaginative embrace of her love and hope.

With my yearly returns home, the photo albums, the shoe boxes and envelopes of old photographs, and dusty canisters of film ritually make their appearance at our family gatherings. They are a catalyst for more participatory talk-story. We gather to recall the names and the related stories of the formal, serious faces of our relatives in the old photographs, to resurrect a word or story, a kinship tie, a locale or smell, an emotion or feeling, an eccentricity, a secret tragedy, desire, or cruelty that after all these years still hauntingly resonates in the family's stories. One looks for signs of affiliation in the faces, for who is standing next to whom, the hierarchy or rank, the setting and objects, the clothes and posture, the date and names and place noted on the back of photo, who took it and why. This must be a gathering or ceremony, a strategic belonging by memory to renew and honor the past, present, and future reciprocal obligations that order and account for our various dispersed selves and very social lives. Through talk-story, a collective politics of memory and desire is negotiated that continually narrates our suffering and healing, especially as they are felt in times of trauma, violence, displacement, and oppression. It is evidently a very significant part of the critical construction and maintenance of identities and cultural memories in my family.

One of my favorite photographs is the sepia passport portrait of Popo as a young woman—just before she left her mother and sisters in China to come to Hawai'i in an arranged marriage. I see a face that looks wistful and solemn, sad almost; it is the face of a delicate girl-turning-woman too abruptly, contemplating the unknown alone. There are pictures of my young dumpling of a mother—the beloved only girl-child—for whom Popo made an embroidered cap with soft dog-furred tufts to protect her and to whom she gave the tiny Chinese bracelets, soft-gold charms, and jade necklace, passed from mother to daughter in each generation. In one photograph, she already has the mischievous look of the tough little tom-girl who as an only child had to fight her own battles among the country kids in Kalihi. In her talk-story, I can still see and hear my mother doing her wild Tarzan calls in the mango trees, affirming a rebellious self she still relishes to this day. It is evident that my mother was no delicate or passive lotus blossom, but a rebel, a risk-taker, in the school of hard knocks. Yet, she has shared some of her private secrets, the fears and vulnerabilities, in a slow smoldering telling over the years.

There are other favorite pictures of my mother as a smiling young woman, leaning against a coconut tree in Hawai'i in her twenties—very much with the pose of a Hollywood actress; jitterbugging on a dance floor with friends; or walking down a street as a stylishly dressed working woman in the late 1940s. I love her confident gait and the seductive tilt of her hat and the black netting over her dark eyes and full red lips. On my mother's days off from her accounting job, we would have lunch in town with her girlfriends, Alma, Becky, or Dot, then walk down Beretania Street to the newsstand to buy a bouquet of tightly budded gardenias so sweetly scented in its ti-leaf wrap, then off to buy a new dress for me.

My mother has her stories to tell about growing up in China and in Hawai'i. She and I have an ongoing conversation about her life—the story is in process. My mother, for example, has happy, carefree memories of a childhood in China as the much loved daughter of both her parents. There were visits to the Chinese fair and to her maternal grandmother's home where she played in the courtyard under the watchful eyes of a household of women. As a young schoolgirl in America, she confronted the isolation and challenge of learning a new language, of negotiating the dilemmas of acculturation and assimilation, of dealing with an immigrant mother who did not speak English and who did not share the same Americanization process she experienced growing up in a new homeland, of the divisive struggles between an immigrant mother and a filial-rebellious daughter stubbornly attempting to carve out breathing spaces while forging a new hybrid identity as a Chinese American woman in Hawai'i—one snapshot at a time.

There is a favorite picture of me in Popo's arms; my mother, Popo's only child, is at our side. I am the first daughter of my mother, born in the United States. Popo, mother, and I are best friends and loyal allies, hard-earned over a lifetime of conversation and commitment to each other: It would, however, be very naive, romantic, and wrong to assume that we do not have fierce personal struggles and disagreements with each other. Certain boundaries are difficult to cross over; others remain adamantly uncrossed.

On certain quiet evenings, we range farther afield, talking stories about the secret angers and sorrows of my mother and Popo's girlhood and early womanhood. Their stories attempt to remember specific people, deaths, war, hunger, dates, brutalities, villages, provinces, ships, immigration buildings, humiliations, homes, trees, bottled curiosities that have never been forgotten. Such traumatic remembering "is never a quiet act of introspection or retrospection. It is a painful re-membering, a putting together of the dismembered past to make sense of the trauma of the present" (Bhabha 1994, 63). Over a lifetime, they trace and retrace a survivor's tracks, the remnants of selves and communities, traveling within and through the vast, and often jarring, disjunctions of time and space, attempting to capture the ever-elusive meaning of it all. Mom and Popo tell me, each in her own haunting silences and volcanic eruptions of emotion, of the fierce desire to tell their stories and of their inability to do so fully. They cannot even agree to the same telling of their shared experiences together. Sometimes, the longings as well as the suffering and satisfactions of their lives are not possible to order or reduce into the bone-dry logic of words and sentences. However, they can sometimes be intuited and felt in the thoughts of the heart. The emotional wounds still fester in the process of telling, repressing and resurrecting profound feelings in nuanced variations.

Popo records the archive of tragedies in our Chinese family and community—of women acquaintances in the Chungshan district whose men left in search of work and better opportunities in Gum san; of the terrible loneliness, courage, and endurance of women left behind; of the young women who made the rough Pacific crossing to join stranger husbands in foreign lands; of lives of backbreaking work within the home and outside as domestic workers, laundry women, factory workers, and sewing women; and of the displacement of individuals and their families in the face of war, poverty, racism, as well as opportunity. Such an archive does not narrate history solely in a formal, objective, or factual manner; rather, it tries to recover the fragments of the everyday marginalized subjects who intimately *inhabit* history, with their bodies and minds, hearts, and spirits.

Popo has had her share of memories in China and the United States: She speaks fondly of a household of women in China; her beloved mother and three sisters occupied the social and emotional center of her life. (Her loved father was a traveling merchant who was away for long periods of time.) She talks of her desire to continue her education, of her excitement in learning to read and write. Her hopes and dreams were cut short despite her pleadings. A "Gold Mountain" man had come to the village to seek a refined, proper Chinese woman to take back to Hawai'i with him. He wanted Popo; the marriage was arranged after much heartbreak in her mother's home.

She tells me of her own long seasick Pacific voyage to Hawai'i as a naive young bride with a worldly husband. She talks of the rage and humiliation of detainment and deportation back to China by the Immigration office in Hawai'i. The Immigration Act of 1924 had just recently prohibited the alien Chinese wives of U.S. citizens from entering United States.[3] Popo and my young mother finally did come to Hawai'i in the early 1930s, but their happiness was short-lived. There were difficult adjustments and sorrows to be negotiated in her married life. She also remembers the trauma of being a young Chinese immigrant mother widowed and alone in an alien country. In her deeply embittered moments, she reveals a history of depression and struggle to endure her daily circumstances, working in pineapple factories and as a sewing woman to support my mother, as well as her own sisters in China.[4] In Kingston's *The Woman Warrior*, Brave Orchid, laundry woman and tomato-picker, tells her daughter that life in America—not China—has made her old and very tired. In Fae Myenne Ng's *Bone*, Dulcie Fu, garment worker, is frightened and angry that her life and hopeful desires and dreams will simply pass under the relentless stamping needle of the sewing machine.

My Popo has certainly gained some hard-earned freedoms as a woman, and gained a supportive network of Chinese friends in the United States—that should not be denied; but the various traumas of her life in the United States do not fully endear this country to her. After all these years, Popo's linguistic, social, cultural, and psychic home is still very much rooted in the China of her young girlhood and womanhood. She still speaks to us in Cantonese, dresses in cheongsams, and keeps to the memories of a Chinese culture and tradition that have sustained her in this country. In her closets are the weathered leather suitcases filled with her favorite childhood books, Buddhist tracts and artifacts, her early calligraphy from school, embroidery samples, pictures, a stringed amulet of old Chinese coins, ivory figurines, silk pillow covers, a wedding garment, sandalwood fans, heirloom jewelry, a photograph of her mother and sisters—the reminders of a happier childhood. The older grandchildren can still haltingly converse with her in the now archaic forms of Cantonese she taught us. We still keep Popo's memories of a place called China as a symbolic geopolitical ancestral homeplace even as we live our lives dispersed throughout other homeplaces.

In Popo's Chinatown

As a young girl, I remember accompanying my Popo to Chinatown almost every week. It was a morning bus adventure to gather the fresh ingredients for our meals in the open-air Oʻahu markets. The city bus slowly meandered through the city gathering pockets of local folk—a lively plenitude of cultures, generations, and languages in the island community. At the Ala Wai and Ala Moana bus hubs, the malihinis boarded, escaping the Waikiki tourist trap for a day visit to the local marketplace. In Chinatown, the locals gathered on sidewalks and at bus stands, park benches, plazas, language and martial arts schools, eateries, theaters and temples, lei stands, pool halls, and grocery stores. In these public spaces, the sounds of island pidgin jostled with other languages as people shopped and bartered in the open market for the freshest seafood, meats, vegetables, fruits, and flowers.

The white plastic buckets at the entrances held glorious bundles of bird of paradise, torch ginger, protaea, heliconia, and red anthuriums. In the refrigerators, white ginger, pikake, tuberose-carnation, and maile leis invited customers with their fragrance, reminding them of celebratory occasions, the graceful markers of local life. Behind the glassed stalls, dangling skewers of Peking duck, roasted chickens, char siu, and crackled roast pork tempted the passersby. Blood-wet pig carcasses dangled blatantly on the hook, ready to be bought and buried in the hot imu for a backyard birthday luau. Ah, kalua pig, laulau, and poi! The early morning Pacific catch of iridescent ulua, ono, ahi, mahimahi, onaga, opakapaka chilled glassy-eyed, as if still stunned by their capture, on beds of cracked ice. Wood crates and half barrels overflowed with choi sum, gai lan, ong choi, black fungus, dried oysters, pickled turnips, boiled peanuts. Bottles of Horlick's malted tablets, jars of preserved plums and packages of sweet milk and jelly candies (boxed with a small toy) were the main attractions for us kids. In the back of the grocery store, amid

Chinese kitchenware and assorted bric-a-brac, fierce Kwan Kungs, gentle-faced Kwan Yins and other spiritual items catered to the more specialized needs of the Chinese shopkeepers and clientele alike.

Popo patronized her favorite old time merchants; she knew where to find the best selection of produce and talk-story. This Chinatown community was a part of her extensive social and global network. As a child, I was lost in the dizzying, sensuous exuberance of sights, sounds, smells, swirls of people. Hand in hand, she guided me through her daily world; it has become a familiar part of my world too. There were visits to the bookstore for newspapers, magazines, and videos from China, Hong Kong and Taiwan; and sometimes, if we had time, we would catch a cheap double feature at a seedy theater located in a Hotel Street alley—squeezed among deteriorating tenements, pool halls, jukebox bars, porno and strip joints, massage parlors, curtained fortune-teller booths, and tattoo parlors. The stench of sour booze and urine mingled with spittle and garbage on wet pavement, and startled the senses as we made our way through the alley world.

In the darkness, Popo and I sat together with other Chinese immigrant families and Chinatown workers, temporarily freed from their monotonous low-paid work in restaurants, laundries, grocery stores, sewing shops, and pineapple and tuna factories; with the old-timers from the bachelor units and tenements a few blocks away; and with a motley assortment of local gang toughs, martial arts buffs, and patrons waiting for the next showing of porno films. Cheap double features were a big hit. The movies would often feature some sad classical Chinese opera drama about a handsome scholar-poet and a woman separated by unrequited or doomed love, a contemporary soap opera or comedy and/or a rousing kung-fu-sorcery movie with Chinese male and/or female heroes fighting the bad guys.

The films created a space to momentarily affiliate with some former world Popo had known as a girl but which no longer existed exactly as she left or remembered it. Popo would patiently explain the movie narrative in Cantonese as the fractured English subtitles whizzed by too quickly for me to read. At times, the movies were in Mandarin, which added a whole other layer of translation dilemmas for my Cantonese-speaking Popo, especially if the stories were not subtitled in Chinese or based on familiar stories she already knew. As a child, I would constantly use my fractured "Chinglish" pidgin to pester Popo for details to help me piece together the fragments of story, at least until the next major plot complication. The movie's storyline was negotiated and renegotiated within the constantly fluctuating conversations on screen and off. When the movie ended, the sticky floors of the theatre were sure to snap-smack us back into the late afternoon realities beyond the dingy red exit door.

If we did not go to the movies, it would be a trip to the noodle factory to select specialized noodles for soup or chow mein. Then we would make our way down the street to the powder-pink Chinese bakery Shung Chong Yuein Ltd. or Lin Fong Confectioners to collect a local assortment of sweets: gin doi, banana mochi rolls, lotus seed cakes and sticky rice wrapped in leaves—these would be the late night snacks that fueled the evening's conversations. I also enjoyed the visits to the Chinese herbalist—not because I was a particularly sickly child: I was more intent on getting the wrapped white li-see packet of plump yellow raisins, a small treat from the doctor. The herbal shop Fook Sau Tong on King and Maunakea streets was the world of physiological charts, pungent medicinal smells, and tiny drawers full of cures stacked to the ceiling. It took me a long while to appreciate how well versed my Popo was in preparing folk remedies; she was a storehouse of information about cures for a wide range of illnesses, both physical and spiritual.[5]

It is no surprise that Popo traveled to Chinatown weekly to renew her contacts with the fragments of her earlier world. In Chinatown, Popo and I would stop off for lunch to visit with her Chinese women friends who were living reminders of her women's culture and community in China—a network of women like Suyuan Woo's Joy Luck club, or Brave Orchid's colleagues at the midwife school, or Dulcie Fu's circle of cooing-consoling sewing women. Popo's group would gather at a friend's restaurant for a bowl of noodles or dim sum and talk-story; and as they chatted I would observe them. Peeking under the table, I could see the once prized but crippled tiny-lily feet of her more elderly friends. The women appeared formal and proper with necklace and earrings of jade, hair buns neatly tucked above the stiffly starched collars of their dark-colored cheongsams. Some of the younger women wore drab-colored slacks and small-print blouses. But they were all exuberant like little girls in each other's company and in their shared confidences and giggles behind cupped hands.

The Cantonese talk could turn boisterous, emphatic, emotional, advisory, sympathetic. The conversation grew hush-hush on more private matters. More than or before the words, they looked at, gestured, and touched each other as if assuring one another of their full embodied attention and their relational commitments and responsibilities. It was evident these women were friends of long standing who understood, analyzed and valued each other's intimate cartographies of experience. Each had weathered diverse experiences of sorrow, alienation, dispersion, and relocation. In telling and retelling their women's stories, they continue to disentangle the layered meanings of their experiences. They share and witness secret suffering and desire in the intimate company of women friends. In these daily social acts, they create supportive, subversive spaces to assert and contest their own sense of their personal and collective memories and experiences.

The Politics of Women's Talk-story Culture

It is difficult to capture the profound meanings of Popo's or my mother's life experiences and traumatized yet resilient histories through such vast and fluctuating expanses of space, time, and context. Moreover, these talk-stories often come by *necessity* with a complicated vocabulary of rupture—heavy sighs, silences, trembling lips, downcast eyes, weeping, and wringing of hands—the "dis-ease" of the great unsaids. To understand this nuanced language of embodied feeling is to develop a level of sensitivity and patience for the details in the developing patterns of love and intimacy that structure intricate relationships and identifications. Yet, the final intelligibility or mastery of these intimate life stories or, for that matter, relationships, seems always tantalizingly out of reach—perhaps as it should be. The desire to continuously tease out intentionality or truth in human experience in these stories is simultaneously incorporated and resisted in the fictional and textual fragments that narrate memory, experience, and the effects of emotional loss and pain.

Such talk-stories cannot be comfortably forced into the traditional categorical straitjackets of linear, coherent, and objective telling or writing. They do not seamlessly rearticulate or reenact the privileged white masculinist capitalist requirements for identity, visibility, material success, and citizenship defined in mythic American ideological formations. These conversational texts are the critical personal and collective stories of Chinese American women like my Popo and mother. They require a nuanced attention to the complex social and emotional dynamics derived at homeplaces and border sites they inhabit and from which they construct their understandings of the world. To understand these multi-dimensional texts, composed of overlapping sedimentary discursive fragments of history, race, ethnicity, culture, class, sexuality, and gender, requires a permeable negotiation among multiple positionings within and beyond the United States. Moreover, these talk-story texts require not just more radically diversified interpretive strategies but also politically and ethically responsible, as opposed to indifferent and impersonal, ones. They require an active attention to the theorizing practices and sites of communities that have been excluded from or marginalized within privileged sites of power in society and history. On a very profound level, they may demand personal and institutional accountability and justice in their traumatized narration of memories and experiences that cannot be legitimated or authorized, cannot be thought, spoken, or acted upon, in the dominant discourses and power distributions in a society.

At the politicized site of my Popo's or her friends' complicated experience of the personal, one can better understand the struggle of Chinese American women to define their own experiences and tell their critical stories from the specific, embodied sites from which they negotiate and define an understanding of the social. They inhabit the material and psychosocial spaces at which to expose the stone-cold heart of dominant institutional practices that have ignored or made normal, comfortable, rationalized sense of their experiences and critical standpoints. The politics emergent from their individual and collective locations can provide ways to rethink masculinist, nationalist, and/or capitalist configurations of the social body politic.

Writing Mother-Daughter Stories: Maxine Hong Kingston, Amy Tan, and Fae Myenne Ng

There are so many questions to ask my mother and Popo. What were their dreams, and those of their foremothers when they were girls? What were their joys and disappointments in life? What secrets did they keep? How did they deal with their families and relationships with men and women? Did they accept or challenge what they had been taught about "true womanhood" or "true motherhood" in a traditional

Chinese society and in an Anglo-American one? What were their strategies or tactics of resistance? How did they manage to survive all these years of being insiders-outsiders in the United States? In what ways did they pass down the multiple cultures and traditions of their mothers and of the China they experienced and which are now a part of my "imagined community"? What do they want us to remember and what do they want us not to know about them, and why? And what might this have to do with self-invention and the erasure or remembrance of historical suffering, violence, or injustice? Do they think we are like and unlike them? Did they fight with their mothers? Did they love them? Did they understand them as women?

And what, then, have been the advantages and the disadvantages of changes—social, economic, cultural, and political—for Chinese American women in their American incarnations? And for myself, the fruit of their expectations, the daughter-writer who attempts to articulate their talk-stories here? What becomes of the remnants of kept memories, identities, and histories across generations and wide expanses of psychosocial and geopolitical space?

These are the intriguing questions that Chinese American daughter-writers—Maxine Hong Kingston, Amy Tan, and Fae Myenne Ng—explore in their women's stories. That is why, as a Chinese American woman remembering my relationship with my own mother and Popo, I find that the mother-daughter stories in Kingston's *The Woman Warrior*, Amy Tan's *The Joy Luck Club*, and Fae Myenne Ng's *Bone* resonate for me. These stories are located in the contemporary struggles of Chinese American women—mothers and daughters—to come to some understanding of each other at the sites they inhabit as women. I am not saying that their stories are exactly my stories, nor am I claiming that these mother-daughter experiences and stories are universal or representative for all Asian American women. None of these writers claims to represent all of Asian American womanhood or culture in their texts—although they are frequently situated in this role by various mainstream and oppositional audiences. But it is a helpful catalyst to critical reflection to consider some of the social, economic, cultural, political, and historical dilemmas these stories represent, dilemmas that do significantly impact on our "real life" concerns as women and our relationships with one another, our families, and communities.

To be sure, what Ramon Saldívar had noted about Cherríe Moraga's standpoint in her mother-daughter stories is applicable to my exploration of mother-daughter relationships and texts as well—as an early caveat against superficial glorification of mother-daughter or women's stories and culture. He notes that Moraga's women's stories were not about romanticizing mother-daughter genealogies as a "sojourn into the motherland of harmony"; rather, her interest was in recovering the "problematical site of ambiguous struggle among sedimented levels of conflicting ideologies of the self." Furthermore, "mother-daughter nurturing, the sisterhood of women, the idealization of an essential Woman should not be regarded as transhistorical concepts that uniformly liberate women from oppression, but as constructions that acquire specific political meanings at different historical moments and under different economic and racial conditions" (Saldívar 1990, 191).

The mothers and daughters in Kingston, Tan, and Ng tell stories of betrayal and complicity within oppressive systems, not just about satisfactions, resistance, and empowerment. They portray the cruelties that women (and men) can inflict on each other and their families; they tell the stories of the social, economic, and historical deformation and exhaustion of women, men, their families, and ethnic communities. They represent the complicated struggles women confront in naming desire, self, and community in ways that better approximate their embodied understanding of experience.

I regret not making the time or effort to understand the stories or contexts of my mother and foremothers with the care and specificity they deserved. I understand Kingston's portrayal of the elderly mother, Brave Orchid, in conversation with her grown-up, gray-haired daughter, who has returned home for a yearly visit. From the distance of time and space, the daughter-narrator sees her mother in another guise—not as a powerful dragon-doctor-shaman—but as a "sad bear" of a mother, who has lived a hard existence in the barbarian lands of the United States. Amy Tan remembers her mother continually telling her, "I think you know only [a] little percentage of me" (Pearlman and Henderson 1990, 19). Once, when Tan thought her mother was dying, she began to think seriously about how her life intersected with her mother's life as a Chinese immigrant woman. One Joy Luck daughter, Waverly Jong, risks stepping out of childish stereotypes in order to see her mother anew. Now as a grown woman, Waverly finally looks over her self-erected psychological barriers and sees not an enemy chess-queen of a mother but a tired old woman "getting a little crabby as she waited patiently for her daughter to invite her in" (JLC 184).[6]

In Fae Myenne's Ng's Bone, the three daughters, Leila, Ona, and Nina spend a lifetime negotiating their difficult relationships with immigrant parents, Dulcie Fu and Leon Leong, who have endured lives of punishing work, failure, psychic trauma, and social humiliation in the United States. Each of these Chinese American daughters—in her own way and degree—attempts to escape (and not escape) the difficult familial responsibilities and stories that haunt their lives and bind them to their parents and San Francisco Chinatown. Given opportunities their parents did not have, the daughters attempt to live individual lives while maintaining links with family and community. The back and forth social and cultural border crossings of these women are hard-earned commitments to each other, and to their families' and ethnic community's history of struggle and resistance against various forms of injustice and destruction.

While recovering their mothers' stories, the daughter-writers, to varying degrees, also recover the stories of Chinese American immigrant fathers. The mother-daughter stories and standpoints that Kingston, Tan, and Ng construct are inclusive of the stories of Chinese American men. They recuperate the homeplace as a heroic and political site for work not only by women but by men as well. They seek to recover the stories of those Chinese American immigrant fathers who, in their own ways, cared for their families while confronting the daily anger, frustrations, and degradations of racism and sexism. The fathers, represented in the daughter-writers' cultural texts, come to understand the importance of the social and affective work within domestic-familial spaces as part of a conception of responsible and meaningful manhood. These writers construct and root these imaginative narratives of men and women, self and family, within the daily negotiations of psychosocial and cultural life that are intimately intertwined with the turbulent history of global migrations and its relations to inequitable political and economic systems.

Through these writers' various narratives of a self-in-process, the Chinese American mothers and daughters learn to name and to compassionately understand their differences as well as similarities as women and to gradually extend this critical political practice to an understanding of men, family, and community. It can therefore be empowering and heroic for women to tell their diverse stories and attend to one another. In this way, women engage and challenge the institutions in society that would define, exploit, deny, or isolate their experiences and standpoints. As bell hooks has powerfully stated, talking back is an oppositional stance, a way of speaking up for oneself as a woman, boldly and defiantly. It is "not solely an expression of creative power; it is an act of resistance, a political gesture that challenges politics of domination that would render us nameless and voiceless. As such it is a courageous act—as such, it represents a threat. To those who wield oppressive power, that which is threatening must necessarily be wiped out, annihilated, silenced" (hooks 1994, 8).

Engaging Those Who Would Name Us or Render Us Nameless and Voiceless

In telling mother-daughter stories, I believe that Maxine Hong Kingston, Amy Tan, and Fae Myenne Ng continue to challenge the politics of domination from multiple discursive communities and institutions—in other words, challenging that which makes difficult the building of political solidarities within and among diverse racial-ethnic groups, classes, genders, sexualities (chaps. 5–7). In the following three chapters, I situate these writers and their cultural texts within three interrelated social-political communities that attempt, consciously and unconsciously, to erase, appropriate or trivialize their mother-daughter stories; and examine how these three writers, in their mother-daughter narratives, vibrantly engage and challenge such perspectives.

The first of these "communities" comprises feminist discourses, which suppress the specificities of Asian American women's social realities, especially in their white middle-class and Western-based representations of "woman," and in their recovery and reception of mother-daughter relations and texts. Chapter 2 explores in particular Kingston's and Tan's work in this context.

The second takes the form of dominant Eurocentric historical and cultural discourses and representations of the Chinese, which led to exclusionary immigration policies and prohibitions well into the twentieth century. These representations denied not only Chinese American men their histories, but even more so denied Chinese American women's substantial struggles and contributions to the making of family, community, and history (chap. 3).

Finally, Asian American cultural nationalist discourses, which, though continually critiqued, are still persuasive or resonant with certain Asian American constituencies and within cultural politics circles. I discuss some of the important issues that emerged in the 1960s and 1970s, which specifically engaged not only white feminism but also racist characterizations of Asian Americans in popular and academic representations. Though many writers have critiqued this cultural nationalist discourse as racialized, sexualized, and gendered, as articulated by Frank Chin and his coeditors in the classic Asian American literary anthologies, *Aiiieeeee!* (Chin et al. [1974] 1991d) and *Big Aiiieeeee!* (Chan et al., 1991), I wish to explore how cultural nationalist concerns impact on the mother-daughter texts, especially of those of Kingston and Tan (chaps. 2, 4).

Cultural nationalist discourses, like their mainstream counterparts, struggle to exert cultural power and hegemony over their subjects. At certain crucial junctures, the formation of racial-ethnic nationalist identities became strongly gendered and sexualized; more specifically, they developed powerful and ultimately problematic masculinist associations (see Kim 1998). As we will see, such cultural nationalist discourses can codify rigid and restricted identifications, which negate or dismiss significant oppositional—and perhaps more emancipatory—discourses and practices from serious consideration on the part of even those who identify as Asian Americans.

Kaimuki Homegirl: Moral Accountability and the Seductions of Becoming a "Gentleman"

As a daughter-writer and scholar, I wonder how the experiences of Chinese mothers and daughters in the United States could ever be illuminated by writing a formal, abstract critical text, especially inside mainstream academic institutions. Such institutions are often embedded in Eurocentric and masculinist paradigms that have historically devalued and alienated our experiences. Under such circumstances, how does one maintain identities and fluencies in a Chinese American women's talk-story culture, derived from a homeplace outside these institutions?

I find myself asking how and where does one situate oneself, especially as an outsider-insider in relation to these often conflicting sites of production and resistance? How does one write about these vibrant differences or rich experiences and histories, which are rooted in a fluid, social and dialogical talk-story tradition? Does one use the language of its experience, Cantonese, the language of my Popo and mother? Or local island pidgin, the language of a lifetime together in Hawai'i? Is the public language of the adopted country, standard English, the appropriate choice? And more profoundly, I wonder too if there is language enough in any of these to resurrect their stories or feelings through such an expanse of space and time, of destruction and coercive forgetting. What about the untranslatable ruptures and fragments—the unknowable—that fail to cross the borderlands of these social or cultural systems or languages?

As a scholar of color, it is not an easy task to move between and across economic, cultural, and intellectual borders and resituate oneself within elitist institutions—

institutions that often seek to reproduce and reward socialization into dominant models of scholarly life. Lani Guinier, the Black female law professor and author, remembers her educational training at Yale into becoming a "gentleman" (Guinier 1997, 73). This is the honorific term that her white male Yale professor applied to both his male and female law students; it referred to those who

> shared a certain civilized view of the world and who exhibited a similarly civilized demeanor. If we were not already, law school would certainly teach us how to be *gentlemen*. Gentlemen of the bar maintain distance from their clients, are capable of arguing both sides of any issue, and, while situated in a white male perspective, are ignorant of differences of culture, gender and race. That lesson was at the heart of becoming a professional. . . . It evoked the traditional values of legal education to train detached, neutral problem solvers. It anticipated the perception, if not the reality, of all of us becoming *gentlemen*. (ibid.)

This was, as Guinier realized, an elite white male academic training ground into the loss of her voice and visibility; it was a training into the absence or amnesia of a self and community as a Black woman. In "La Güera," Cherríe Moraga talks about years of "anglocized" education, which seemed to promise that she would more effectively be allowed to pass into the white world by denying her Chicana mother and an integral part of herself. "If I got educated enough, there would never *be any telling*" [italics mine] (1981, 31). The institutions of white privilege, power, and identity are profoundly constituted on the continuing invisibility, silencing, and exclusion of women of color—except, of course, as not quite white "gentlemen."

More broadly, many scholars of color become the "one-of-a-kind" exotics—isolated, monitored, and ill-funded in the diversity display of the Western academic zoo (see, for example, Wing 1997, 69–122); the *gentlemanly* ones are especially valued, tolerated, and exhibited as window-dressing for a comfortable "civilized" form of "multiculturalism" (see Hage 1993). Despite the rhetoric and display, many academic establishments remain, in their deep foundational paradigms, racist and sexist locations that do not like challenge to their power and privilege. Such elite institutions exist mainly to oversee and encourage the reproduction of privileged forms of knowledge that, in turn, validate dominant social identity formations and institutions of the capitalist nation-state. It is important to be skeptical of such institutional knowledge production, which subordinates the voices and standpoints of the disenfranchised. At such sites, radical scholar-activists of color, who come with diverse experiences, theorizing practices, and moral commitments to their oppressed communities, risk struggle to resist duplicating these dehumanizing forms of knowledge and socially and emotionally brutalizing sites of alienation, containment, and injustice.

For me, thinking, remembering, writing, speaking, and professing are difficult, painful tasks in these ambiguous and problematic environments. They are never free of risk or qualification, of complicity, violation, and loss. They necessitate continual cultural and political negotiation and contestation against the traumatic forgetting that denies the self in order to maintain visiblity or validity in privileged hegemonic institutions. To remain grounded and affiliated with my central, personal, intimately known reference points is a complex form of criss-crossing that seeks to transform the exclusionary academic spaces I inhabit as an activist scholar and teacher.

"What We Hold in Our Hearts is What Matters. . ."

After the academic year comes to a close—the papers graded, the committee work completed, and the lectures filed neatly in folders—I look forward to my return to family and to my home in the islands. It is another world, another rhythm, another language and identity. I hope that the heart work of this primary homeplace, amid the women of my family, will keep me honest and morally accountable wherever I might be, and nourish my life and vision in all their forms. My Popo and mother guide my process of writing and theorizing talk-story, in the threading and suturing of my eclectic quilt of narrative, language, images, and collective political vision. I am a prodigal-faithful daughter, who promises to resurrect the remnants of their often untold stories of continued struggle, resistance, and transformation; who promises never to forget them.

As they continue to speak themselves into my life, I see the women of my family as strong and complex, not as simple passive victims to be pitied or exotics to be "othered" as I had often been taught. They are women of multiple worlds, like Brave Orchid and the Joy Luck mothers and Dulcie Fu, who survive and resist as best as they can, given their individual strengths and weaknesses; given their difficult and contradictory positions and circumstances.

Gloria Anzaldúa refers to the border crossers who negotiate new identities and practices between and within ambiguous cultural and geopolitical borders; that is, the borders that are "physically present wherever two or more cultures edge each other, where people of different races occupy the same territory, where under, lower, middle, and upper classes touch, where the space between two individuals shrinks with intimacy" (Anzaldúa 1987, preface). As well, Anzaldúa notes that individuals must also struggle with the psychic, sexual, and spiritual borders derived from living and working within these borderlands. Through such struggles and commitments, Chinese women like my Popo and mother were able to endure by rooting themselves and bearing fruit in inhospitable soil. In return, they hope that their daughters would love and cherish them for their rich and complex work and love.

I have learned to listen more attentively to their stories. At the same time, I am exploring my own complex positions in examining Chinese American mother-daughter stories, to name the discourses and struggles that are mine and that continually remind me of my not always harmonious or stable frames of reference. As part of a new practice of talking about mother-daughter stories, I use autobiographical writing as one critical tool to ground my "narrative of self" or my "narrative of struggle" (hooks 1991). "Subjective, engaged, personal, anecdotal, testimonial, narrative, mixed genre—these are but some of the terms used to designate a form of writing at the crossroads of autobiography and criticism, a form that works against the premise of more putatively objective, impersonal, legalistic, abstract kinds of critical practice" (Henderson 1995, 13). I do this not in order to privilege my own position and create a narcissistic metanarrative, but as a way to interact with the reader and the various mainstream and oppositional discourses I foreground in the chapters of the book. I like the potential in critical "talk-story" theorizing that challenges the more traditional and abstracted academic practices.

The attempt to range beyond my self to connect with another woman's multiple ways of being—starting in my own bountiful backyard—is a difficult, yet liberating, practice.[7] It is one way to actively and creatively engage discourses that have attempted to define Asian American women and men in delimiting and debilitating ways.

It has taken many years to critically absorb the rich legacy and meanings of oral stories and epic life experiences as part of a more comprehensive understanding of history. As Joan Scott (1989) reminds us, history is not just to be defined in terms of war, diplomacy, or high politics—the public spheres most traditionally identified with men. Historians need significantly to examine the diversity of women's experiences that have often been erased or dismissed from privileged social and public discourses and sites. Furthermore, there is a need to attend to the often neglected, invisible histories of subordinated racial-ethnic women as part of a new, more comprehensive understanding of history. In retheorizing history from women's experiences and standpoints, one becomes more sensitive to their contributions not only to formations of individuals, families, and communities, but also to the theorizing of the political and public.

A fluid, open-ended, feminist "politics of location" can suggest a way to become less arrogant, as María Lugones (1990) asserts, and to be more loving and understanding as a woman toward not only other women but also toward men and other peoples. Teresa de Lauretis provides us with a concept of a feminist critical practice with the potential to be part of a liberating politics of location.[8] She locates the specificity of this feminist practice

> not in femininity as a privileged nearness to nature, the body, or the unconscious, an essence which inheres in women but to which males too now lay a claim; not in a female tradition simply understood as private, marginal and yet intact, outside of history but fully there to be discovered and recovered; not, finally, in the chinks and cracks of masculinity, the fissures of male identity or the repressed of phallic discourse; but rather in that political, theoretical, self-analyzing practice by which the relations of the subject in social reality can be rearticulated from the historical experience of women. (de Lauretis 1984, 186)

Thus, talk-story is part of the process of rethinking the fierce heart of the matter, the politics of mother-daughter writing and its potential for radically rethinking the ways we experience our lived realities.

Notes

1. Maxine Hong Kingston says that she writes in the "peasant talk-story Cantonese tradition ('low,' if you will), which is the heritage of Chinese Americans (see chap. 5, n10). In this tradition, stories change in the flux of social-historical circumstances. She alters or reconstructs Chinese myths, legends, folklore. For this reason, Kingston states

that her new stories should not be seamlessly traced back to ancient, scholarly stories derived from a 'high culture' or a purist classic Chinese tradition or past. It is not her intent to simply duplicate or appropriate Chinese myths and legends as Chinese American or Asian American ones" (see Cloutier 1984, 291).

Furthermore, Kingston expands the talk-story definition, especially to include women's experiences and imaginative stories as part of an expanded notion of a community's "story roots." She retells traditional stories and/or invents subversive stories to account for the varying social, economic, cultural, and historical circumstances of Chinese women, families, and communities in the United States.

The talk-story tradition can also be linked to the local oral traditions in Hawai'i. "Talk-story," a pidgin expression, is a social or communal oral exchange in which people gather to "chew the fat" or "shoot the breeze" with friends and family. As Steve Sumida notes, this term was further popularized in a 1978 conference entitled "Talk Story: Our Voices in Literature and Song; Hawai'i's Ethnic American Writers' Conference."

We were already finding by mid-1978 that "talk story" also characterizes much of Hawai'i's contemporary written literature: anecdotes, vignettes, sketches, short fiction, both lyrical and narrative poetry, monodramas filled with central character's reminiscences directly addressed to the audience and entire novels told by a speaker whose genuine voice sounds like someone talking story. For instance, Murayama's Kiyo and Holt's Mark talk story; not only the dictions but the very structures of these works indicate so. (1991, 240)

Kingston lived in Hawai'i in the mid-1960s and 1970s, and had exposure to local writing communities and the local oral traditions of talk-story, a term she used in *The Woman Warrior* (1976) to name the "verbal style and form which the narrator learns from her Cantonese immigrant mother" (Kingston 1977, 240).

Such oral traditions, of course, are not unique to the Chinese or local folk in Hawai'i. There are, for example, very rich and distinct oral traditions in Native American and African American cultures as well. See, for example, Silko (1981, 1986) and Jones (1991).

2. See Ng (1993). All references to this edition will appear in the text with abbreviation B.

3. It was only after Chinese American men and their white allies vigorously protested this situation that Congress amended the Act to allow Chinese women who had already married U.S. citizens before 1924 to come into the country (S. Chan 1991a,106).

4. According to a study of Asian and Pacific Island women's health, Chinese Americans experience depression at an equal or greater level than the general population, and elderly Chinese and Japanese women have the highest suicide rates of all ethnic groups, including whites (APIAHF, Fact Sheet on Mental Health, 1990 qtd. in Luluquisen, Groessl, and Puttkammer: 1995, 25).

5. Besides the ingredients from the herbalist, the nondescript plants that grew in the corners of our yard were her medicinal cabinet. I have had to rethink my normal routine of yanking out the pesky weeds in the backyard. Weeds, as they were named in Western garden guides, needed to be removed immediately since they had no place in traditional garden-lawn aesthetics. But Popo's garden was always stubbornly different, based, as it

was, on another way of constructing the world and its possibilities. She kept all sorts of rangy-weedy plants in a maddening collection of pots and tin cans all over the yard, which seemed to constantly subvert the presumed order of my father's yard.

Popo knew the chants to draw out the poisons, fevers, and evil spirits as well; and she observed a calendar of festival rituals, foods, and days to honor the community of our dead and the special personages of her Buddhist religious tradition and culture. The grapes, oranges, pomelo, and oolong tea would be displayed on the card table on the veranda; the red candles and joss sticks would be lit for the day, long before most of us were awake in my parents' Catholic household.

6. See Tan (1989). All references to this edition (hardback) will appear in the text with abbreviation *JLC*.

7. For prime examples of leaving home—literally and figuratively—in order to review the world in which one lives, see Ang (1994, 1995, and 1996); Anzaldúa (1990a); Bulkin, Pratt, and Smith (1984); Gilroy (1991); and Hoffman (1989).

8. There are a number of exciting critics writing on the politics of location and identity: see, for instance, Alcoff (1988), Alexander and Mohanty (1997), Anzaldúa (1990a), Bhabha (1994), Bromley (1989), Caraway (1991), Chow (1991b and 1993), de Lauretis (1986), Fregoso and Chabram (1990), Giroux (1988), Goldberg (1993 and 1994), Grewal and Kaplan (1994), Hall (1989), hooks (1990), Kosasa-Terry (1991), Lavie and Swedenburg (1996), Lowe (1996a), Mani (1992), Mohanty (1984), Reed (1997), and Thompson and Tyagi (1996).

2

Feminist Recovery and Reception: Chinese American Mother-Daughter Stories

> . . . you would think Daisy Tan is a very shy, quiet woman. But if you would have lunch with her, go shopping with her, you would see her in action; her personality would come out. I mean, it used to embarrass me, how she would fight back. Every Chinese woman that I know is strong like that. Just determined as hell.
>
> Amy Tan, in an interview with Barbara Somogyi and David Stanton

In the 1960s and 1970s, a number of diverse social and counter-culture move-ments were vibrantly engaging multiple, entertwined forms of injustice—the Civil Rights, Black Power, Third World revolutionary and nationalist movements; as well as the anti-Vietnam War, Peace, Free Speech, and Women's movements. Stuart Hall outlines the way in which these movements were often opposed to corporate liberal politics of the West or the "Stalinist" politics of the East, and were wary of all bureaucratic forms of organization. These movements affirmed the "subjective" as well as "objective" dimensions of politics; they favored sponta-neity and acts of political will; they had a powerful cultural emphasis and form (such as the "theatre" of revolution); they reflected the weakening or breakup of class politics and its corresponding alignments with mass political organizations; and they appealed to a social identity of its supporters, often one identity per movement (Hall 1996, 610–11).

This contentious, revolutionary milieu profoundly affected women's under-standing of their own locations in the complex dynamics of gender, sexuality, class, and race in this country and abroad. The Women's Liberation Movement of the

1960s and 70s, the second-wave of the predominantly white U.S. women's move-ment, opened up for activism such arenas as sexuality, family, employment, social welfare, violence against women, and others. It politicized subjectivity ("personal is political"), identity, and the practices of self-identification. It refused reductive binary forms of thinking between inside/outside, subjective/objective, private/public and men/women, and forefronted the formation of new ways of articulating sexual and gendered identities and theorizing practices. Feminism, moreover, challenged the notion that men and women were simply the Same; that is, differences —not just similarities—must be significantly accounted for in history, law, health, education, employment, sports, politics, and other arenas of life.

Asian American women shared and were influenced by these issues and concerns circulating in the mainstream Women's Liberation Movement. But they were comfortable neither with a feminist notion of "sisterhood" based on superficial sentimentality, nor with a gender unity based solely on the experiences and concerns of predominantly middle-class white women. Their interest lay in a politically earned notion of sisterhood that would acknowledge similarities and differences and radically retheorize and critique oppressive institutions, attitudes, and power relations among diverse communities in the United States and abroad.[1] Like other women of color, many did not choose to separate themselves from the struggles of racial-ethnic men; rather, they continued a tradition of working and dialoguing within their subordinated communities.[2] That the Women's Liberation Movement was stereotyped as being anti-male did not sit well with many Asian American women. Many Asian American feminist-activists understood the intimate links between race, ethnicity, class, gender, and sexuality in their daily life, having witnessed the oppression of not only Asian American women but also men—fathers, husbands, sons, brothers, lovers, friends. They deeply understood the destruction and violation within their racial-ethnic communities.

Amid these complex and multiple concerns and affiliations, Asian American women were compelled to situate their theorizing practices at more than one site.[3] In "Letter to Ma," the Asian American feminist Merle Woo talks about her definition of a "Yellow Feminist,"

> being a Yellow Feminist means being a community activist and a humanist. It does not mean "separatism," either by cutting myself off from non-Asians or men. It does not mean retaining the same power structure and substituting women in positions of control held by men. It does mean fighting the whites and the men who abuse us, straight-jacket us and tape our mouths; it means changing the economic class system and psychological forces [sexism, racism, and homophobia] that really hurt all of us. And I do this, not in isolation, but in the community. (Woo 1981, 142)

Audre Lorde (1984) noted that coalition-building requires a multiple issue rather than a single-issue orientation. Women of color feminists understood the importance of a more permeable political and collective front from which to challenge the multiple systems of oppression of their men, families, and communities.

Sexism and gender issues were important to women in the Asian American Movement, who were also deeply invested in the struggles against racism and its vicious links to capitalism, colonialism, and imperialism in the U.S. and abroad. Their concerns were also for the social, economic, and political well-being of their communities, concerns which were not being addressed in mainstream feminist discourses and practices.

> More specifically, Asian American women who are committed to fighting sexism and racism feel that white feminists are not aware of or sympathetic to the differences in concerns and priorities of Asian American women. Although Asian American women share many common issues and concerns with white feminists, many tend to place a higher priority on eradicating racism than sexism. They prefer to join groups that advocate improved conditions for people of their own ethnic background rather than groups oriented toward women's issues only. (Chow 1989, 371)

White women were perceived as exclusionary and racist in their organizations and representations of women of color. Merle Woo tells her exploited, working-class mother why she takes issue with white feminists: "I can give you so many examples of groups which are "feminist" in which women of color were given the usual least important tasks, the shitwork, and given no say in how that group is to be run. Needless to say, those Third World women, like you, dropped out, quit" (Woo 1981, 143, and see duCille 1994 and Quan 1990).

The representations of women of color as "those poor victimized, traditional, backwards women" were, and still are, alienating. Chandra Mohanty discusses the concerns of women of color about the "colonization" of their voices and struggles— by not only the white, Western, imperialist/colonialist hegemony, but also by "hegemonic white women's movements." "This colonization," according to Mohanty, "implies a relation of structural domination, and a suppression—often violent—of the heterogeneity of the subject(s) in question." She critiques feminist work that sees women of color as an "already constituted, coherent group with identical interests and desires, regardless of class, ethnic or racial location or contradictions" (Mohanty 1984, 333; 336–37). There is, for example, a tendency to lump all of us as "Asian women," "Third World women," or "women of color," which denies the significance of our experiences and histories. On the one hand, Mohanty is wary of theoretical and critical perspectives that implicitly represent Anglo American or Western women as "educated, modern, as having control over their own bodies and sexualities, and the freedom to make their own decisions;" while on the other hand, representing the average woman of color as "ignorant, poor, uneducated, tradition-bound, domestic, family-oriented, victimized" (ibid., 337). The binaries privilege the voices and experiences of middle-class white women as the norm. Moreover, Elaine Kim notes that such Western perspectives are often recycled in portrayals of Asia as a feminized landscape of passivity, weakness, and decadence in counterpoint to the West, which is depicted as civilized, rational, strong, moral, and assertive.[4] The diverse specificities, for example, of Chinese, Japanese, Korean, Vietnamese, Hmong, Cambodian, Filipina, and South Asian women—their culture, history, language, and strategies for resistance—are dismissed or made invisible in these stratified binaries.

Contrary to Eurocentric imperialist representations, Chinese and Chinese American women have maintained a level of power in their families as well as in their social, cultural, and political affiliations. For example, Chinese women have a long, complicated history of agitation for women's and human rights through the nineteenth and twentieth centuries in various social, nationalist, and revolutionary movements in China.

Kumari Jayawardena notes that throughout the mid-nineteenth and into the twentieth century "women's struggles [were] an essential component of the political struggle. . . . The remarkable and continuous struggles of Chinese women in the years before 1911, in the uprisings led by Sun Yat-sen against the Manchu government in 1911, and in the revolutionary struggles for liberation from the war-lords, the Japanese aggressors and the right-wing forces of Chiang Kai-shek (from the 1920s to 1949), serve to show that the issue of women's liberation *was an issue of the revolution* and not a side issue to be tacked on after the revolution" (Jayawardena 1986, 194–95). During the Chinese Revolution, women learned to tell their stories at various sites and to find ways to confront and resist multiple forms of inequity: Women learned to speak the bitterness of their daily lives (e.g., Frenier 1984 and Ono 1989). Historians have noted that within early critical consciousness-raising groups in the Chinese countryside and cities, women learned to speak up about the poverty, the hunger, and the physical and psychological abuse and fear in their "indictments of bitterness."[5] In having access to each other's experiences of oppression, women from different backgrounds learned they were not alone, not separated from other women (such as by language, ethnicity, class, geographic regions) or other groups seeking social changes.

Furthermore, progressive Chinese women and men formed alliances to fight against footbinding, concubinage, arranged marriages, and women's illiteracy. They sought practical ways to deal with husbands, arranged marriages, and families, as well as with landlords, factory bosses, and imperialists.[6] They agitated in a variety of social and public forums for women's rights to an education, marriage and divorce reform, paid employment, property rights, and the vote. These struggles, emanating from China and other Asian countries, are a significant part of the complex transnational legacies that have affected the development of Asian American women's social and political activism in the United States. Into the twentieth century Chinese immigrant and American-born women were greatly inspired by the various struggles in China to fight against imperialism, to transform China into a modern nation, and to improve the condition of women.[7] Judy Yung (1990, 205) analyzed one of the oldest Chinese language newspapers in the U.S., *Chung Sai Yat Po* (1900), with special attention to its coverage of women's emancipation in China. In part, through the advocacy of the ethnic press and its readers for change in early twentieth-century China, Chinese American women, especially second-generation women, began to refashion themselves as "new women" who each "sought education for herself and her daughters [and took] advantage of resources in America, to work outside the home, and to participate in community affairs" (ibid., 205).

As we enter the twenty-first century, Asian American historians are continuing their research into the often-neglected lives and histories of Chinese women in the United States. They are forefronting the significance of women's experiences and standpoints among and within diverse racial-ethnic, gender, socioeconomic class, and transnational/diasporic formations. Other historians are recovering and retheorizing how and where women through Chinese history have articulated and enacted practices to exercise agency and power despite ideologies, discourses, and institutions that attempt to limit their activities and life options (see Chow 1991b, Ko 1997, and Mann 1997).

Feminist Recoveries of Mother–Daughter Stories

As part of the recovery of women's social realities, feminists have focused on the primary relationships between mothers and daughters. Adrienne Rich emphasizes the importance of exploring this neglected bond between mother and daughter: "The loss of the daughter to the mother, the mother to the daughter, is the essential female tragedy. We acknowledge Lear (father-daughter split), Hamlet (son and mother), and Oedipus (son and mother) as great embodiments of the human tragedy; but there is no presently enduring recognition of mother-daughter passion and rapture" (Rich 1986b, 237).[8] As Marianne Hirsch states, "there can be no systematic and theoretical study of women in patriarchal culture, there can be no theory of women's oppression, that does not take into account woman's role as a mother of daughters and as a daughter of mothers, that does not study female identity in relation to previous and subsequent generations of women, and that does not study the relationship in the wider context in which it takes place: the emotional, political, economic, and symbolic structure of family and society" (Hirsch 1981a, 202).[9]

The care and education of children, especially daughters, has often been socially and historically assigned to women at domestic-familial sites. In such embodied, immediate, and permeable social spaces, many women construct and situate their understanding of a personal self and its relations to the family, community, and larger society. In naming the domestic-familial site, I am not suggesting that this is the only place from which women can form their critical standpoints. In addition, I do not define the domestic-familial as a restricted site of private, neutral relations or activities, separated from racial-ethnic, economic, social, or political issues in the broader society. In terms of the long history of denying the Chinese access to their families and communities in the U.S. (see chap. 3), this domestic-familial site becomes even more significant to reclaim and retheorize. It reveals a painful and conflicted space for many subordinated racial-ethnic groups who have shared or share similar concerns and histories.

Women writers such as Maxine Hong Kingston, Amy Tan, and Fae Myenne Ng situate their mothers and daughters at domestic-familial sites, which are complicated by race, ethnicity, gender, sexuality, and social-economic issues. In their stories are opportunities to analyze the ways Chinese American mothers and daughters construct and reconstruct their understandings of the conflicted self in relation to multiple homeplaces and borderlands. These experiences of women may suggest different and potentially oppositional practices and standpoints to those constructed within hegemonic social, cultural, historical, and political understandings of the U.S. nation-state. In a patriarchal-capitalist labor economy, constituted upon profit, labor, efficiency, governmental/bureaucratic control, and commodity consumption, writers like Kingston, Tan, and Ng suggest ways of organizing and enacting social and emotional relations that may counter those constituted within such an economy.

Early U.S. feminist literature and theorizing was significantly focused on examining the experiences and dilemmas of white, middle-class mothers and daughters oppressed in a white male patriarchal system. Gloria Wade-Gayles comments on Adrienne Rich's discussion of the mother-daughter relationship in *Of Woman Born:* According to white female interpretations of motherhood, "mothers and daughters are estranged by patriarchal norms for female behavior and self identity." The "good" mother in a patriarchal society teaches her daughter to conform "to female stereotypes such as passivity, spirituality, or irrationality" (Wade-Gayles 1984, 11). In her recent review of the literature on mothering, Alice Adams notes that women, whether feminist or not, have also duplicated similar discourses on mothering, which suggest that the primary task of the "prototypical [white] middle class daughter" is to separate from mother, who is perceived as the "key pathogen" in her daughter's life, the primary psychological source of her anger and emotional pain (Adams 1995, 414–15). From such a perspective, "the choice that daughters seemed to face was either to reject Mom or to replicate what was identified as her limited identity as homemaker, her economic dependence on men, her annoying and fruitless attempts to live through her children, her years of thankless, stultifying service as wife and mother, and especially her lack of a sense of individual self-worth, the result of her oppression" (ibid.).

Bonnie Thornton Dill describes the positioning of white women within a social, economic and legal system based on patriarchal familial and state authority during the eighteenth and nineteenth centuries in America:

> The society was structured to confine white wives to reproductive labor within the domestic sphere. At the same time the formation, preservation and protection of families among white settlers was seen as crucial to the growth and development of American society. Building, maintaining, and supporting families was a concern of the State and of those organizations that prefigured the State. Thus while women had few legal rights as women, they were protected through public forms of patriarchy that acknowledged and supported their family roles of wives, mothers, and daughters because they were vital for building American society (Dill 1988, 415–16).

In contrast, subordinated racial-ethnics, according to Dill, were often brought here as an exploitable labor force to work within a white capitalist economy (see ch. 3). They were often perceived as inhuman, as commodities to be exchanged and exploited, enslaved, and indentured. There was little regard for their families and the welfare of their communities; their families were not constituted to survive or to gain significant access to the power networks of mainstream white society. Out of such histories of injustice and oppression, women of color foregrounded issues important to their racial-ethnic families and communities, issues that were not centrally addressed in mainstream feminist or women's discussions.[10]

Wade-Gayles believes that Black women have not been treated as "fragile figurines on pedestals white feminists seek to dismantle" (1984, 12). Because of multiple inequities in U.S. society which affected their personal lives, Black women taught their daughters "to be independent, strong and self-confident" very early in their lives. In fact, they are "suffocatingly protective and domineering precisely because they are determined to mold their daughters into whole and self-actualizing persons in a society that devalues Black women" (ibid.). They trained their daughters in social, economic, cultural, and political survival and resistance not practiced by or fully understood or visible to white middle-class or elite women (Hurtado 1989, 170). "Black women have not been," as Margaret Andersen asserts, "segregated within the home; they were denied participation in social and economic affairs outside their own communities; and their psychological roles within the family have not been culturally glorified" (1988, 127). They have had to confront social-economic disadvantages based on race and gender, single parenthood, low-paid factory or housekeeping jobs, and poor access to health services and educational opportunities. They have had to face condemnation by a mainstream media and society that continues to replicate discourses on Black mothering as psychosocially dysfunctional or pathological.

In the 1960s, 1970s, and 1980s, there were increasing concerns among women of color that their diverse stories and issues were not an integral part of the central theorizing on mothers and daughters or women. There has been much research on white middle-class mothers and daughters, especially from psychoanalytic and literary perspectives, but there are few full-length studies, for example, that deal with the struggles between Chinese or Asian American mothers and daughters.[11] At the same time, there was a growing desire to question and challenge Western discourses that might not be totally useful when applied to an understanding of the bonding between mothers and their daughters of color: Their frames of reference may not be applicable when significant differences exist in conceptions of family dynamics, social structure, and the construction of a mature adult identity. Many women writers of color sought ways to articulate their specific concerns and contradictions in the telling of their mother-daughter experiences in ways that did not replicate or depend upon white mainstream feminist models and narratives. As much as there were intense conflicts with mothers, they emphasized the mothers' powerful social and emotional presence in nurturing their creativity and in establishing the homeplace as a political space for survival and resistance for their subordinated racial-ethnic families.[12]

Alvina Quintana's discussion of the predicament faced by Chicana writers hints of the predicaments confronted by other women of color writers at this historical juncture of the 1960s and 1970s: "Chicano cultural productions moved closer to legitimacy by developing ideological systems which represented predominantly masculine interpretations of history and culture. Paradoxically, Chicanas were subordinated and repressed by the ideologies of resistance. On one side they were marginalized by the traditional masculine interpretation of their respective culture and on the other by the future dreams and aspirations of a feminist utopian vision which allowed no space for cultural, racial, or class distinctions among women" (Quintana 1990, 258). That is, Chicanas "are faced with the prospect of developing a liberation strategy that either sells out to one of these outside forces or contributes to a new perspective which is influenced by, but not limited to, either Anglo-feminist or traditional Chicano ideologies" (ibid., 259). Quintana, however, does note that space between these two ideologies does contribute inventive opportunities, "as it provides the writers with the strategic position to enhance or refute two outside sources and thereby contribute to the emergence of a new culture, a culture which by its very nature is characterized by a multiplicity of voices and experiences" (ibid.).

In her essay "Homeplace (a site of resistance)," bell hooks discusses the great efforts by exhausted Black mothers, who worked outside of their home tending to white people's children and homes, to "conserve enough of themselves to provide service (care and nurturance) within their own families and communities. . . . Contemporary Black struggle must honor this history of service just as it must critique the sexist definitions of service as women's 'natural' role" (hooks 1990, 42).

> Historically, African-American people believed that the construction of a homeplace, however fragile and tenuous (the slave hut, the wooden shack), had a radical political dimension. Despite the brutal reality of racial apartheid, of domination, one's homeplace was the one site where one could freely confront the issue of humanization, where one could resist. Black women resisted by making homes where all Black people could strive to be subjects, not objects, where we could be affirmed in our minds and hearts despite poverty, hardship, and deprivation, where we could restore to ourselves the dignity denied us on the outside in the public world. (hooks 1990, 44)

hooks constructs such women's care at the homeplace as a "radically subversive gesture" toward nurturance, developing degrees of Black female critical consciousness, and for organizing political resistance. Such work cannot be defined in essentialist terms; for example, in terms of a notion of self-sacrifice that is "not reflective of choice and will" in difficult circumstances (ibid., 45). Alice Walker talks about the poor, working class mothers and grandmothers, who were denied education, economic support, privacy, encouragement and opportunities to develop their creativity. Nevertheless, these hardworking women of color managed, often against circumstances "cruel enough to stop the blood," to find outlets for their art. "By any means necessary" (*pace* Malcolm X), they did find ways—through language, before language, and beyond language—to pass on their hopes, creative spirit, culture, and history to their daughters.

Asian American women have shared in this retheorizing, actively engaging in collecting oral histories and critically re-envisioning women's histories and experiences (see Chen 1976 and Chu 1976). Many recovered their mother's experiences, as central to their distressed families, often supporting and compensating for their husbands, who were not simply psychologically oppressed but also socially, economically, and politically oppressed and humiliated in Anglo-American society. Asian American and other women of color can thus expand our understanding of the complex, difficult, and valuable work of "preservative love, nurturance, and training" that arises out of women's familial roles that constitute the daily, lived "maternal practice" of mothers and other women (Ruddick 1989, 17). Race, ethnicity, and class factors, at varying times, need to be considered in examining women's diverse nurturing and caregiving practices in American society.[13]

Formations of Asian American Mother–Daughter Writing: Maxine Hong Kingston, Amy Tan, and Fae Myenne Ng

Asian American women also claim the in-between spaces as sites on which to resignify themselves and their cultures, distinct from white mainstream feminist and Asian American masculinist nationalist discourses and practices. Influenced (directly and/or indirectly) by the early Asian American cultural nationalist call to construct an Asian American cultural politics, Maxine Hong Kingston, Amy Tan, and Fae Myenne Ng sought to recover the neglected stories of their Chinese immigrant and American-born communities. At the same time, they responded to the mainstream feminist call to reclaim women's stories. But in keeping with the emerging critiques by many women of color feminists in the 1970s and 1980s, these writers reclaimed their mother-daughter stories not only from masculinist traditions but also from elitist, capitalist, nationalist, and imperialist traditions. Theorizing the plurality of identity and cultural-political formations at women's diverse and often ignored social locations, and its complex imbrication in race, ethnicity, class, and gender, are some of the major contributions of women of color to contemporary discourses on knowledge formation. This is a theorizing in which Kingston, Tan, and Ng participate in through their mother-daughter narratives.

Kingston's *The Woman Warrior* (1976), Tan's *The Joy Luck Club* (1989) and Ng's *Bone* (1993) focus on the struggles encountered by mothers and daughters in contemporary Chinese American contexts.[14] Each constructs a representation of the ordinary activities and dilemmas of living in an American culture-in-the-making, and examines the complex negotiations that Chinese immigrant mothers and their Americanized daughters perform daily in dealing with diverse, and often conflicting interpretive systems and cultures. This "borderland" existence, Gloria Anzaldúa tells us, can lead to *un choque*: "Like others having or living in more than one culture, we get multiple, often opposing images. The coming together of two self-consistent but habitually incompatible frames of reference causes *un choque*, a cultural collision" (1990a, 378).

Kingston (b. 1940) grew up in Stockton's early Chinatown where her family has lived in the same house for over fifty years. Presently, the area is in the heart of one of the poorest and roughest parts of downtown Stockton (see Loke 1989). Kingston's father Tom Hong was the youngest son of a peasant family, who had been prepared for life as a scholar. Having failed to attain a government position, he left China for New York City's Chinatown in the 1920s, leaving behind a young wife and children. He spent fifteen years toiling as a laundryman, sending back remittances to his wife in China. He later moved to Stockton in 1940 with his wife and became a manager of a gambling house. Kingston's mother Chew Ying Lan arrived in 1939 to join her husband. She had six children in the United States (her first two children died in China). Kingston was born a year after her mother's arrival in the United States. Chew Ying Lan is listed as a practitioner of medicine and midwifery, a field hand and a laundry worker.

Amy Tan was born in Oakland, California in 1951. Her parents had arrived in 1949 and were Mandarin-speaking, as opposed to the Cantonese-speaking families who settled Chinatown in earlier migration phases. (Kingston's family speaks the Say Yup dialect.) Tan's parents John and Daisy, first-generation Chinese Americans, met and were married in the United States. It was a second marriage for Daisy, who had left three children in China as the price for leaving a bitter and abusive arranged marriage. Daisy Tan came from a wealthy Shanghai family. John Tan was an electrical engineer, trained in Beijing, before his immigration to the United States. He later became a Baptist minister. Her mother Daisy was a vocational nurse. They had three children. Tan's father and brother died tragically of brain tumors in 1968. Tan describes her early childhood as nomadic; her family moved frequently and she states that she often felt like an outsider. As her family moved into better neighborhoods, she was further isolated as the only Chinese girl in class or in her school (Tan 1990a, 5). In 1987, Tan visited China for the first time with her mother and husband and met her fall-sisters for the first time.

Fae Myenne Ng (b. 1957) grew up with immigrant parents and among male old-timers in San Francisco's Chinatown during the late 1950s. As a child, Ng assisted her mother, who was a sewing woman in a Chinatown sweatshop. As she remembers, "I got a penny for each buckle. . . . Many women had cradles next to their machines. The shops were open all night, and then the women went home and sewed more" (Hunnewell 1993, 9). As a child, she also witnessed Chinatown folk sending the bones of relatives to China for burial. It was a sight that deeply moved her, reminding her of the Chinese men she knew in the community, who had come to the United States in the earlier immigration phases, and suffered greatly without the comfort of their families. "They came to this country to make a living and to bring it home and to raise their families, but in the end they couldn't do that. The working class . . . find themselves at the end of their lives in these SRO [single room occupancy] hotels with only their pennies" (Stetson 1993, 3). In many ways, Ng honors not only these men but also the women and families affiliated to this community of men; she compassionately witnesses their hardships and notes their passings (Ng 1994, 87). Ng's *Bone* explores these earlier Chinatown formations of family, which have been profoundly affected by the Chinese American history of immigration, exclusionary, and anti-miscegenation laws; as well as by wars and economic chaos and exploitation (see chap. 3).

Kingston, Tan, and Ng came of age during and after the social-political upheavals of the 1960s and 70s, namely the period of the Civil Rights and Black Power Move- ments, the Asian American and Third World Movements, the Women's Liberation Movement, and the anti-Vietnam war protests.[15] All three writers spent time at the University of California (UC), Berkeley, a hub for social and political ferment of the time (see chap. 4). Maxine Hong Kingston was immersed in the Berkeley culture of sit-ins, love-ins, Third World strikes (for ethnic studies, for example) and activism (see her novel *Tripmaster Monkey* [1989a]). Kingston continued her anti-war activism in the Sanctuary Movement at the Church of the Crossroads in Honolulu. She aided U.S. soldiers who were going AWOL from the military bases in Hawai'i. Berkeley, like San Francisco, was the site of intense struggles and debates by students and community activists in the emergent Asian American Movement. Kingston received a B.A in English in 1962 as well as a teaching certifi-cate in 1965. Throughout the 1960s, she worked in California as well as in Honolulu as an English and language teacher; she became a visiting associate professor of English in 1977, and is now teaching in the English Deptartment at UC, Berkeley. Tan entered in a doctoral program in 1974–76 after receiving an M.A. degree in linguistics from San Jose State. Ng was a graduate in English at UC, Berkeley, and she also received an M.F.A. in writing from Columbia University in 1984. She has taught courses in creative writing and in Asian American literature in California.

In representing the painful struggle of mothers and daughters to articulate the social spaces for themselves and for their interactions, Kingston, Tan, and Ng portray a vibrant, contentious, and vital women's subjectivity-, culture-, and history-in-the-making. On the one hand, Tan's Joy Luck daughters are Chinese American women who love but do not easily or comfortably identify with their immigrant Chinese mothers or with their families and racial-ethnic communities. In *The Woman Warrior*, the young female narrator wants to escape the "hating range" of Chinese mother and home: "Concrete pours out of my mouth to cover the forests with freeways and sidewalks. Give me plastics, periodical tables, TV dinners with vegetables no more complex than peas mixed with diced carrots. Shine floodlights into dark corners: no ghosts" (*TWW* 1976, 237).[16] Ng's narrator Leila, the oldest daughter in the household, attempts to mediate between the burden of family responsibilities and tragedy as well as her own needs for a separate life in more diversified and eclectic homeplaces and borders. She does this within earshot of a mother, who uses her impatient, accusatory "sewing-factory voice" to reduce her daughter to edgy silence, guilt, frustration, and anger.

On the other hand, the Chinese immigrant mothers' experiences in these writers' stories are significantly embedded in Chinese traditions and ways of being and thinking, which have been further dislocated and relocated—culturally, geopolitically, and historically—in the U.S. Sadly, many of the daughters do not understand the value of this legacy: They have lost or devalued the meanings of their mothers' stories in their Anglo-American translations. Kingston, Tan, and Ng portray how difficult it is for daughters and mothers situated in alienating societal structures to reclaim a significant bond with one another and to meaningfully share their conflicted experiences and stories. The painful distances and tensions between their private communication and its comprehension are intimately intertwined with the social-political world in which their personal dialogue and relationships are situated. Despite the difficulties, these communications are still vital to their daughters' material and social-emotional survival in the United States. Kingston, Tan, and Ng imagine more flexible forms of bonding that can potentially help readers to rethink their own particular relationships to the world. Their stories can provide a powerful counter-memory to the prevailing ideologies, discourses, and institutions that continually attempt to appropriate, trivialize, commodify, or destroy the stories and standpoints of women.

Reception to Chinese American Mother–Daughter Stories

Maxine Hong Kingston

Maxine Hong Kingston was not, as a number of critics have already noted, the first Chinese American woman to write about mother-daughter relationships and the struggles within Chinese American families (see Ling 1990, Kim 1990, Lim 1992, Cheung 1993, and Wong 1995). In the latter, Sau-ling Wong mentions the few "antecedents for Kingston's strong Chinese women" such as Su-ling Wong and Earl Cressy's autobiography *Daughter of Confucius* (1952), Helena Kuo's *I've Come a Long Way* (1942), Jade Snow Wong's *Fifth Chinese Daughter* (1989), Chuang Hua's *Crossings* (1986) (Wong 1995, 177–78).[17] Kingston acknowledges Jade Snow Wong as "the Mother of Chinese American literature," the only Chinese American author Kingston read before writing her own book, "I found Jade Snow Wong's book myself in the library, and was flabbergasted, helped, inspired, affirmed, made possible as a writer—for the first time I saw a person who looked like me as a heroine of a book, as a maker of a book" (Ling 1990, 120).[18]

In 1976, Maxine Hong Kingston published her memoir *The Woman Warrior* to critical acclaim in mainstream and Asian American communities. According to Thomas Ferraro, "Kingston's timing was right. The 1970s feminist readership was ready to hear her, and she had strong material" (Nguyen 1997, 48). The reading public, more specifically a diverse female readership (including baby-boomer women), ethnic Studies and various other programs and departments (such as American and Women's Studies, English, Sociology) helped to construct a consumer market for women's writing and for investigations of mothers and daughters.

No one expected a women writer —least of all a woman of color writer—to do very well in a mainstream market. While writing her first book, Kingston was supporting herself as a typist and schoolteacher in Honolulu. "No one in New York, the publishing citadel, knew who the hell this Maxine Hong Kingston was; her publisher Alfred Knopf, couldn't even find her!" (Talbot 1990, 12) As Kingston remembers, "My publisher initially published 5,000 copies thinking there was no market, nobody's going to read this work by an unknown person. . . . But those 5,000 copies sold overnight" (Milvy 1994, 38). Nowadays, 50,000 copies of *The Woman Warrior* are sold every year in this country alone (ibid., 38).

Kingston's first book was the winner of the National Book Critics Circle Award in 1976; the *Mademoiselle* Magazine Award (1977); and the Anisfield-Wolf Race Relations Award (1978). It was named one of the top ten nonfiction works of the decade by *Time* Magazine (1979). In 1980 Kingston became a writing fellow of the National Education Association and was named a Living Treasure of Hawai'i in 1980. Her second book *China Men* (1977) won a National Book Critics Circle Award and an American Book Award in 1980, and was a runner-up for the Pulitzer Prize. Kingston was honored with the American Academy and Institute Award in Literature, California Governor's Award in the Arts, the Hawai'i Award for Literature, and the California Arts Commission Award.

Maxine Hong Kingston's books have received both criticism and praise from a variety of audiences (see Lim 1991). Her texts are often canonized in curricula, and are taught as if they are representative of Asian American writing and the experiences of Asian American mothers and daughters, or of Asian American families and communities, a bone of contention for some Asian American critics. Kingston's *The Woman Warrior* has been heavily anthologized; and it is used in many first-year composition classes as an introduction to Asian American culture or to women's writing. According to Lim's study (1991), the most frequently excerpted sections from the book are the chapters, "No Name Woman," "The Misery of Silence," "The Quiet Girl," and "White Tigers" (ibid., 3). *The Woman Warrior* is one of the books canonized by the Modern Language Association in its series *Approaches to Teaching World Literature*, and, as Lim further notes, it is situated within a group that includes Chaucer, Dante, Shakespeare, Ellison, Achebe, Keats, and Dickinson. With all the success and adulation accorded to Kingston's texts, the hope was to turn both *The Woman Warrior* and *China Men* into a single film or play; but it has been extremely difficult. The inventive narrative content and structure of Kingston's memoir has been difficult to translate into a filmic or play medium. Terry Hong (1994, 54–57) traces the saga of Kingston's text in the cultural marketplace: Martin Rosen, a movie producer, bought the stage and film rights to *The Woman Warrior* and *China Men* in 1982. Rosen states that he was the only one to make a serious bid to Kingston for the novels' rights with the intention of having them made into films. Over the years he has conducted an international search for a writer, eventually reading 80 scripts. Rosen describes how difficult it has been to find someone to work on the memoir: "'I didn't get any calls from interested Asian American directors or writers in all the time that I had the rights'" (ibid., 55). The controversy generated by Frank Chin and other critics about her book did not help. Rosen, as show producer, finally settled on a script by the writer Deborah Rogin (ibid., 54) and on Sharon Ott of the Berkeley Repertory as director for the play. It premiered in mid-1994 to lukewarm reviews.

Kingston's critical acclaim and media exposure promoted, in part, the growing interest in Asian American writers. Mainstream and independent publishers sought out new Asian American voices for this cultural consumer market. Despite the growing market for mother-daughter stories, it took over a decade before another Chinese American mother-daughter book was singled out and published in a major publishing venue (with the accompanying mainstream media hype)—Amy Tan's *The Joy Luck Club* (1989).

Amy Tan

Amy Tan drew inspiration from *The Woman Warrior:* "A friend gave me *The Woman Warrior* and I devoured it in one sitting. . . . I felt amazed and proud that somebody could have written this" (Talbot 1990, 8). Like Kingston, Tan captured the attention of not only a mainstream audience but also an Asian American female readership. As we will see, she also encountered a number of Asian American critics who disliked her work. As Tan's and Kingston's literary agent Sandra Dijkstra opines, "People were very excited by everything that [Maxine] had done, but she was looked upon as an anomaly. . . . Years later, Amy was also a bolt out of the blue, but for some reason, society was ready. All of a sudden, they could see that this wasn't foreign, this was American" (qtd. in Nguyen 1997, 48–9). There was a consumer market for Tan's mother-daughter text that the major publishing houses were happy to accommodate (the nature of the beast) and the mainstream, sometimes tributary, media were happily recommending to readers, unfortunately in rather stereotypical ways (see Ho 1996 and Wong 1995).

In 1989, *The Joy Luck Club* was the longest running hardcover on *The New York Times* bestseller list (34 weeks), and was on the paperback list for another nine months. The book was also chosen for the Commonwealth Club Gold Award for fiction and the Bay Area Book Reviewers' award for new fiction, and received nominations for the National Book Critics Circle award for best novel and for a *Los Angeles Times* book award. It was also translated into several languages; and book club rights for the novel sold for a reported $425,000—an astonishing amount (Tan 1991, 25). The softcover rights sold for a reported $1.2 million (ibid., 25). As of early 1997, the book had sold over 4.5 million copies.

In addition to literary audiences, the dramatic and filmic interpretations of her books have created global audiences for her work. In 1993, Amy Tan's *Joy Luck Club* was made into a mainstream movie by Hollywood Pictures, an affiliate of Disney Productions. The film was a four-year project, made on a budget of $10.5 million—a small figure by Hollywood standards (Armstrong 1993, D1). It became an instant hit in terms of box office receipts, grossing $14.9 million dollars in its first six weeks and $32.9 million in 1993. There is already talk of turning Tan's second book *The Kitchen God's Wife* (Tan 1991c), another mother-daughter story, into a film. She has also published *The Hundred Secret Senses* (Tan 1995) and a number of children's books.

Fae Myenne Ng

Fae Myenne Ng is a new voice among a contemporary group of young Chinese American women writers. Her first full-length work of fiction is *Bone*, published in 1993, the same year that the *Joy Luck Club* film hit the theaters. Ng took ten years to compose this novel while supporting herself through teaching, waitressing, and temp work (Jones 1993, 9). Her short stories have appeared in a number of Asian American literary anthologies, as well as in magazines. On the dust jacket of *Bone*, there is advance praise from a variety of critics, who had disagreed on their reviews of Kingston and Tan's first works of fiction. For example, Sau-ling Wong, who situates a reading of Tan's *Joy Luck Club* within an ethnographic, Orientalist perspective, forefronts Ng's work as an "instant classic" and a "stunning novel, a work of great wisdom and compassion" about life in San Francisco's Chinatown. The writer Ishmael Reed, a longtime supporter of Frank Chin's perspectives, commented favorably on the tough and realistic portrait of Ng's Chinese American family, feeling that her representation counters the dominant model minority one constructed within mainstream culture. The lives of the Fu-Leong family are grounded in the localities of Chinatown and its environs (e.g., the Tenderloin and Mission districts). As the critic Alvin Lu notes, the author does not construct China as a "mythical presence" in the telling of her story as do Kingston and Tan; rather, "it is a real, even dismissable, place. The novel's focus is entrenched firmly within the alleys of Chinatown, in memory and experience" (Lu 1993, 1).

In *Bone*, Chinatown is a central site at which the experiences of a Chinese American family and community are lived, felt, and understood—within the "details of sewing ladies gossip, funeral preparations for a kinless old man, and a community dealing in tragedy" (ibid., 1, 4). Ng's early Chinatown is a fluid and dynamic site that is inclusive of male history. For example, Ng situates her narrative at the San Fran hotel, Universal Cafe, and Portsmouth Square, which are frequented by Chinese American male old-timers in her story. Chinatown is central to the formation of homeplaces for immigrant working class families and ethnic communities (for example, the Nam Ping Yuen housing project, Dulcie's Baby store, and garment sweatshops). In addition, Ng's contemporary Chinatown is reflected in the eclectic characters who curse and gamble and fight; drive fast American cars; use recreational drugs; have names like Zeke, Priscilla, and Mason; work in fast-food joints and mechanics' garages; get drunk on Tom Collinses; get married in Reno; rebel against seeming "too Chinesey"; and watch a lot of *I Love Lucy* (Garcia 1993, 8).

Both immigrant parents and second-generation children, each in their own individual contexts and as a familial-social community unit, struggle and resist within a bittersweet history in this country. The family members vacillate between love and hate, the fierce desires to stay bonded together, to escape and travel across borders (physical and psychosocial), and to envision (or remake) communities and identities for themselves in the United States. As Leon notes, the difficult work of the heart fluctuates in negotiating these complicated and contentious sites, "forward and forward and then back, back" (*B* 145). The vacillations and displacements are evident in the intense struggles of the daughter-narrator Leila, who attempts to articulate the psychosocial and economic traumas haunting her family and history as a Chinese American woman. On the dust jacket, the writer Joel Agee states that the characters in *Bone* drift through time and memory, moving through "the quarrels, griefs, hopes and loves of its characters—who are not types or policy statements, but wonderfully alive and particular people." Moreover, the spare style of writing, according to Ng, emphasizes the frugality and regulation of working class immigrant Chinatown families, and how economics and racism bleed into the private and domestic lives of subordinated minority communities in America.

Moreover, the favorable reviews for *Bone* reflect the shifts in Ng's work toward more comprehensive articulations of social-political struggles, which include the stories of men as well as women, especially within the critical and conflicted site of the homeplace. *Bone*, as Laureen Mar states, "does not follow the formulaic Chinese American woman's novel of misogyny and victimization (and it eludes that strangely consistent propensity of female characters in such works to spout proverbs throughout)" (Mar 1993, 185). In her interviews, Ng discusses her desire to tell and honor the stories of an earlier Chinatown, of men who lived and died in this country, often without means to return to China and without the comfort of their families. She places Leon Leong within psychosocial contexts in order to relate the complex range of his life as a man, father, husband, son, hopeful dreamer, rebel, and inventor— not just his history as an exploited victim-worker within a racist capitalist system. In this way, we can begin to explore the depths of Leon's anger, frustration, guilt, vulnerability, and silences as well as the power of his love and search for forgiveness and justice. Ng, through her daughter-narrator Leila Fu, reclaims the specificities of men's histories as central to understanding the formations of family and community. Ng's first novel suggests the continual potential of women's writing in redefining an understanding of self-in-community both as a legacy and project into the new century.

Perils of Mainstream Publishing: Orientalists, Traitors, and Whores

Some Asian American male and female critics dismissed Kingston's *The Woman Warrior* and Tan's *The Joy Luck Club* as Orientalist commodities produced by a mainstream publishing industry for predominantly white audiences (see chap. 4). In a reductive critique, Gloria Chun asserts that Asian American female critics and scholars (such as Elaine Kim, King-Kok Cheung, and Nellie Wong, who have written about Kingston's work) "ignore the detrimental, self-hating, assimilationist view of Chinese American" that she believes Kingston's text depicts (Chun 1991, 90). Kingston has, in Ng's critique, destroyed Chinese history and myths and defined the Chinese as "extremely patriarchal, barbaric, authoritarian, uncivilized, irrational and backward" and deserving of blame from the dominant society (ibid., 92). Furthermore, she claims that Asian American scholars who use Kingston's book become "effective agents in perpetuating the dominant society's view of Asians in America as the inferior and exotic Other" (ibid., 90).

Sau-ling Wong asserts that in examining Tan's usage of Chinese and Chinese-seeming details as well as her stylistic and narrative formats, she believes that Tan's texts enable a culturalist reading that "must ultimately be situated in quasi-ethnographic, Orientalist discourse" (Wong 1995, 181). She believes that Tan's work is bought and read by a white mainstream readership, who find her work comforting in its reproduction of stereotypical images, and who are attracted to Orientalist fantasies of Old China (primitive, superstitious, mythic, traditional, disempowered) versus the United States (progressive, civilized, rational, modern) (ibid., 186). More specifically, she concludes that the "Amy Tan phenomenon" is supported by a predominantly white middle-class female readership. Wong takes to task the feminist or "sugar sisterhood" readership of Tan's mother-daughter stories, which she asserts "allegorize a Third World/First World encounter that allows mainstream American feminism to construct itself in a flattering, because depoliticized, manner" (ibid., 181). Though I am sure that many readers, white and non-white, may reproduce the familiar, comfortable Orientalist codes, it is hard to believe that such a massive generalization could be made about how diverse individuals and social audiences may engage these texts, especially since the specific research with audience receptions has not yet been substantially explored. Wong's and Ng's concerns seem to also concern Kingston and Tan.

In a 1982 essay discussing the cultural misreadings of *The Woman Warrior*, Kingston had already expressed her own frustrations at being praised for all the wrong reasons. She had expected her work to "be read from the women's lib angle and the Third World angle, the *Roots* angle" (Kingston 1982, 55). Kingston found it depressing to see mainstream and oppositional critics assessing her and her book in relationship to the exoticized and inscrutable Oriental/Other.

> I had really believed that the days of gross stereotyping were over, that the 1960s, the Civil Rights Movement, and the end of the war in Vietnam had enlightened America, if not in deeds at least in manners. Pridefully enough, I believed that I had written with such power that the reality and humanity of my characters would bust through any stereotypes of them. . . . The critics who said how the book was good because it was, or was not, like the oriental fantasy in their heads might as well have said how weak it was, since it in fact did not break through that fantasy. (ibid.)

Like Kingston, Tan has stated her objections to the reproduction of Orientalist and/or ethnographic characterizations of her writing by various audiences of *The Joy Club*. Tan believes some Asian American critics have interpreted her work as catering specifically to the profound Orientalist fantasies of a white readership because her fictional work constructs a sense of a less than perfect China past through the memories and experiences of the Joy Luck women and because she discusses sexism within Chinese culture. She is critical of audiences who choose to interpret her stories as fixed, monolithic ethnographic descriptions of the Chinese or China. They treat her fictions as a scholarly text and/or tourist guide, which directly and continuously references back authoritatively to Chinese culture, legends, society or history. Tan asserts that these readers reduce her personal fiction into "cultural lesson plans."

> Contrary to what is assumed by some students, reporters, and community organizations wishing to bestow me with honors, I am not an expert on China, Chinese culture, mah jong, the psychology of mothers and daughters, generation gaps,

immigration, illegal aliens, assimilation, acculturation, racial tension, Tiananmen
Square . . . human rights, Pacific Rim economics, the purported one million missing
baby girls in China . . . or, I am sorry to say, Chinese cooking. (Tan 1997, 136-37)

She may have personal opinions on a number of these topics, but she insists that
her sentiments and "make-believe" world do not make her an authority in any of
these areas.

Tan is also concerned that some Asian American readers claim that her book
is not "authentic" or "representative" of Chinese American or Asian American
experiences. She has asserted that she does not want to be representative of all
these experiences. "Is Jane Smiley's A Thousand Acres supposed to be taken as
representative of all of American culture? If so, in what ways? Are all American
fathers tyrannical? Do all American sisters betray each other. . . . Why do readers
and reviewers assume that a book with Chinese American characters can encompass
all the demographics and personal histories of Chinese America?" (ibid.) She also
recalls an encounter with an unnamed professor of literature, who insisted that
Asian Americans maintain their marginalism and dissociate from the mainstream,
perceiving the dominant class as the "enemy" (ibid.). This is not a positioning
which Tan wishes to claim for herself or her work. "If your work is inaccessible to
white readers, that is proof that it is authentic. If it is read by white people, then
that is proof the work is fake, sellout, and hence the writer is to be treated as a
traitor, publicly branded and condemned. While the numbers within this faction
are small, their influence in academia and the media is substantial" (ibid., 143).
Tan is suggesting such discourses can reproduce simplistic, totalizing binaries
between "them" versus "us" in their own critical paradigms. In this contentious
cultural and historical milieu, Tan's book, like Kingston's, became a cultural
commodity and a media event, generating publicity and controversy in mainstream
and Asian American cultural venues and communities.

By the 1980s and 1990s, the targeted audiences were more racially-ethnically
diversified and more multiculturally (in different degrees) literate and college
educated, having been affected, directly or indirectly, by the social-historical changes
of the 1960s and 70s. There were also continuing changes in feminist theorizing
and practices, especially in light of the numerous critiques by women of color. In
some ways, the tendency to clump white readers (including white feminists) as
predominantly depoliticized Orientalist readers of Tan's text, or other women of
color mother-daughter texts, denies the possibility that they might have a more
expansive range of readings strategies for these diverse texts. A few reviews in
mainstream venues can not quite speak to the variety of interpretations of Kingston's
and Tan's texts by diverse feminist scholars and critics.

To be clear, I am not attempting to claim that Tan's work is without flaws or
multiply inflected codes. I am not disputing the possibility that Orientalist codes
and images might be recalled in their work by readers in various locations. There
are readings that reinterpret these texts predominantly within Orientalist paradigms
that replay, consciously and/or unconsciously, the typical racist, sexist narratives

and images. This may speak to some segments of the female (and male) readership who are culturally and critically open to the barrage of scripts and images that construct the "Oriental." I would not disagree with this point. I do not contend that it is the greatest book ever written or the last word on Chinese American mother-daughter relationships.

However, I do think the text can be interpreted in multiple ways by audiences from a variety of social-cultural and political positionings. Sau-ling Wong mentions this in passing but does not fully explore in focussing predominantly on the ways an Orientalist, depoliticized, white middle-class feminist "sugar sisterhood" would read Tan's text (Wong 1995). In replaying such Orientalist interpretations as predominant, Wong, Chin, and others do not consider the growing segment of other female readers whose experiences of the cultural texts of Kingston and Tan do not simply duplicate reductive Orientalist readings.[19] It is not my intent to conduct an exhaustive study of the audience reception of Tan's text. I wish only to suggest the possibilities of socially and politically more resistant critical readings, especially by a diversified Asian American women readership, as a significant way to re-think these popularized texts.

Another Kind of Sisterhood: Preliminary Reflections on Asian American Female Readership

An Asian American female readership is increasing (we have not even addressed the possibility of a male readership for these texts) and major and independent (and Asian American) publishing houses are not only targeting more diversified audiences but also marketing to this ethnic female readership.[20] According to the 1990 census, the Asian population in the U.S. has increased to 7.2 million, constituting 3 percent of the total U.S. population. They are the fastest growing and the third largest minority group after African Americans and Latinos (Glenn and Yap 1998, 125). And according to the *Chronicle of Higher Education*, Asian Americans constitute 5 percent of the nation's 14.3 million college and university students, a sizable source of potential readers (Nguyen 1997, 48). Some of the readership for *The Joy Luck Club* are comprised of baby-boomer women of varying backgrounds going through mid-life changes and phases. "I [Tan] think I wrote about something that hit a lot of baby boomer women whose mothers have either just recently died or may die in the near future. They felt that their misunderstandings, things that had not been talked about for years, were expressed in the book. There are so many mothers I know who gave the book to their daughters, and daughters, who gave the book to their mothers, and marked passages of things they wanted to say" (Tan 1991d, 29). In many ways, Tan's text was ready for this market of women who were reassessing their adult lives, careers, relationships, and, of course, their mothers.

Furthermore, there were shifts in terms of the Chinese population in the United States that may also account for a more diversified and growing Chinese American female readership. By this I mean the development of a female readership, who differ in such factors as age, socioeconomic class, immigration phases, degrees of acculturation and assimilation, and links to home countries. The mother-daughter narratives, for example, portray types of dilemmas and tensions that can arise between immigrant parents and American-born children and within dual-wage or multilingual Chinese American families and communities. The gender ratios between Chinese men and women in the United States, which were historically skewed, have evened out, especially with the immigration of increasing numbers of women in the 1940s and 1950s as well as with the immigration of family units post-1965 (Glenn and Yap 1998, 141). By 1980, the ratio between Chinese women and men was nearly evenly balanced. According to the U.S. Census 1992, the Chinese American population alone nearly doubled between 1970 and 1980; and it doubled again by 1990 to 1,645,472 (ibid., 145). This increase was mostly due to immigration and it has radically altered the composition of the Chinese population in the U.S. "Whereas in 1960, more than 60 percent of the Chinese population were born in the United States, by 1980 the ratio had shifted in the other direction, so that 63.3 percent were foreign born" (ibid.).

A majority of these immigrant families are bilingual, speaking Chinese at home and English elsewhere, and maintaining various levels of traditional culture. Overall, Chinese Americans have lower divorce rates, maintaining their family units for a variety of social, cultural, and economic reasons. As often portrayed in the mother-daughter narratives, the children translate and mediate their parents' transactions with the English-speaking public world, feeling a range of frustration, guilt, anger, and love for their parents and communities. In Chinatowns and in broader Chinese American communities, the issues of social fragmentation, poverty, gang violence, discrimination, frustrated expectations, and restricted life options may also accentuate the readers' need to explore the issues in multiple homeplaces and bordersites. This process can be complicated, painful, and debilitating, as well as protecting and nurturing.

Under these circumstances, it is worthwhile to explore the effects of these mother-daughter texts on an Asian American women readership, and expand our understanding of these Chinese American mother-daughter stories and their interest to this particular audience. After all, Tan's and Kingston's books were a catalyst for many Asian American women readers, encouraging them to become more critical of their lives and to start discussions and renew social, emotional, and political networking. To begin to recognize one's personal agency in an oppressive system—even when compromised and conflicted—can provide fruitful opportunities for individual and collective action and change. Political agency and resistance do not come naturally or ready-made; they do not materialize or function in a vacuum. Rather, they are continually forged and re-forged in passionate struggle and recreation at many different political sites. Few critics write about this growing constituency of Asian American female readers and their specific interactions with these texts.

Kingston has stated she writes for herself as well as for a broad reading public and for specific audiences. She specifically addresses, for example, Chinese

Americans in her text. She states that the majority of her mail is from Chinese and Chinese American women answering back with their personal critiques, opinions and stories. They address "how similar their childhoods were to the one in the book, or they say their lives are not like that at all, but they understand the feelings; then they tell me some stories about themselves" (Kingston 1982, 63).

Likewise, Tan received letters, especially from Asian American women, who had been deeply affected by *The Joy Luck Club*: Ordinary women readers critically responded to what they liked and disliked in the mother-daughter stories. Many wrote about how true the portrayals of the mothers were (Tan 1991d, 29), and about identifying with the struggles between mothers and daughters, about feelings of alienation and isolation, about cultural dislocation, and about concerns about their assimilation-acculturation process in the United States. Their readings of her text were not romanticized or apolitical in the memories, feelings, and experiences they recovered.

> I [Tan] received many letters from young readers, most of whom wrote, 'I thought I was alone. I thought I was the only one who felt this way about my mother or about being Chinese. And I know I'm not alone now'. . . . I received a lot of letters from readers—both here and overseas—who tell me they had read the book to a parent in the hospital, and they were looking for a connection. . . . And usually—thank God—they found something. I don't take credit for it, because I wrote the book for my own reasons, not to save the relationships of other people. But readers add their own imagination and own set of experiences, so it becomes *their* book. You can't control or plan it. And that's part of the wonderful magic of books. (Younger 1993, 35)

For many, these works had an "emotional verism," something that corresponds to what Ien Ang defines as a subjective experience of the world; that is, it is a form of psychological reality, or an inner realism, rather than a reality based solely on an externally perceptible (social) reality (Ang 1985, 44–45). As a way to counter the language barrier between the Joy Luck mothers and daughters, Tan states that she tries to write without relying on "fancy five-dollar words." She intended the language of the Joy Luck women to be intensely visual and emotional, and wanted to allow the images' power to create an intense feeling of intuitive truth. The intimate audience that grounds her work is her mother, whose traumatic talk-story (sometimes on shopping trips) provided Tan the seeds for her responding talk-stories: "I really was writing *The Joy Luck Club* for my mother. And I thought, here's this intelligent person, and I want to write for her in a way that the emotions come through and the story comes through and the words are never more important than the story. I wanted to convey images through the language, and I believe that you can do this in a way that is very clear and accessible to the reader" (Tan 1990b, 256).

In a review of *The Woman Warrior*, Suzi Wong discusses her own response to Kingston's text: "Let others praise *The Woman Warrior* for its literary achievement, its dazzling and subtle use of English—I only hear a familiar dialect. Nor can I laud the story for its 'truthfulness,' 'representativeness' or 'politics'—all I know is that in a strange, yet gratifying way, Maxine Hong Kingston's story slowly revealed itself to be my own. For me, the book was an exhilarating and powerful experience, for it validates not only a commonality of our lives but indeed, our lives themselves. In her telling, there is existence; in giving voice, she gives credence to the reality of our lives" (Wong 1977, 165). Wong proceeds to discuss the "emotional reality" or the embodied feeling of the text and to specify what evokes the specific memories of childhood for her—the *sounds* of a village dialect, the *touch* of maternal hands on her earlobes, and the *taste* of medicinal herbal tonics (ibid., 165). Wong's responses—the pleasures of recognition, sensual involvement—have a subjective and emotional reality both in terms of her own experiences and her potential affiliations with other women.

Likewise, Amy Tan cites a letter from a young Missouri teenager who related to the details in *The Joy Luck Club* in observing her own Chinese family; and who developed an emerging critical awareness of ethnic pride in the midst of racist isolation:

> I had never read a book like yours that I could relate to—from the dumplings that were made with the expert twist of chopsticks to the ways the 'formica table was wiped down twice after dinner.' I also lived with my grandma who liked to say "Ai yaa!" quite often! A few ignorant students mocking me would always cause me to wish that I had blonde hair instead of dark brown. . . . You wrote many beautiful things in your book that made me realize that I was lucky to have two cultures that some traits in the Oriental culture could never be traded for an American one. (Streitfield 1989, F9)

The young letter writer recalls the details of the homeplace, which becomes a nurturing site for the reformation of identity and subjectivity against the taunts outside (see hooks 1990). Both Wong and the young Missouri teenager accent the ordinary daily details of life that often seem mundane. Yet, within these domestic-familial sites, the social, emotional, and political are critically merged.

Janet Yang, who produced the *Joy Luck Club* film with Oliver Stone, spoke of the original impact of the book on her personal life. "It was like seeing my deepest and most private moments in writing. . . . I felt my interior life exposed to light. I immediately contacted Amy and she continued to send me chapters" (Buena Vista Pictures, Inc. 1993, 11). Yang, an American-born second-generation Chinese daughter, discussed her childhood difficulties of reconciling the family values of modesty, duty, and familial piety with those of others around her. At the time, it never occurred to her to explore her heritage or question the differences between herself and her peers: "I was somewhat in denial of the fact that I was Chinese. I didn't ask my parents . . . what it was like being Chinese. I was, I think, more interested in trying to be a chameleon . . . not be Chinese . . . to blend in with the rest of the crowd" (Moore 1995, 431). This beginning self-critique does not sound apolitical, passive, or assimilationist. For better and worse, it moved Yang enough to become involved with the making of the film: At the time she reflected, "Although I dreamt I would one day help make it into a movie, I wasn't sure exactly how with all the obvious strikes against it. It is now years later—the climate has changed, and all the right forces have comes together" (Buena Vista Pictures, Inc. 1993, 12).

Another Chinese American woman "heard [her] mother's voice and mine, sometimes speaking to each other, more often missing the words that are spoken and not heard" (Y. S. Fong 1990, 122). Like other readers, Ms. Fong identifies with the conflicts generated by daily transnational border crossings—the emotional, social-economic, cultural, and historical ruptures—between her experiences in the United States and those of her immigrant mother. "I never understood my mother. I just wanted her to be like Donna Reed in the "Donna Reed Show" or Jane Wyman in "Father Knows Best". . . . I was to talk to the shop owners in English while she loudly told me in Chinese what to say. Like the daughters in The Joy Luck Club, I was embarrassed by my Chinese mother" (ibid., 123).

These stories provide women an opportunity to rethink what is repressed in model minority representations of the successful assimilated-acculturated life, especially as it appropriates and exploits Asian American women as the ideal feminized representation of the model minority citizen for the white nation-state. Such dominant discourses can obliterate alternate ways of thinking, speaking, representing, and enacting self in relation to the world. They literally can authorize and regulate what can and cannot be said or thought in order to maintain specific power arrangements in a society.

The actress Ming-Na Wen, who played June Woo in the Joy Luck Club movie, records her first reactions to reading Tan's book: "For the first time, I felt I was reading something that was completely talking to me" (Avins 1993, 14). She remembers "crying and laughing because it [the book] opened a whole new awareness for me: that I wasn't the only one living this kind of life. . . . I was trying so hard to balance my Chinese background with being very Westernized. I was feeling so isolated and alone . . . and here was this book saying, 'You're not alone'" (Chambers 1993, 82).

Another indication of Asian American women's involvement in Tan's book is found in the response to the casting calls for the movie. The casting director, Heidi Levitt, set up audition notices in San Francisco and New York, Los Angeles, Chicago, Seattle, Vancouver, and Toronto. They advertised in Chinese newspapers and various cultural organizations for leads. The first open casting call for mothers brought out nearly 400 women. "I've never seen people so happy and so touched to come in and read for a part," remarked Levitt afterward. "This was directly reflective of Amy's novel. The auditions attracted serious, educated and emotional people who loved the book and wanted to bring this experience to the American public. And I've never conducted auditions where people cried so much. . . . Every woman who came in had a story, whether it was about a sister, aunt or grandmother, that reflected these characters. Whether they were born here or in China, they all could relate to the script" (qtd. in Buena Vista Pictures, Inc. 1993, 13). "Word spread to so many ears in New York's large Mandarin-speaking community that 2,000 people showed up for an open call in the ballroom of the Sheraton Hotel in Flushing, Queens, in July 1993" (Avins 1993, 14). The auditions brought out not only Chinese but

Japanese, Filipinos, and Koreans to the Sheraton for the audition (Smith 1992, A12). According to the San Francisco casting director Robin Gurland, "When I initially read the book and then the screenplay, I thought that the characters' tragic lives were unique. . . . If anything the stories in the novel were minimized compared to the ones I heard from the women who auditioned. They would inevitably leave the audition in tears" (ibid., A12).

Wayne Wang, the film's director, noted that there were a lot of real mothers and daughters who had read the book and felt it reflected their own experiences (Avins 1993, 14). People wanted to meet the filmmakers because they felt an affinity for the themes in Tan's book. One journalist noted that many of the auditioners clutched "copies of The Joy Luck Club like talismans" (Smith 1992, A12). As Heidi Levitt states, "Their attitude wasn't, 'I want to be in a movie,' . . . It was, 'I want to be in *this* movie. This is my story'" (qtd in Buena Vista Pictures, Inc. 1993, 14). At a casting call, June Yee "says she felt 'split' growing up in an upper-middle-class suburb of Pittsburgh. In school, she was just another American kid, but at home she was surrounded by 'moon cakes and thousand-year-old eggs.' Acting in the movie would be one way to draw on her rich Chinese side, long neglected in her life as an investment banker, 'I'm really here because of the book'" (Smith 1992, A12).

Asian American female readers and filmgoers are constructing spaces at personal, domestic-familial, and social-public sites to talk-story about their lives. They don't feel alone or emotionally isolated or paralyzed in "developing a context of action and response in which [they] could make sense to others and to themselves" (Smith 1990, 138). This is the critical heart work that could potentially enable women to perhaps actively re-envision themselves and the world in more constructive and collective ways.

The Opiate of the Duped?

Asian American female readers have commented on the pleasures of recognition in Tan's mother-daughter stories, which confirm their dilemmas and provide them spaces to critically assess their perspectives and practices. The traumas of everyday life that were experienced separately are now shared by women situated in an imaginative and/or actual social community or readership. They see their individual suffering and conflicts as part of a shared community, and they have the urge to bear witness—in letters, in interviews, in the making of films, in social bonding with other women, in the buying of books. Where once they suffered alone and in silence, or where they once did not know exactly the nature of their unhappiness or discomfort, they are now beginning to think in critical personal and social terms. Where certain female readers may have once perceived themselves or their ethnic culture as the lone cause of their alienation or exclusion from mainstream society, they now situate their individual dilemmas within a broader social and public context. They can speak and be heard and validated by others who know and share similar desires, conflicts, alienation, and resolutions, creating a social and political culture in opposition to the one articulated and enforced by the dominant culture.

Major publishing venues rarely gave Asian American writers opportunities to have their work received by a broad audience. Further, in Hollywood movies, Chinese American women were rarely visible and central to a mainstream film; nor were they employed in roles supposedly expressing Asian or Asian American female experience. Visibility was really constructed through a racist cosmetology that inscribed the illusion of an Asian woman for a white mainstream audience. As it was for roles like Charlie Chan or Fu Manchu, where white men depicted Chinese American males, Caucasian women—Myrna Loy, Ruby Keeler, Loretta Young, Angie Dickinson, Katherine Hepburn, Luise Rainer, Shirley McClaine, Ona Munson, and Jennifer Jones—were often used for Asian roles. This contributed to a long history of aesthetic imperialism for Asian and Asian American women. *The Joy Luck Club* brought together Asian American female actresses and gave them employment and presence on the screen as had never been seen in the long history of Hollywood movies. The pleasure of recognition on the part of female Asian American readers and film audiences was therefore understandable.

In providing access to Chinese women's silenced and invisible stories, Tan's and Kingston's stories are a source of pleasurable recognition for some Asian American women readers, recognition that needs to be taken seriously. Such responses, of course, are sometimes quickly and smugly dismissed in elitist critiques as part of the culture of the unsophisticated reading masses or as part of the sentimental, melodramatic narratives favored by nonintellectual or apolitical women.[21]

Ien Ang notes, "the way in which a cultural product is consumed [cannot] be directly deduced from the way in which it is produced; it is also dependent on all sorts of sociocultural and psychological conditions" (Ang 1985, 18–19). What, for example, is its entertainment value, its pleasure value to a reader or a community of readers? Ang emphasizes the importance of examining the mechanisms that lie at the basis of that pleasure, how that pleasure is produced and how it works. Pleasure from such a perspective is not natural and automatic, it is constructed and functions in specific social and historical contexts .

The narrow and reductive classification of their stories as "sentimental," "melodramatic," or "emotional," or dismissal as typical "mother-daughter" or "women's" stories places Kingston, Tan, and Ng in danger of being trivialized or ignored by "high culture" or academic discursive communities that devalue women's culture or mass popular appeal as non-intellectual and non-political. Scholars who study popular culture are rethinking the complex ways it can be "manipulated by various desires that are encoded" (Henderson 1995, 19). While this culture may appeal "to repressed, regressive fantasies and [reinforce] race, gender, and class stereotypes, it also has the ability to deconstruct or subvert popular stereotypes, especially when these cultural forms . . . embody a self-critique." Furthermore, as Henderson rightly notes, "it is in cultural critique that the intellectual as an interpreter of cultural forms and expressions (whether regressive or progressive) plays a central role" (ibid.). In interpreting the relationships of these popular texts to specific communities, critics can produce deforming (as well as transforming) social and political narratives and practices. There exists the notion that these stories are "sell-out" fictions, produced by white mainstream publishers, which do not represent the interests of the Chinese American "community" but rather reinforce hegemonic institutions. One must ask whose community is being referred to? And does this community take seriously women's various viewpoints, practices, and experiences as significant?

While pleasurable responses do merit substantial analyses, condescending or dismissive criticism does not serve to illuminate the significance of cultural texts for a diverse Asian American women reading public who may not be circulating their viewpoints in elite academic journals or mainstream media venues. They circulate their feelings and viewpoints in homes, grocery stories, offices, buses and carpools, schools, in phone discussions, book readings and lunches with mothers, families, and friends.

Far from being duped into an ahistorical, apolitical amnesia of thought, Asian American women readers of these mother-daughter texts form a fluid and eclectic community of women who ask questions about their own relationships with their mothers, families, and hybrid communities. Cultural critic Jacqueline Bobo articulates a more nuanced consideration of the audience reception to popular cultural forms produced by mainstream institutions for a broad audience. In her study, Bobo suggests that Black women could engage with certain aspects of a film without totally forgetting the long Hollywood history of racist and sexist narratives and representations of Black people.

> Members of a social audience—people who are actually watching a film or television program—will utilize interpretive strategies that are based upon their past viewing experiences as well as upon their personal histories, whether social, racial, sexual, or economic. This is the cultural competency, the repertoire of background knowledge, that is brought to the act of making sense of a particular text. . . . Black women's negotiation of a controversial mainstream film allowed researchers to understand that audiences had more control over their reactions to mainstream cultural forms and to other's opinions about how they should react than had been previously assumed, and that their historical and cultural knowledge played a significant role in their responses. (Bobo 1995, 87–8)

That is, even though Hollywood (or a mainstream publishing firm) might attempt to produce certain popular seductive codes that make a cultural text accessible to a broader reading audience, the audience may not read it as exactly within these codes. Like Black women, Asian American women can negotiate their problematic and multiple positioning to life as well as to a film or book by bringing their own personal experiences and historical and cultural knowledge to the critical evaluation of dominant or oppositional cultural products.

Into the Twenty-first Century with a Fruitful Lineage

On a more promising note, Kingston's and Tan's texts have helped to open the door to, and generated a market for, mother-daughter stories. Despite being exoticized by mainstream publishers and media and damned as mostly popular Orientalist fare for evidently uncritical Anglo (and Asian American) audiences, the mother-daughters stories are part of a thriving community of women readers. The Asian American women's community generates not just readers of these stories but literary sisters. These social cultural texts beget a fruitful lineage of talk-stories among readers and writers who preserve and continue women's specific stories and histories into the future. Rather than simply classifying and dismissing these stories in universal and conventional mother-daughter schema, which some critics are doing, I believe they are worth serious critical attention. The new narratives are vibrant, and aesthetically idiosyncratic. They include Chinese American: Sara Chin's *Below the Line* (1997), Gish Jen's, *Typical American* (1991) and *Mona in the Promised Land* (1996); Fae Myenne Ng's *Bone* (1993), Mei Ng's (1998) *Eating Chinese Food Naked*, Lan Samantha Chang's *Hunger: A Novella and Stories* (1998), Belle Yang's *Baba: A Return to China Upon my Father's Shoulders* (1994); Japanese American: Cynthia Kadohata's *The Floating World* (1989), R. A. Sasaki's *The Loom and Other Stories* (1991), Kiyoko Mori's *Shizuko's Daughter* (1993) and *The Dream of Water* (1995), Julie Shigekuni's *A Bridge Between Us* (1995) and Lois-Ann Yamanaka's *Wild Meat and the Bully Burgers* (1996) and *Blu's Hanging* (1997); Korean American: Ronyoung Kim's *Clay Walls* (1987), Nora Okja Keller's *Comfort Woman* (1997), Patti Kim's *A Cab Called Reliable* (1997); Vietnamese American: Lan Cao's *Monkey Bridge* (1997); Filipina American: M. Evelina Galang's *Her Wild American Self* (1996); and South Asian American: Ginu Kamani's *Junglee Girl* (1995) and Chitra Divakaruni's *Arranged Marriages: Stories* (1995). There are also several Japanese and Chinese Canadian mother-daughter stories to be found in Joy Kogawa's *Obasan* (1981), Sky Lee's *Disappearing Moon Cafe* (1990), Evelyn Lau's *Runaway: Diary of a Street Kid* (1995), Denise Chong's *The Concubine's Children* (1994), Ying Chen's *Ingratitude* (1990), Judy Fong Bates's *China Dog and Other Tales from a Chinese Laundry* (1997), and Elaine Mar's *Paper Daughter: A Memoir* (1999).

On the down side, the mother-daughter narratives have become so chic and profitable that non-Asians (as well as Asians) want a share of the market for things Asian and Asian American (Nguyen 1997, 47). Elaine Kim "recalls a conversation she had recently with a [non-Asian] writer who asked to interview some of her students. At the urging of a literary agent, the writer hoped to write a version of Amy Tan's *The Joy Luck Club*, using Korean, Chinese, Vietnamese, and Filipino characters. Unfamiliar with these backgrounds, she needed to do some research" (ibid., 47). Mainstream publishers, of course, are on the prowl for marketable, proven formulas and genres by which to woo broad audiences to their multicultural commodities. Putnam's Faith Sale, who handled Tan's book, acknowledges that one of the reasons Putnam picked up the rights to the book was because of its exotic appeal for a mainstream audience (Feldman 1989, 26). The "tributary media" hype, associated with the publishing industry, augments the commodity appeal (see P. Smith 1993). Tan was called "the flavor of the month, the hot young thing, the exotic new voice" (Streitfeld 1993, F8); the book "snappy as a fortune cookie and much more nutritious" (Koenig 1989, 82). The writer and her text have been appropriated, advertised, and exoticized for mainstream consumption. The comfortable, exoticized "visibility" constructs readers as Orientalist tourists being guided into the lives of the Joy Luck women.

Even though Tan's (or Kingston's) work was marketed as exotica, readers should not capitulate to and reproduce such a comfortable racist, sexist reading. Like a number of Asian American women readers, they may instead accept the challenge of reading these polysemic texts actively and subversively. In such ways, we can begin to construct alternative interpretive strategies for understanding these texts rather than duplicating the popular mainstream readings that apply inappropriate and distorting assumptions that erase or foreclose on their myriad possibilities. We are, after all, in the process of challenging hegemonic and privileged meanings that have profoundly affected our private and public lives and positionings in American society.

Fae Myenne Ng

Fae Myenne Ng, even more so than Kingston or Tan, significantly recovers and incorporates the struggles (interior and exterior) of Chinese immigrant men as they transition from a predominantly male Chinatown society to one that includes women, families, and permanent communities. She critiques the notion that Chinese men and women were cold and heartless toward their children, especially to their female children—a viewpoint lacking an understanding of the everyday strains of survival that marginalized people suffer within distressed communities. Having learned a great deal in the contentious debates within Asian American cultural politics, Ng is sensitive not only to mother-daughter trauma but also to the specific trauma of men in their multiple transitions to different familial and social sites in Chinatown and in the larger public world.

Ng, like Kingston and Tan, revisits the domestic-familial site in order to articulate the heroic, epic lives and struggles of trail-blazing mothers, daughters, and fathers. She explores the relationships between Dulcie, Leon, and their daughters. The marriage of Leon Leong and Dulcie Fu is described as "marriage of toil—toiling together" in the interests of their family of daughters (see also Kam 1989, Quan 1990, Nunez 1995, Yang 1994). Their form of heroism involves sustaining families and, in this case, having to confront hard labor, humiliation, and sometimes defeat and rejection in the process. Through her daughter-narrator Leila, Ng gives us an insider's sympathetic sense of how the changing power relations in China and the United States have serious consequences for Chinese American immigrant families in San Francisco's Chinatown. In the long history of excluding Chinese American families and communities in the U.S., the struggles of these women and men to maintain selves and families are a badge of heroism and resistance. Ng explores the psychic terrain of a family's collective and individual past. The manifest story is about the trauma of confronting the terrible death a beloved daughter and sister. But the profound subtext is rooted in the traumatic injustices in the United States that haunt this family's intimate spaces.

Ng's writing is spare in its respectful recovery of the community of suffering. In fact, she states in an interview that the discipline of sewing helped her learn to write (Hunnewell 1993, 9). She wanted a language that reflected the Chinese working class. The English language, as she says, had to be "lean, unsparing, even brutal in its bareness because it was meant to reflect honestly the harshness of immigrant livelihood" (Ng 1994). The drudgery and suffocating monotony of their daily work eat up their lives and dreams. This work is wearying to the bone; and chips away at their stamina and their ability to continue struggling to survive, especially for their children. Yet in the poetic nature of Ng's language and images, Ng resurrects the memories of a homeplace that Leila can still speak of with great love and pride. Her work is imaginatively sensitive in its social and emotional recuperation of the complex terrain traveled by immigrant women and men, as well as their American-born children.

Through their mother-daughter talk-stories, Kingston, Tan, and Ng challenge the representations of women that they find within their own communities in China and America as well as in dominant U.S. culture. They forefront the struggles of Chinese women, whose voices and standpoints have long been silenced, devalued, and appropriated. They reveal and challenge the debilitating, masochistic, and dysfunctional definitions of womanhood that situate Chinese women as purely and forever second-class citizens—psychosocially, economically, culturally and politically—under the authority and protection of men. In opposition to the simplistic stereotypes of obedient, self-sacrificing women and heartless, violent, tyrannical Chinese American men that resurrect dominant society's "contempt and pity" (see Scott 1997), these writers present varied and complex portrayals of the ways that Chinese Americans construct and maintain complex positions to survive the multiple oppressions of their daily lives.

Notes

1. See Alexander and Mohanty (1997); Allen (1986); Anzaldúa (1990b); Asian Women United of California (1989); duCille (1994); Gordon and Newfield (1996); Guy-Sheftall (1995); Hull, Bell, and Smith (1982); Lim, Tsutakawa, and Donnelly (1989); Lorde (1984); Lowe (1996a); Mohanty, Russo, and Torres (1991); Moraga and Anzaldúa (1981), Reagon (1983); Rebelledo and Rivero (1993); Sandoval (1991); Smith (1983); Spelman (1988); Spivak (1998); Wing (1997); Zinn and Dill (1994, 1996).

2. Likewise, other women of color struggled to keep the dialogue going with their men. See, for example, Cade (1970), Combahee River Collective (1981), Davis (1983), Fregoso and Chabram (1990), hooks (1990, 15–22; 1992), Pesquera and Segura (1993), Powell (1983), Quintana (1990), Wallace (1990), and Wei (1993).

3. See Allen (1986), Anzaldúa (1987, 1990b), Asian Women United of California (1989), Cade (1970), Moraga and Anzaldúa (1981), and Smith (1983).

4. See Kim (1982, 1986); see also Said (1978).

5. See Belden (1949) on the story of Gold Flower and her escape from her dehumanizing conditions. For a description of "indictments of bitterness," *suku*, see Ono (1989, 170–75). See also P. Chin (1931).

6. See Emily Honig's discussion (1986) about the impact of the YWCA, more so than that of the Chinese Communist Party, on developing the political consciousness of the women in the Shanghai Cotton Mills, 1919–1949. "Beginning in the 1930s the YWCA night schools taught women workers how to read, how to speak in public, and how to analyze the social structure of which, as women and as workers, they were a part. The YWCA schools were the first to arrange social activities with women from various mills and industries. In due course some graduates of the YWCA schools became political activists. By the 1940s many of those women had joined the CCP; even more interestingly, many women Party members had joined the YWCA" (p. 248). In order to organize women, the Party also instituted changes, which were similar to those being practiced in the YWCA and in the sisterhoods formed by factory women (ibid., 249). Party members visited women workers at their home sites, helped them with daily laundry and shopping and went with women to social activities (p. 249).

    See also Janice Stockard's discussions (1989) of marriage resistance formations like "sworn sisterhood" and on "delayed transfer marriage" alternatives in the Canton Delta, 1860–1930.

7. On the specific history of Chinese women's experiences, see Wolf and Witke (1974), Croll (1978 and 1995), Siu (1981), Honig (1986), Jayawardena (1986), Stockard (1989), Ono (1989), and Ebrey (1991). Also see Chen (1976), Lott (1989), Chow (1989), S. Ling (1989), Yung (1995), and Wei (1993) for discussions of the impact of the revolutionary developments in China on Chinese women in the United States.

8. Rich does mention the Demeter-Persephone story, ritualized in the religious mysteries at Eleusis and an element of Greek spiritual life for over two thousand years. However, she states that this recognition of mother-daughter "passion and rapture" is lost to us in present day society (1986b, 237–40).

9. There is a large body of critical work being produced on the topic of mothers and daughters. For some useful introductory surveys on the mother-daughter literature, consult Andersen (1988); Bassin, Honey, and Kaplan (1994); Chodorow (1978); Daly and Reddy (1991); Davidson and Boner (1980); Dill (1988); Dinnerstein (1976); Freidan (1963); Friday (1977); Flax (1978); Gardiner (1985); Glenn, Chang, and Forcey (1994); Hirsch (1981a and 1989); Jelinek (1980); Kaplan (1987); Thurer (1994); Umansky (1996); and Walters (1992).

10. See Abel, Christian, and Moglen (1997); Anderson (1988); Collins (1987, 1990, and 1994); Dill (1988); Glenn (1985, 1986, 1990, and 1994); Hurtado (1989); Spelman (1988); and Wade-Gayles (1987).

11. In the process of writing this book an ever increasing number of articles on mothers

and daughters have appeared, attesting to the growing interest in this area. However, there are still no full length studies on the topic of Asian American mothers and daughters or on mother-daughter writing by Asian American women writers. There are a number of articles and sections in books that include critical discussions of mother-daughter writing by Maxine Hong Kingston such as Bannan (1979), Barker-Nunn (1987), Cheung (1988), Friedman (1988), Ho (1991), Juhasz (1985), Kim (1990), Ling (1990), Rabine (1987), Schenck (1988), S. Smith (1987), and S. Wong (1988, 1995).

In regard to Tan, there are even fewer critical discussions of mother-daughter writing; however, see Heung (1993), Ho (1996), Kim (1990), Ling (1990), Lowe (1991), Schueller (1992), and S. Wong (1995). See Lim (1990), Cheung (1993), and T. Yamamoto (1998) on mother-daughter writing by Japanese American women writers.

12. See Black feminist writers such as Toni Cade Bambara (1992), Toni Morrison (1973 and 1987), June Jordan (1994), Paule Marshall (1981), and Alice Walker (1983). See also Anzaldúa (1987 and 1990b), Fernández (1990), Giddings (1984), Lorde (1982, 1984), Moraga and Anzaldúa (1981), Mohr (1985), Yamamoto (1988), Yamauchi (1994), and Woo (1981).

13. There has been some interesting recent work done on the caregiving and nurturing abilities of men, especially as single fathers or as caregivers for elderly people. See Wood (1999, 60–61).

14. The American-born Chinese writer, Jade Snow Wong, also writes about the dilemmas of being between two worlds (Wong 1989). Kingston herself has referred to Wong as one of her literary mentors. Wong's autobiography is more fully discussed by Amy Ling in comparison with Kingston's text (Ling 1990). I do not include Wong's autobiography for a number of reasons.

As Ling points out, even though Wong does bring up her difficulties and frustrations as a woman between Chinese and Anglo-American cultures, the text is less personal and more traditional, modest, and respectfully filial in regards to her father and her Chinese cultural roots. Wong's autobiography is written in the formal third person.

Kingston, Tan, and Ng focus on Chinese American mother-daughter struggles in the contemporary milieu of Chinese America, write from a more idiosyncratic point of view, and suggest innovative narrative and political strategies in their texts.

15. Kingston is currently working on a "global novel" that will foreground more peaceful strategies to become a more humane person rather than strategies to glorify tragedy, violence, and war as the end result of life.

16. See Kingston (1976). All references to this edition will appear in the text with the abbreviation *TWW*.

17. See Hisaye Yamamoto's *Seventeen Syllables and Other Stories* (1988), Wakako Yamauchi's *Songs My Mother Taught Me* (1994) and Monica Sone's *Nisei Daughter* (1953), which explore the experiences of Japanese American mothers and daughters during the pre-war and internment years, and also preceded Kingston's work.

18. Ling 1990, 120. Ling's volume on Chinese American women writers includes an extensive annotated bibliography.

19. Rooks and Pannish note that Asian American women reviewers in particular find a solidarity with Maxine Hong Kingston (1993, 136).

20. For example, see Horton's interview in which Kingston discusses the appeal of *The Woman Warrior* for men, who also bought it for their wives, daughters, and girlfriends to read (Kingston 1998, 7).

21. On popular culture see Ang (1985), Bourdieu (1984, 1993).

3

THE TRAFFIC IN WOMEN:
MIGRATION AND REPRESENTATION

> To assess the damage is a dangerous act.
> Cherríe Moraga, from "La Güera"
>
> Systematically incorporating hierarchies of race
> and class into feminist reconstruction
> of the family remains a challenge, a necessary
> next step into the development of theories of
> family that are inclusive.
> Evelyn Nakano Glenn, from
> "Gender and the Family"

Any account of the women's culture that Chinese American mothers and daughters make together—"talking-story beneath a mango tree"—must be rooted within the larger and more complex history of the formation of Chinese communities in China and the United States. It is a history in which social and family relations and the prohibition and subordination of these relations are central. We know a part of this oppressive history from the Chinese American male perspective. But part of this story, the less visible part, is that which has to do with the social realities of women in China and in the United States.

Early Migration to the United States
The Chinese were one of the earliest Asian groups who began significantly migrating to California during the early 1850s Gold Rush period. The first groups of Chinese were predominantly male; most came from China's Guangdong Province and spoke Cantonese.[1] Like European Americans, the Chinese had hoped to find work and better circumstances in the United States, especially during periods of hardship in

the home country. By 1852, twenty thousand Chinese had arrived to join in the search for gold, encountering a great deal of hostility and violence from white miners. California attempted to legalize harassment of Chinese miners by enacting the Foreign Miner's Tax in 1852.

With waning mining opportunities, many Chinese men contributed to the infrastructure of the country through their dangerous, backbreaking labor in building the transcontinental railroad (1866–1869), and in the agricultural and fishing industries (see Takaki 1983, S. Chan 1986). After the completion of the railroads, many Chinese men took low-paying work in the increasingly segregated manufacturing sector (such as the cigar, shoe, and woolen goods industries) in San Francisco and other large cities.

From the 1870s into the early 1900s, white-supremacist politicians, settlers, nativists, and craft and labor unions such as the American Federation of Labor agitated forcefully against the so-called "hordes of coolie laborers" or "Yellow Peril" competing for jobs with immigrant white European-Americans in an increasingly depressed economic market.[2] Labor organizations in San Francisco, for example, formed the Asiatic Exclusion League to fight for the exclusion of the Chinese, who were perceived as inassimilable workers who could not understand or cooperate with white working-class labor demands for better wages, hours, and compensation. Furthermore, the privileged white racist narratives, which circulated in mainstream culture and by which exclusion was justified, maintained that Chinese men chose to be "sojourners" or "bachelors" and that they "came to America without. . . women (a sign that [they] had no intention of settling here); refused to assimilate, were alien and incapable of accommodating the democratic, individualistic manly ideals that throbbed in the guts of every American word, breath and deed, established [their] own clannish social structures in defiance of the laws of the land, robbed America of her wealth and took it home to China and [their women]" (Chin 1972, 63). Such interpretive narratives attempted to suppress racial-ethnic individuals and groups and their histories in order to maintain and justify the inequitable power arrangements of the nation-state.

As a result of anti-Chinese hysteria, there was a great deal of racial violence against individual Chinese and their communities: They were burned out of town, murdered, and legally hounded by the government (see Wu 1972, Daniels 1988, Takaki 1993, and Almaguer 1994). "This terrorism and violence resulted between 1890 and 1900 in the first real drop in the Chinese male population in California. Those who could afford it returned to China, many others departed for the East Coast. Still others sought refuge in the crowded Chinese settlements of the large cities from which it had become unsafe to venture without fear of being beaten as late as the 1920s. . . . " (Nee and Nee 1972, 55). In a racially- and gender-stratified white capitalist-patriarchal labor economy, Chinese men, for the most part, found themselves restricted to restaurants and other domestic settings as launderers, house servants, cooks, dishwashers—cheap labor jobs most often held by women and defined as "women's work." Moreover, these jobs were often located within Chinatown enclaves where co-ethnic employers were not above exploiting their workers' desperation. Into the early decades of the twentieth century, Chinese men who contemplated bringing their families to the United States found it socially, economically, and politically difficult—if not impossible—to do so.

In Chinatown, the crowded urban ghetto of the Chinese/Other within the heart of the white city, there was little freedom, safety, or privacy. Those who lived there found that their psychosocial and physical needs were exploited and monitored. The Chinese were governed by laws concerning immigration, miscegenation, and citizenship; there were regulations that governed their work, hygiene, sexuality, behavior, travel, leisure, and environment. For example, there were "poll taxes, license taxes on . . . laundry men, measures regulating sleeping quarters, theaters, the location, construction, and operation of places of business, of recreation, and of indulgence" (Sandmeyer 1973, 110 and see Yung 1995, 21–2). In the hostile environment of nineteenth-century struggles to advance a homogeneous and dominant national identity, actually based on racialized white ethnic notions, it is not surprising that the Chinese were the first of many Asian groups to be excluded by law on the basis of race and nationality. These exclusionary and stratified racialized practices were also used against other ethnic groups— Native Americans, Black and Mexican/Latino Americans—who were constructed as alien, inferior and marginal to an Anglo-American notion of citizenship and national identity.

Despite legal challenges and resistance from Chinatown associations and individuals, a number of exclusionary policies were passed that made it very difficult for most Chinese males (except a small elite class of wealthy merchants who were allowed to bring their wives, concubines, and children) to survive and to bring women and families to the United States. One of the major outcomes of the anti-Chinese hysteria was the Chinese Exclusion Act of 1882, which prohibited the immigration of Chinese laborers to the United States and banned Chinese from becoming naturalized citizens. This Act had a dramatic effect in isolating a predominantly aging Chinese male population, dying alone in the tenements of Chinatowns, and in curtailing the development of Chinese families in the U.S. (see Nee and Nee 1972). "Among most immigrant groups, working-age men tend to precede women, children, or older people to a new land, but in the case of the Chinese, exclusion was imposed just at that point in the immigrant community's development when men might have sent for their wives and children. Exclusionary policies therefore truncated the natural development of the community" (S. Chan 1991a, 105). There were few Chinese women in America in the nineteenth century; in fact, between 1860–1910, the gender ratio between men and women fluctuated between 13 and 27 men for every woman (Glenn and Yap 1998, 132). And according to Roger Daniels, even as late as 1920, seventy years after migration began, women comprised less than 10 percent of the Chinese American population (1988, 16). Women, children, and families were still a rare sight in Chinatown into the 1930s. Babies were such a rarity that they were doted upon by single and married Chinese men (see Chu 1961). In 1900, the Chinese population consisted of less than 4 percent children 14 and under, compared with 37.4 percent of the U.S. whites of native parentage (Glenn and Yap 1998, 132). In 1900, only 11 percent of the Chinese population were American-born; by 1930, this number rose to 41 percent, and 52 percent ten years later (Takaki 1989, 254).

Thus, a majority of immigrant Chinese men—single or married with wives, and families in China—were denied the traditional heterosexual markers of masculinity well into the twentieth century: fatherhood, providing for women and families, companionship-sexuality, citizenship (Naturalization Act of 1790), and ownership of land (following the 1913 California Alien Land Act barring aliens from owning land).

Maxine Hong Kingston and Fae Myenne Ng are particularly sensitive to this early male history in their mother-daughter stories. In her second memoir, *China Men* (1989c), Kingston imaginatively portrays the struggles of Chinese American men who toiled on railroads and sugar plantations and in Chinatown laundries, often separated for long periods from children, wives, and kin. She portrays their sorrow and loneliness as well as their courage and rebellion in the face of American social, economic, and political oppression. In *Bone*, Fae Myenne Ng bears witness to the tragic impact of exclusionary laws and economic exploitation on the lives of not only women but also men. Like Kingston, Ng's great-grandfather crisscrossed the Pacific in order to maintain contact with his family in China while keeping an economic foothold in California during the Gold Rush period. She depicts the experiences of old-timers living in Chinatown tenements, a motley family of men who cared for one another in the absence of wives and families and who lavished attention on the few children living in their fragmented community.

Ng and Kingston, more so than Tan, significantly include the stories of Chinese men, especially in their expansive and compassionate exploration of the psychosocial and political formations of self and family in Chinatown. Theirs are stories of men's heroic endurance in a hostile, emasculating society. With their critical stories, they challenge the inadequate traditional historical narratives that marginalize the struggles and legacies of Chinese (and Asian) Americans in the making of the United States.

Women, Migration, and Capitalism

An even more neglected part of the oppressive history of Chinese American families has to do with the experiences of Chinese women in China and in the United States. Gender, sexuality, race, class, and legal status affected the lives of Chinese immigrant women as profoundly as they affected the lives of the men. In order to begin the radical project of rethinking and reformulating critical forms of knowledge, social identities, and political alliances, it is important to consider women's experiences, which have been largely erased or repressed within traditional Western and masculinist ideologies, discourses, and institutions.

Because of perceptions that filtered into the United States through missionaries, diplomats, and travelers, Chinese women were stereotyped as heartless mothers, prostitutes, victims, and slaves in a patriarchal society. There were sensationalized accounts about Chinese mothers killing their babies, especially girl children. Stuart Creighton Miller in his book *The Unwelcome Immigrant* (1969) describes, for example, the observations of various missionaries: "Before the carts go around in the morning to pick up the bodies of infants thrown in the streets . . . dogs and swine are let loose upon them. The bodies of those found are carried to a common pit without the city walls, in which the living and the dead are thrown together." Another missionary, a Reverend James Nevius, wrote of "baby houses" into which the infants could be discarded so that they would not be eaten by dogs in the last moments of life. There were articles and illustrations of places where "heathen mothers without natural affection" would abandon or kill their children. Other missionaries are quoted as estimating that up to 40 percent (if not more) of all female infants born in China were "murdered" by their parents (Miller 1969, 67–68). In 1856, an American editor in China noted that "in China, whose ditches, canals and rivers are reported to be strewn ever and anon with the bodies of infants that of course have been killed by their horrid mothers. . . . Is it possible that, in the breasts of the Chinese, there can be one drop of the milk of human kindness, at least for children?" (ibid., 147). Miller concludes that "most other Western travelers to China who reported on infanticide understood it to be the consequence of poverty. However missionaries claimed it was a result of paganism, and hence infanticide was perceived as a 'universal practice in the Celestial Empire'" (ibid., 67–68). These representations attempted to describe Chinese women, families, and culture as perversely immoral and inherently alien to nineteenth-century Victorian notions of "civilization," which saw ideal women as upholders of Christian notions of moral purity, piety, and culture, especially in the care of their families.

The domestic sphere, which was constructed as separate from the public sphere of men, was emphatically identified as the special and naturalized domain of mothers, wives, and children. Good women tended not only to the care and education of children but also to the upkeep of their homes for the nation-state. The Anglo wives of missionaries, according to Miller, commented on Chinese domestic life and habits: "Their reports of the filth that permeated the Chinese home and the horrors of opium smoking, polygamy, and infanticide found a ready outlet in the ladies' magazines which were multiplying with such fecundity in the middle of the nineteenth century. . . . Their wives stipulated that the Chinese were both physically and morally unclean" (ibid., 147). These reports also contributed to perceptions of Chinatowns in the United States as sites of inferiority, difference, dirt, disease, and depravity. Thus, racist ethnocentric reports about the nature of Chinese society fueled the anti-Chinese hysteria, which contributed to the exclusion of the Chinese and their families from the United States into the early half of the twentieth century.

Another damaging perception was that all Chinese women who entered the United States from the late nineteenth into the twentieth century were prostitutes. In 1854, for example, Horace Greeley reported his fears over the immigration of the Chinese, especially Chinese women, into the U.S.: "The Chinese are uncivilized, unclean, and filthy beyond all conception without any of the higher domestic or social relations; lustful and sensual in their dispositions; every female is a prostitute of the basest order" (qtd. in Miller 1969, 169). To raise the pitch of anti-Chinese hysteria even further, Chinese prostitutes were believed to have brought into the United States "especially virulent strains of venereal diseases, introduced opium addiction, and enticed young white boys to a life of sin. In short, Chinese prostitutes were constructed as potent instruments for the debasement of white manhood, health, morality, and family life. Thus, their continued presence was deemed a threat to white civilization" (S. Chan 1991b, 138). The discourse on the Chinese prostitute is related to the larger discourse on the containment of the Chinese in general. These racialized, sexualized, and gendered constructions of the physical and moral pollution of the virtuous, libidinally-disciplined, civilized body politic reflect deep fears about the breakdown of a dominant white ruling order, and its control over the stratified classification and enactment of racialized ethnic identities and social relations within its capitalist and patriarchal power formations. Such cultural discourses, which incite mainstream societal anxieties about morality and well-being, suppress the actual ideological and institutional practices that promote and discipline the exploitation of subordinated racialized communities in the United States. Representations of prostitutes and Yellow Peril "coolies," for example, narrate the fears in the disintegration of the *white* family, economy, culture, and nation-state—not the destruction of racialized ethnic others and their families.

Because American capitalists sought to exploit a cheap male labor force in the early immigrant phases, they created circumstances that also exploited poor Chinese girls. Chinese social-cultural values as well as the rigors and hostilities of frontier life were factors in discouraging many Chinese women from immigrating to the United States. However, there were a number of women who came to this country as single and married women. Their histories have yet to be fully accounted for in this early period of Chinese immigration history, which has frequently been represented as a male "bachelor" or "sojourner" society. Moreover, numerous racist, sexist laws and immigration policies enacted against the Chinese resulted in a very imbalanced ratio between men and women in the United States. A number of Asian American historians such as Judy Yung, Sucheng Chan, Gary Okihiro, Lucie Hirata, Cheng Tsu-wu, and Ronald Takaki have documented the specific forms of discrimination and coercive regulations practiced against the Chinese in these early immigration phases. For example, anti-miscegenation attitudes were institutionalized in the amended 1880 California Civil Code that prohibited "the issuance of a marriage license to a white person and a 'Negro, Mulatto, or Mongolian'" (see Yung 1995, 29–30). Many Chinese men were stranded in America and financially unable to return home or to bring their families. As a result, both heterosexual married and single Chinese men "found it difficult to establish conjugal relationships or find female companionship. . . . The demand for Chinese prostitutes by both Chinese and white men intersected with an available supply of young women sold in servitude by impoverished families in China" (ibid., 29–30). Chinese male workers, therefore, needed to be "managed": "Whether the bodies of the racialized Other were to be killed or colonized, slaughtered or saved, expunged or exploited, they had to be prevented at all costs from polluting the body politic or sullying civil(ized) society" (Goldberg 1993, 187).

Chinese women were often imported as unfree labor, indentured or enslaved for a very profitable prostitution and *mui tsai* (female domestic servants) trade in the United States (Yung 1995, 27, 37–41). They were lured, kidnapped, or bought by procurers who worked within a lucrative prostitution trade that often included a network of importers, brothel owners, criminal tongs (for example, the Hip Yee Tong), landlords, police and immigration officials (Hirata 1979).[3] It is estimated that "in 1870, there were 159 brothels in San Francisco's Chinatown alone, and almost two-thirds of the Chinese women in the city worked as prostitutes" (Amott and Matthaei 1991, 202). Not only were Chinese prostitutes providing companionate-sexual services to a predominantly male society, they were also exploited as domestics and garment workers in the labor economy.

Following historical notions about women's ideal social roles and responsibilities in a patriarchal society, many Chinese prostitutes felt they were enacting their filial duties as good, self-sacrificing daughters to families who were often economically distressed. Furthermore, many had "no political rights and limited access to legal recourse within or outside the Chinese community" (Yung 1995, 31). This made it difficult to consider alternative options seriously. Some prostitutes, depressed and humiliated by their servitude, escaped their dismal circumstances by taking opium or by committing suicide. Others were able to escape the brothels with lovers or flee to Christian rescue missions. Sadly, despite their sacrifices for their families, the bodies of Chinese women were rarely sent back to China for burial as was customary for Chinese men who died in the United States (Almaguer 1994, 177). Within interlocking Chinese and Anglo-American frameworks, the prostitution of Chinese women was accepted as a tolerable alternative to meet the temporary needs of men separated from their families and communities.

The prostitution trade in Chinese women had a specific impact on the history and representation of Chinese female immigration to the United States. Sucheng Chan notes that "beginning in 1875, federal laws forbade most Chinese women— all of whom the government suspected of being prostitutes—from entering" and these regulatory laws were a factor that made the settlement history of the Chinese different from that of Europeans (Chan 1991, 105). Tomás Almaguer notes that "between 1866 and 1905 at least eight California laws were passed designed to restrict the importation of Chinese women for prostitution or to suppress the brothel business. . . . Such sentiment . . . led the California state legislature in March 1870 to enact an 'anti-prostitution' measure that required any Chinese or Japanese woman entering the United States to present satisfactory evidence that she had 'voluntarily' immigrated and was 'a person of correct habits and good moral character'" (Almaguer 1994, 178). In 1875, the federal government established the Page Law, which prohibited prostitutes and coolie labor entry to the United States. "Between 1870 and 1880, the percentage of Chinese women in San Francisco who were prostitutes had declined from 71 to 50 percent, while the percentage of women who were married had increased from 8 to 49 percent, most likely owing to the enforcement of anti-prostitution measures, the arrival of wives [of the elite merchant class] from China, and the marriage of ex-prostitutes to Chinese laborers" (Yung 1995, 41).

Christian missionaries, like Rev. Otis Gibson of the Women's Missionary Society and Donaldina Cameron of the Presbyterian Mission Home (1874–1939) in San Francisco, established "rescue homes" specifically for Chinese prostitutes. Missionaries focused on Chinese women, who came to symbolize the degradation, confinement, and enslavement of women by Chinese men. "If not murdered at birth, they were shabbily treated until sold to the highest bidder as wives, concubines, and prostitutes. . . . Even as a legal wife, the Celestial female lived in 'perpetual humiliation and wretchedness'" (Miller 1969, 68). Chinese women were often represented simplistically as helpless victims, slaves and chattels of Chinese men and patriarchy, a totalizing view that historians such as Dorothy Ko (1997) and Susan Mann (1997) are dismantling in their nuanced studies of Chinese women in seventeenth- and eighteenth-century China.[4]

In light of the racist and sexist images and discourses about Chinese women, the missionaries worked vigorously to reform Chinese women into strong Christian mothers and wives. According to Peggy Pascoe, the mission homes attempted to prepare Chinese women and their families for life in mainstream white American society and to develop a Protestant Chinese middle class in San Francisco and elsewhere (Pascoe 1990, 131; see also Mason 1994). Pascoe notes that between 1874 and 1928, several hundred marriages between rescued prostitutes and small merchants in Chinatown were registered by the Presbyterian Mission Home. Many Chinese women in mission homes did not convert to Christianity and married nevertheless. But to ensure that those Chinese women who did convert would follow through with Christian principles "only those Chinese men who fit the white Protestant ideal of the Christian gentleman were allowed to write or call on Mission Home residents" (Pascoe 1990, 130). The missionaries based their understanding of gendered identities and social relations on the Victorian ideals of "true womanhood" and the "cult of domesticity." The women converts were socialized to perceive themselves—and not patriarchal husbands—as the center of "moral authority" in the home and family. However, as we noted earlier, for a long period in U.S. history, many Chinese men did not have the same patriarchal privileges over their families or lives as did white men under U.S. capitalism.

Although the missionary women did afford some Chinese women an escape from the prostitution trade and opportunities for education, domestic work, and marriage, they also created dilemmas for many Chinese women by turning them against "traditional Chinese marriages and family life, alienating the Chinese community and subjecting the women to cultural conflict and social ostracism. . . . Moreover, by choosing to focus only on transforming the gender roles of wives, excluding husbands in the process of change, they further alienated the men and jeopardized the long-term efficacy of their work" (Yung 1995, 36). However, a number of historians have noted that the dilemmas were not purely negative for Chinese women (see Pascoe 1990, Mason 1994, and Tong 1994). Many Chinese women did not simply end up mimicking the Victorian ideals of womanhood or domesticity. In the new social realities of America (where they were fairly free from in-laws and were valued as wives, mothers, and workers), Chinese women had potential spaces for the exercise of power and innovation in their personal, familial, and social lives.

Into the early twentieth century, there were laws specifically aimed at restricting not only immigration but also the citizenship and naturalization rights of Chinese women in the United States. These discriminatory policies resulted in a long history of split households, which made the lives of Chinese men in the United States, as well as the lives of women in the home country, extremely difficult. On one hand, these women were often denied the sexual and companionate comforts of a husband and stable breadwinner. They endured long, lonely separations; and societal prohibitions against adultery were severe. Consider the severe punishment of Kingston's No Name Woman in the opening chapter of *The Woman Warrior* or the fact that Kingston's mother Brave Orchid was separated from her husband for 15 years before she came to the U.S. in the late 1930s to join him. Other women saw their husbands more rarely or never again.

On the other hand, a woman left behind—*the gum san po* (Gold Mountain woman)—had to be strong and independent to survive: She shouldered the care of her husband's kin, nurtured and educated their children, made important decisions in his absence, and labored inside and outside the home, especially if the "Gold Mountain" remittances were not forthcoming from their husbands.[5] Out of need, women often achieved a level of resilience, independence, and power in maintaining their families and making decisions in their husbands' absence. Gary Okihiro reminds us:

> Asian men in America were not solitary figures moving in splendid isolation but were intimately connected to women in Asia. . . . Re-centering women extends the range of Asian American history, from bachelor societies in Hawaii and the U.S. mainland to the villages and households in Asia, in an intricate and dynamic pattern of relations. Transcending American exceptionalism is but one of the consequences of a woman-centered history. While Asian American historiography might have begun with Europeans and European Americans imagining and witnessing Asia, the primary contexts of Asian American history . . . comprise that entrance of Asians into the European consciousness, together with the intersection of Asians with Africans, and the agency of generative societies in Asia, where women held up half the sky. (1994, 68)

A reconsideration of the transnational dimensions of Asian American history, in this case Chinese American women's history, can assist in challenging the stereotypical Orientalist accounts of Chinese women as passive victims in an absolute and ahistorical patriarchal culture and society. In revealing the significant and diversified identities of Chinese women in relation to women, men, children, and extended networks within overlapping structures of oppression, I think we vastly enrich our understanding of the complex dynamics of women making culture and community.

The Cable Act of 1922 stipulated that American-born Chinese women would lose their U.S. citizenship if they married aliens ineligible for citizenship. In contrast to white women, these women could not regain their U.S. citizenship through naturalization (Yung 1989, 426). There was also the Immigration Quota Act of 1924 which excluded all aliens ineligible for citizenship (all Asians except Hawaiians and Filipinos) and allowed entry of alien wives of Chinese merchants, but not alien wives of U.S. citizens until 1930, when Public Law 349 admitted wives married before May 26, 1924 (ibid.). All these restrictions significantly contributed to the harassment of Chinese women and the slow formation of Chinese families in the United States in the early decades of the twentieth century.

Family development in Chinatowns increased more significantly in the period between 1930 and 1960 with changes to the Immigration Quota Act of 1924 as well as other immigration policies. In the 1940s, the U.S. was at war with the Japanese, which resulted in a favorable change in sentiment toward the Chinese, who were also fighting the Japanese. In recognition of the bond between China and the U.S., the 1882 Chinese Exclusion Act was repealed in 1943. The War Brides Act, the GI Fiancées Act, and the Act of August 9, 1946 were also enacted to allow the entrance of Chinese war brides, fiancées, and children, often after rigorous investigation and detention by the FBI and INS. Political and student refugees were now able to enter as refugees or displaced persons. In the midst of war and turmoil in China, the Joy Luck women make their way to the United States in 1949. The McCarran-Walter Immigration and Nationality Act of 1952 allowed Chinese to leave China after the establishment of the People's Republic of China under Chairman Mao Zedong in 1949. These various institutional policies helped to balance the long skewed male-female ratio in the Chinese community and encouraged the formation and reunification of families. Furthermore, it diversified the population of Chinese women (and men), who were now entering the U.S. in consideration of factors such as socioeconomic class, education, dialect, and geopolitical distribution.

Some immigrant women were gradually reunited after long years of separation from their husbands. Many were detained and subjected to degrading physical searches and interrogation at the Angel Island Immigration Station in San Francisco Bay (1910–1940). On the bittersweet soil of America, they raised and educated children and contributed, with their husbands, to the economic and political survival of their families here and in China. Low Shee Law, the wife an American citizen who came to San Francisco in 1922, remembers: "We rented a room on Stockton Street for eleven dollars a month. We did everything in that one room—sit, sleep, and eat. We had a small three-ring burner for cooking, no ice box, and no hot water. We would hand-wash our clothes and dry them on the roof or in the hallways. Those were poor times and it was the same for all my neighbors" (Yung 1986, 43).

Marriages were a matter of collective survival. For some of the older women who rejoined husbands in the post-WWII period, it was a mixed blessing. They could not speak the language and were socially, economically, and culturally struggling to adapt. According to Stanford Lyman, the percentage of suicides of Chinese women rose from 17.5 percent in the 1950s to 28.3 percent in the 1960s (qtd. in Yung 1986, 82). Most Chinese immigrant women worked even after the birth of their children, typically ranging from six to thirteen in number (ibid., 43), and the wives of the merchant class often contributed to the family income by taking in sewing and embroidery (S. Chan 1991a, 109). In urban areas, many Chinese immigrant women worked long hours for little pay in domestic services or in restaurant, garment, and canning factory work. Family life suffered under these debilitating circumstances, and some women began to organize and strike to unionize for better pay, hours, and working conditions in the garment industry.[6] Women and children also contributed to the agricultural work and economic survival of their families in rural areas (see S. Chan 1986).

In order to counter the racism and discrimination in mainstream society, a number of Chinese families pulled together to open family-owned laundries, grocery stores, and restaurants, non-competitive with whites and situated within the protective, and sometimes exploitative, confines of Chinatown communities. Families worked long hours under miserable conditions (see Nee and Nee 1972, Siu 1987, Yu 1992). Children witnessed at an early age the grinding social realities of their parents' lives as well as their own. For example, John Gee, a laundryman, testifies to his parents' lives in the laundry business and how he has gradually developed his own politicized social consciousness about Chinese American experiences:

> Growing up and living in my parents' laundry, I did not fully understand how they worked and struggled. I would not stop to consider that my father immigrated to America as a teenager and could not go to high school because he had to work in a laundry to make money. Yet, he had learned to speak English well, and people were surprised when they discovered that he was not born in this country. Accordingly, watching my mother ironing hour after hour, I would forget how laundry work limited her abilities. Anyone who saw her laboring over the ironing table would not know that she had received a fine education in China and had worked as a teacher. However, I always realized that they worked very hard. I saw that every day. Years later, I began to understand that my parents' struggles were not isolated from those of other Chinese. Now I view Chinese laundry work as an important part of the Chinese American experience and as a reflection of people's struggle against social and economic oppression. (1976, 338)

In the mother-daughter narratives of Kingston and Ng, the daughters Maxine and Leila witness their mothers toil exhausting hours side-by-side with their husbands and children in Chinatown laundries while also assuming the more traditional responsibilities for the care of their families and the housework. They are intimately aware of the exploited human labor (productive and reproductive) and social-emotional suffering that occur within the confines of their emergent ethnic families and Chinatown communities. At the same time, the daughters know that the Chinatown community's defensive wariness, fear, and hostility towards "white devil outsiders" limit their social interactions, options, and perspectives in mainstream American society. Chinatown is the continual reminder of Anglo-America's repressed history of economic exploitation, racism, and indifference toward the Chinese in the United States. While the larger mainstream American society can provide these second-generation daughters with more options than their parents had, the daughter-narrators cannot fully escape or deny the legacy that intimately haunts their subjectivity and their collective and political identity.

The writers work to do justice to women's histories in their stories of the complicated formation of racial-ethnic families and communities. In opposition to the Eurocentric portrayals, many Chinese women were actually deeply devoted to their husbands and children. They cared for husbands who were continually negotiating anger and frustrations, the result of the everyday racisms that denied them visibility as men and as providers. Chinese American women were social and emotional anchors, as well as disciplinarians, and struggled actively to maintain their families and communities under very difficult circumstances and conflicting frames of reference. Moreover, continuing research on Chinese and Chinese American social history suggests a complex child- and family-centered culture and society not acknowledged in racist and sexist Eurocentric paradigms, discourses, or practices.

Through Chinese women's significant contributions to the social, cultural, and economic survival and development of their families and communities, they were sometimes able to challenge patriarchal domestic-familial authority and construct more fluid relationships with their husbands as well as with other women in their community. Pierrette Hondagneu-Sotelo, in her study of the migration of Mexican women and men and its impact on changing gendered dynamics, noted that "both single and married Mexican women [were] contesting patriarchal dictates in the process of U.S.-bound migration, and men, as fathers, husbands, and brothers, [were] responding in various ways. Just as women often comply with their own subordination in patriarchal institutions, so conversely do men participate, albeit sometimes unwittingly, in the dismantling of patriarchy. Migration and settlement introduce new challenges and pressures for change in both women's and men's behavior" (1994, 192). As will become evident in the stories of Kingston, Tan, and Ng, many Chinese American women (as well as men) carved out distinct spaces within multiple patriarchal structures to enact various strategies for survival and creative resistance. Women also established strong, mutually supportive networks outside their marriages and/or familial-kinship ties that helped them to care for themselves, their families, and communities, often under difficult contexts.

Thus, to suggest that Chinese or Chinese American social-familial dynamics are purely oppressive and debilitating to women (and to men) is an ahistorical and truncated approach to understanding the creative ways people negotiate their lives and circumstances. Furthermore, to suggest that Chinese American families have a desire to totally assimilate into white middle/upper-class identities and lifestyles (e.g., the "model minority" stereotype) blinds us to how racial-ethnic families enact new, eclectic, and practical ways to negotiate their everyday lives and circumstances. The mother-daughter stories of Kingston, Tan, and Ng contribute to a more complex and transformative project, which is to articulate Asian American women's specific contributions to the theorizing on identity formations and on social-cultural and political life.

Until World War II, immigrant and American-born Chinese women confronted significant discrimination in employment and social mobility outside of Chinatown. Before the 1940s, even with the best education, many American-born women found it hard to find jobs outside of Chinatown as clerical workers or professionals.[7] If they did find outside work, they were likely to get jobs that emphasized their erotic-exotic image in the mainstream or catered to the specific needs of their ethnic community (such as language translation services at banks or phone companies). Some Chinese American women (and men), disappointed with the lack of employment and acceptance in United States, departed with their American educational degrees to work and agitate in China and other countries (see Chun 1998).

However, with a male labor shortage during the war years, Chinese American women began to find more job opportunities outside of their Chinatown communities, in the defense industries, civil services, and professional fields (see Amott and Matthaei 1991, and Zhao 1996). According to Judy Yung, the views on sex/gender identities and relations changed more so for a significant number of educated, middle-class women "owing to the influences of Chinese nationalism, Christianity, and acculturation into American life. . . . Through church, school, and the popular media, the second generation was encouraged to challenge traditional gender roles at home and discrimination outside, to shape a new cultural identity and lifestyle for themselves" (1995, 6; see also Chan 1998).[8] With increasing work opportunities for women after the war, there came more economic independence, social mobility, and leisure. Immigrant and American-born Chinese women moved into the public domain and became increasingly involved in the social and political issues of their communities. They joined such groups as the Chinese YWCA, the Square and Circle Club, and several others.

Another new generation of Chinese American women found various ways to construct more hybrid identities as their lives were influenced by the revolutionary transformations in China and the United States. The communist scare and Cold War period of the conservative 1950s and subsequent social and political ferment of the 1960s generated diverse ideologies and discourses in American society. This created potential spaces for second-generation women to articulate and enact more liberating changes in their everyday lives.

The "Oriental" in American Popular Imagination

American literature and media have presented a range of dominant images of Asians that have become the staples of not only elitist culture but also American popular culture. The persistent construction and recreation of racist and sexist representations to define subordinated racial-ethnic groups have helped to ensure the continued deformation and/or erasure of their diverse experiences here. According to Patricia Hill Collins, as well as others, the objectification of subordinate groups through the application of "controlling images" helps to justify their exploitation, which is in turn related to a system based on such factors as race, class, sexuality, and gender (qtd. in Hamamoto 1994, 2). These hegemonic representations are deeply inscribed and legitimated in mainstream institutions; they are often constructed as if they are "objective" or "apolitical" understandings of the individual and social relations in society. They are, in part, a way for dominant group interests, aligned in power blocs with other diverse interest groups, to control the power relations among all groups within and outside the late capitalist nation-state.

For example, cultural representations of Chinese and Asian Americans have profound consequences not only for the perceptions of the dominant ruling group and its interactions with marginalized groups, but also on the self-perceptions and behavior of Asian Americans and their relationships to dominant society and to their specific ethnic community. Richard Delgado and Jean Stefancic have noted that

> the mechanistic view of an autonomous subject choosing among separate, external ideas is simplistic. In an important sense, we *are* our current stock of narratives, and they us. We subscribe to a stock of explanatory scripts, plots, narratives, and understandings that enable us to make sense of—to construct—our social world. Because we live in that world, it begins to shape and determine us, who we are, what we see, how we select, reject, interpret, and order subsequent reality. [italics mine] (Delgado and Stefancic 1998, 213)

Thus, to examine the history of these representations and to understand the complicated ways they construct and organize our psychosocial world is to create hopeful, active, and critically conscious sites at which to discover more emancipatory ways to live and to challenge society's injustices.

American Made Chop Suey: Villians, Houseboys, and Wimps

In the popular American imagination, Chinese men were depicted as alien, inferior, grotesque, immoral, and decadent—skulking in dark, wretched Chinatown alleys, frequenting brothels, smoking opium and gambling, or salivating lasciviously at a distance over white women, whom they could not have. Chinese men were represented as vicious, inscrutable, and clever criminals or gangsters; Hollywood films still portray martial-arts/triad/clan stereotypes in a decadent, alien Chinatown environment. Late nineteenth-century articles and illustrations incited fears about the "consequences of coolieism" or the "Yellow Peril" invasion, which would result in the horrific ruination of the Anglo-American family. In such representations, Chinese and Chinese American men were constructed as a dangerous corruptive influence not only on the morality of white women but also on white men and the development of their social and familial units. The caption under one typical illustration in *The Wasp* (1885) reads:

> [the Asian interloper] is the ruin of the household. . . . The wreck of the white workingman's family is graphically depicted. The leering, idiotic and immodest

attitude of the daughter of the house shows the damning influence of the opium-pipe; the father, driven from employment, despairingly seeks relief in a suicide's death, leaving his widow destitute, famished and despondent; the son, driven to stealing bread for himself and mother, finds himself a felon. . . . the Chinese are driving out the white men from employment, hurling them from windows and kicking them out of doors. Surely such a spectacle must stir the blood in the veins of either Saxon or Celt. (Choy, Dong, and Hom 1994, 126)

The images of evil villains are sometimes intermixed or qualified with racial-ethnic images of effeminacy and homosexuality. For example, the evil, cold-blooded villain Dr. Fu Manchu, created by the British author Sax Rhomer, was popularized in Hollywood films of the early 1920s through the 1940s. "Evil Dr. Fu Manchu and Chan are visions of the same mythic being. . . . Devil or angel, the Chinese is a sexual joke glorifying white power. Dr. Fu, a man wearing a long dress, batting his eyelashes, surrounded by muscular Black servants in loin cloths, and with his bad habit of caressingly touching white men . . . with his long fingernails is not so much a threat as he is a frivolous offense to white manhood" (Chin 1972, 66). Chinese males were also often represented as deferential, non-threatening sidekicks to the major Anglo male characters; as effeminate, obedient domestics; as wise but unattractive detectives; and as model minority types. The role of the good Chinese male was not to be the movie hero and get the girl, which would usurp the role of the white male hero, but rather to die or get killed off conveniently.[9] Mainstream cartoons, books, magazines, and films depict Asians as "natural" houseboys, cooks, gardeners, and restaurant and laundry workers, reinforcing notions that affected their social and economic mobility. The Charlie Chan character, created by the writer Earl Derr Biggers, was portrayed in films (1926–1950) as a comically wise detective, who spoke fortune cookie aphorisms. Chan is also a pudgy, sexless father to a number of Americanized sons, who appear as awkward, childish bumblers. Ironically, a number of white actors impersonated Charlie Chan in films, producing the racist characteristics most often identified in the national consciousness as "Asian." The various restricted, ambivalent representations of Chinese males pale next to the more glamorized and diversified portrayals of white males in mainstream American culture, who are constructed as the ideal masculine American hero-subject-citizen of the U.S. nation-state.

The Model Minority: Narrating Honorary Whiteness

In addition, there are the "model minority" discourses and images that depict Asian American individuals, families, and communities as holding to a complete faith in white culture and government. According to cultural nationalists, the model minority's American middle-class dream is to acculturate and assimilate into the visibility and affirmation of the white mainstream. For example, the white model minority version of Chinese manhood, family and culture is characterized by obedience, filial piety, hard work, self-respect, and self-reliance, which are not rooted in China but in racism (Chin 1972, 63). In disciplining the "heathen Chinee" into civilized, moral Christian men caring for model minority families, Asian men were taught cultural genocide and self-hate. That is, Christian missionaries in America contributed to the disciplining and reformation of Chinese men into soft, emasculated workers—obedient subordinates of a patriarchal white male capitalist economy and nation-state.[10] Thus, the dominant and privileged representations of the Asian American model minority were used to reproduce a capitalist version of the American Dream, to affirm the foundational metanarratives and practices of a seemingly enlightened meritocratic society. Within such metanarratives, Chinese and Asian Americans were characterized as apolitical citizens, socially mobile, educated, more interested in "making it" materially—finding good jobs and enjoying the fruits of their hard work in an American consumer lifestyle and culture. This pervasive representation of working- and middle-class Chinese American hard work and aspirations is indeed damaging, especially as it erases or appropriates the more diversified experiences of poor and working- and middle-class Chinese and other subordinated racial-ethnic groups in this country and elsewhere. Further, reactive cultural nationalist "outlaw" discourses, which contrast this mainstream model minority ideology, have the damaging potential to erase the stories of citizens who actively struggle to enact more transformative and ethical forms of psychosocial, economic, and political life within the same hegemonic field of contestation. Both mainstream and countering discourses need to be critiqued on the bases of their ideological assumptions and narration of the relations among such slippery factors of race, ethnicity, social-economic class, gender, and sexuality.

The "positive" image portrayed in mainstream culture sharply contrasted with the images of rioting, rebellious, and politically resisting Blacks and Chicanos emerging during the ferment of the 1960s (see Osajima 1993). It was used to exemplify a form of acculturation and assimilation as well as "acceptable" manhood for other subordinated racial-ethnic groups to emulate. In response, "real" Chinese men, according to cultural nationalists, needed to join up with a brotherhood of outlaws to recover their "authentic" Chinese manhood and fight against the incursions of the white nation-state. In the process of constructing this oppositional manhood, they sought to escape from the confinements of the domestic-familial sites, often associated with effeminized or model minority Chinese fathers and emasculating Chinese mothers, wives, and sisters, in order to be free of their painful humiliation as men (see chap. 4).

The Exotic Other

It was not just male stereotypes of Charlie Chan, Fu Manchu, and Hop Sing that were demeaning. This oppressive history is also carried over into literary and visual representations of Asian women. Over sixty-five years of American media entertainment have constructed a range of inaccurate and demeaning representations of Asian women that have become the staple of the popular American imagination. Eugene Wong (1978), Elaine Kim (1982, 1990), and others have concisely noted a whole set of limiting stereotypes by which the West has tried to label all Asian women.[11] These pervasive portrayals make the experiences and histories of Chinese American women invisible; if Asian women do appear, it is ironically often as the exoticized Other. As Kingston has noted:

> To say we are inscrutable, mysterious, exotic denies us our common humanness, because it says that we are so different from a regular human being that we are by our nature intrinsically unknowable. Thus the stereotype aggressively defends ignorance. Nor do we want to be called not inscrutable, exotic, mysterious. These are false ways of looking at us. We do *not* want to be measured by a false standard at all. . . . By giving the 'oriental' (always Eastern, never *here*) inhuman, unexplainable qualities, the racist abrogates human qualities, and, carrying all these extremes, finds it easier to lynch the Chinaman, bomb Japan, napalm Vietnam. (Kingston 1982, 57)

The point is not to deny the mysteries or differences that might exist in one's self, but to examine how they are constructed, sometimes into false and debilitating binarisms that thwart self-knowledge. As cultural critic Deborah Root notes, the problem should not be that differences are noticed, but rather how these come to be aestheticized and by whom. A major issue is "how a culture comes to be aestheticized by people who have no stake in that community and in particular by those who exercise authority over the culture of people being rendered exotic" (Root 1996, 31).

Renee Tajima describes two basic types of female stereotypes that have been fixated in the American popular imagination: the Lotus Blossom Baby (a.k.a. China Doll, Geisha Girl, shy Polynesia beauty) and the Dragon Lady (Fu Manchu's various female relations, prostitutes, devious madams) (Tajima 1989, 309). In mainstream discourses and images, Asian women are frequently portrayed as docile, obedient, and erotic-exotic women; their raison d'être is to serve their men. In the film *The World of Suzie Wong* (1960), Nancy Kwan portrays a hooker-bargirl-mistress in love with an Anglo-American played by William Holden. In the film musical *Flower Drum Song* (1961), Kwan plays a nightclub dancer, who is a manipulative femme fatale or dragon lady type while Miyoshi Umeki plays the quiet, soft-spoken, subservient long-suffering Asian woman, happy to serve her Asian man in a traditional family-arranged marriage. Sometimes these two stereotypes would be combined. As the actress-director Thi Thanh Nga comments, "Moviegoers were fed erotic images of the China Doll as concubine, supple in cheongsam attire, secret danger cocked in her eyes, graceful as a snow leopard. But look out! There's a dagger up her silk sleeve" (Nga 1995, 38). Asian and Asian American women are continuously constructed as a "chop-suey" of ambivalent racialized, sexualized, and gendered male (dominant and subordinated) desires, romances, and dilemmas, none of which address the social realities of Asians and Asian American women.

Asian women have not been portrayed in significant companionate and/or sexual relationships with Asian men (see Marchetti 1993 and Espiritu 1997); and have rarely been complexly portrayed in familial and social relationships with Asian men, children, or both. The "model minority" familial discourse as well erases or distracts from the discussion of diverse Chinese American familial formations (see chap. 6).

Moreover, it is the exotic-erotic relationship or romance between Asian females and white males that is foregrounded in a number of mainstream cultural constructions ad nauseam. Asian women are objectified as one-dimensional objects or trophies who fulfill the pornographic sexual and power fantasies of white males.

The typical narrative and images are derived from *Madame Butterfly–Miss Saigon* cultural productions: despite war, abandonment, death, and tragedy, the long-suffering and self-sacrificing Asian woman is aligned to a white man as her way to escape the totalizing oppression of Asian males, culture, religion, nation. Angelo Ragaza protested the romanticized Orientalist discourse and representations in both Puccini's opera and the award-winning Broadway musical *Miss Saigon*:

> Butterfly is a woman who can only exist for a man, not for herself. She symbolizes a Japan who cannot join the modern world without America's "help," and an "East" which has no identity without the benediction of the West. Everything about Butterfly's demise sublimates Western frustration about Eastern impenetrability. From her defloration by an American military official to her ritual suicide with a dagger, Butterfly's tragic death reasserts the primacy of Western virility and, in the mind of the spectator, erases the challenges to that virility posed by the East. . . . (qtd. in Yoshikawa 1994, 279)

In these racialized, sexualized, and exoticized stereotypes that construct a debilitating notion of femininity (and masculinity), Asian women cannot realize themselves as human beings, whether in terms of identity, sexuality, power, or options in life. For Asian women to name their own experiences and standpoints would destabilize and contradict the discursive masculinist symbolic binaries that have already foreclosed on their rights to access culture, society, history, and politics, to access life rather than "death-oriented" narratives and identities.

Though Asian women may have children by white men and though they may be depicted as loving mothers and faithful wives/lovers, they are also frequently depicted as giving up their interracial children to be raised by their former white husbands/lovers and their white wives in the West. The outcome of their fidelity and self-sacrificing love is suicide and death, the "fitting" resolution for the desired *and excluded* Other. The Asian woman living in U.S. militarized, war, or sex tourism zones (e.g., in Korea, Japan, Vietnam, and Philippines) is often constructed as a racialized and sexualized object, representing fantasies about Asian femininity, masculinity, and nationhood in relation to white American heteronormative masculinity and imperialism. She is the girlfriend, lover, temporary "wife," domestic worker, entertainer, or prostitute for white males from the First World supposedly there to save and protect her and her poor, backward, childlike "Third World" country. However, the usual narrative ends with the death of the Asian woman, who as a predominantly eroticized and exoticized fantasy lover in a primitive, foreign land and traumatic war zone, cannot be comfortably or seamlessly domesticated in white, nuclear, Christian family-oriented America. As it was for the loyal-faithful Asian male sidekick or wannabe hero in mainstream representations, the loyal-faithful Asian lover, wife, and mother dies, allowing the white male (and his white wife and the "rescued" biracial child) to return home as the privileged family unit. The Asian woman as mother and wife has no legitimate, normal or stable social-familial presence in such American family romances. Thus, the biracial child, the rescued and subdued symbol of white America's pseudo altruism abroad, accompanies his white parents "home" and is raised under the disciplining and restrictive panoptic gaze of the white family and nation—like, but not ever quite, an American. The Asian woman, excluded as wife, mother, and lover can only haunt the suppressed bloody, violent, and pornographic foundations of such racialized, heterosexualized, and nationalized white family romances. And sadly, as we will see, Chinese American women were often marginalized or dismissed in Asian American outlaw cultural representations as well (see chap. 4).

Like a form of cultural cannibalism, exotic images feed particular cultural, social, and political needs of the appropriating culture or discursive community. Orientalist spectacles about Asian women enact acceptable, rationalizing narratives about race, gender, sexuality, national identity, and power in the popular imagination. Stereotypical discourses and images of Asians are replayed in sophisticated and updated variations and distortions in high and low culture even as we move into the twenty-first century (see Moy 1993). They encourage a sense of difference, mystery, peculiarity, and visibility that continues to suppress and delimit the actual realities of Chinese Americans.

The implications of these diverse stereotypes and discourses are evident in the thriving pornography, sex tourism, and mail-order or foreign bride industries in the United States and globally, which exploit a mutually generative storehouse of cultural narratives and representations of the Orient/Orientalized women. Besides the field of erotic-exotic seductresses and the toxic dragon lady representations, there are popular forms of Orientalized femininity that project the visibility of a traditional, sometimes foreign, Asian woman as the feminized model for a dominant and conservative nationalist notion of family values in the United States. She comes with an array of prized feminine virtues of obedience, gentleness, passivity, vulnerability; she is not materialistic or assertive like Anglo American women, so the story goes. However, Bonnie Honig astutely notes how foreign brides' voices, experiences, and practices are appropriated and redefined as a specific form of domesticated femininity within dominant white ideologies: "A foreign bride's perceived family priorities may be less a matter of feminine affect than of necessity" (Honig 1998, 11). The newly immigrated Asian bride may not speak the language of her new country. She may be isolated, especially if she lacks extended kin or social networks to support the transition from her home country. She may not fully understand the social or cultural values in the United States. The foreign Asian wife is often dependent upon her American husband. Honig notes that the foreign wife's "subject position mimes that of the traditional feminine wife, but foreignness abets or trumps femininity as the real and reliable cause of her dependence and acceptance, her so-called family values. What is labeled feminine is the foreign bride's would-be powerlessness, her confined agency and her limited alternatives" (ibid.). Honig asserts that such "perceived powerlessness is why the husbands, who believe their foreign wives are feminine and unmaterialistic, are undisturbed by the knowledge that these women—who are seeking to escape poverty, after all—are actually quite interested in the very thing to which they are supposed to be indifferent. . . . What is most important is not finally whether the woman is interested in money but whether she has the power to pursue that interest by way of employment for herself or ambition on her husband's behalf" (ibid.). Such cultural constructs define and valorize disempowering forms of traditional femininity for Asian and Asian American women as well as other women. They misname the various and permeable positionings Asian and Asian American women have negotiated to ensure the survival of their families and communities. In this process, they exploit women's significant identities as workers (paid and unpaid) while constricting their agency, rights, and options. Such traditional global patriarchal-capitalist formations can have serious consequences, especially for poor, immigrant Asian female domestic and factory workers as well as migrant sex-workers and entertainers, who (with their families and communities) are often socially, economically, and politically disempowered and vulnerable to exploitation and sexual abuse.[12]

Thus, the mother-daughter stories of Asian American women writers like Maxine Hong Kingston, Amy Tan, and Fae Myenne Ng are an achievement in light of the long neglect and invisibility of Chinese women's diverse experiences, histories, and standpoints. Their stories challenge the Orientalist characterizations of Chinese American women by representing them in their protean complexity and power. They re-signify and centralize women's affiliations and alliances with each other rather than simply recovering the heterosexual relationships and identities that are constructed within patriarchal, capitalist and/or imperialist frames of reference. In traditional Chinese stories, the swan symbolizes married, heterosexual love. In *The Joy Luck Club,* Tan reinterprets this symbol and applies it to the silenced and intimate pairings between and among women in Chinese and U.S. contexts. Traditional symbols, stories, and sayings are being appropriated and reconstructed by writers like Tan, Kingston, and Ng who wish to tell the powerful stories of love and struggle between mothers and daughters, between women in China and in America.

Finally, these writers challenge the cannibalizing and abstracted representations of Orientalist/touristic fascination such as Chinatown, which obliterate the true dynamics of Chinese American life within Chinatowns and other sites. Their mother-daughter stories are an achievement in light of the obstacles confronted by the Chinese in establishing, nurturing, and representing their families and communities in the United States as well as in China. The stories these writers tell are not only about women's issues, but also about the ceaseless struggle to define an understanding of self in relation to the social and political life of their multiple communities.

Notes

1. With the liberalization in immigration policies post-1965, Chinatowns grew dramatically more diversified by class, language, gender, race, ethnicity, and national origins.

2. See K. Scott Wong (1998) as well as S. Chan (1986) on a discussion of the distinctions between two streams of Chinese emigrants: the Chinese who were taken to Cuba and Peru in the coolie trade and those who came to the United States as free or "semi-free" emigrants through the credit-ticket system. See also Kwong (1997) on the exclusion of Chinese labor from the United States, especially pp. 139–159.

3. Hirata (1979) discusses the role of the Hip Yee Tong, a Chinese fraternal organization, which was influential in the prostitution trade. It is estimated that they imported six thousand women and made large profits between 1852 and 1873. There were also a number of "underworld" tongs, who warred with each other to establish control over the lucrative prostitution, gambling, and drug trades.

4. For example, Dorothy Ko's discussion of a Chinese women's culture in the seventeenth century counters reductive imperialist depictions of Chinese women as passive victims living in an absolute patriarchy in an uncivilized and primitive Old China. She also counters the symbolic positioning of Chinese women as subjugated victims of a feudal China in nationalist and Chinese communist discourses, which were attempting to define the modernization and liberation of an "Old China" (1997, 1–5). See also Chow (1991a, b).

5. See Denise Chong's discussion of her grandmother May-Ying, who was a concubine in Canada, and her relationship to the First Wife Huangbo in China (*The Concubine's Children* [1994]). The sojourning husband Chan Sam travels back and forth over a period of years to look after his two families. Both wife and concubine had hard lives. Huangbo was burdened with the care of her husband's children, his in-laws, and his property through war, famine, poverty, and the socialist revolution without her husband. May-Ying, the concubine, waitressed and prostituted herself in order to make ends meet for her family in Canada as well as the one in China.

6. See, for example, Yung for discussion on 1938 garment workers' strike against National Dollar Stores (1995, 209–22).

7. Even in the contemporary period, Elaine Kim reminds us, "it is not coincidence that the majority of Asian women in America today, no matter what their level of formal education and work experience, are clustered in either sewing factory and food services work or in low-profile, low-wage, low-mobility clerical jobs requiring hard work, attention to detail, and low autonomy—the qualities of good subordinates" (1986, 108). Asian women are also located in global assembly factory work. See also Alexander and Mohanty (1997), Applebaum and Scott (1996), Bonacich (1996), Hossfeld (1994), Louie (1992), Lowe (1996b), Wong and Hayashi (1989), and D. Woo (1989).

8. See Matsumoto (1990 and 1991) on the dynamic changes among second-generation Japanese American women. See also the changing gender dynamics in immigrant communities such as the Vietnamese (Kibria 1990 and 1998), Hmong (Donnelly 1994), Punjabi Mexican (Leonard 1992), and South Asian (Dasgupta 1998).

9. Consider D.W. Griffith's well known classic movie *Broken Blossoms* (1919) which features a kind Chinese man, portrayed stereotypically by a white actor named Richard Barthelmess, who takes in an abused white girl (Lillian Gish) and who kills himself because society cannot tolerate their love for each other.

10. See Frank Chin's critique of mission homes such as Charles Shepherd's Chung Mei Home for Chinese Boys (1923), which attempted to reform young boys. The Home raised money by forming the "first Chinese black-faced minstrel troupe." Chin's Uncle Paul was one of the first Chung Mei Minstrels (1991b, 17–19).

11. See, for example, C. Chow (1988); Hamamoto (1994); Marchetti (1993); Moy (1993); Root (1996); and Tajima (1989, 1991).

12. For more on this, see Constable (1997), Enloe (1989), Matsui (1987), and Sturdevant and Stoltzfus (1992).

4

OUTLAW BROTHERHOOD:
CULTURAL NATIONALISM AND THE
POLITICS OF MOTHER-DAUGHTER DISCOURSES

> So used to being unwhole and unwell, one forgot
> what it was to walk upright and see clearly, breathe
> easily, think better than was taught, be better than
> one was programmed to believe—so concentration
> was necessary to help a neighbor experience the best
> of herself or himself. For people sometimes believed
> that it was safer to live with complaints, was
> necessary to cooperate with grief, was all right to
> become an accomplice to self-ambush.
>
> Toni Cade Bambara
> The Salt Eaters

Yellow Power: Asian American Movement Liberation Politics

The 1960s and 1970s saw significant social and political ferment in the U.S. This was due in part to the rise of critical racial-ethnic consciousness, and anger about the racism suffered by various historically subordinated groups, such as African Americans, Asian Americans, Mexican/Latino Americans, and Native Americans in this country. In this vibrant historic milieu of change, Asians, like others, sought to construct and define racial-ethnic, cultural, and political identities and practices for their diverse communities.

Asian American student activists were politicized in sit-ins and be-ins on college campuses during the Third World Strike (1968–69) at San Francisco State College and University of California, Berkeley and Davis; they participated in anti-Vietnam war efforts and the establishment of Asian American ethnic studies programs and curricula. Students aligned themselves with grassroots community activists to improve the material circumstances within their communities, especially among poor and immigrant members (see Tachiki et al. 1971, and Wei 1993). They established social service programs, sought federal funding and litigated for their civil rights in legal institutions. At the same time, others sought more revolutionary critiques of power and privilege, and fought against inequities in American society and elsewhere. As Glenn Omatsu states,

> Those who took part in the mass struggles of the 1960s and early 1970s will know that the birth of the Asian American Movement coincided not with the initial campaign for civil rights but with the later demand for Black liberation; that the leading influence was not Martin Luther King, Jr. but Malcolm X; that the focus of a generation of Asian American activists was not on asserting racial pride but reclaiming a tradition of struggle by earlier generations; that the movement was not centered on the aura of racial identity but embraced fundamental questions of oppression and power; that the movement consisted of not only college students but large numbers of community people, including the elderly, workers, and high school youth; and that main thrust was not one of seeking legitimacy and representation within American society but the larger goal of liberation. (Omatsu 1994, 20–21)

Omatsu asserts that many Movement activists understood "the urgency of Malcolm X's demand for freedom 'by any means necessary,' Mao's challenge to 'serve the people,' the slogans of 'power to the people' and 'self-determination,' the principles of 'mass line' organizing and the 'united front' work, or the conviction that people, and not elites, make history" (ibid., 21). This interpretation of Asian American Movement politics challenges the notion that it was dominantly focused on building racial identity-pride or racially-based forms of nationalism or culture. Rather, activists sought ways to develop diverse macro- and micro-coalitions (within and across racial-ethnic communities, classes, genders and geopolitical borders) in order to develop shared forms of identification and resistance against multiple and interrelated injustices in society. Furthermore, Omatsu's analysis challenges the more tepid, reformist, liberal 1980s reconstructions of Asian American Movement history as purely involving "advocacy," "access," "legitimacy," "empowerment," and "assertiveness."

In confronting the policies and practices of Western-based educational institutions, the Asian American Movement of the late 1960s and 1970s aligned itself with other coalitions who shared a historical understanding of oppression in the United States to agitate for radical changes in curricula, recruitment of faculty of color, and the reorganization of university administrative institutions. Furthermore, it aligned itself with revolutionary or nationalist movements and ideologies in Africa, Latin America, and Asia—the "Third World" coalitions, who agitated against imperialism, capitalism, and colonialism. Asian American activists drew from Marx, Lenin, Stalin, Mao, Frantz Fanon, Malcolm X, Che Guevara, Kim Il-sung, Amilcar Cabral, Kim San, W. E. B. Dubois, Frederick Douglass, Paulo Freire, the Black Panther Party, the Young Lords, the women of color liberation movements, and other resistance struggles as part of their eclectic search to define the "Asian American" experience (ibid., 31).

In line with these multiple struggles, cultural activists sought to challenge the cultural, ideological, and psychosocial elements that were debilitating their communities from within and without. "Inspired by a vision which seems not so much an alternative to that of the political radicals but complementary to it, 'cultural radicals' in the Asian American Movement see a new exploration of their ethnic tradition and its deep roots in American soil as essential to the restoration of integrity and dignity to American Chinese life" (Nee and Nee 1972, 359). That is, in coming to recognize the power of the dominant culture's influence in the shaping of their personal and collective identity, many Asian Americans began to feel that they had no self-defined identity. Cultural activists set out to construct oppositional identity practices that would establish a sense of racial-ethnic group solidarity and power in their communities.

In situating an oppositional stance, cultural nationalists deconstructed the history of dehumanizing and debilitating characterizations of the "Oriental" in popular and elitist representations. They realized how dominant cultural discourses could contribute to the inequitable circulation of power within mainstream society and within their own ethnic communities. At the same time, they recovered and reclaimed the histories of Asian Americans, which had been erased or marginalized from the American historical record. In the ruptured spaces created by these multiple challenges, cultural nationalists urged writers to construct an Asian American sensibility that could be related to but distinct from Asian and white America.

Aiiieeeee!: Constructing an Asian American Cultural Politics

Some of the early critical voices who attempted to define a new Asian American aesthetic included Frank Chin, who, along with fellow writers-editors Jeffrey Paul Chan, Lawson Fusao Inada, and Shawn Wong, assembled in 1974 one of the first literary anthologies featuring the work of Asian American writers—*Aiiieeeee! An Anthology of Asian American Writers* (Chin et al., eds. 1991). The editors had difficulty getting their project published because it was considered "too ethnic." In this anthology, the editors outline the long history of racism against Asians in the United States, and discuss the erasure of "real," "more authentic" forms of Asian American history, literature, and culture by the film and publishing industries, and by the educational and capitalist systems. They discuss how difficult it was to convince the white male-dominated publishing industry to consider the literature of Asian American writers. The anthology was most likely framed as too aggressively hostile, alien, and marginal to the interests of an American reading public. That is, it did not present the "Oriental" in ways that were familiar and comfortable for the mainstream reader. In the volatile period of the 1960s and 1970s, this anthology did not represent similarity and difference in acceptable or tolerable forms of cultural-political visibility and identity for subordinated racial-ethnic groups or general reading audiences. It is no wonder that it was repeatedly turned down by mainstream presses in the early 1970s, until its publication in 1974 by Howard University Press.

Like others of the period, Asian American cultural nationalists urged writers to recover and articulate authenticating cultural identities and histories that reflected voices and experiences not bounded by a "white racist love." Such "love" left Asian

Americans not only marginalized and invisible within mainstream American culture but also in a "state of contempt, self-rejection, and disintegration" (Chin et al. 1991a, xii).[1] According to the editors, their anthology was for and by Asian Americans:

> That means Filipino, Chinese, and Japanese Americans, American-born and raised, who got their China and Japan from the radio, off the silver screen, from television, out of comic books, from the pushers of white American culture that pictured the yellow man as something that when wounded, sad, or angry, or swearing, or wondering whined, shouted, or screamed "aiiieeeee!" Asian America, so long ignored and forcibly excluded from creative participation in American culture, is wounded, sad, angry, swearing, and wondering, and this is his AIIIEEEEE! It is more than a whine, shout, or scream. It is fifty years of our whole voice. (ibid., xi–xii)

In sum, there was a strong desire to build and fortify a political group identity that would be able to counter the racist ideology and oppression Asians experienced in this country. They were formulating an Asian American cultural politics which claimed its roots in the United States, a contested and fragmented homeground in which young Asian American writers could nevertheless construct their distinct, multiply situated and diverse critical fictions. Naming this as a site of struggle over cultural power and self-determination for Asian Americans in the United States, theirs was a substantial, trailblazing contribution to the making of identity and culture.

Outlaw Brotherhood:
Racialized Masculinist Identities and Discourses

Asian American cultural nationalists like Frank Chin and his colleagues, while calling for a radical redefinition of identity in terms of an Asian American sensibility and culture, actually discouraged any literary exploration of, for example, gender, sexuality, or class that would complicate a rigid, narrowly-defined notion of "Asian American" culture and solidarity. While inspiring artists to articulate the experiences of Asian Americans, Chin's (and others') restrictive discourses also created obstacles to understanding and appreciating the work of writers such as Maxine Hong Kingston and Amy Tan. In the revised and expanded *The Big Aiiieeeee! An Anthology of Chinese American and Japanese American Literature* in 1991, the editors restated their oppositional Asian American standpoint. Significantly, in Chin's chapter entitled "Come All Ye Asian American Writers of the Real and the Fake, " he condemns Kingston and Tan as "fakes" and "white racists" who do not meet the editors' criteria for insertion into the latest edition (see Chin 1991b). Though these writers also worked to portray diversified and potentially resistant images of Asian Americans that could counter those stereotyped ones constructed within mainstream U.S. society, they were and still are condemned by some critics as inauthentic and dishonest, not worthy of recognition as "Chinese American" or "Asian American" writers.

The objections to these writers' texts still resonate in varying degrees in Asian American cultural politics and communities (see Cheung 1990). These critiques situate Chinese American mother-daughter texts in cultural discourses that erase or trivialize women's experiences, practices, and standpoints as a serious subtext of their oppositional paradigm. This power to name an oppositional Asian American cultural politics as well as a personal and collective identity needs to be more carefully examined, and its discourses considered in relation to others that circulate within the contested terrain of Asian American cultural politics. Furthermore, such discourses must be critically resituated and understood within the inequitable social-economic and historical power dynamics from which they are derived and in which they articulate and enact understandings of race, ethnicity, class, gender, and sexuality in society. Finally, they must be critically examined to reveal the emancipatory dimensions, *if any*, of their social, economic, cultural, and political project.

Frank Chin and his colleagues constructed a cultural discourse of identity and solidarity based on intersecting racialized, masculinist, and heterosexist ideologies and practices, which dismissed or marginalized other significant formations of gender, sexuality, and class that were also emergent within Asian American Movement critiques.[2] In essence, they constructed an Asian American cultural politics based on "positive" and hypermasculinized representations of men (and women). For example, the warrior self is represented as the model for the unified "Chinaman I," coherent, stable, and known (Chin 1985). When it was first articulated it seemed like a breath of fresh air in its angry warrior stance. In *The Woman Warrior*, Maxine Hong Kingston constructs one early image of a feminist woman warrior in masculine terms, warring through the world seeking revenge for the wrongs against women and families. Some found a liberating or political component in this projection of a unified warrior self—especially in the way it countered images of the model minority, as well as of Asian American men, as the emasculated Other; and women as passive sexualized and victimized lotus blossoms. Chin's construction of racialized heteronormative masculinity, however, later operated as a dogmatic restriction on other Asian American female *and* male writers, who did not share this particular stance (e.g., Kim 1998). His work argued against explorations of the significant differences and contradictions within emerging Asian American Movement politics that could potentially destabilize a monolithic, narrowly defined conception of a cultural nationalist identity—one that was substantially vested within racialized masculinist and heterosexist institutions.

Mainstream American nationalism, of course, is also constructed in similar terms. The U.S., for example, or the model U.S. citizen has been frequently represented by strong, heroic male figures—the rugged and stoic individualist on the physical or metaphysical frontier of the American West. These fictional and real figures are socially and emotionally independent, self-made individualists, hard-working and endlessly resourceful larger-than-life characters—explorers, pioneer heroes, frontiersmen, cowboys, warriors, tamers of the wilderness—and constructors of a mythic white nation-state (see Bederman 1995). Such representations provided the basis upon which white European male immigrants differentiated themselves from women and from the diverse racial-ethnic populations they encountered during their myriad expansions (Almaguer 1994, 7; and see Omi and Winant 1986).

Teddy Roosevelt, for example, advanced the notion of a virile nationalism and imperialism by building a "claim to political power on his claim to manhood":

> Roosevelt drew on 'civilization' [meaning Western] to help formulate his larger politics as an advocate of both nationalism, colonialism and imperialism. As he saw it, the United States was engaged in a millennial drama of manly racial advancement, in which American men [meaning white men] enacted their superior manhood by asserting imperialistic control over races of inferior manhood. To prove this virility, as a race and a nation, American men needed to take up the 'strenuous life' and strive to advance civilization—through imperialistic warfare and racial violence if necessary. (Bederman 1995, 171 and see also n4)

As American history demonstrates, warfare and exploitation of non-white ethnic groups is an integral part of the narratives of public culture and nation and empire building. That is, the representatives of a certain type of white American (and European) heroic manhood also manifest a dark side in its practice—the arrogant and brutal massacres of indigenous peoples and their culture; the slavery, internment, and exploitation of non-white ethnic groups; the corrupt accumulation of massive fortunes; and the sexual violence, possession, and degradation of women.

Native Americans, Mexican/Latino Americans, African Americans and Asian Americans were exploited as slaves or as cheap labor, made to toil without families, citizenship, or basic legal and human rights; or hounded by racist governmental policies, lynchings, rapes, and massacres. This white heroic manhood was appealing, for example, to racist white males in the state of California, whose nineteenth- and twentieth-century origins were very much embedded in racialized white supremacist and nativist ideologies, discourses, and institutions. These ideologies were used to construct racial difference and enact the separation of humanity into distinct stratified categories of people with unequal social, economic, and political power and opportunities in society (see Almaguer 1994; Delgado and Stefancic 1998; Lipsitz 1998; Lowe 1996b; Romero, Hondagneu-Sotelo, and Ortiz 1997). Thus, "race as a cultural construct" must not be separated from its "structural causes and consequences" (Lipsitz 1998, 2). "Conscious and deliberate actions have institutionalized group identity in the United States, not just through dissemination of cultural stories, but also through systematic efforts from colonial times to the present to create economic advantages through a possessive investment in whiteness for European Americans" (ibid.).

Despite its attack on Asian American men—the Chinese being one of the first—this ugly side of white patriarchal masculinity (and its linkages to nationalist, colonialist and imperialist projects) did not make Asian American men immune to this psychosocial, sexual, economic, cultural, and political model of male identity. It did not make them immune to the seductive and "possessive investment in whiteness" that infects their oppositional stances (see Lipsitz 1998). Many nationalisms have embraced a violent, aggressive heterosexual masculinity as representative of their actual and imagined communities; Asian American male nationalists have been no different. Chin, Chan, Wong, and Inada have envisioned a unified oppositional life as militaristic phases of war and revenge, have embraced male warriors as representatives of Asian American activists, and have employed a discourse that implicitly identifies the nationalist citizen in racialized and sexualized masculine-identified terms:

> all of us—men and women—are born soldiers. The soldier is the universal individual. No matter what you do for a living—doctor, lawyer, fisherman, thief—you are a fighter. Life is war. The war is to maintain personal integrity in a world that demands betrayal and corruption. All behavior is strategy and tactics. All relationships are martial. Marriages are military alliances. Fa Mulan and her captains were allies, fighting shoulder to shoulder in war for twelve years. (Chin 1991b, 6–7)

Women and men live as warriors in a community based on military discipline, heroism, and an "ethic of private revenge" (Chin 1991b, 37). The domestic, social, and political worlds are constructed and lived predominantly within the ideologies and realities of war.

According to the critic Dorothy Ritsuko McDonald, Chin defines an authentic, reintegrated Asian American narrative of self, group identity, and political struggle as intimately linked with the war god Kwan Kung, who is portrayed as militant, loyal, vengeful, selfish, and individualistic (McDonald 1981, xxvi). He is the "god of war to soldiers, the god of plunder to soldiers and other arrogant takers, the god of literature to fighters who soldier with words, and the patron protector of actors and anyone who plays him on stage" (ibid.). From an Asian American male cultural nationalist perspective, the individual "Chinaman I" trains to fight like the war god Kwan Kung. Living is male camaraderie, fighting, honor, and revenge. Life is war against corrupt warriors, states, and nations (Chin 1991b, 35). The "Yellow Power" movement of Asian Americans of the 1960s and 1970s gradually becomes allied with racialized, sexualized, and gendered discourses projecting and glorifying the power of the warrior life of Asian American men and their loyal male-identified kung-fu warrior women. These metanarratives of war have serious consequences not only for defining a public and political culture but also for structuring the social relations within private, domestic, and familial sites.

In a number of Chin's stories, the Chinese American male protagonists are portrayed as escaping pathologically dysfunctional Chinatown parents and family—defined as passive, hardworking, assimilationist, model minority types. The American-born Chinese male characters such as Tampax Lum, Fred Eng, and Ulysses Kwan seek to escape the feminized spaces that have defined their history of humiliation in the United States as Chinese men. Men flee castrating, bitchy, or silly Chinese women—mothers, daughters, wives, girlfriends—women who remind them of their lack of manhood. Elaine Kim also notes that in *Three Kingdoms*, a classic text that Chin references, only two or three women can be found—a faithless wife or the mother of a valiant son (1990, 78). In Chin's *Donald Duk* (1991a), Donald's father claims descent lines from one of the outlaws from *The Water Margin* (Shih 1972), Lee Kuey, nicknamed the Black Tornado. This Tornado is so "tough" that while in a tavern talking to his male friends of his exploits, he becomes very annoyed by a singing girl who distracts their attention. He gets up from the table and knocks her out cold in order to shut her up. Donald's father also silences his twin daughters, who seem to babble like space-cadets, in order for his son Donald to talk. (At this point, I can't help but think of this episode in relation to Kingston's ending to *The Woman Warrior,* in which the singing voice of the warrior woman is privileged.) Donald's mother Daisy Duk also encourages her daughters to listen to their father in order to learn about family and history, which is not what the daughter-writers are forefronting in their texts. There is a sense that Chin believes that women should stand by their men and be silent.

The heroic literary landscape of the male romance narrative is inhabited by railroad men, old-time "bachelor" loners, and virile macho wannabes who hang out with trophy-blondes, Chinatown cowboys, boxers, and angry outsiders. In the absence of "manly" and "strong" father-models, honor and loyalty are transferred to a predominantly fraternal, rather than paternal, culture of brotherhoods and outlaws who inhabit marshes, woods, or urban ghettoes, wreaking havoc and vengeance on the corrupt ruling white patriarchal, imperialist nation-state.[3]

Michael Kimmel, in his study of the mainstream mythopoetic men's movement, critiques its belief in rescuing men from their "father wound." Like Chin and his colleagues, contemporary mythopoetic men believe that men have become feminized, passive, and disempowered. They believe the problem is the absence of strong father models in the lives of men, who are emasculated in society as well as in their homeplaces. The claim is that men have not separated psychosocially and emotionally from mothers, and have learned their sense of manhood from mothers and other women. Chin and Chan allude to this discourse in their depiction of a maternalized form of "racist love": "It is well known that the cloying overwhelming love of a protective, coddling mother produces an emotionally stunted, dependent child" (Chin and Chan 1972, 69). They assert that such "sissifying" maternal love fails to develop a "hatred for whites," which would "free" Chinese Americans "to return hate with hate" and to develop "their own brigand languages, cultures, and sensibilities, all of which have at their roots an assumed arrogance in the face of white standards, and defiant mockery of white institutions, including white religion" (ibid.). Mothers are to blame primarily for discouraging the specifically violent emotions and practices needed to establish a warrior culture and to forge the fierce mentality of the warrior, who battles his way through life.

The solution of such male cultural nationalists and the mythopoets is to run "to the woods, where they can escape the emasculating world of women—mothers, wives, and children—and workplace responsibility and drudgery. In the forests, men can come together and be mentored by men into manhood and heal from their 'father wound'" (Kimmel 1996, 317). The idea is to escape personal domestic-familial attachments and sites and quest for authenticity, freedom, and meaning among men.[4] According to Kimmel, some feminists have argued that men's problems are perhaps not the result of incomplete separation from mothers, but rather that a " 'self-made masculinity'. . . constantly tested and proved, becomes equated with a relentless effort to repudiate femininity, a frantic effort to dissociate from women" (ibid., 318). This masculinist discourse and enactment is evident in cultural nationalist discourses that attempt to define a legitimate, authentic Asian American identity and cultural politics.

In their anthologies, cultural nationalists assert that "real" heroic literature is found primarily in traditional Japanese and Chinese classics such as *Chushingura*, *Momotaro*, *Three Kingdoms*, *The Water Margin*, and *Journey to the West*, popularized in oral culture, theater, and comics. The texts of the historians Ssu-ma Ch'ien and Confucius, and the military strategists Sun Tzu and Wu Chi, also become part of the Asian American heroic canon.[5] This recuperated "Asian American" legacy is constructed in opposition to the humiliating legacy of "white racist love" that reproduces self-hate and cultural genocide. Cultural nationalists were attempting to recover distinct and specific social-historical and cultural legacies that were lost or appropriated in racist discourses and institutions. This in itself is a laudable and difficult effort. However, these texts were then further constructed as the immutable and essential foundational texts for situating and referencing a resisting Asian American sensibility for men and women. This would become problematic for writers like Kingston, Tan, and Ng, for example, who were recovering Asian American women's stories, experiences, and standpoints as a significant form of cultural and political resistance as well.

Within cultural nationalist discourse, the elements of writing, language, and creativity become symbolic of an aggressive reclamation of Asian American culture and of the verbal spectacle of refashioning a manhood not identified with women or feminine-identified domestic culture: "Language coheres the people into a community by organizing and codifying the symbols of their own common experience. Stunt the tongue and you've lopped off the culture and sensibility. On the simplest level, a man, in any culture, speaks for himself. Without a language of his own, he no longer is a man but a ventriloquist's dummy at worst and at best a parrot" (Chin and Chan 1972, 77). Eva Hoffman speaks eloquently to this longing in the disenfranchised to "give voice accurately and fully to [themselves] and to their sense of the world." When this voice is denied, it can erupt in hatred and rage:

> Linguistic dispossession is a sufficient motive for violence, for it is close to the dispossession of one's self. Blind rage, helpless rage is rage that has no words— rage that overwhelms one with darkness. And if one is perpetually without words, if one exists in the entropy of inarticulateness, that condition itself is bound to be an enraging frustration. In my New York apartment, I listen almost nightly to fights that erupt like brushfire on the street below—and in their escalating fury of repetitive phrases ("Don't do this to me, man, you fucking bastard, I'll fucking kill you"), I hear not the pleasures of macho toughness but an infuriated beating against wordlessness, against the incapacity to make oneself understood, seen. Anger can be borne—it can even be satisfying—if it can gather into words and

explode in a storm, or a rapier-sharp attack. But without this means of ventilation, it only turns back inward, building and swirling like a head of steam—building to an impotent, murderous rage. If all therapy is speaking therapy—a talking cure—then perhaps all neurosis is a speech dis-ease. (Hoffman 1989, 124)

As their talking cure against rage and disempowerment within society, male cultural nationalists speak and strut the language of the phallus—full of cocky streetwise rap and working-class grit, full of bawdy and pornographic sex-talk, violence and swearing.[6] Violent racist and heterosexist stereotypes are replayed in Chin's sensationalized oppositional forms of manhood—the "evil Black stud, the Indian rapist, the Mexican macho" (Chin 1972, 66). "Real," as opposed to "fake," writing is about warfare, "the fighter writer uses literary forms as weapons of war, not the expression of ego alone, and *does not fuck around wasting time with dandyish expressions of feeling and psychological attitudinizing.* The individual is found in the act of war, *of not selling out, not in feelings*" [italics mine] (Chin 1985, 112). Rather than kowtowing to humiliating white racialized notions of Asian manhood and to debilitating and humiliating forms of assimilation and acculturation, these cultural nationalists responded by representing themselves as Yellow Power warriors or outlaws in a constant state of war. The formation of an oppositional *binary* discourse on Asian American identity, culture, and sensibility is translated into an essentialized battle between white men and Asian American men. It becomes hypervirile—a hostile, competitive response to a white male hierarchy in which Asian males have been historically portrayed as the feminized, passive, and obedient Other. It is their aggressive reaction to the appropriation of their experiences and voices—to continually being denied a language and style of their own, to being denied a body and sexuality (often defined as the loss of rights over the bodies and services of Asian women and their families), to being denied social and public power and visibility.

However, in choosing this response to articulate an Asian American sensibility, they neglected to consider Chinese American women's (and other men's) specific and diverse experiences and standpoints. Elaine Kim notes that "what Frank Chin eulogizes as the 'Confucian ethic of personal revenge, friendship, and military alliance' is basically just another old boys' club for male bonding; sworn brother-hoods have never spelled freedom for women. To accept the contention that a revival of these patriarchal signifiers is all that is needed for Asian American empowerment is to accept political invisibility for Asian American women" (Kim 1990, 78). I assert that writers such as Kingston, Tan, and Ng, in differing degrees, attempt to articulate in their cultural texts other potential formations of oppositional *and* transformative subjectivities, social identities, and cultural politics that are derived from women's critical standpoints. I think we need to consider these writers and their cultural narratives in relation to various discourses: feminist (chap. 2), mainstream historical and cultural (chap. 3), and Asian American cultural nationalist, that were contesting for cultural-political power within Asian American communities and the larger culture of the 1960s and 1970s.

Asian American Women in the Movement: Grunt Work and Secondary Status

Women who supported the various revolutionary, New Left and racial-ethnic politics and movements of the 1960s and 1970s began to see that they were not being treated equally but subordinated within these movements. Asian American women began to perceive that the racialized form of Asian American cultural nationalism was also organized around a male hierarchy—an outlaw brotherhood. Asian American women worked diligently in the Asian American Movement; they understood the racial politics of the Movement and fought against racial injustices suffered by their communities. They understood the importance of building familial and communal solidarity and sought to change relations from within their families and communities. But just as Chin and his colleagues named their anger as Chinese American men so did Asian women name their anger at the masculinist articulations and practices within the Movement, which denied them power and visibility.

Their critiques often paralleled those made by Chicana and Black feminists in El Movimiento and in Black nationalism: "When words like castration, emasculation, impotency are the commonly used terms to describe the nature of male suffering, a discursive practice is established that links Black male liberation with gaining the right to participate fully within patriarchy. Embedded in this assumption is the idea that Black women who are not willing to assist Black men in their efforts to become patriarchs are 'the enemy'" (hooks 1990, 76). Similarly, there existed a

> feeling among some Asian males, similar to the mood in the Black civil rights movement, that their "manhood" had been oppressed for decades and that this discrimination thus gave them the right to dominate Asian women. Second, in attempting to show strength while confronting institutionalized racism, the movement was strongly identified with a ghetto image that was largely "macho" and male. Third, a large part of the civil rights movement emphasized finding oneself and discovering one's ethnic identity within the minority culture, an identity that had been historically denied to minority people by the dominant culture. But, for Asian *women*, much of Asian culture offered only secondary status. (Chu 1986, 96–7)

Asian American women did not feel that they were a substantial part of the decision-making processes in the Asian American Movement or within mainstream culture and society. They did not feel that they were recognized for their contributions in the making of culture and social and political life. They grew tired of being confined to subordinated roles of "taking minutes, making coffee, typing, answering phones, and handling the mail" (Ling 1989, 54). Ling quotes one woman who referred to herself in a poem as a "toilet cleaner" (ibid., 53). One Asian American woman felt that there was a "subtle attitude that men had a right to women, sexually;" another woman said that she became "concerned about women's issues after working with a 'lot of male chauvinist pigs. The guys were young and they were the most macho'" (ibid, 54). Women experienced the differences between the ideals of the

Movement and the actual inequitable sex-gendered relations of power in their everyday interactions with their male "allies" within the Movement.

Furthermore, concern with sexism and women's issues could bring on resentment and accusations of betrayal. Asian American Movement brothers labeled assertive women "dragon ladies," the same stereotype used in the mainstream media (Chu 1986, 97). The editorial staff of *Rodan*, an Asian American newspaper, commented on the behavior of Movement men toward women leaders: "They will frown on women who take on a lot of responsibility (and the authority that goes along with it), labeling them as 'unfeminine'. . . . Some [women] find themselves labeled as Bitches. . . . Some women gain respect only by putting up with put-downs on other women, i.e., 'you're not one of those bird-brained little girls,' or 'You're as strong as a man!' . . . Once women get into leadership positions, they find that their ideas are usurped by the men, who then take credit for the idea as being their own" (Tachiki et al., 1971, 297–8). Sexist and racist language and representations were used to put women in their place and to construct and validate "authorized" forms of femininity, masculinity, and sexuality that seemed to replay the same old traditional binary scripts between men and women.

The feminist socialist Merle Woo takes to task the "Asian American brother [Frank Chin]," who feels "pussywhipped" by a long line of Chinese American woman writers and who does not support the Asian American women who support their men, brothers, fathers, sons, and lovers.

> According to him, Chinese American women sold out—are contemptuous of their culture, pathetically strain all their lives to be white, hate Asian American men, and so marry white men (the John Smiths)—or just like Pochahontas: we rescue white men while betraying our fathers; then marry white men, get baptized, and go to dear old England to become curiosities of the civilized world. Whew! Now, that's an indictment! (Of all women of color). . . . The Pochahontas image used by a Chinese American man points out a tragic truth: the white man and his ideology are still over us and between us. These men of color, with clear vision, fight the racism in white society, but have bought the white male definition of "masculinity": men only should take on the leadership in the community because the qualities of "originality, daring, physical courage, and creativity" are "traditionally masculine." (Woo 1981, 145)

Who indeed has bought white male notions of masculinity? Woo believed that Asian men needed to understand that in supporting Asian women and their struggles against the interlocked oppressions of race, ethnicity, class, and sex-gender that these men were potentially helping themselves out of oppressive circumstances as well.

Woo recognized this fact in an intimate way—in witnessing her father's treatment in this country. "To be a Chinese man in America is to be a victim of both racism *and* sexism. He was made to feel he was without strength, identity, and purpose. He was made to feel soft and weak, whose only job was to serve whites" [italics mine] (ibid.). Woo admits to being ashamed of her father after watching him being humiliated by two white cops; so ashamed, in fact, that she never held his hand again. It isn't until later that she makes the realization that Asian men suffer in this country too: "I didn't know that he spent a year and a half on Angel Island; that we could never have our right names, that he lived in constant fear of being deported; that, like you [her mother], he worked two full-time jobs most of his life; that he was mocked and ridiculed because he speaks 'broken English'" (ibid., 145). She recognizes the importance of critically dismantling the psychic and emotional defenses and self-abuse, which misname, misrecognize, and misuse differences (Lorde 1984) in order to alienate subordinated racial-ethnic men and women, families, and communities. Woo's theorizing practice resituates her own family's debilitating psychosocial struggles within the structural inequities of society.

In rethinking an understanding of community, Movement women and men were opening up more plural sites of resistance at which to theorize and enact identity, and politics that were not derived from a racialized masculinist standpoint. They understood that oppressions needed to be addressed within their communities as well as within the larger society. As an Asian American socialist feminist, Woo calls for a movement toward more expansive forms of community and coalition-building within and among social-economic classes, genders, sexualities, and racial-ethnic groups.[7]

The Daughter-Writers and Cultural Nationalist Critiques

In attempting to be the dominant creators of cultural narratives and in perceiving culture as a battleground on which to defend their racialized manhood and honor, Chin and colleagues developed an outlaw brotherhood, made up of men (and loyal women) in a state of warfare. The tradition of military culture was constructed as the only "real" form of political activism and authentication. They did not find broad audiences for their message even though some shared their analysis; they did not attract the audiences that women writers like Kingston and Tan had for their work. Instead of attributing this, in part, to Kingston's and Tan's mainstream publishing and academic markets and to a growing women's readership (see chap. 2), Chin and others accused the writers of betraying the cause of the Movement as well as Asian manhood.

What became a sore point for male cultural nationalists was that Chinese American women activists and writers were also claiming the rights to language, writing, creativity, culture, and politics, the assumed essential traditional prerogatives of manhood. Frank Chin and Jeffrey Chan note that "the white stereotype of the Asian is unique in that it is the only racial stereotype completely devoid of manhood. Our nobility is that of an *efficient housewife*. At our worst we are contemptible because we are *womanly, effeminate,* devoid of all the traditionally masculine qualities of originality, daring, physical courage, creativity. We're neither straight talkin' or straight shootin'. *The mere fact that four of the five American-born Chinese-American writers are women reinforces this aspect of the stereotype*" [italics mine] (Chin and Chan 1972, 68). In this definition of manhood, women are stripped of a number of important human—not just male—traits (i.e., originality, creativity, courage). Instead, women in such a masculinist world, possess the "negative" traits a manly man cannot accept in himself and yet, cannot live without. As we will see, these

Chinese American women writers recuperate the stories of women and men in ways which do not try to follow but rather rethink the discourses and prescriptions which were defined and valorized by these early male cultural nationalists. In the heart of a war culture, this is seen as disloyalty and betrayal.

African American women writers have also faced accusations of selling out to white male institutions when constructing images of Black men in their work.[8] bell hooks notes that "whether or not images of Black femaleness in contemporary work by Black women are 'positive' is never a concern voiced by Black men" (hooks 1990, 70). Rather, it seems that the Black men are more interested in controlling their rights to representation, especially the "dissembling image" of Black masculinity. "Those Black men who approach the issue from a patriarchal mindset fundamentally disapprove of autonomous Black women creating images without first seeking their approval. From a sexist perspective, that in and of itself is seen as an indication that Black men have no power, since it suggests that they can't control 'their women'" (ibid.). Setting up rigid authenticating regulations to buttress forms of masculinity that silence or alienate women from their own experiences and representations is not a particularly fine way of building community or solidarity among women or men.

Maxine Hong Kingston and Amy Tan have both received a barrage of criticisms from male cultural nationalists like Chin, Chan, Wong, Inada, and others.[9] There are five major lines to this cultural nationalist critique, which still have a lively currency in late twentieth-century debates and critiques in Asian American cultural and political circles, even among those who do not claim a direct genealogy or association with Chin's cultural nationalist discourses or politics.

One line of argument claims that Kingston and Tan betray the Chinese community and manhood by acting as Orientalists for white folks (including white feminists) and a white publishing industry. In this way, they become the "poster girls" for a more acceptable (feminine) or apolitical version of Asian American identity, acculturation, and assimilation. This claim is sometimes amplified by a second claim that in their narratives about women and their personal and familial struggles, Kingston and Tan display hatred for Asian men and betray the cause of the Asian American community. Third, critics argue that Kingston's and Tan's focus on feelings or emotions and the imaginative interior life is self-indulgent and not the business of "real" politics. As a warrior who is a law unto himself, Chin hates the spilling of one's guts—the "psychological attitudinizing," which he claims their texts are all about. Fourth, Chin and others vehemently object to the autobiographical fictions these writers produce as a humiliating form of Western, Christian confessional. And finally, that Kingston and Tan are said to write "fake" stories, which distort Chinese American culture, and, in their cultural and Orientalist stupidity, they dream up and distort not only Chinese language, myths, and histories, but also the social realities of Chinese Americans.

The cultural nationalists claim that Kingston's and Tan's "Orientalist" critique of Asian patriarchy is an indication of their hatred for their Chinese community and for Chinese manhood. They are said to have betrayed the Asian American cause, and are constantly labeled "traitors," "white racists," and "whores." As a form of "prostituted" writing, they play to the racialized and sexualized fantasies of a white readership. In *The Big Aiiieeeee!*, the writer-editors are highly critical of what they perceive as Kingston's and Tan's exoticization of China and the Chinese. Their books resurrect images of an inscrutably corrupt East and of fragile, lotus-blossom women who appear to be too good for the decadent, ignorant society and culture from which they come. Tan and Kingston, along with a number of other writers, are accused of buying into the "same old white Christian fantasy of little Chinese victims of 'the original sin of being born to a brutish, sadomasochistic culture of cruelty and victimization' fleeing to America in search of freedom from everything Chinese and seeking white acceptance, and of being victimized by stupid white racists and then being reborn in acculturation and honorary whiteness. . . . The China and Chinese America portrayed in these works are the products of white racist imagination, not fact, not Chinese culture, and not Chinese or Chinese American literature" (Chan et al. 1991:xi–xii).[10] Kingston's and Tan's texts cater to a mainstream readership who are hungry for Orientalia, for accessible, familiar, safe, and pleasurable ways of "knowing" and possessing the erotic-exotic Other in the *corpus* of women's writing.

Frank Chin and other critics also believe that Kingston and Tan, like the Chinese American writer Jade Snow Wong, make Chinese men appear evil and misogynistic.[11] In "Come All Ye Asian American Writers," he takes these writers to task for grossly distorting the original stories and legends (such as Fa Mu Lan or the Kitchen God's wife) and the roles of women in Chinese society simply to make women appear oppressed by coarse, tyrannical Chinese men.[12] "She takes Fa Mulan, turns her into a champion of Chinese feminism and an inspiration to Chinese American girls to dump the Chinese race and make for white universality" (Chin 1991b, 27). "Misogyny is the *only* unifying moral imperative in this vision of Chinese civilization. All women are victims. America and Christianity represent freedom from Chinese civilization. In the Christian yin/yang of the dual personality/identity crisis, Chinese evil and perversity is male. And the Americanized honorary white Chinese American is female" [italics mine] (ibid., 26). From this perspective, Kingston and Tan replay the emasculating narratives and stereotypes about Asian men and patriarchy that already abound in American popular cultural representations and discourses.[13] Stephen Sumida accuses Kingston of indicting "only male chauvinism in Chinese America, and not the chauvinism and xenophobia of the America that created the bachelor society by excluding Chinese women" (Sumida 1992, 220). Benjamin Tong interprets *The Woman Warrior* as "a fashionably feminist work written for white acceptance in mind" (Tong 1977, 6). Jeffrey Chan asserts that white feminists have simply latched on to Kingston because she castigates sexist Chinese men, thereby confirming their racist notions of Asian depravity and of women's universal oppression (ibid.). Sau-ling Wong (1995) also replays a number of these critiques in regard to Tan's texts (see chap. 2). These critics would have us believe that Kingston and/or Tan have sold out the Chinese community and its manhood in order to get published and to assimilate wholeheartedly into Euro-American culture.

The critiques interpret Kingston's and Tan's stories as substantially about passive, abused Chinese female victims rescued by the superior, civilized empire of the West (and/or Anglo male), which I will argue they are not. The dominant cultural discourses and representations in the American popular imagination do replay privileged Orientalist codes in which Kingston's and Tan's texts could be selectively interpreted. Their cultural texts could also be used, for example, by Orientalist readers to arrogantly or smugly access the Chinese American experience as part of a pseudo "redemptive national narrative" of multicultural and multiracial-ethnic inclusion or diversity (see Ang 1996). It is a redemptive narrative that can easily obliterate or marginalize the pyschosocial and historical realities of Asians and Asian Americans in this country. Furthermore, in situating Kingston and Tan predominantly within an Orientalist frame of reference, they become the updated feminized (and supposedly safer and more acceptable) embodiment of the Asian American model minority within both hegemonic *and* oppositional cultural-nationalist discourses and representations.[14] At the edge of these ambiguous, multiply disempowering and dangerous discursive borders, they are *framed* as not only exotics, but also as educated, hardworking yuppies and thoroughly assimilated and acculturated partners to the ruling white capitalist patriarchy. None of these interpretations do justice to their mother-daughter experiences, stories, or standpoints.

I agree with some aspects of the cultural nationalist analysis of how Asian Americans have been made invisible in society—how their history and voices are either not represented, or if represented are often stereotypical and humiliating. In addition, I share their serious concerns about the damage that these Orientalist images and discourses do to the Asian American community. There are always readers, *including* Asian Americans, who read Kingston's and Tan's texts primarily in an exotic, stereotypical manner (e.g., Kingston 1982 and Tan 1997). Like Chin and his colleagues, I think it is vitally important to recover the social and historical realities of Chinese Americans as well as to know about Chinese cultural heritages and histories. However it is critical to bring this cultural, social and historical knowledge to a complex situated analysis of Kingston's and Tan's writing from women's standpoints as well. Cultural nationalists also remind us of the serious political implications and dilemmas in making choices about the style, language, and content by which we construct and articulate oppositional forms of subjectivity against hegemonic discourses and practices. Finally, they legitimately stress the need to interrogate and challenge how and why publishing institutions, consumers and critics might choose one writer or text over another—sometimes for very racist and sexist reasons.

Sadly, however, the cultural nationalists also reinscribe old master narratives tied to essentialized constructions of race, masculinity, and aesthetics. Their derivative discourse mimics in many profound ways the "same old same old" hierarchy of power relations and creates a space for racialized hypermasculine, and often intensely homophobic, displays that are part bravado posturing, part revolutionary theatrical spectacle, and part linguistic pyrotechnics and sensationalism. The enactment of this heterosexual masculine code may provide temporary relief for the grinding realities of institutional exclusion and racial domination within the United States. That is, Asian men, like other men of color, can internalize aspects of the dominant definitions and categories of masculinity in order to contest the conditions of dependency and powerlessness that racial oppression intensifies and enforces in U.S. society (Zinn 1995). Maxine Baca Zinn, for example, notes that

> perhaps manhood takes on greater importance for those who do not have access to socially valued roles. Being male is one sure way to acquire status when other roles are systematically denied by the workings of a society. This suggests that an emphasis on masculinity is not due to a collective internalized inferiority, rooted in a subcultural orientation. To be 'hombre' may be a reflection of both ethnic and gender components and may take on greater significance when other roles and sources of masculine identity are structurally blocked. . . . My point that gender may take on a unique and greater significance for men of color is not to justify traditional masculinity, but to point to the need for understanding societal conditions that might contribute to the meaning of gender among different social categories. It may be worthwhile to consider some expressions of masculinity as attempts to gain some measure of control in society that categorically denies or grants people control over significant realms of their lives. (Zinn 1995, 39)

Cultural nationalists, while reconstructing race relations and reversing historically white discursive and social constructions of Asian and white manhood, do not go as far in questioning traditional definitions of masculinity and writing new masculine (or feminine) endings as Kingston, Tan, and Ng attempt to do. Their form of resistance to the socially dominant white patriarchy is oppressive to Asian women, children, and Asian men themselves.

Contested Terrain: The Cultural Politics of Chinese American Mother–Daughter Stories

Patriarchy, as a system of men's domination of other men as well as women, divides the community, and therefore weakens the potential for more plural forms of resistance and solidarity. Chinese American men are victims of sexism too. They have often been stereotyped as feminine and despised for not fitting into dominant masculine codes. "America has locked the whole race into the same housewife stereotype women are running out of town. Our lack of manliness, and all that manliness means in this culture . . . aggressiveness, creativity, individuality, just being taken seriously . . . is subtly but visibly confirmed in the movies, and life imitating the dark art. . . . We've always been ridiculous with men and still outnumber our women, but in Hollywood, we as men count for nothing" (Chin 1972, 67). In relational power terms, patriarchy is a system that not only pits men against women, but some groups of men against others. Chin's rearticulation of dominant forms of masculinity, then, detracts from the search for more liberatory ways to think, live, and produce meanings.

Kingston, Tan, and Ng, to varying degrees, extend women's talk-story to include the stories of Chinese American men, especially grandfathers and fathers, as heroic men. Kingston, for example, attempts to articulate a father's stories in China and the United States, and in the process, she carries on an interactive dialogue with her own father. In *China Men*, Maxine, the narrator, extends a challenge to a silent father to tell his own stories if he does not think the ones women tell are correct (see chap. 7). In *The Joy Luck Club*, June Woo's father plays a key role in helping June to re-envision her relationship with her mother. He tells his daughter of his long, loving relationship with Suyuan and he takes care of and accompanies his daughter to see the lost twins in China. Fae Myenne Ng continues this tradition of recovering not only the mother-daughter stories but also the father-daughter stories in *Bone*. In telling Leon Leong's story, Ng speaks about the silence, distance, rage, frustration, guilt and the unknowability of this Chinese American father-man (see also Nunez 1995). But, at the same time, she portrays his indomitable, rebel will to survive in physical, socioeconomic, emotional, and creative terms against over-whelming odds and without the sweet certainty of success.

Unlike racialized masculinist cultural nationalist discourses, these women writers represent Chinese American men as complex and heroic within the feminine-identified domestic and familial site, which has often been devalued or rejected as not heroic enough for the enactment of cultural nationalist manhood. Daughter-writers address the courage and love of Chinese American men in the face of personal humiliation and hardship. This becomes one significant site on which to reclaim and redefine an alternative sense of heroic manhood as well as womanhood.

Kingston, Tan, and Ng, therefore, help us to rethink the nature and politics of self, family, culture, and community. As Raymond Williams has noted "social experience, just because it is social, does not have to appear in any way exclusively in . . . overt public forms. In its very quality and social reality it penetrates, it is already at the roots of relationships of every kind. We need not look only, in a transforming history, for direct or public historical event and response. It can appear as radically and as authentically in what is apparently, what is actually, personal or family experience" (Williams 1970, 65).[15] In writing stories about personal and domestic-familial relations, Kingston, Tan, and Ng suggest ways for women and men to re-envision themselves psychosocially and politically outside mainstream images and narratives. They articulate the private and domestic/familial experiences as significant sites in which identity and culture are negotiated and contested. They challenge the discourses which attempt to naturalize or biologize these women-identified spaces (which Chinese American men have shared) or to depoliticize and dehistoricize women's experiences. For such reasons, I think there is critical space in these mother-daughter stories for women to articulate moral or ethical standpoints that have their own specific structure, coherence, and practice. Such work is of a piece with the more radical goals and struggles of women and men in the Asian American Movement, who understood the serious consequences of the multiple oppressions of race, class, and gender, and who understood the importance of nurturing strong social and emotional alliances with their families and communities.

Thus, to focus on critiques of patriarchal formations is not to express hatred of all Chinese (or Asian) men or their communities, but to explore the profound and complex nature of the suffering, cruelty, and violence (psychosocial and physical) that multiple patriarchies exact and the ways in which they disrupt unity and solidarity. Kingston, for example, seeks ways to write that use nonviolent means to get to nonviolent ends—a task that she admittedly finds difficult.

> We are addicted to excitement and crisis. We confuse "pacific" and "passive," and are afraid that a world without war is a place where we will die of boredom. A tale about a society in which characters deal with one another nonviolently seems so anomalous that we've hardly begun to invent its tactics, its drama. There's a creative-writing adage that the loaded gun in an early chapter has to go off later on. How to break that rule? The loaded guns—and the first-strike and second-strike bombs—are ready. How to not shoot and not launch, and yet have drama? The writer needs to imagine the world healthy, nurturing young Wittman [in *Tripmaster Monkey*] to be a good man, a citizen whose work improves life. (Kingston 1989b, 37–38)

War, hate, and revenge as a way of life, as the ultimate and only viable answer to our issues or needs, is deficient (see Moyers 1990, Easley 1987, and Aubrey 1989). Kingston as well as Tan and Ng hint at the alternative social realities by writing new stories that counter unjust and destructive ones. These stories inspire and enact complexly nuanced social bonds and practices in the act of telling. A search for ways to build and maintain more genuine, satisfying diversified communities and alliances is certainly worth serious consideration.

As we have seen, masculinist nationalist discourses assert that Kingston and Tan express hatred for men and betray the cause through their woman-centered narratives. I argue that they work on behalf of the community; and that their work is not nationalist but transnationalist in its multiple perspectives. Thus, Kingston and Tan focus on the way mothers "forge and sustain multi-stranded social relations that link together their societies of origin and settlement" (Basch, Schiller, and Blanc 1994, 7). That is, they struggle to understand and articulate the multiple worlds and processes of mothers who "take actions, make decisions, and develop subjectivities and identities embedded in networks of relationships [familial, economic, social, organizational, religious and political] that connect them simultaneously to two or more nation-states" (ibid.). Kingston and Tan challenge the sexist and racist stereotypes of women that they find within their ethnic culture and community in China and in the United States, and within white ethnic mainstream American culture. At the same time, they challenge the oppressive racist Western hegemony that has affected them and their families here and abroad in so many ways. In other words, Kingston's, Tan's, and Ng's stories do not explore the racialized, genderized, and sexualized subjectivities of women in isolation or alienation from the larger community.

Chinese mothers in Kingston and Tan are champion-talkers and therefore makers of culture and society. Their Chinese voices, moreover, according to Kingston, are loud and brassy in the home and in their extended social networks even though they may be silenced and devalued in mainstream American society. Through talking, Brave Orchid, like the Joy Luck mothers, passes on heroic myths, languages of survival, and oppositional strategies to women—not just disempowering ones such as those found within patriarchal discourses. African American writer Paule Marshall also refers to the "poets in the kitchen" whose talk

> served as therapy, the cheapest kind available to [her] mother and friends. Not only did it help them recover from the long wait on the corner that morning and the bargaining over their labor, it restored them to a sense of themselves and reaffirmed their self-worth. Through language they were able to overcome the humiliations of the work-day. But more than therapy, that freewheeling, wide-ranging, exuberant talk functioned as an outlet for the tremendous creative energy they possessed. They were women in whom the need for self-expression was strong, and since language was the only vehicle readily available to them they made of it an art form that—in keeping with the African tradition in which art and life are one—was an integral part of their lives. (Marshall 1990, 653)

Similarly, bell hooks remembers fondly the language of her home—the woman talk that taught her to realize that language was a birthright:

> It was hard not to speak in warm rooms where heated discussions began at the crack of dawn, women's voices filling the air, giving orders, making threats, fussing. Black men may have excelled in the art of poetic preaching in the male-dominated church, but in the church of the home, where the everyday rules of how to live and how to act were established, it was Black women who preached. (hooks 1989, 5)

At these sacred domestic-familial spaces, women spoke in a "language so rich, so poetic, that it felt to me like being shut off from life, smothered to death if one were not allowed to participate. It was in that world of woman talk . . . that was born in me the craving to speak, to have a voice, and not just any voice but one that could be identified as belonging to me" (ibid.).[16] Women's talk is social; it accesses a nuanced range of emotions, desires, and intentions. In gathering to talk-story, they console, advise, argue with, critique, delight, and support each other. Kingston, Tan, and Ng also make clear that women's stories are often so compromised and entangled in patriarchal discourses and institutions that it is very difficult for Chinese American mothers and daughters to locate and decipher their meanings. Nevertheless, these stories are vital to their bonding as women and allies and vital to the political mobilization of community.

Emotional ties and relations are crucial heart work for building—brick by brick— a strong social and political community as well. Political activism is not just about the practice of fighting or about recuperating narrow racialized or masculinist understandings (or a "socially deformed theorizing") of what constitutes privileged "discursive," "social," "economic," "public," and "political" sites. Over a lifetime, through critical heart work, the daughters come to understand their mothers' daily practical activities of negotiating life and work in diverse contexts. The mothers and daughters in the stories of Kingston, Tan, and Ng are working through their social and emotional dilemmas in order to begin to act rather than re-act, to free themselves to become allies.

To critically examine the psychic formations of subjectivity, identity, and community is also to examine one's social, economic, and political positionings in mainstream and marginal ideologies, discourses, and institutions. In discussing Fanon's theorizing on colonial relations, Diana Fuss asserts that his most important contribution to political thought was his "critical notion that the psychical operates precisely as a political formation." Fanon's work foregrounds the historical and social condition of identification, which is "never outside or prior to politics. Identification is always inscribed within a certain history: Identification names not only the history of the subject but the subject in history. What Fanon gives us, in the end, is a politics that does not oppose the psychical but fundamentally presupposes it" (qtd. in K. Chen 1998, 12).

From this perspective, the excavation of the psychic and the engagement with work done by mothers and daughters in these talk-story cultural texts comprise a political formation grounded in the cultural and political spaces in which affiliations or identifications are disarticulated, rearticulated, and enacted. This is a different reading from a reductive cultural nationalist one, which constructs all life and literary activity as "weapons of war . . . and does not fuck around wasting time with dandyish expressions of feeling and psychological attitudinizing. The individual is found in the act of war, of not selling out, not in feelings" (Chin 1985, 112). In such constricted spaces, there is little room for the range of experiences, discourses, and standpoints of women to be examined or taken seriously.

Raymond Williams observes how people are sometimes trapped in the discourse and practice of the "old consciousness," which makes a clear division between what is "emotion" and "intelligence."

> It is understandable that people still trapped in the old consciousness really do see the new movements of our time—peace, ecology, feminism—as primarily "emotional." Those who have most to lose exaggerate this to "hysterical," but even "emotional" is meant to make its point. The implied or stated contrast is with the rational intelligence of the prevailing systems. . . . it is in what it dismisses as 'emotional'—a direct and intransigent concern with actual people— that the old consciousness most clearly shows its bankruptcy. . . . But where people actually live, what is specialized as 'emotional' has an absolute and primary significance. . . . If our central attention is on whole ways of life, there can be no reasonable contrast between emotions and rational intelligence. (Williams 1983, 266)

In this perspective, the psychic, emotional, and spiritual arenas are integral to more complex understandings of subjectivity, identity, and community formation. Furthermore, the "deformed social order," which is, in part, the result of such foundational, binary theorizing about emotion and intelligence, "is not particularly rational or intelligent," according to Williams, "It can be sharp enough in its specialized and separated areas, but in its aggregates it is usually stupid and muddled. It is also, in some of its central drives, an active generator of bad emotions, especially of aggressiveness and greed. In its worst forms it has magnified these to extraordinary scales of war and crime. It has succeeded in [the] improbable combination of affluent consumption and widespread emotional distress" (ibid., 266–67). The point is that emotional and social relations really matter in politics; that serious attention to feeling and connection is the crucial brickwork that builds and sustains a more transformed world.[17]

War as the ultimate metanarrative and as a way of life does not speak to the loss, rage, alienation, terror, confusion, sorrow, guilt, vulnerability, and the need to love and nurture, which are central to the lives of marginalized people and indeed to all humans. War, revenge, violence, and death as a way of life deforms and destroys the potentially constructive *social* and *political* resolutions of such emotions and needs within a society.[18] Audre Lorde, for example, noted the constructive uses of anger in clarifying differences and in noting one's passionate displeasure. But when anger turns to "metabolizing hatred like daily bread," one can "eventually come to value the hatred of one's enemies more than one values the love of friends [or allies], for the hatred becomes the source of anger, and anger is a powerful fuel." In the long view of things, anger is an "incomplete form of human knowledge." "Strength that is bred by anger alone is a blind force which cannot create the future. It can only demolish the past. Such strength does not focus upon what lies ahead, but upon what lies behind, upon what created it—hatred. And hatred is a deathwish for the hated, not a lifewish for anything else" (Lorde 1984, 152). Moreover, within a racialized masculinist culture, which cruelly disparages men's emotional vulnerabilities and dependencies as well as their affiliations with feminine-identified discourses and sites, it becomes crucial to re-examine possibilities at these specific marginalized sites for potentially transformative options for men and women, for society.

For this reason, the home is often constructed by women of color as a major space in which to nurture skills of survival and political activism. Although home is not free of internal physical and psychic struggle and violence, or free from the racism and sexism either, "home" has been identified as a source of individual and community strength. bell hooks writes:

> In our young minds houses belonged to women, were their special domain, not as property, but as places where all that truly mattered in life took place—the warmth and comfort of shelter, the feeding of our bodies, the nurturing of our souls. There we learned dignity, integrity of being; there we learned to have faith. The folks who made this life possible, who were primary guides and teachers, were Black women. . . . This task of making a homeplace was not simply a matter of Black women providing service; it was about the construction of a safe place where Black people could affirm one another and by so doing heal many of the wounds inflicted by racist domination. We could not learn to love or respect

ourselves in the culture of white supremacy, on the outside; it was there on the inside. . . . This task of making a homeplace, of making home a community of resistance, has been shared by Black women globally, especially Black women in white supremacy societies. (1990, 41–2)

Perhaps it is time for women, men, families, and communities to rethink what keeps us divided and alienated, enemies so close to home, so murderously close to the heart.

Cultural nationalists' discourses also condemn Kingston's and Tan's use of the Western autobiographical genre on the grounds that autobiography is not a true Chinese genre.[19] Autobiography is narrowly and monolithically defined as a Christian and Western form of confession and of capitulation to imperialists. Autobiography, according to Chin and colleagues, presumes self-contempt and a confessional need for forgiveness. It is a form of writing that trains individuals "to better express faith, belief, and submission to a higher moral authority, to overcome reality with dreams, and to defy the effect of knowledge with belief" (Chin 1991b, 35). According to Chin, this genre is appropriated by Chinese Americans to deny or devalue their Chinese community and heritage.[20] "A traditional tool of Christian conversion, the autobiography became the sole Chinese American form of writing, with Yung Wing's mission-schoolboy-makes-good Gunga Din licking up white fantasy in the first Chinese American autobiography, *My Life in China and America*. Every Chinese American autobiography and work of autobiographical fiction since Yung Wing, from Leong Gor Yun and Jade Snow Wong to Maxine Hong Kingston and Amy Tan, has been written by Christian Chinese perpetuating and advancing the stereotype of a Chinese culture so foul, so cruel to women, so perverse, that good Chinese are driven by the moral imperative to kill it" (ibid., 11).[21]

The use of autobiographical fiction, however, is not a "western form" in Kingston's or Tan's work. Rather, the texts of Kingston, Tan, and Ng represent disunified selves talking-story, attempting to construct a temporal and imaginative coherence for the complex experiences that constitute their social-historical circumstances. Their autobiographical fictions are built on a collective sense of self rather than on an individualistic and autonomous one.[22] "Individualistic paradigms of the self [in the Western autobiographical tradition] ignore the role of collective and relational identities in the individuation process of women and minorities" (Friedman 1988, 35). Kingston and Tan as well as Ng define a new sense of the self that is not unitary, immutable, or isolated. Indeed the emerging concept of self they engage may best be described in Teresa de Lauretis's words: "What is emerging in feminist writing is, instead, the concept of a multiple, shifting, and often self-contradictory identity, a subject that is not divided in, but rather at odds with, language; an identity made of heterogeneous and heteronomous representations of gender, race, and class, and often indeed across languages and cultures; an identity that one decides to reclaim from a history of multiple assimilations, and that one insists on as a strategy" (de Lauretis 1986, 9). These writers' narratives of a self-in-process—the self talking-story—inventively engage the ongoing dilemmas, ruptures, and forms of alienation and trauma that arise in attempting to construct a strategically negotiated oppositional subjectivity, which is accountable to one's self, family, and diverse communities.

Such an autobiographical project cannot be seamlessly unified in its positioning because it inhabits the psychosocial, cultural, historical, and geopolitical borders of conflict and confusion and names this as an important site of recreation and resistance. It cannot be hegemonically rational, linear, or stable, for it includes the recovery of the trauma, rage, and resistance of those whose experiences and histories are constantly and violently embedded in, and yet denied access to, not only memory, culture, and history, but human dignity and justice as well. Lacan ironically restates the rational Cartesian *cogito* of "I think therefore I am," proposition as "I think where I am not, therefore I am where I do not think" (qtd. in Gandhi 1998, 9). Thus, the public enactment of the disunified self talking-story can be a site of remembering resistance in the way it deconstructs and reconstructs the complicated formation of subjectivity, identity, and community.

Another critique of Kingston and Tan is that they distort Chinese American culture and dream up Chinese histories, myths, and social realities as well: "Myths are, by nature, immutable, and unchanging because they are deeply ingrained in the cultural memory, or they are not myths" (Chin 1991b, 29). In covering up their own cultural ignorance, both writers are accused of suggesting that Chinese immigrants have forgotten the original culture and that "faulty memory combined with new experience [produces] new versions of the traditional stories" (ibid., 3). For Chin, the "real" history and myths are clearly and forever inscribed in the heroic tradition of Chinese and Japanese popular classics, which are faithfully recovered and remembered by authentic, "real" Chinese Americans versus "fake" ones. To combat Kingston's and Tan's cultural ignorance in the recovery of their heritage, he also recommends reading the texts of the historians Ssu-ma Ch'ien and Confucius, and the war strategists Sun Tzu and Wu Chi. Kingston and Tan, according to Chin, are blasphemous and ethically irresponsible to their Chinese community in not knowing and failing to report the "real" myths as well as "real" history and culture.

Contrary to the claims of Chin and others that Kingston's imagination is entirely informed by non-Chinese and Orientalist images and stereotypes, I argue that Kingston (as well as Tan and Ng) are rooted in and informed by a Chinese oral tradition, within which there is no fixed, unitary story, no one "right" story. Each revision of an ancient story has its own validity in the continuum of cultural survival. Indeed, the point of talk-story is to *retell* the stories—not simply to reproduce them. Talk-story, therefore, provides space in which Chinese women may tell their own stories, instead of being told how to think, write, or tell. Kingston also draws upon traditional Chinese myths that have experienced change and rupture upon the soil of the United States; her talk-stories are vibant hybrids created out of her diverse cultural landscape in this country. They represent the heart of a living, therefore changing, Chinese American culture that is *not* seamlessly continuous with Chinese culture or history. The daughter-narrator's talk-stories are not attempting to reproduce or recover a clear-cut ethnography of Chinese identity, language, culture, or history; they instead articulate the narrator's psychosocial and emotional relationship with, and a cultural-political imaginary of, an important but problematic site for her and her Chinese family and community. It is a place to which she had not actually been to physically, but with which she nevertheless chooses to negotiate and maintain an affiliation.

These talk-stories model the nature of culture as a whole: Culture and history are syncretic—changing, adapting, and retaining all at once. As Stuart Hall notes, "[The past] is always constructed through memory, fantasy, narrative and myth" (1989, 72). This is especially true for lives, cultures, and histories that have been disrupted or resituated in new circumstances and subjected to various forms of domination and violence. Charting the psychosocial, cultural, and political changes at such ruptured sites can challenge hegemonic narratives and institutions that also are working to define and order these peripheral, hybrid sites. As a political project, the mother-daughter stories recover this contested terrain for exploration.

Although I share with cultural nationalism a desire for the inauguration of new histories and cultures, new senses of subjectivity and assertions of agency, these new histories and cultures cannot be dictated or certified as authentic by a few individuals. A single political identity or solidarity, based on narrow racialized or masculinist configurations, may be not wholly useful in the complex, far-reaching trajectories of inequitable power relations we confront in this period of globalization and transcultural border crossings. Even the term "Asian American" homogenizes and obscures the complex nature of the differences and the similarities among the Asian racial-ethnic groups in the United States.[23] Cultural nationalists and other like-minded critics do not seem fully aware of the serious consequences of political discursive communities and practices, which stifle rather than encourage a more strategic, liberatory, and practical range of alternatives for writers and communities.

To be clear, it is not my project to substitute all Chinese American mother-daughter writing or women's writing as the privileged or romanticized discourse for theorizing or resolving the complex issues about identity, resistance, or political solidarity. As Ramon Saldívar has pointed out in his discussion of feminist Chicana writers, "mother-daughter nurturing, the sisterhood of women, the idealization of an essential Woman should not be regarded as transhistorical concepts that uniformly liberate women from oppression but as constructions that acquire specific political meanings at different historical moments and under different economic and racial conditions" (Saldívar 1990, 191). My explorations are meant to begin rethinking the political potential in Asian American mother-daughter stories rather than to summarily dismiss them as nostalgic Orientalist fare geared predominantly toward white mainstream audiences.

In his theorizing of the politics of location, Stuart Hall eloquently defines two important historical forms of cultural identity. The first model defines "cultural identity" in terms of the idea of one, shared culture, a sort of collective "one true self," hiding inside the many other, more superficial or artificially imposed "selves," which people with a shared history and ancestry hold in common. Within the terms of this definition, our cultural identities reflect the common historical experiences and shared cultural codes which provide us, as "one people," with stable unchanging and continuous frames of reference and meaning, beneath the shifting division and vicissitudes of our actual history. (Hall 1989, 69)

Such an important archaeological form of cultural identity is busy excavating indigenous formations and legacies—that which the colonial and imperialist experience brutally attempted to suppress, appropriate, or destroy.

The second form of cultural identity

encompasses the matter of "becoming" as well as of "being." It belongs to the future as much as to the past. It is not something which already exists, transcending place, time, history and culture. . . . But, like everything which is historical, they [cultural identities] undergo constant transformation. Far from being eternally fixed in some essentialized past, they are subject to the continuous "play" of history, culture and power. Far from being ground in a mere "recovery" of the past which is waiting to be found, and which, when found, will secure our sense of ourselves into eternity, identities are the names we give to the different ways we are positioned by, and position ourselves within, the narratives of the past. (ibid., 70)

This second understanding of culture describes the experiences of Chinese Americans, whose identities are formed in cutting across national-cultural-geopolitical frontiers. Lisa Lowe notes that "once arriving in the United States, very few Asian immigrant cultures remain discrete, impenetrable communities. The more recent groups mix, in varying degrees, with segments of the existing groups; Asian Americans may intermarry with other ethnic groups, live in neighborhoods adjacent to them, or work in the same businesses and on the same factory assembly lines. The boundaries and definitions of Asian American culture are continually shifting and being contested from pressures both 'inside' and 'outside' the Asian origin community" (Lowe 1991, 35–6).

While Chinese Americans retain affiliations with an originary homeland, languages, and traditions to varying degrees, many are without the fantasy of a return to the past; moreover, they come to terms with the new cultures they inhabit, without simply assimilating or acculturating and losing their identities or cultural traditions completely (Hall 1996, 629). As Fae Myenne Ng states: "Assimilation is often the first filter used to look at literatures of communities outside of the mainstream, the Other Americans. The world the sisters [inhabit] is clearly defined and culturally specific, but it is a world in the remaking. An old world is being broken down and a new world is to be created. None of the sisters want to enter Middle America. Each sister has a heroic dream of remaking her world with hope and courage, in the tradition inherited from their old-timer ancestors. *Bone* hopes to describe that journey, the personal and spiritual cost of leaving one life in order to make another" (Ng 1994, 87).

Kingston's, Tan's, and Ng's stories in all their diversity of homeplaces, generations, genders, and dreams are the products of several intimately interlocked histories, cultures, and communities, in China and in the United States (Hall 1996, 629). Individual identities and communities are contingent, relational, flexible, and syncretic—continually and passionately negotiated and reinvented as a result of the circumstances and tensions from which they are in part derived.

To explore the complex site of the recovery and formation of multiple identities in open-ended, non-essentializing or totalizing grids is a political necessity. To do so is not a naive, individualistic celebration of free-floating dislocation, home-lessness, or hybridity. It is not a touristic luxury for some of us, who intimately inhabit these sites. The cultural critic Inderpal Grewal has written that a non-essentialist subjectivity does not imply that one does not desire to affiliate with a group or community; it does not imply the impossibility of agency or coalition-building or political solidarity. She states the very rich possibilities from such a post-modernist standpoint:

> For some feminists of color, identity politics remains central, though the identity may be multiple. . . . There can be syncretic, "immigrant," cross-cultural, and plural subjectivities, which can enable a politics through positions that are coalitions, intransigent, in process, and contradictory. Such identities are enabling because they provide a mobility in solidarity that leads to a transnational participation in understanding and opposing multiple and global oppressions operating upon them; that is, these subject positions enable oppositions in multiple locations. Multiple locations also enable valuable interventions precisely because the agendas of one group are brought along to interrogate and empower those of another group. (Grewal 1994, 234)

Such a radical political project, which is rooted in the issues of social justice and human dignity, seeks practical, provisional formations of strategic identification and solidarity that respects and works with the commonalities and differences among people in varying localities.

In telling the history of individuals and communities, these writers articulate a sense of life-in-process that includes feelings, gestures, silences, fragments, contradictions, talk-stories, and everyday social activites. In particular, the writers foreground the often neglected arena of personal experiences and feelings. They attempt to capture a new "vocabulary of feeling," according to Fae Myenne Ng, which can express the nuanced constitution of identity and social interactions within family and community. They focus first of all on their mothers' complicated lives and puzzling, fragmented stories as a source of meaning for themselves as women. The battlefield of cultural nationalists is redefined as the interior wilderness of the self talking-story—the heroic male self is redefined as the female self which explores this wilderness and the wilderness in myths and stories that Chinese immigrant mothers tell.

Women have been crucial to creating and recreating culture. Telling and retelling stories are essential to this process. Thus, the excavation of the stories and oral traditions passed from mothers to daughters is not the egotistical, self-serving "psychological attitudinizing" that Chin and others claim, but an exploration of the making and remaking of culture and society. As the persons most often assigned primary care of children, Chinese American women have played a central role in preparing their children to live in changing circumstances, in teaching strategies of survival and in maintaining traditional culture and values as well. In understanding the struggles of Chinese Americans to establish families and communities into the mid-twentieth century, it becomes clear that private-domestic and social sites cannot be constructed as immune to debilitating practices and institutions of a racist nation-state. To do so would be to replicate traditional and reductive binaries that situate a woman's naturalized sphere in home and family and a male's purely in the public, and more privileged, world that constructs culture, society, nation, and history. This binary erases and alienates the intersecting, multiple, and permeable sites that women as well as men, families, and communities inhabit in their everyday social life. Private, domestic-familial, and communal sites play an important part in the formation of subjectivity, individual and social identities, and political affiliations. In looking at history, it is not only at traditionally authorized social-public sites that Chinese men and women have known the disciplining power of the white nation state; they have felt it *socially and publicly* at their most intimate physical and psychosocial interactions with each other. They have felt it most profoundly in their interior struggles—the heart of darkness within.

To foreground and examine the often silenced or marginalized standpoints, experiences and sites that women inhabit provides the potential to enrich our understandings of social and political practices. To learn to negotiate multiple standpoints at various sites, as Homi K. Bhabha notes, is what politics is all about: "Subversion is negotiation; transgression is negotiation; negotiation is not just some kind of compromise or 'selling out' which people too easily understand it to be. . . . Political negotiation is a very important issue, and hybridity is precisely about the fact that when a new situation, a new alliance formulates itself, it may demand that you should translate your principles, rethink them, extend them" (qtd. in Reid 1997, 22). Gary Okihiro also hints at the nature of women's complex activities in the preservation, transmission, and formation of culture. Women pass on a culture encrusted with patriarchy and women's oppression but also a culture that resisted European American racism and colonization. "Is it possible that women, in passing on Asian culture to the next generation, 'Americanized' (not in its usual meaning of assimilation or Anglo-conformity, but in the sense of transformation and democratization) that culture by subverting its patriarchal forms and meanings and thereby helped to liberate themselves?" (Okihiro 1994, 92). Certainly, Kingston, Tan, and Ng search for distinctive personal, communal and public voices that can speak to the diverse circumstances of living as Chinese American women in the United States. Their mother-daughter stories *are* rich, vital, and interactive stories about the intensely difficult task of naming our social and political practices in ways that heal rather than destroy our complex communities.

Notes

1. William Van Deburg states that the Black Power movement nationalists, unlike assimilationists and pluralists,

   are suspicious of claims that radically divergent groups long can live in peace and on a basis of equality while inhabiting the same territory or participating in the same society institutions. Eventually, they believe, one component of the social matrix comes to dominate and oppress the others, eradicating important subgroup mores in the process. The result is assimilation by fiat and should be avoided at all costs. To avert this end, nationalists seek to strengthen in-group values while holding those promoted by the larger society at arm's length. Withdrawing from the body politic as much as practicable, they hope to win and maintain sociocultural autonomy. (Van Deburg 1992, 25)

2. Masculinism, as practiced in American culture, is "in part the mistaking of male perspectives, beliefs, attitudes, standards, values, and perceptions for all human perceptions" (Ruth 1990, 7).

3. See also Ehrenreich (1983) or Buhle (1998) on this escape model in the 1950s-60s, which seems to have made a reappearance in our time.

4. See Rutherford's fascinating discussion of the development of "imperial manliness" in nineteenth-century England, which was an attempt to socialize and discipline boys into an elite force of future administrators and soldiers of the imperial nation. Part of this project involved weaning boys from domestic spaces identified with mothers and into the public culture of fathers, who would discipline their sons into robust manhood.
   "Consequently the language of emotions—expressions of need, pleasure, pain and vulnerability—were feminised in a domestic world clearly delimited from the public world of men and masculinity." Futhermore, he asserts that these Victorian bourgeois patriarchal sons, separated from their mothers, developed an "autarchic emotional economy." "In childhood, solitude created anxiety, in adulthood it became a virtue. In his aloneness the man imagines himself freed of social relations and untied from all emotional dependency on women. But, in spite of adopting the defensive ego boundaries and manly postures prescribed him, he could never fully repress the trauma of maternal loss, nor succeed in establishing an unambiguous adult heterosexuality" (Rutherford 1997, 19–23).

5. Modern sources for these classical works include Takeda, Shoraku, and Senryu (1971); see also Ssu-ma Ch'ien (1961), and Wu Cheng-en (1977–1983).

6. See Chin's portrayal of Tampax Lum in the play *Chickencoop Chinaman* or Fred Eng in *The Year of the Dragon* (Chin 1981). Tam, for instance, speaks buck buck bagaw:
   I am the natural born ragmouth speaking the motherless bloody tongue. No real

language of my own to make sense with, so out comes everybody else's trash that don't conceive. But the sound truth is that I AM THE NOTORIOUS ONE AND ONLY CHICKENCOOP CHINAMAN HIMSELF that talks in the dark heavy Midnight, the secret Chinatown Buck Buck Bagaw. (Chin 1981, 7)

7. Socialist feminists situate the sexual division of labor within capitalist modes of production. However, they also see that patriarchal formations are connected not only to sex-gender oppression but also to racial-ethnic and social-economic oppressions. These multiple forms of oppression require radical structural changes in society. Moreover, family is constructed as a key site of the oppression of women *and* men, which needs to be significantly transformed in order for more liberating options to be created for all.

8. Charges of demeaning African American men in their works have been lodged against African American writers Toni Morrison and Alice Walker by writers such as Ishmael Reed. Reed and Chin were part of a panel discussion entitled "Has the Feminist Movement Victimized Third World Men?" (Chung 1991). See, for example, Bobo (1995), hooks (1989, 1990, 1992, and 1996), Powell (1983), Wallace (1979), White (1995). Chicana writers have also faced the similar accusations from Chicano/Latino men: see Fregoso and Chabram (1990), Pérez-Torres (1995), Pesquera and Segura (1993), and Quintana (1990).

9. For more information on the Asian American debate between Frank Chin and Maxine Hong Kingston, Amy Tan, and other writers on the issue of race and gender, see Chan (1977); Chan et al. (1991b); Cheung (1990); Chin (1997); Chung (1991); Fong (1977); Kim (1982), Lowe (1991), Tong, (1977), Sumida (1992), Wei (1993), and Wong (1992 and 1995).

10. See other literary critics who argue against Chin and other critics' narrow reading of Kingston's *The Woman Warrior*: Cheung (1988), Fischer (1986), Friedman (1988), Ho (1991), Kim (1981, 1982 and 1990), Juhasz (1980 and1985), Lim (1992), Ling (1990), Rabine (1987), Schenck (1988), Smith (1987), and Wong (1988, 1992, and 1993). For literary critical discussions on Tan, see Heung (1993), Ho (1996), Ling (1990), Lowe (1991), Schueller (1992), and Wong (1995).

11. See Fong (1977) for her criticism of the portrayal of all Chinese fathers as cold and authoritarian "assholes" in Kingston's *The Woman Warrior.*

12. Despite Chin's assertion that there is one "real" version of the Fa Mu Lan story, Jingshen Zhao contends that there are many versions of this story dating back to the Tang dynasty (qtd. in Wong 1992, 275).

13. Chin and others seem to forget that the complement to *The Woman Warrior* is *China Men,* which details the suffering and heroism of Chinese men who endured the hardships of life in a racist America. In *China Men,* men as fathers, sons, brothers and husbands are given space to tell their stories from multiple perspectives. I think these points need to be taken into consideration in light of their generalizations about her negative perspective on Asian men. See also Kingston's *Tripmaster Monkey* (1989a).

14. Ien Ang talks about her own ambivalent positioning as an "Asian" woman in the Australian multicultural narrative. As she notes, certain forms of difference are more acceptable for inclusions than other forms.

    > Why? Why is the Australian image of the ideal (as well as the ideal-typical) "Asian" migrant more often than not feminized? . . . the appearance of an "Asian" woman on the government poster should not just be seen as a feminist triumph, but as a symptom of the particular national desires invested in the image. . . . The "Asianness" imagined and represented . . . is one which is useful and flattering for Australia's self-image and projected future: not quite the same, but almost. To put it differently, I am not a dispossessed refugee with no job and no proper linguistic skills living on welfare, but a "westernized," highly educated professional whose English is almost fluent, a presentable and articulate "Asian" whose presence is arguably of economic and social benefit to the nation. That the image of the desired "Asian" other is feminized, however, might be precisely a sign that "Asians," no matter how desired, can still *not quite* be imagined as integral to the national self. No matter how "multicultural," Australian national identity still bears the trace of orientalism—a Eurocentric discourse renowned for its feminization of the "Orient"—despite all well-intentioned efforts to wipe them out. (Ang 1996, 46–7)

15. I wish to thank my colleague Judy Newton at the University of California, Davis for sharing this quote and her interest in Raymond Williams with me.

16. See Audre Lorde's biomythography *Zami: Another Spelling of My Name* (1982) in which she pays high tribute to her mother's language, which allowed her to access not only her rich matrilineal culture on the island of Carriacou but also the culture of Caribbean and African women. From her mother Linda, she inherited the sensual images and aesthetics that influenced her own writings.

17. See Alexander and Mohanty (1997), Jordan (1984), Lorde (1984), Moraga and Anzaldúa (1981), and Moraga (1983). See Robnett (1997) for Black women as bridge builders in the Civil Rights Movement.

18. Kingston's *Tripmaster Monkey* (1989a) discusses Wittman Ah Sing's production of *Three Kingdoms*, which made him realize the futility of war. He decides to become a pacifist. The book recovers an anti-war tradition not only during the anti-Vietnam protest era in America during the 1960s but also in Chinese culture and history.

19. There is evidence that Chin is not totally correct in claiming that autobiography is not a Chinese genre. See Wu (1990).

20. Chin severely criticizes Jade Snow Wong's autobiography *Fifth Chinese Daughter* for selling out Chinese community, heritage, and men. However, as Amy Ling notes, Kingston has expressed a very different perspective: Kingston considers Wong her literary mentor and the "Mother of Chinese American literature" (Ling 1990, 120). One begins to see how narrowly Chin defines "Chinese community," "Chinese heritage" or an "Asian American sensibility" and "aesthetics" in his denunciations of Chinese female writers such as Jade Snow Wong, Maxine Hong Kingston, and Amy Tan.

21. See also K. Scott Wong's re-assessment of Yung Wing's life and career as a cultural broker (1998).

    According to Walter K. Lew, Chin's original reaction to Kingston's work as fiction was actually fairly positive, but "when it [Kingston's *The Woman Warrior*] was marketed as a memoir, and therefore had the status of transmitting, documenting, describing Chinese American experience to the American reading public," he condemned the book (Yang 1996, 38).

22. Tan states that the stories in *The Joy Luck Club* are true emotionally to what happened in her life. "The heart of *The Joy Luck Club* is definitely autobiographical, but I could list factual things that are not true—that I did not grow up in Chinatown in San Francisco, that I have never played chess. My mother did not lose her babies in (Guay Lin); she's never been in Guay Lin except with me in 1987. But she did lose three daughters in China in 1949. She was the little girl watching her mother cut a piece of flesh from her arm to make soup, and she was the little girl watching her mother die when she took opium because she had become a third concubine" (Tan 1991d, 28).

23. See Ang (1994), Chow (1993), Lowe (1996a), Ono (1995), and Yanagisako (1995).

5

DESIRE IN THE DESERT:
THE SELF TALKING-STORY IN
MAXINE HONG KINGSTON'S
MOTHER-DAUGHTER STORIES

I lay claim to this being which I am; that is,
I wish to recover it, or more exactly,
I am the project of the recovery of my being.
Jean-Paul Sartre, *Being and Nothingness*
(trans. H. Barnes)

the barbarians heard a woman's voice singing,
as if to her babies, a song so high and clear,
it matched the flutes.
Maxine Hong Kingston,
The Woman Warrior

The Daughter's Recovery of Mother-Daughter Stories

In *The Woman Warrior*, Maxine Hong Kingston eschews the one-dimensional representations of Asian American women as victims, lotus blossoms, or erotic seductresses and prostitutes to focus on the complicated dilemmas and traumas in the experiences of a Chinese American mother and her daughter. Kingston neither exoticizes nor sentimentalizes the intense and often brutal conflicts that take place between Brave Orchid and the daughter-narrator Maxine. Her cultural text testifies to the complicated work of constructing a self talking-story that re-envisions and enacts a more transformative social and political subjectivity in the face of considerable psychosocial, as well as cultural and historical, disorientation, violence, and loss experienced by the Chinese in America. Kingston's autobiographical fictions reveal the oppressive *and* empowering interpretive possibilities, life choices, and locations for women and communities in negotiating and challenging dominant and marginalized ideologies and institutions that would define them.

Mothers and daughters are not distinct, autonomous individuals. According to Marianne Hirsch, to study the mother-daughter relationship is to "plunge into a network of complexities, to attempt to untangle the strands of a double self, a continuous multiple being of monstrous proportions stretched across generations, parts of which try desperately to separate and delineate their own boundaries. It is to find continuity and relationship where one expects to find difference and autonomy. This basic and continued relatedness and multiplicity, this mirroring which seems to be unique to women have to be factors in any study of female development in fiction" (Hirsch 1981b, 73). In *The Woman Warrior*, the autobiographical "I" is both self and Other, intimately linked to and separated from the (m)other in the formation of its own distinct talk-story narratives.

Throughout the text, Kingston imaginatively portrays the mother-daughter relationship as an ambiguous, permeable, and precarious territory in which to work. In the case of daughters with immigrant mothers, the task can be especially difficult, but it is a necessary project. Maxine, the daughter persona, must crisscross the borders and ruptures among different generations, classes, languages, cultures, constructions of selves as well as geopolitical space in order to access her mother's stories and to construct her own unique voice. It is, however, in the processes of the self talking-story that Kingston's mother-daughter pair can begin to discover their complicated sites of conflict as well as opportunity for connection and alliance as women.

Through Maxine, Kingston provides herself the psychosocial and aesthetic distance necessary for exploring the profoundly intense relationship between a champion-talking mother and a young daughter coming into her own voice and stories. Kingston's autobiographical self talking-story is the vehicle by which the daughter-writer, Kingston, through her daughter-narrator Maxine, continuously deconstructs *and* reconstructs her confusing childhood memories and her mother's ambiguous stories. In this way, she tries to sort out what it all means and how it branches into her own life story. Maxine processes the memories of her childhood, which are located in the multiple traumas of dislocation and relocation of her family, culture, and community. Under these ruptured circumstances, it is difficult for the young narrator to articulate her complicated "real" in a purely factual, linear, and unified manner. Moreover, her stories chart the interior vacillations and vulnerabilities of the autobiographical subject in excavating and resurrecting the fragments of self and desire that have been lost or silenced.

Deciphering Her Mother's Many Voices

It is not easy for a Chinese American daughter to decipher her immigrant mother's stories, which are profoundly situated in and disrupted by social, economic, cultural, and historical circumstances. Brave Orchid, for example, speaks in a multiple-voiced discourse, which reflects her complex social identities at different locations.

On one level, Brave Orchid is portrayed as a traditional Chinese woman who has been socialized into her role as keeper and transmitter of the "traditional ways" of her Chinese culture and village community. Among the village families, "the heavy, deep-rooted women were to maintain the past against the flood, safe for returning" (*TWW* 9). Traditionally, women were to stay in their father's home until they married, whereupon they would most likely enter their husband's home to care for his family, to bear and teach his children, and carry on his name in a patrilineal, patrifocal, and patriarchal society. As a symbolic and public representation of society, she is empowered as the keeper of the private-domestic life, of family secrets and stories; a guardian of male descent kinship lines; and a performer of rituals, values, language, and culture. As an immigrant mother, Brave Orchid attempts to pass her knowledge and experience to her second-generation Chinese American daughter as part of a shared notion of identity, despite the inequitable circumstances for women within this patriarchal structure.[1] This Chinese homeland and culture are integral parts of her first world, a world in which Brave Orchid continually negotiates her "official" duties as well as her transgressions as a woman.

Aside from fulfilling the demands of a Chinese patriarchal tradition, the Chinese immigrant mother preserves her family and traditions against the dominant culture of Western "ghosts" in the United States—often perceived as a greater common enemy to the family collective. Euro-American "ghosts" introduce a different value system, language, and culture found in the United States. Brave Orchid herself knows well the hardships suffered by her family and community, as well as the caveats of a white capitalist patriarchy that imposes silence on Chinese women and men. She is a woman who suffers within the overlapping networks of power in her adopted country.

In 1939, Brave Orchid arrives in the United States as an adult after a long separation from her husband, who arrived in the 1920s. Her memories are haunted with her fears of being deported to China and of being jinxed by white "ghosts." Her fears are reflected in mainstream America's growing concerns about the formation of a communist government in China and its severe anti-communist paranoia at home during the 1950s. This paranoia was enacted in the subcommittee of the Senate Committee on Governmental Operations (chaired by Senator Joseph McCarthy); the House Un-American Activities Committee; the Senate Internal Security Subcommittee; the FBI (directed by J. Edgar Hoover); and the INS, which deported or denaturalized suspected communists (see S. Chan 1991a, 141).

Brave Orchid and her family, like many working-class immigrant Chinese and peoples of color before them, are marginalized and restricted to a lifetime of menial jobs such as in laundries and in tomato fields, monotonous work that meant long hours and low pay (or no pay in a family business). Brave Orchid, who works in the family laundry in Chinatown along with her husband, children, and co-ethnic workers, gives her woman's testimony about her harsh life to her daughter:

> This is terrible ghost country, where a human being works her life away. . . . I have not stopped working since the day the ship landed. I was on my feet the moment the babies were out. I shouldn't have left, but your father couldn't have supported you without me. I'm the one with the big muscles. . . . I put you babies in the clean places at the laundry, as far away from the germs that fumed out of

> the ghosts' clothes as I could. Aa, their socks and handkerchiefs choked me. I
> cough now because of those seventeen years of breathing dust. (*TWW* 122–23)

This embodied witnessing counters the capitalist-nationalist myth that the Chinese, through their racial, ethnic, and cultural contexts, have all succeeded in American society.

Maxine testifies to the truth of her mother's testimony: Though a small, middle-aged woman, Brave Orchid could "carry a hundred pounds of Texas rice up- and downstairs. She could work at the laundry from 6:30 a.m. until midnight, shifting a baby from an ironing table to a shelf between packages, to the display window, where ghosts tapped on the window glass" (*TWW* 122). Brave Orchid assumes the care of children as well as her home. In this exhausting environment, Brave Orchid suffers the stereotypes of her customers, "No tickee, no washee, mama-san?" (*TWW* 123) Her social and work life are not easily divided into the binary of private/domestic versus public/political spheres. Her exploited labor—reproductive and productive—exhausts her body, mind, and spirit, profoundly affecting the survival and well-being of her family and community.

For Brave Orchid, preserving the remnants of Chinese social and cultural traditions in the United States, even though they place limits on women, becomes a means of constructing, reinforcing, and commanding family-communal loyalties and socioeconomic survival. Immigrant Chinese families and Chinatown communities provide networks for mutual support and economic assistance that help them survive, grow, and resist a hostile environment in America. Evelyn Nakano Glenn sheds light on the double bind:

> When individuals and their families confront economic deprivation, legal dis-
> crimination and other threats to their survival, . . . conflict over inequities within
> the family may be muted by the countervailing pressure on the family to unite
> against assaults from outside institutions . . . the family [becomes] a "culture of
> resistance." The locus of conflict . . . lies outside the household, as members en-
> gage in collective attempts to create and maintain family in opposition to forces
> that undermine family integrity. (Glenn 1986, 192)

Under these difficult circumstances, Brave Orchid is represented as transmitting the importance of preserving ties with a Chinese history, culture, and family to an American-born daughter as a strategic form of social, economic, and political survival in the United States, and, as we will see, in China.

Maxine's parents, disillusioned by life in America, fantasize temporarily about returning home to China and feel a need to prepare their children for this possibility. During the pre-WWII period, Chinese immigrant women and men were disappointed with their marginalization in the United States. In this period, second-generation American-born Chinese were also deeply disappointed in a racist culture and society that denied them access and opportunities despite their assimilation and acculturation into mainstream societal norms. Many Chinese parents reconstructed a diasporic social and political imaginary of a homeland for themselves and for second-generation children who had never been "home" before. As Gloria

Chun (1998) argues, many Chinese of this period, racially and economically segregated in Chinatowns, maintained a strong nationalist and racialized ethnic identification with Chinese culture and society. Some second-generation American-born Chinese left the States to live and work in China, employing their American education and skills in the revolutionary-nationalist Chinese cause, especially during the pre-WWII period.

Maxine, born in the middle of WWII, inherits an ambivalent and fragmented storehouse of her mother's China and Chinatown stories as she matures in the post-war milieu of the 1950s, 1960s, and 1970s. She moves between the world of her Chinese immigrant parents and Chinatown community and the social and cultural world and movements of a Berkeley in ferment. Another "culture of resistance" (see chap. 4) was being constructed by early Asian American cultural nationalists in opposition to the dominant forces in mainstream America that attempted to brutally contain, destroy, or exploit subordinated racial-ethnic families and communities in the United States.

In the milieu of multiple signifying practices and sites, the narrator Maxine portrays her dilemmas with her mother's efforts at transmitting the remnants of a Chinese identity and cultural legacy half-embedded in the specific and complex psychosocial context of turmoil within China. Brave Orchid attempts to articulate her understanding of this transforming world to her daughter. Her efforts erupt in cryptic warnings and discontinuous story fragments constituted, contradicted, and protected in duplicity: It is hard to get the stories of relatives straight from her parents; and news from China and about China is confusing. Maxine learns that good things are unspeakable and Chinese holidays and customs are kept but their meaning never explained (*TWW* 215). The Chinese American daughter is at a loss, for example, to explain her mother's desire for retribution from the pharmacist who jinxed their house by sending a wrong prescription. The "bad guys and good guys" in China are hard to determine, especially with the chaotic winds of war and political change sweeping through the country, constantly refiguring and contesting, for example, who the "enemy" was or what was to be identified as "feudal" or "modern." "It is confusing that my family was not the poor to be championed. They were executed like the barons in the stories, when they were not barons" (*TWW* 61). Her mother's expectations for her, moreover, are not clear. Does mother want her to be a wife-slave or a swordswoman? Does she think her daughter is ugly and clumsy? Brave Orchid protests that she did not actually call Maxine ugly: "That's what we're supposed to say. That's what Chinese say. We like to say the opposite" (*TWW* 237). When the young narrator asks for information, she is frustrated and confused by adults who get "mad, evasive, and shut you up if you ask" (*TWW* 215). Answers are not always forthcoming or totally accessible to Maxine; these are the ambiguous and dislocated fragments of culture and history the narrator grapples with in her desire to articulate a self, story, and history.

Maxine is frustrated in her attempts to infer how this Chinese world fits into her own life. "Those of us in the first American generations have had to figure out how the invisible world the emigrants built around our childhoods fit in solid America" (*TWW* 6). There are disturbing hints from her parents of returning to China one day. She has never been to China and worries about the consequences for a girl who does not behave like a "good Chinese-feminine girl." This Chinese world is part of the collective diasporic imaginary of her parents and an "overseas Chinese" community. "Diasporas always leave a trail of both collective memory about another place and time and create new maps of desire and attachment. It is the myth of the (lost or idealized) homeland, the object of both collective memory and of desire and attachment, which is constitutive of diasporas, and which ultimately confines and constrains the nomadism of the diasporic subject" (editors of *Public Culture* qtd. in Ang 1994, 5). The immigrant Chinese mother selectively reconstructs her past life while Maxine tries to understand the complicated meaning of her mother's stories in relation to their present life in the United States. In the process of articulating her conflicted narratives of self, Maxine depicts her ongoing struggles with this polysemic originary myth of a past homeland as part of re-envisioning a more radical politics of memory, identity, culture, and community in the United States.

To further complicate the communications between mother and daughter, the daughter herself is continually advised not to tell the truth, and to hide her name and history; to remain silent and insular. This is a trickster's advice for survival in a racist society. Lying, for example, has a long tradition in the political memory of the Chinese living in this country; it stems from America's history of violence and discrimination against the Chinese. "Lie to Americans. Tell them you were born during the San Francisco earthquake. Tell them your birth certificate and your parents were burned up in the fire. Don't report crimes; tell them we have no crimes and no poverty. Give a new name every time you get arrested; the ghosts won't recognize you. Pay the new immigrants twenty-five cents an hour and say we have no unemployment. And, of course, tell them we're against Communism. Ghosts have no memory anyway and poor eyesight. And the Han People won't be pinned down" (*TWW* 214–15). Maxine begins to realize that "the emigrants confuse the gods by diverting their curses, misleading them with crooked streets and false names. They must try to confuse their offspring as well, who, they perceive, threaten them in similar ways—always trying to get things straight, always trying to name the unspeakable. The Chinese I know hide their names; sojourners take new names when their lives change, and they guard their real names with silence" (*TWW* 6). Duplicity protects the powerless or subjugated by ensuring survival when one feels threatened or has something to hide from the powerful— whether we are speaking of jealous ghosts or a hostile community or country. Nevertheless, all these layers of duplicity, silence, and injunction seriously affect the young daughter's understanding of her history as a Chinese American: "Sometimes I hated the secrecy of the Chinese. 'Don't tell,' said my parents, though we couldn't tell if we wanted to because we didn't know" (*TWW* 213).

Another reason for the daughter's inability to fully comprehend the knowledge of her history here in the United States is that she is not "Chinese" enough for her parents and ethnic community. "They would not tell us children because we had been born among ghosts, were taught by ghosts, and were ourselves ghostlike. They called us a kind of ghost. Ghosts are noisy and full of air; they talk during meals. They talk about anything" (*TWW* 213–14). Maxine's family constructs and situates her as a partial outsider, half Chinese, half barbarian, raised among and taught by white ghosts, who threaten her parents and their way of life as well as their security in this country. Brave Orchid's American-born daughter, like the half-barbarian children of the poet Ts'ai Yen (of whom more later), speaks the English language and has, in part, assimilated Euro-American ways of seeing the world. She cannot fully understand her mother's Chinese dialect and must use a dictionary to figure out the meanings of curses or words that frighten or diminish her. She tells her story as an insider-outsider engaging subjective and objective elements, making disturbingly visible an ambiguous border identity that is not quite Chinese (or Anglo-American) enough for comfort. Under these circumstances, who can trust such a daughter not to betray her mother, her family and community? Who can be sure of or even understand the filiality or the "legitimacy" or "authenticity" of such a hybrid daughter? Thus, they do not entrust the whole story of the family, especially their secrets, to such a ghostly daughter who haunts the interior and exterior border zones of everyday life.

Yet, like her dragon mother, Maxine wants to be a storyteller and heroic fighter of ghosts that terrorize or hurt people. She wants to "shine floodlights into dark corners: no ghosts" (*TWW* 236). But rather than fight the bad Chinese warlords or hairy ghosts and ape-men that inhabit her mother's imaginary, Maxine wants to make some coherent, strategic sense of her various worlds by defining and explaining the mysteries and terrible secrets in her family, by breaking the imposed silences and speaking the grievances that have shaped and haunted her life.[2] As a young daughter, Maxine learns that the difference between the sane and the insane is that the insane have only one story to tell which they repeat over and over again.

Talk-story with its fluid, organic form, is continuously open to the speaker's embellishment and transformative imaginative power, and becomes a way of telling *and* enacting stories that are not one story but many. To claim multiple positions as a woman, writer, and individual in society, Maxine critiques, rejects, and lovingly transforms her mother's stories, eventually learning to speak and write a new language of self-in-community that is intimately linked to the life and stories of her mother, a champion performer in a vibrant Chinese oral tradition.[3] It is through telling and transforming her mother's stories that she breaks her own suffocating silence, vindicates the ancestral women in her family and culture, and reclaims their names and stories for herself and for other women in socially and politically creative ways. Maxine learns to assert her identity against the institutions that seek her erasure, marginalization, and confinement as a Chinese American woman. She is no longer the absolute silent/silenced object of racist or sexist culture or history. Hers is not a passive, ahistorical positioning of self, but an actively subversive and difficult one.

In order to begin this difficult task, Kingston as daughter-writer realizes that she must excavate the ambiguous and discontinuous remnants of a Chinese heritage as well as take an active role in articulating the cultural and historical fluctuations of a vibrantly contentious Chinese and Asian American community. How else, Maxine thinks, could five thousand years of culture have survived—"maybe everyone makes it up as they go along. If we had to depend on being told, we'd have no religion, no babies, no menstruation (sex, of course, unspeakable), no death" (*TWW* 216). For the rebel-filial daughter-writer, the task is also a vital form of enacting survival and cultural power in hegemonic mainstream American society. All these multiple dilemmas bring to the forefront the particular practices, ways of thinking, and understandings of life that are constantly being negotiated in Maxine's construction of a standpoint from which to speak and enact herself.

No Name Woman: Living in Patriarchy in China and the United States

It is a difficult and risky negotiation for Brave Orchid and Maxine to preserve a patriarchal Chinese culture and history as part of a "culture of resistance" against a dominant Eurocentric culture in America. For in preserving certain aspects of traditional Chinese culture and history, they are confronted with the dilemma of maintaining the oppression of women and of each other within this system. Kingston makes clear that the responsibility of cultural preservation is certainly not without cost to Brave Orchid, to her daughter, to other Chinese women, and to their communities. In her work of preservation, Brave Orchid is implicated in the culture or Law of the Father, the patriarchal ("official") stories and non-stories (silence) about fallen women and useless girl children in traditional Chinese society.[4]

Kingston gives us a powerful example of how women collude in the disempowerment of one another in the opening chapter of *The Woman Warrior*. For over twenty years Brave Orchid has been silent about No Name Woman, her husband's sister. She has never discussed the violent reactions of the village women and men against No Name Woman for committing adultery, and she does so only when her own daughter has begun to menstruate. In the Chinese community, the valuable work of preserving family and culture was linked physically and symbolically with women. If women stepped out of the restricted boundaries of their assigned roles they had the power to cause significant social disruption or destruction. Ideally, women were to be defined and valued according to their obedience, passivity, and maintenance of the traditional ways within a patriarchal societal system. As Hélène Cixous bluntly states: "Either the woman is passive; or she doesn't exist. What is left is unthinkable, unthought of" (Cixous 1981, 92). In a village beset by poverty, hunger, plagues, floods, and war, such things as frivolity, individuality, a private life, adultery were anathema; they were considered dangerous extravagances and weaknesses.[5] "The round moon cakes and round doorways, the round tables of graduated size that fit one roundness inside another, round windows and rice bowls—these talismans had lost their power to warn this family of the law: a family must be whole, faithfully keeping the descent line by having sons to feed the old and the dead, who in turn look after the family" (*TWW* 15). When No Name Woman broke the rules by her adultery, public censure and disorder followed, destroying the social and familial bonds that had kept her rooted to an identity and community.

No Name Woman's husband, however, like the other village men who were "hungry, greedy, tired of planting in dry soil," was a sojourner in America in search of "food-money" for the family in China (*TWW* 15). No Name Woman was left at home, barely married, young and restless, but expected to "maintain the real"—to preserve his family, home, name, and culture until his return (*TWW* 14). Thus, No Name Woman's private and imaginary life as well as her "real" life as a woman—her desires, sexuality, dreams, emotional needs—are doubly silenced: "The work of preservation demands that the feelings playing about in one's guts not be turned into action. Just watch their passing like cherry blossoms" (*TWW* 9). Kingston reveals how patriarchal codes along with the discriminatory policies of the late nineteenth to mid-twentieth century in America added to the oppression of women left behind in China and not only to the single and married men who journeyed here.[6]

Brave Orchid witnessed with her own eyes how the consequences of disobeying the Law of the Father can mean isolation, violence, insanity, or death. For women whose lives were intimately tied into familial and communal networks, there is the haunting terror of being "a bright dot in blackness, without home, without a companion, in eternal cold and silence" (*TWW* 16). It is no wonder that a Chinese immigrant mother attempts to instill in her young daughter (even in America) the virtues and habits that are considered ideally feminine in traditional Chinese culture (Bannan 1979, 172). The mother tells her daughter that "what happened to her [No Name Woman] could happen to you. Don't humiliate us. You wouldn't like to be forgotten as if you had never been born" (*TWW* 5). Brave Orchid attempts to shame and discipline her daughter into obedience just as the villagers did on a larger scale to No Name Woman. In addition, the daughter is warned by her mother not to tell anyone the secret about her father's sister. The frightening lesson is not totally lost on the daughter: No Name Woman had "crossed boundaries not delineated in space" (*TWW* 9). For this reason, no word, name, or memory is allotted her. It was as if she had never been born.

Thus, learning about patriarchal relationships within the family or community coincides with learning names and non-names and rules of naming and non-naming implicit in patriarchal discourse. To have no name is the punishment; to be remembered as a patriarchal caveat to other women is the punishment. Such traumatizing practices often dictate that women inhabit silence and inhibit action.

The young Maxine's mother can be terse and rough in her admonitions to behave like a good Chinese daughter, but Brave Orchid's warning stories are often rooted in the powerful laws of survival that govern a Chinese woman's life and options in a patriarchal structure. "My mother has told me once and for all the useful parts. She will add nothing unless powered by Necessity, a riverbank that guides her life. She plants vegetable gardens rather than lawns" (*TWW* 6). The stories with their

their austere, practical attitude have an affect on Maxine, who as a young child still remembers the price of guilt in doing things that were considered "frivolous"—flying a kite, eating ice cream, going to a movie, enjoying a carnival ride, and speaking out. It is no wonder that Maxine identifies with her outcast Aunt, who defied community norms, since she too subverts both her mother's and her family's injunctions to be silent in telling and writing.

Kingston, however, complicates Brave Orchid's message: It could represent a warning based simply on fear or acquiescence to tradition; it could also represent a form of love, practicality, and personal and political survival for herself and daughter within racist and sexist systems. "Whenever she had to warn us about life, my mother told stories that ran like this one, a story to grow up on. She tested our strength to establish realities. Those in the emigrant generations who could not reassert brute survival died young and far from home" (*TWW* 5–6). Kingston politicizes the complex social and historical work and agency of Chinese women who often bear the responsibility of maintaining the survival of their families and culture under difficult circumstances, but she does not ignore the limiting and compromised discourses mothers might pass to their daughters in the process.

Maxine identifies a Chinese word for the female "I" with a female slave—*mui*. For Maxine this word becomes symbolic of women's trauma and powerlessness. That is, women seemed to be rewarded for subordinating themselves as slave to master. In many ways, patriarchal societies are set up to "break women with their own tongues!" (*TWW* 56). In reaction, Maxine, for example, wants to remain single and independent and yet she finds herself feeling envious, bitter, and unloved because she is not a wife supported by a man. The "slave mentality" of women is just below the surface, waiting to make an appearance; even as an adult, the daughter feels that "China wraps double binds around [her] feet" (*TWW* 57).[7]

The meanings of her mother's discourses powerfully resonate in Maxine's life. They remind her of boundaries and obstacles, affecting her psychosocial and emotional life as a woman in self-abusive ways. Internalized, the weighty legacy of her mother's ambivalent and ambiguous stories traumatically inhibits Maxine's ability to imagine and enact more liberating possibilities within her own circumstances. She is continually reminded of the social and cultural codes and demands that have a strong hold not only on her mother's life and stories but also on her own.[8]

Maxine, moreover, must deal with sexist definitions of ideal feminine behavior not only from Chinese culture but also from mainstream American society. She resents the oppressions located in both patriarchal cultural systems; and she is not satisfied with either/or choices between a Chinese and Euro-American heritage. This rigid binary does not do justice to the complicated and permeable positionings she maintains in her daily life. In this ruptured space of painful yet hopeful difference, the self talks-story in order to begin to stretch and re-imagine her multiple legacies. "Women looked like great sea snails—the corded wood, babies and laundry they carried were the whorls on their backs. The Chinese did not admire a bent back; goddesses and warriors stood straight. Still there must have been a marvelous freeing of beauty when a worker laid down her burden and stretched and arched" (*TWW* 11). If given opportunity, how does one enact the "marvelous freeing of beauty" of the goddess-warrior in one's own psychosocial and cultural locations?

Seductive Night Songs of the Shaman: Brave Orchid's Talk-Story

Brave Orchid's life and stories do not present a simple and unambiguous mirror for patriarchal Chinese culture. Subordinated or silenced subtexts seep through the dominant texts, making for contradictions and ruptures in her stories and injunctions.[9] The mother speaks with a polyvocality that she hopes her daughter will inherit. On the one hand, Brave Orchid seems to reinforce the laws and ideals of society by repeating the caveats of patriarchal society in talk-story, but as Sara Ruddick has noted, "children are shaped by—some would say imprisoned in—the stories they are first told. But it is also true that storytelling at its best enables children to adapt, edit, and invent life stories they can live with" (Ruddick 1989, 98). Thus, despite the fact that Brave Orchid tells her daughter she will end up "a wife and a slave," the daughter distinctly remembers following her mother around the house chanting the song of the warrior woman (*TWW* 24). She learns that she fails if she becomes just a wife or a slave.

Brave Orchid has a rich imaginative life, which extends its explorations to a female self not fully confined within masculinist values and norms. Like No Name Woman and even Fa Mu Lan, she is able to cross "boundaries not delineated in space" (*TWW* 9).[10] She tells her daughter fabulous stories about female heroes and their extraordinary adventures; the transformative stories signify or suggest a woman's resilience, courage, freedom, and potential. She tells about a Chinese woman who was not only a superb pole fighter but also the founder of white crane boxing. She provides a subversive prepatriarchal story to explain the subjugation of Chinese women—"that they were once *so dangerous* that they had to have their feet bound" [italics mine] (*TWW* 23). This is Chinese cultural talk-story that incorporates the potential to express a mother's powerful transgressive desires and discourses for herself and for her daughter in its Chinese American translation.

The visionary stories seduce and unbind her daughter's mind, allowing it to move critically beyond daily limits, beyond the patriarchal heterosexist "real" that attempts to constrict her physical and psychic freedom, and at times beyond Western notions of time, space, and perspective. "I learned to make my mind large, as the universe is large, so that there is room for paradoxes. . . . The dragon lives in the sky, ocean, marshes, and mountains; and the mountains are also its cranium. . . . It breathes fire and water; and sometimes the dragon is one, sometimes many" (*TWW* 35). In this social-political imaginary, mother and daughter are dragons, reborn as fierce and powerful in the Year of the Dragon. The daughter feels the magical power in her mother's talk-story, and in her singing, which has the power to bring her "out of nightmares and horror movies" and make her feel safe and loved (*TWW* 24). The visionary and mythic world evoked by her mother's stories does not seek to recover an immutable China past; rather, these stories recover the marginalized formations of cultural knowledge and resistance of those subordinated and distressed within racist and sexist ideologies, discourses, and institutions.

In this sense, the power of the mother's imaginative stories are *not* escapist fantasies that invite the daughter to immerse or lose herself in Orientalist exotica, nostalgia, or cute bedtime stories. bell hooks notes that "all too often the colonized mind thinks of the imagination as the realm of the psyche that, if fully explored, will lead one into madness, away from reality. Consequently, it is feared. For the colonized mind to think of the imagination as the instrument that does not estrange us from reality, but returns us to the real more fully, in ways that help us to confront and cope, is a liberatory gesture" (hooks 1991, 55). Through her mother's multiple stories, Maxine learns to talk-story herself; to learn the processes for re-envisioning the universe; and to survive, contemplate, and enact alternative realities or futures for herself and her community.

This subjective and cultural site which reveals her mother's conflicted feelings and experiences allows the daughter to further explore these conflicts and what they mean for herself and her mother, as well as for women. Such a psychosocial exploration by the self talking-story is a political legacy and project as it continually examines and critiques its relationships within culture, society, and history. Told to her nightly, these are the stories the young Chinese female narrator hears over and over until she could no longer distinguish hero from mother. The mythic and visionary world is made flesh in the mother as hero; the daughter-writer recuperates the mother's devalued and complex historical presence in the making of identity and culture. Maxine is not a passive listener; rather she enacts a critical social practice of imaginative intervention, empathy, and political resistance. She re-envisions the exhausted and devalued Chinese immigrant mother as a heroic individual in her own fictive realities *as well as* in her diminished and complicit social, economic, and historical contexts in America.

The mother, who is a woman warrior, champion-talker, and bully, is worn down and lonely in her old age and hardscrabble life in the United States. She is tired of unsuccessfully fending off the mundane "ghosts" (such as shopkeepers, mailmen, police, winos) who occupy her ordinary life. But Kingston constructs this mother as a complicated woman who does not wish to leave her daughter with this humiliating portrait of herself. Brave Orchid is concerned that Maxine knows very little about her Chinese life as an educated, independent woman and feisty ghost-fighter at the height of her powers in a changing China. Thus, in the chapter "Shaman," Kingston also has Brave Orchid dramatically portray herself as a successful shaman and midwife-doctor with status and power in her Chinese community.

Brave Orchid's earlier life story counters the Anglo-American version of her identity and experiences in China as a woman. In China, she experiences the destructive forces that can be used against a woman in a village community, but she also develops a feisty sense of self and gains a level of independence from her sojourner-husband. In recovering the formative and progressive aspects of her earlier life in China, Brave Orchid reinvents herself in her time as a hero in a genealogy of heroic women. This is her way of subverting the discourses and institutions that have restricted and demeaned her in China and in this country. Through the art of talk-story, Brave Orchid maintains her power to tell the stories that track the wide range of her social actualities and the imaginary life that sustains her spirit—as well as her daughter's—across the fluctuations of space, time, and history.

In "Shaman," the daughter-narrator tells the heroic story of her mother's life, thereby merging the mythic, epic world of heroic swordswomen with the actual world of her mother's lived experience. She recuperates her mother's autobiographical fictions, the imaginative reconstructions of the self talking-story, which are a crucial element in understanding the experiences and histories of oppressed individuals and groups. These stories are complex historical remnants and legacies of her mother's experiences, situated within multiple frames of reference and meaning, which the daughter seeks to decipher as part of a critical and situated dialogical and political practice.

In "Shaman," Brave Orchid tells about her earlier life in China, which was, like No Name Woman's, Fa Mu Lan's, and Ts'ai Yen's, a "private life, secret and apart from them [an oppressive village or community]" (*TWW* 14). The daughter-narrator portrays her mother as a practical, feisty modern woman. Brave Orchid's life suggests the massive changes coming for women in her society at a time when China is in a revolutionary period, socially and politically transforming itself. Brave Orchid's husband is a laundryman in New York and her two children have died in China. Given the financial opportunity by her husband (who wishes to prepare her to join him in the United States) and by societal changes in China, Brave Orchid seizes the chance to get a scientific education and work as a doctor *prior* to her arrival in the United States in 1939. She takes leave from her husband's family home, makes her way alone to the capital city, and goes to school, something that was not possible for No Name Woman.

At To Keung School of Midwifery, Brave Orchid lives two years without servitude, acquiring a job, a room of her own, and new women friends. Her colleagues are also modern women blazing trails of freedom and independence and pursuing scientific inquiry. Brave Orchid's factual and rational approach to the "realities" of her world view, however, do not exclude her dealing with the psychological, spiritual, or imaginary world. As a shrewd and practical woman, she deals with all possible contingencies. During this time, for example, Brave Orchid displays her abilities as a shaman—fearless in battling the unknown and coming out victorious among her women colleagues. After the battle with the ghost, these new women chant Brave Orchid back from the spirit world by shouting out magical spells and prayers: "They called out their own names, women's pretty names, haphazard names, horizontal names of one generation" (*TWW* 89). They chant her back through her homosocial affiliations with women—not through the names of fathers. In contrast to Chin's search for self in a narrowly selected range of Chinese classics, these women remake themselves by calling out each others' names.

Such a woman's culture might be akin to what Elaine Showalter means when she talks about the muted culture of women "the boundaries of whose culture and reality overlap, but are not wholly contained by, the *dominant (male) group*" (Showalter 1985, 261). Within this world of women, Brave Orchid constructs a spectacle that displays her ability to make herself courageous—in fighting the unknown as a shaman, undertaking an education as an older married woman, gaining fame as a doctor, and coming to the United States.

In reconstructing her mother's story, Maxine engages in collaboration and bonding with her mother as well as in brutal resistance and disengagement from her. Brave Orchid is a formidable role model and hero to Maxine, who acknowledges her affiliation: "I am practically the first daughter of a first daughter" (*TWW* 127). Like the magical stories of swordswomen, Brave Orchid's autobiographical fictions, blossoming as they do from the heart of her own daughter's, provide a stimulus and "pre-text" for her daughter's explorations. According to critic Bella Brodzki, a daughter-narrator's "linguistic disability or instability and cultural disorientation" pivots around her desire to communicate with a distant or absent mother, who becomes the "pre-text for the daughter's autobiographical project." Moreover, "as the child's first significant Other, the mother *engenders* subjectivity through language; she is the primary source of speech and love. And part of the maternal legacy is the conflation of the two. Thereafter, implicated in and overlaid with other modes of discourse, the maternal legacy of language becomes charged with ambiguity and fraught with ambivalence. In response (however deferred), the daughter's text, variously, seeks to reject, reconstruct, and reclaim—to locate and recontextualize—the mother's message" (Brodski 1988, 246). The daughter presents her mother as a ghost-fighter, a doctor, a survivor, woman warrior; and as a champion talker and storyteller who transmits complex messages in difficult circumstances. This is the awesome dragon-mother who tells her daughter that she cut her frenum in order to free her tongue to "speak languages that are completely different from one another" (*TWW* 190).

However, Brave Orchid is also portrayed as a repressive, egotistical, insensitive tyrant who is quite capable of victimizing, silencing, and destroying other women, such as her fragile sister Moon Orchid and her daughter Maxine, in the name of bully love.[11] We learn, as Maxine does, that her mother and her stories can sometimes do real harm in the lives of ordinary people. For example, Moon Orchid does not have the strength or will to survive the aggressive woman warrior scenario that Brave Orchid has mapped out for her to play in order to win back her bigamist husband in the United States: "A long time ago . . . the emperors had four wives, one at each point of the compass, and they lived in four palaces. The Empress of the West would connive for power, but the Empress of the East was good and kind and full of light. You are the Empress of the East, and the Empress of the West has imprisoned the Earth's Emperor in the Western Palace. And you, the good Empress of the East, come out of the dawn to invade her land and free the Emperor. You must break the strong spell she has cast on him that has lost him the East" (*TWW* 166). Furthermore, Brave Orchid's powers as a shaman are useless when she tries to call Moon Orchid's lost spirit home after the shock of losing her husband. Brave Orchid's awesome power and love have constructive and destructive consequences within her own family. Maxine has felt the silencing power of her mother.

Brave Orchid is a complicated, powerful woman whose ambiguous stories of truth and fiction are fascinating and extremely frustrating to her daughter, who seeks to sort out mother and a cultural legacy from the precarious border standpoint of an insider-outsider, a second-generation half-barbarian, half-Chinese American daughter-writer. In constructing a damaging portrayal of Brave Orchid alongside the one that glorifies her as a protective mother, shaman, warrior woman, and champion talker, the daughter-narrator represents the dilemmas in reconstructing and understanding Brave Orchid's multifaceted positionings within the interstices of desire, experience, memory, and culture.

I do not think that Kingston's mother-daughter stories are meant to naively romanticize or celebrate universalized, ahistorical, and seamless enactments of harmonious mother-daughter or women's nurture and understanding, or to suggest an automatic or essentialized sisterhood—global or local. Rather, I think these stories are honest in their specific refusal to romanticize the stories of matrilineal descent, of mothers and daughters, as fairytale stories with happy endings. These mother-daughter stories interrogate the multiple dilemmas and traumas at women's sites of struggle within conflicting discourses and institutions that continually interact to delimit their power and options in society.

The Self as Project: A Daughter's Quest to Find Her Own Voice and Stories

Searching for self-expression—breaking oppressive forms of silence and victimization —becomes a way for Maxine to process identity. She must find a new language within which to articulate discoveries about herself and her world as a Chinese American woman. As Maxine says to another silent Chinese girl, who seems to mirror the narrator's own anger and self-abuse: "If you don't talk, you can't have a personality. . . . Talk. Please talk" (*TWW* 210) or "I thought talking and not talking made the difference between sanity and insanity. Insane people were the ones who couldn't explain themselves" (*TWW* 216). Yet, how to transform silence, invisibility, and desire into a language? And what to say?

In the search for a personal voice and self, the daughter's awkward first steps are mirrored in her voice. Her voice is not loud and brassy like her Chinese mother's voice. Rather, it is the self-conscious, awkward voice of an immigrant daughter attempting to assess her mother's truths and fictions. The frustrations between daughter and mother are very evident. There is a point in the story when the daughter wishes to escape the "hating range" of home and her mother's stories which appear to have no logic. These Chinese stories scramble her up. She tells her mother, "You lie with stories. You won't tell me a story and then say, 'This is a true story,' or, 'This is just a story.' I can't tell the difference. I don't even know what your real names are. I can't tell what's real and what you make up" (*TWW* 235). To worsen her confusion, there is no unified, centered tradition in her communities in America that allows her as a Chinese American woman to speak easily and forthrightly in her own person.

Through the narrator, Kingston is engaged in a constant struggle to break from the various communities and legacies of "we" that exclude or devalue her experiences, in order to negotiate another liberating understanding of herself as an individual "I" in a more fluid and hybrid notion of community.[12] She does not construct this fragmentation of self and community as a naive apolitical or ahistorical celebration of homelessness, or as a playful exercise in hybridity or dislocation. Rather, this ongoing and fluid engagement with the dilemmas of self in relation to family and community is grounded in surviving and resisting disempowering monolithic mainstream *and* oppositional discourses and institutions which would erase or represent her voice and story in constructing their own exclusive narratives. Disempowered within these racist and sexist discursive communities, the narrator's talk-story is not a luxury, as Audre Lorde (1982a) has often reminded us.[13]

As a silent child in school, Maxine paints layers of black paint over pictures of houses and flowers and suns. And when her confused parents take them home, she "spread them out (so black and full of possibilities) and pretended the curtains were swinging open, flying up, one after another, sunlight underneath, mighty operas" (*TWW* 192). There is indeed a rich creative life masked under darkness and absence. Later, she describes her voice as "a crippled animal running on broken legs," "a small person's voice that makes no impact" (*TWW* 196, 57). Her voice is a squeaking, quacking, ugly duckling voice. She says there were "splinters in [her] voice, bones rubbing jagged against one another" (*TWW* 196). She protests typing invitations for her boss in words "whispered, voice unreliable" (*TWW* 58). Finally, she accuses her mother of cutting her frenum, destroying her ability to speak and to acquire language. In her crippled, sickly voice, she struggles to confess to her mother "true things" about herself and to get rid of her throat pain; her mother, caught up in her own world of frustrations and patriarchal stereotypes, fails to understand the sane-crazy, lonely babbling of her awkward daughter.

Paula Gunn Allen notes that people caught between two languages and cultures are often "inarticulate, almost paralyzed in their inability to direct their energies toward resolving what seems to them insoluble conflicts" (Cheung 1988, 163).[14] At home, for example, Maxine is confronted by prejudices against girls from China that seep into conversations in America. She must deal with the image of girls as useless maggots, stink pigs, or cow-birds, fit to be killed or sold. At school and work—the outside world—she is silenced not only by sexist but also by racist stereotypes that haunt her childhood and womanhood. She is doubly silenced by "Chinese-feminine" and "American-feminine" models of behavior for young girls. She is considered retarded by some of her teachers, handicapped and silenced in her second-language English.

Maxine cannot fully articulate the experience or nature of her trauma. That is, her narrative *is* traumatized in attempting to make rational sense of trauma. She suffers years of angry silence, withdrawal, and finally emotional breakdown; she spends years enjoying the silence and the world of her imagination, the world of Chinese operas and crazy women where there is space for the repressed and resisting self to explore its desires and potential. But this world, covered under black paint, also mirrors the trauma, the inner fears and anxiety, of a daughter coming into being and creative voice in ways which are not legitimated, authorized, or deemed normal, healthy, or functional in her multiple communities. Maxine has more than enough ghostly models of lost, marginalized, or traumatized women in memory and language: No Name Woman, Moon Orchid, silent Chinese schoolgirls, crazy women who can tell only one story. The silent anger and depression are not psychological or pathological symptoms that Maxine must manage or work out in order to return to a functional state of "normality," "health," or "proper" behavior. The symptoms of illness reflect a struggle to resist the violent and debilitating forms of her socialization that attempt to *make* her ill, to alienate her experiences and suppress her ability to realize alternative realities or futures as a Chinese American woman. Having resisted in isolating silence, she gradually decides she has either to talk in school to establish an "I" identity or be a non-person with no language to define herself or her social relations.

The daughter's throat pain symbolizes her struggle to articulate how she really thinks, feels, acts—to articulate, though never fully recuperate, the invisible world under the black paint as well as the repressed anger and fears, and to come against her loud, bossy mother, the champion-talker, again and again through the power of self talking-story. At the laundry, Maxine's throat bursts open—comes crazy clean—after dinner with her family. She looks directly at her mother and screams out her anger and long list of grievances in a torrent. She *knows* there's nothing wrong with her: she's smart; she *can* write, win scholarships and go to college; she *won't* let them turn her into a slave or a wife. "Ha! You can't stop me from talking" (*TWW* 235). As Audre Lorde recognized in her discussion on the constructive uses of anger: "Every woman has a well-stocked arsenal of anger potentially useful against those oppressions, personal and institutional, which brought that anger into being. Focused with precision it can become a powerful source of energy serving progress and change. And when I speak of change, I do not mean a simple switch of positions or a temporary lessening of tensions, nor the ability to smile or feel good. I am speaking of a basic and radical alteration in those assumptions underlining our lives" (Lorde 1984, 127). That is, anger, can be strategically redirected more constructively at its roots in the violence and injustice of social practices and institutions.

Outlaw Knotmaker: Maxine Tries Out Her New Voice and Stories

Throughout the book, Kingston portrays the young Chinese American daughter-writer imaginatively testing and positioning her rebellious new voices and stories.[15] At first, like Fa Mu Lan, Maxine appropriates patriarchal rhetoric and codes of behavior in order to speak heroically. She fights in the guise of a male warrior, adventuring and bloodthirstily warring and lopping off heads. Fa Mu Lan wears armor while pregnant which makes her look like a "powerful, big man" (*TWW* 47). She gives up her child to fight in the wars as a "slim young man" (*TWW* 48). Upon her return home, she impresses her son not so much as a mother but as a war general (*TWW* 53). In this male disguise, she learns to articulate and redress her community's rage and grievances on the battlefield; at the same time, she wins the love and respect of her family and community as a powerful warrior. For a time, she revels in the life of the privileged male sex—the apple of her mother's, father's, country's eye.

But even a courageous woman, masquerading as a male warrior in defense of her country, must contend with the dilemmas and oppressions of being a woman within her family and society, especially if both race and gender are important to her. Kingston embellishes the story of Fa Mu Lan by exploring the personal tensions of a woman appropriating the male stance. In a face-off with a bad baron who has drafted her brother, Fa Mu Lan tells him that she is a "female avenger" and plans to kill him for the crimes committed against her family and community. But he makes a final appeal to her "man-to-man": "Oh, come now. Everyone takes the girls when he can. The families are glad to be rid of them. 'Girls are maggots in the rice.' 'It is more profitable to raise geese than daughters'" (*TWW* 51). As Linda Hunt has noted, this retelling of the swordswoman's story suggests that Fa Mu Lan (and Maxine) cannot "overlook the patriarchal biases of Chinese culture. The enemy of her village seeks to create an alliance with the defender of family and community on the common ground of misogyny. No wonder Kingston exclaims just after the swordswoman's tale is finished, 'I could not figure out what was my village'" (Hunt 1985, 8). Maxine comes to learn that the story of Fa Mu Lan as a heroic model for women has "provided neither an alternative rhetoric nor a practicable role model [to enable] daughters to become a woman different from that defined by Confucian rhetoric" (Croll 1995, 17). That is, "if stories like that of Mulan juxtaposed messages of the filiality of 'good' daughters and wives with the exercise of agency of the 'warrior' woman free of body and roaming in the guise in wide-open spaces, the split between fantasy of fable and reality of rhetoric [of Confucian gender-differentiated norms and behavioral expectations between males and females] broadened as daughters grew up" (ibid., 17). The stories are about girls who momentarily enact masculine-identified heroic fantasies that do not substantially change the gender and social actualities of women in culture and society.

The masculinized and racialized ethnic discourses of Asian American cultural nationalists also marginalized the concerns of women in their recuperation of a male-identified heroic life and literary canon or oral tradition. This recognition of the ruptures between these revered canonical fictions and the actualities of women's lives in China and in the United States raise the level of anger, frustration, and depression of a young narrator attempting to tell her own story in the spaces of difference.

There are no easy ways to resolve contradictions or to be all things to all people and to oneself in actual life. The narrator Maxine tells us that life in kung-fu–

sorcery movies or mother's myths and legends about heroic swordswomen are difficult to situate in her own life. Like Fa Mu Lan, Maxine initially wants to become a boy—or at least a tomboy. Or even a lumberjack. It is an early rebellion against her mother and her harping on the uselessness of girls, especially bad ones. It is a way for Maxine to deny her connection with what is devalued in her society. To be a bad girl is almost like being a boy, she rationalizes, but it does not seem to make her a loved child. Maxine tells us about her pathetic interactions with her boss. She objects to his racist jokes and actions but in such an "unreliable, small-person's voice" that it makes little impact on him. "If I took the sword, which my hate must surely have forged out of the air, and gutted him, I would put color and wrinkles into his shirt." She wonders about how she will fight the "stupid racists" and the "tyrants who for whatever reason can deny my family food and work" (*TWW* 58). For unlike Fa Mu Lan, Maxine has no supporting pop-out casts of eighty pole fighters or kung-fu training for the kind of social and cultural wilderness a Chinese American woman must negotiate in the United States. Neither straight As at Berkeley nor working for change in her daily life can make her a loved boy, Chinese-feminine, or the fabulous swordswoman of old. Her mother's stories are not easily translatable into her life in the United States.

Instead, Maxine must learn to tell and write her own stories in Asian America—just as her own mother Brave Orchid did in her own contexts in China and in the United States. Despite the fact that she must challenge her mother in order to establish her own personal identity, Maxine is still intimately linked to her Chinese mother's talk-story tradition. It is this talk-story tradition that introduces her to the aesthetic forms and vibrant images she uses to construct her own alternative selves. Talk-story, therefore, becomes a heroic and subversive form of verbal expression—passed on from one woman to another across dislocations and relocations, generations, cultures, and continents. In Kingston's autobiographical fiction, a quiet but imaginative young girl learns ways to defend herself discursively against the cruel savagery of various systems that would silence her or appropriate her story. Maxine learns agency in the process of actively learning to articulate herself. Talk-story becomes a courageous act that leads to transformation and discovery, to the inscriptions of self.

Maxine learns from the Fa Mu Lan story that the Chinese idiom for revenge literally means to "report a crime"—to witness and record—the injustices suffered by the community and by Chinese women ancestors and herself. It is the *language* of sexism and racism—painful, ugly words and images that maim and kill—that she as a woman warrior attempts to purge, to decapitate with fiery vengeance: Roiling anger erupts when she remembers past put-downs and the images of the "cowering, whimpering women" Fa Mu Lan discovers in a locked room. Maxine conjures up a legend about a group of wild women, "witch amazons" who "did not wear men's clothes," but "rode as women in black and red dresses. They bought up girl babies so that many poor families welcomed their visitations. When slave girls and daughters-in-law ran away, people would say they joined these witch amazons. They killed men and boys" (*TWW* 53). Maxine discursively inserts this wild mythical group of women who did not hide themselves as women, but aggressively recruited and reclaimed lost women and killed men outright for their crimes in the Fa Mu Lan story, thereby subverting her mother's story of Fa Mu Lan, the filial male-identified hero of her community.

The image of wilderness, inherited from her own mother's stories and life, is reclaimed and adapted by the daughter-writer in her own subversive talk-stories, in her legend about "witch amazons," who rupture the boundaries of patriarchal discourse and society. "Wilderness" is the home of the female avenger and outlaw storyteller, an unexplored space beyond the prison house of racist, sexist images and narratives. This wild territory is to be appropriated and transformed into a rich and imaginative female space that displaces male power. This awareness of potential female space enriches the daughter's sense of identity: The self is not fully solid, unified or defined; it is more provisional, fluid, a decentralized entity, without hard boundaries, the outcome of multiple social, cultural, and historical dislocations and relocations. The narrator learns to traverse this unexplored territory in speaking and writing as a woman, and not disguised as a male warrior.

In *The Woman Warrior*, the daughter-narrator acknowledges her mother's formidable power as champion-talker, but she continually struggles to name her own social realities as a Chinese American woman by retelling the stories that she first heard from her mother. Maxine, for example, takes the tantalizing secrets of No Name Woman and embellishes and transforms them to make them resonate in her own Chinese American life. In opening her book with this story, she subverts her mother's more practical, austere telling of the story and makes extravagantly visible the secret that her parents and Chinese village have kept hidden. She also demonstrates her affinity for the ostracized Aunt by exploring versions of her story that are different from the patriarchal one. Thus, Maxine imagines her Aunt's positioning as outcast, as wild woman, as lover of beauty, as sensuous woman, as beloved daughter, as adventurer and as risk-taker. Like her mother, the daughter imagines more than one way of seeing a situation, a person, and even her own life. As Sidonie Smith has noted, Maxine re-envisions her Aunt as an agent rather than a helpless victim. A spite-suicide, who refuses to name the paternity of her child, she contaminates the community well in vengeance and takes her baby with her out of mother love and concern for her welfare in the community (Smith 1987, 155). In another version of the story, Maxine wonders whether this Aunt was an unusually beloved and precious only daughter sheltered by a loving family rather than the despised woman she is made out to seem. She suggests that her father's injunction to silence about his sister may have been a reflection of his jealousy or hate. She reveals, for example, how her father had once been traded for a girl by her grandfather and that when her grandfather finally had a daughter, he "doted upon her" (*TWW* 12). Maxine reveals the significant but often neglected and unspoken social-emotional investments that often underpin individual decisions, actions and/or group identifications and alliances.

Such a resurrection of No Name Woman is a subversive form of ancestor worship that would not have the authorization of the Father. It takes its form not with paper boats, clothes, or money to honor the dead but with the power of the written word, the discursive power to name and order the world that had predominantly belonged to males in Chinese and American society. Writing talk-stories, which value women's oral cultures and practices, is a multiple transgression of patriarchy: in naming No Name Woman and in breaking the family's silence about her very existence from a woman's standpoint.

Just as Kingston has suffered condemnation for her imaginative reconstructions of Chinese American women, so the persona Maxine is haunted by consequences for resurrecting a ghost Aunt. To resurrect the restless dead in a patriarchal society by boldly bringing them into living memory and history is a serious, subversive act with many possible consequences. The stories do not always guarantee good, liberating or transformative results; they do not guarantee freedom from further hauntings by old and new ghosts; and they do not guarantee truth. "The Chinese are always very frightened of the drowned one, whose weeping ghost, wet hair hanging and skin bloated, waits silently by the water to pull down a substitute" (*TWW* 19). Maxine herself, moreover, fears turning out to be a crazy woman, just like the other crazy women in the book. She already perceives telltale signs: she is sickly, clumsy, messy, her hair is tangled; she limps. She talks to "adventurous people inside [her] head" and she had a mysterious illness (*TWW* 220). No wonder Kingston's book is subtitled a "memoir of a girlhood among ghosts." Ghosts in China and in the United States profoundly complicate her ability to think, feel, and act; they haunt the construction of her own fictive realities.

The daughter-writer carves out new territory in alien lands (literally and figuratively) as an intricate knotmaker of stories in her own right, a position she inherits from her champion-talker mother. She participates in and re-signifies heroic Chinese culture through the transformed voices of ancient heroes, the Fa Mu Lans and Ts'ai Yens; the ceremonial voice of the family storyteller rehearsing the matriarchal genealogies into the collective family and historical memory; and the shamanic voice that chants magical incantations and women's names to keep away ghosts, demons, and nightmares.

Out of the "Hating Range" of Home: Reconnoitering in Other Barbarian Lands

In *The Woman Warrior*, Maxine finally comes to provisional terms with her Chinese heritage and her mother through intense and painful struggle. Stifled and frustrated, she initially escapes home and mother in order to see the world differently, finding breathing spaces outside of her Chinese world—out of "hating range" of mother and the Chinatown community—in which to review the complex worlds in which she lives. She explores other parts of America "where the 'I' is a capital and 'you' is lower case" (*TWW* 193). The American "I" is straight, assertive and capitalized;

it is not written in small, crooked strokes as in Chinese. The symbolic language of the barbarians or foreigners—the white "ghost" people—suggests other possibilities of using language to talk about self in new ways. The language gives Maxine aesthetic distance in which to analyze the world as well as the narratives of mother, ethnic community, and dominant society.

In the mainstream culture of the United States, Maxine learns a logical, rational language that may explain the terrorizing ghosts and the other frustrating mysteries of her Chinese American life: "I learned to think that mysteries are for explanation. I enjoy the simplicity. Concrete pours out of my mouth to cover the forests with freeways and sidewalks" (*TWW* 237). In this larger society, the grown-up daughter-writer can come home to visit her family and "wrap [her] American successes around [her] like a private shawl; I *am* worthy of eating the food. From afar I can believe my family loves me fundamentally. They only say, 'When fishing for treasures in the flood, be careful not to pull in girls,' because that is what one says about daughters. But I watched such words come out of my mother's and father's mouths. . . . And I had to get out of hating range" (*TWW* 62). As Elaine Kim notes, however, Maxine's desire simply to relocate herself in an antiseptic American mainstream and to explain the world in purely logical, concrete, "no ghosts" terms could also diminish her by robbing her of the profound mysteries, myths, dream visions, and talk stories that are an integral part of her ethnic community and culture (Kim 1982, 206). These struggles are reflected in the writing of this talk-story memoir as the narrator negotiates her complicated relationship to these various discursive communities.

Hannah Arendt has noted that intellectual freedom or a new sense of reality can exist only in the context of psychic space, while psychic space in turn can be created only between distinct and contrasting points of view. In this rich frontier between Chinese and Euro-American ways of seeing, the daughter begins to "sort out what's just my childhood, just my imagination, just my family, just the village, just movies, just living" (*TWW* 239). She can return to the ambiguous, confusing facts and fictions of her life and her mother's raw material and find creative inspiration without losing a developing sense of a separate self in relation to her intersecting communities. Kingston's book seems to explore how to create a third perspective that incorporates various Chinese and Euro-American elements from which to enact new formations of agency and create new stories accountable to her circumstances as an Asian American woman.

This new self-in-process emerges, in part, from the mother-daughter collaboration and bonding process. The ego boundaries between mother and daughter are not clearly defined even in adulthood, and there is an affiliative link between mother and daughter. But there is a sense of separation as well, as the daughter, like her mother before, attempts to disrupt and subvert the discourses that confine her potential. In the daily grind of life, Brave Orchid crams her daughter full of ominous caveats and stories. In contrast, the young daughter chooses to associate herself more with voices of the mother who sings her out of nightmares, with the voices of To Keung School women, and with the songs of the visionary poet Ts'ai Yen.

Maxine struggles as well against the larger prejudices and practices of sexism and racism in the United States. She fights mainstream (American-feminine) ideals of beauty and behavior and her mother's traditional views of female children: that she is a bad girl because she refuses to cook; because she cracks dishes; because she is rebellious, silent, surly, clumsy, ugly—wanting to be a boy and a lumberjack, not wanting to marry. "The swordswoman and I are not so dissimilar. May my people understand the resemblance soon so that I can return to them. What we have in common are the words at our backs. The reporting is the vengeance—not the beheading, not the gutting, but the words. And I have so many words—'chink' words and 'gook' words too—that they do not fit on my skin" (*TWW* 62–63).

As King-Kok Cheung notes, "In reshaping her ancestral past to fit her American present, moreover, Kingston is asserting an identity that is neither Chinese nor white American, but distinctively Chinese American. Above all, her departures from the Chinese legends shift the focus from physical prowess to verbal injuries and textual power" (Cheung 1988, 169). But Kingston is not done with this shift to textual talk-story power. She is aware of the construction of her own positions and processes as a woman continuing the search for more liberating forms of identity.[16]

In an interview with Bill Moyers (1990) Kingston looks back on her retelling of the story of the woman warrior Fa Mu Lan in *The Woman Warrior* and the original emphasis she put on a woman's ability to lead people into bloody righteous battle (whether against bad barons and emperors, or against the language of racism and sexism). Kingston would now add some details she omitted, such as Fa Mu Lan's return home with her army and her transformation into a beautiful woman dressed in feminine clothes and with flowers in her hair. This sight shocked the troops she led, perhaps reconfiguring their sex-gender perceptions. As a warrior-feminist, Kingston thought the more feminine aspects of Fa Mu Lan would distract from her portrayal as a powerful woman. But she reconsidered these details and inteprets their meaning in social-political terms that reconstitute the individual and community after war and violence:

> Even more important, they wanted to say this woman went away to war and came back and was not brutalized. She came back and she could be whole. She could still be a woman, a family person and community person. The reason she went to war was to take her father's place, and when she came back she took another kind of service: she was changed, and she will change the community by her presence in it. She will raise children and teach them new ways. She was not dehumanized or broken by the war. And so it's important to figure out how we can do that. How do you come back from a war and then turn back into a beautiful woman? And give that beauty to your family and community? (Moyers 1990, 16)

Identity is a relational and ethical process, open to continuous critical reflection and interpretation as the new meanings of events become evident. Kingston indicates her constant, permeable negotiations with her own self talking-story as well as in her direct address to Chinese Americans in her work. The growing consciousness of her protean possibilities as a woman—not as subordinate, male warrior, traitor—but as a Chinese American woman who struggles in multiple locations for the transformation of self in community, is manifested through the self talking-story.

Reinventing the Self Writing Talk-Story in the United States

Kingston's quest for narratives by which to represent the formation of a hybrid self could not end in the absolute and unquestioning embrace or recuperation of a cultural legacy or past history, or by a restricted range of traditional Chinese classics—as Frank Chin and other cultural nationalists would have us believe.[17] Kingston cannot apply the past Chinese canon in her life in America wholesale. Many of these canonical works were written from the perspectives of elite men in China who defined women's roles, powers, and visibility within a patriarchal society. It would be naive to think that there was and is no oppression of women among the Chinese, that Chinese history and myths and men have always been non-sexist in their characterization and treatment of women. It would be wrong to assume that a male warrior "real" is necessarily the same "real" for Kingston or for other Asian women.

Corrosive racist, classist, and sexist discourses and institutions eat into the heart of a genuine community; they do not harness the energy in an open-ended coalition politics that is respectful of the differences of its potential allies. Rather, the "wagon train" strategy of containment and resistance stifles writers like Kingston who wish to re-envision themselves, their families, their relationships, and their communities in ways that do not simply duplicate debilitating mainstream practices. Such a politically radical and multiple challenge certainly does not put Kingston in the traitorous camp that cultural nationalists and other critics have so comfortably assigned her.

Moreover, Kingston does not simply turn to a "Western" autobiographical format to construct her story (chap. 4). The more traditional Western mainstream auto-biographies are often chronological, factual, and unitary stories based on a notion of a distinctly individuated and coherent self. Kingston believes that standard autobiography concentrates on the exterior aspects, "like when you were born and what you participate in—big historical events that you publicly participate in" (Kingston 1991, 786). Kingston's interests are instead in inventing a "new autobiographical form that truly tells the inner life of women and I do think it's especially important for minority people, because we're always on the brink of disappearing" (ibid., 786).

In the artistic construction of her subversive autobiographical fictions, Kingston mixes straightforward reporting with the coded talk-story language from Chinese women's social world, such as secrets, dreams, myths and legends, folk wisdom, incantations, singing, gossip, jokes, crazy talk, parables, and poetry.[18] Kingston believes "there are implosions and crazinesses that take place when you keep important energies and forces locked up inside of yourself. . . . I think that dreams are very important to women—and important to everybody's psyche—and to have access to those dreams is a great power. Also visions that we have about what we might do, also prayers—that's another 'silent, secret' kind of thing. I think part of what we have to do is figure out a new kind of autobiography that can tell the truth about dreams and visions and prayers. I find that absolutely necessary for our mental and political health" (Kingston 1991, 786). Kingston also indicates the need to understand the profound mysteries of the exotic, the strange or foreign aspects, which the self must confront in constituting, articulating, and enacting itself in more hopefully emancipatory ways. Kingston's narrator portrays these difficult engagements in the formation of subjectivity and identity. "It's a schizophrenic way of thinking to put the burden of the exotic onto others and not face the exotic and mysterious that's in oneself. Many Asian American artists work in sort of an extreme realism because they don't want to appear exotic. But then what happens is that we deny what's truly exotic and mysterious in ourselves" (Moyers 1990, 15).

Chin rejects autobiography as apolitical and ahistorical psychologizing, favoring the preservation of a selective past history and a fixed interpretation of Chinese textual and oral classics as authenticating reference points for Chinese Americans (chap. 4). Kingston, on the other hand, shifts our attention more toward talk-stories that are constantly reclaiming, deconstructing, and reconstructing Chinese American selves as they are negotiated and transformed by the female narrator's critical memories of her experiences. Stuart Hall reminds us that the self or subject consists of "contradictory identities, pulling in different directions, so that our identifications are continuously being shifted about. If we feel we have a unified identity from birth to death, it is only because we construct a comforting story or "narrative of self" about ourselves. . . . The fully unified, completely secure and coherent identity is a fantasy" (Hall 1996, 598). Maxine's multiple, imaginative stories are a form of mental and political survival and resistance as well as a form of cultural power against that which attempts to erase, marginalize, and appropriate the voices of Asian American women like herself.[19]

Kingston's realistic fiction registers the surface details of daily life; yet, on another level, the traditional unitary conventions of realism are frequently disrupted by shifts into imaginative, magical, and crazy-visionary moments. These are often re-appropriated from her mother's talk-story tradition, which may be truer to her new sense of reality and self within and beyond the oppressive masculinist and Orientalist discourses that attempt to claim the terrain of language or the symbolic. Such legacies haunt her struggles to reconstruct identity and community. Her attempt to recover a self talking-story so sedimented in multiple referential frames is a subversive re-invention of self and history that is not homogenous, not easily placed within such coercive discourses and practices. This style disrupts the storyline of rigid, structured classifications or of traditional power. It disarranges and defamiliarizes and demands new perspectives on questions of power.[20] The emphasis is on process and revision so that absolute truth is only provisional and writing is not transparent and unmediated, but something to be decoded and reconstructed through the reader's or listener's active and collaborative efforts. In other words, the text is not a final recording of actual life or fixed interpretation, but is instead the self talking-story—an enactment of the dynamic processes of constructing and deconstructing the political cartographies of cultural memory and history.

> I believe that the strong imagination imagines the truth, sees a vision of the truth. A good strong imagination doesn't go off into some wild fantasy of nowhere. It goes to the truth. It also tells a lot about the "talk story" tradition. Thousands of years of people passed on history and genealogy by speaking them. When they took these stories across the ocean and gave them to me, I didn't invent what had gone before. I had to invent the next state. I went on. . . .
>
> I continued it. Every human being who speaks the story does it in a new way. We can try to tell the same old story and it will come out different. And so what? It means that human beings carry on the next stage, the next evolution of the story. So what I've told are the new American stories. (Moyers 1990, 13)

Thus, in disrupting genre boundaries, Kingston establishes her rights to the telling of her personal story within her own overlapping frames of references. She ruptures those rigidly rational and authoritarian classifications that attempt to define her and how the world must be conceptualized and experienced. Kingston creates resisting spaces in which to articulate complex multi-layered identities and histories that cannot be fully processed or evoked in traditional autobiographical genres. It is through such innovative strategies and perspectives in multicultural autobiography, Michael Fischer believes, that "ethnic autobiography and autobiographical fiction can perhaps serve as key forms for explorations of pluralist, post-industrial, late twentieth-century society" (Fischer 1986, 195).[21] He states the case that Kingston's autobiographical fictions are inadequately understood through "discussions on group solidarity, traditional values, family mobility, political mobilization or similar sociological categories." Fischer sees Kingston's work as exploring the "paradoxical sense that ethnicity is something reinvented and reinterpreted in each generation by each individual and that is often something quite puzzling to the individual, something over which he or she lacks control" (ibid.). Furthermore, "to be Chinese-American is not the same thing as being Chinese in America. In this sense there is no role model for becoming Chinese-American. It is a matter of finding a voice or style that does not violate one's several components of identity" (Fischer 1986, 196). It is not centrally about looking back to an immutable past for an originary of authenticated self, but projecting, envisioning, and enacting potential, and perhaps more emancipatory, selves in the present and future.

In another vein, David Leiwei Li points out that Kingston transforms traditional Chinese oral talk-story into an inventive form of self-writing that explores the dynamic and radical potential of voicing selves from within an American landscape that is continually in creative, chaotic flux.

> Change results both from transmission and as a direct and positive response to demands of cultures—the collision and negotiation of mainstream American cultural motifs with the Chinese American subcultural motifs which occasion Kingston's works. Moreover, change epitomizes American culture more than

any other in the world, because an economic built-in obsolescence that disposes of anything old has left an indelible mark on the literary production of the country: the constant call to make it new paves the way for a rejuvenation of the American canon that successive generations of literary revolutionaries embrace. (Li 1990, 496)

Far from being informed by anti-Chinese representations, Kingston's imagination is deeply rooted in, and informed by, a Chinese oral tradition that weaves together multiple histories in a living, changing culture.

Within this talk-story tradition, there is no fixed, unitary, or right story to be told through all space and time. Each story has its own validity in the continuum of cultural survival, power, and moral accountability. The point of talk-story is to retell the stories—not to simply reproduce them, and this is one way women create culture. It is the Chinese tradition of talk-story, therefore, that provides the social, emotional, and political space from which Chinese American women continue to tell their stories.

A Woman's Voice in the Wilderness

The final story in *The Woman Warrior* counters a male-identified warrior stance as well as notions of recovering an authentic, purist, and originary identity. Rather than perpetuating imperialist exotica or nostalgia of Chinese people and culture, there is, I believe, discovery and reclamation of psychic territory and of connections for the daughter-writer between China and America; between the individual and her mixed communities, between mother and daughter. Kingston's text challenges the psychosocial and symbolic codes that define the position of women in society. She courageously explores the dilemmas and traumas women must manage in order to maintain not only their families and communities, but also a complex subjectivity and cultural text that can signify their desires, visions, and potential as well as their social actualities as women.

Kingston attempts to reclaim the often delegitimated standpoints of women. Her corrective is a woman's vision of integrity in the fluid process of the self talking-story; of open-ended, multiple roads to meaning, of transformative art and life. Her response to masculinist critics is the singing voice of the Chinese woman poet Ts'ai Yen. Like Fa Mu Lan and Brave Orchid, Ts'ai Yen fights fiercely against the enemy only when she has to—during close combat and in defense of herself and family. Yet unlike Fa Mu Lan, she no longer disguises herself as a male warrior. She bears two children by the barbarian chieftain of the Southern Hsiung-nu, who kidnapped and ravaged her in twelve years of desert exile. Ts'ai Yen's children do not speak Chinese, but they speak their father's barbarian language. "They imitated her with senseless singsong words and laughed" (TWW 242). In the barbarian lands, the hostile and binary parsing of differences in identity, culture, community, politics, and history confuse and divide Ts'ai Yen and her half-Chinese and half-barbarian children.[22] The telling of this final story also evokes the struggles of Kingston's narrator, nomadic and exiled, who is in search of new homes and communities (real and imaginary)—that will not duplicate savage and cruel practices that repress and disempower women or their hybrid families and communities.

At first, the music of the Southern Hsiung-nu barbarians appeared to be the whistling arrows—primitive and hostile war and death sounds. Ts'ai Yen thought this was her captors' only music. One night, she hears another music coming from those very war-flutes which "tremble and rise like the desert wind" (*TWW* 242). It was cold, achingly sharp music "yearning toward a high note"—like "an icicle in the desert" (*TWW* 243). Ts'ai Yen is haunted by this music. In her tent, as the story describes, Ts'ai Yen begins to re-envision this alien, barbarian culture and language, which is also part of her history and her children's. "Then, out of Ts'ai Yen's tent, which was apart from the others, the barbarians heard a woman's voice singing, as if to her babies, a song so high and clear, it matched the flutes. Ts'ai Yen sang about China and her family there. Her world seemed to be Chinese, but the barbarians understood their sadness and anger. Sometimes they thought they could catch barbarian phrases about forever wandering. Her children did not laugh, but eventually sang along when she left her tent to sit by the winter campfires, ringed by the barbarians" (*TWW* 243). It is out of more transformative ways of encountering difference—distinct and contrasting perspectives—that new ways of seeing, communicating, and living are born. In part, paradox is the key that opens the way to a more inclusive understanding of a continually transforming world where things are sometimes one, sometimes many. It confuses the logic of reason, of exclusive binary oppositions as a matter of principle; it encourages flexibility and a willingness to participate in the process of creating and discovering unexpected, surprising meaning.

Like Ts'ai Yen, Kingston's narrator sings of her and her mother's sadness and anger as Chinese women in diverse barbarian lands. As a woman, she sings the yearnings of dislocated communities, isolated and distressed in societies that silence or dehumanize them.[23] She preserves the remnants of a dislocated Chinese heritage as she participates in the making of a vibrant hybrid culture and society here in the United States. Her songs, set to barbarian music, enact meaning through the power of art—the warrior transformed into filial-rebel artist and visionary living in multiple positions and communities.

In *The Woman Warrior*, the daughter-writer has begun to achieve a confidence and power in her own distinctive Chinese American voice—a voice and agency that are not always alienating and destructive, a voice that does not want to channel its anger at injustice through the seductive brutalities of bloody war or violent death. Ts'ai Yen as well as Fa Mu Lan returned home from war and pain to nurture and transform their families and communities. Kingston's narrator also yearns to return home from her wanderings to a family and community that will accept her multiple social identities and contexts. In *Tripmaster Monkey*, Kingston (1989a) defined further the life of a good and heroic individual: "Maybe a good man [or woman] is . . . one who comes into a chaotic scene, a chaotic home, or a chaotic country, and finds a way to bring order, community, peace, harmony. He [or she] is able to establish peace among people in a family. To set up harmonious relationships between people, between countries, within societies. At the core is a spirit of creation" (Moyers 1990, 16). Kingston questions the privileged masculinist war metanarratives and practices that infect her own work, and more importantly, cultures and nations. She reflects on what one might do after we have scorched the earth with the policies of hate, war, and chaos? In returning to relationships, to families, societies, or countries, how does one begin to re-root and cultivate more peaceful, fulfilling, and empowering social-economic and political formations?

Kingston's narrator leaves us with an imaginative story by which to project and enact her own future from the diverse legacies of her past and present. As the story goes, Ts'ai Yen's songs from the savage lands translated well in Chinese and in barbarian terms; she had developed the rich polyvocality to travel in different landscapes, tracing the hauntingly resonant story of loss, anger, and wandering that her children, as well as the barbarians, and Chinese could relate to. Maxine, like her mother before her, searches for an active agency as a Chinese American woman in the making of identity, community, culture, and history. In attempting to free her own voice, she also hopes to free her mother's voice and the oppressed women who continually remind her of the moral and social accountability of her stories.

In contrast to the outcast No Name Woman, Ts'ai Yen is eventually ransomed, returned to the Han homeland and married to Tung Ssu. She is memorialized by name for her own unique and heroic life and songs brought back from the barbarian lands, an acceptance and return the filial-rebel daughter-narrator yearns for from her family and multiple communities. Like Ts'ai Yen, No Name Woman, Brave Orchid and the daughter-writer "[piece] together new directions" from the fragments and silences of women's culture and history and follow them "instead of the old footprints" (*TWW* 89) towards new homeplaces.

Notes

1. For example, see Jaschok and Miers (1994), Ko (1997), Mann (1997), Ono (1989), and Siu (1981), for more information on Chinese women's diverse activities and locations within patriarchal societal formations in different periods of history.

2. This reminds me of bell hooks' memories of growing up. She wanted to talk up and be heard but was put down by her mother and told to speak in a feminine way and not sass. However, she persisted in rebelling against these caveats by talking back and writing (hooks 1989).

3. According to Francis Hsu, traditional "talk-story" refers to the original Chinese tradition that a story is first delivered to a community and then becomes "*Hua Ben*" or "story roots" for later written versions (qtd. in Li 1990, 495). See also chapter 1, n1.

4. Rich provides a useful working definition of patriarchy as "the power of the fathers: a familial-social, ideological, political system in which men—by force, direct pressure, or through ritual, tradition, law, and language, customs, etiquette, education, and the division of labor, determine what part women shall or shall not play, and in which

the female is everywhere subsumed under the male. It does not necessarily imply that no woman has power, or that all women in a given culture may not have certain powers" (Rich 1986b, 57).

5. Wong (1988) has written a very interesting article on the dilemma between necessity and extravagance in *The Woman Warrior* as it reveals itself in the lives of the female characters. She also explains how these terms characterize the burdens on the ethnic writer who must negotiate between the practical survival and the demands of community and his/her own creative needs as a writer.

6. See McClain (1994) and Sayler (1995) on the history of discriminatory U.S. immigration laws against the Chinese, and Yung (1995) and S. Chan (1991b) on the impact of exclusion on Chinese women.

7. Consider the social practice of footbinding, especially among wealthy families in China. A frail, obedient and passive wife with small lotus feet was considered sexually desirable by many men; she was also a sign of his high social status. The practice of footbinding allowed men to confine women at home; many were so crippled that they could not walk beyond their courtyards without assistance. Footbinding confined women in both psychological and physical terms.

8. In a recent essay "Race, Ethnic Culture, and Gender in the Construction of Identities among Second-Generation Chinese Americans, 1880s–1930s," Sucheng Chan describes the different sites of contestation for men and women in history: "Overall, although race and ethnic culture shaped the identities of both the male and female Chinese Americans who came of age during the six decades of Chinese exclusion, race was a more salient feature in the young men's experiences, whereas ethnic culture (and the constraints that it imposed) played a more dominant role in the young women's lives. In short, gender refracted race as well as ethnicity. One result was that male and female narrators often ascribed different meanings to experiences that, on the surface, seemed similar" (Chan 1998, 141).

9. Because many Chinese women were barred from institutions of higher learning and were confined to the home in a feudal Confucian society, they invented their own written language called *nushu*, which was passed down among women through the centuries and was known only to them. According to Vivian Chiu (1992), *nushu* flourished in the multi-tribal southern part of Hunan province for more than 1,000 years. It was a language by which Chinese women shared their joys, hardships, loneliness, and anger in the inequities they suffered. Women gifted other women with *sanzhoushu*—collections of *nushu* poems and essays that recorded a woman's life. They were so valued that these books would be copied from household to household and even buried with the women when they died. Women would transmit messages, letters, and poems through go-betweens in this script (ibid., 50). These secret Chinese *nushu* writings certainly suggest an unbroken, subversive discursive tradition by which women attempted to counter oppressive patriarchal definitions and institutions. In this way, Chinese women asserted the centrality of their experience and the rights to its articulation in language.

10. Besides the Confucian discourse that socialized young girls and women into their ideal roles in Chinese society, there was also an inherited Chinese oral tradition. Croll discusses the oral tradition among daughters in gentry and peasant households. Young daughters were also brought up on heroic stories of warrior women "who roamed in wide open spaces combining male and female roles" (Croll 1995, 14). These stories and the art of storytelling were highly valued by women audiences, who loved to hear the simple stories, which were told in rhythmic and popular language; they identified themselves with the heroines against the growing gender-specific social realities of their lives (ibid., 11–68).

   These popular stories were passed on in domestic settings as well as public spaces (village or town) "from grandmother or mother or daughter and old tales were spun and embellished by amahs [nurse/nanny], servants and itinerant storytellers" (ibid., 14). One older Chinese woman interviewed by Croll recounts her understanding of what these stories meant in the life of her mother, who was the daughter of a general and led an unhappy life: "As a young girl her mother herself had dreamed of freedom and happiness, all dreams which had been frustrated as, physically timid and without education, she had suffered as a junior member of a large stifling household. The girl thought that since her mother was a victim of this and other facets of the system, 'the story of Mulan was actually a projection of the dreams she had originally for herself and later gave to me' " (ibid., 15).

11. Ling correctly identifies Kingston's reclamation of the white stereotyped image of the sinister dragon lady: In contrast to this stereotype, Kingston depicts the "strength of will and courage" of two dragon women—Brave Orchid and Maxine. However I would disagree with Ling's assertion that "Brave Orchid and Maxine do not endanger the lives of others but are fierce in defending their own against encroachments and repressions" (Ling 1990, 129).

12. See Rowbotham: "In order to create an alternative an oppressed group must at once shatter the self-reflecting world which encircles it and, at the same time, project its own image onto history. In order to discover its own identity as distinct from that of the oppressor it has to become visible to itself. . . . People who are without names, who do not know themselves, who have no culture, experience a kind of paralysis of consciousness. [Consciousness] becomes coherent and self-critical when its version of the world becomes clear not simply within itself but when it knows itself in relation to what it has created apart from itself. When we can look back at ourselves through our own cultural creations, our actions, our ideas, our pamphlets, our organization, our history, our theory, we begin to integrate a new reality" (Rowbotham 1973, 27–28).

13. For example, see Lorde "Poetry is Not a Luxury" (1984, 33–39).

14. See Anzaldúa (1990a) for a discussion on the development of new consciousness—*la conciencia de la mestiza*.

15. See Sato (1991) for an interesting link between Maxine's abbreviated name "Ink" and its relationship to inkwell and the community well that No Name Woman drowns

herself in. Sato explores the notion of transformation from violence/death to creation/ art in *The Woman Warrior.* The daughter-writer's pen-water-ink become life giving to Kingston and the silenced women of her past.

16. See Sandoval's theorizing on "a differential mode of oppositional consciousness:" "The differential mode of oppositional consciousness depends upon the ability to read the current situation of power and of self-consciously choosing and adopting the ideological form best suited to push against its configurations, a survival skill well known to oppressed peoples" (Sandoval 1991, 15).

17. Consider Cheung's argument (1990) about the limitations to Chin's search for masculine models in Chinese classical texts about war and revenge, as well as her critique of a Western machismo that seems like a stereotype. She urges a search for more enlightening models for men and women.

18. For example, Celeste Schenck notes how "often modern and contemporary women's poetry and autobiography—as texts recording the negotiation of the female self-in-process between the historical fact of displacement and the possibility of textual self-presence—may be fruitfully conceived of as cut from the same bolt" (Schenck 1988, 287).

19. Kim mentions some critics' inability to read Kingston's text on a metaphoric level because of their "flat-footed facticity" (Kim 1990, 79).

20. See Dasenbrock (1987) on use of "ghosts" as a form of defamiliarization in *The Woman Warrior.*

21. For discussions of feminist and multicultural autobiography, see Ashley, Gilmore and Peters (1994), Benstock (1988), Boelhower (1982), Brodzki and Schenck (1988), Culley (1992), Davidson and Bonner (1980), Demetrakopoulos (1980), du Plessis (1985), Friedman (1988), Jelinek (1980), Payne (1992), and Rose (1982).

   For African American autobiography: Andrews (1986), Fox-Genovese (1988), Hirsch (1990a), Lionnet (1990), McKay (1988), Rampersad (1983), and Reagon (1982). For Chicano/a autobiography: Saldívar (1990). For Native American Indian: Carr (1988), Cheyfitz (1991), and H. Wong (1994).

   For Kingston and autobiography: Barker-Nunn (1987), Homsher (1979), Holte (1982), V. Hsu (1983), Lim (1991, 1992, and 1996), Manganyi (1983), Miller (1983), Myers (1986), Rose (1987), Smith (1987), Ho (1991), and Wong (1992). For Japanese American autobiography, see Lim (1990), Rayson (1987), and Yamamoto (1998).

22. In an interview, Kingston mentions that her own son, a musician, does not speak, read or write Chinese. As a mother, she is concerned about passing on culture to her son, a culture which teaches him to be a good man (Moyers 1990, 16).

23. Kingston has stated that she writes about "the most chaotic, tragic, hard-to-deal-with events, and these events are sometimes so violent and so horrible that they burst through bounds of form and preconceptions. I'm hoping that readers will find how to get the meaning out of those events. How do you find beauty and order when we've had this bloody horrible past?" (Moyers 1990, 11).

6

LOSING YOUR INNOCENCE BUT NOT YOUR HOPE: AMY TAN'S JOY LUCK MOTHERS AND COCA-COLA DAUGHTERS

> . . . now that I am old, moving every year closer to the end
> of my life, I also feel closer to the beginning. And I
> remember everything that happened that day because it
> has happened many times in life. The same innocence,
> trust, and restlessness, the wonder, fear, and loneliness.
> How I lost myself.
> I remember all these things. And tonight, on the
> fifteenth day of the eighth moon, I also remember what I
> asked the Moon Lady so long ago. I wished to be found.
>
> Ying-ying St. Clair
> Amy Tan, The Joy Luck Club

Joy Luck Mothers and Daughters: Excavatory Heart Work

Amy Tan, like Maxine Hong Kingston, is a daughter-writer who tells the stories of women and who sees these stories as ways to confront personal and communal oppression. As in Kingston's work, one is acutely aware that this is painful, complicated excavatory work and that it is also subversive, creative, freeing, and responsible.

The Joy Luck Club focuses on four central pairs of mothers and daughters: Suyuan Woo and Jing-mei "June" Woo; An-mei Hsu and Rose Hsu Jordan; Lindo Jong and Waverly Jong; and Ying-ying St. Clair and Lena St. Clair. The stories of these pairs are interwoven in four major segments with mothers and daughters telling their stories of how it is they came to be where they are in life. Each of the four major segments opens with a vignette, which is then followed by four chapters. In the first and last segments mothers tell their individual stories ("Feathers From A Thousand Li" and "Queen Mother of the Western Skies") and these mother segments figuratively embrace the two middle segments ("The Twenty-Six Malignant Gates" and "American Translation") in which their daughters speak as second-generation Chinese women in the United States.

Tan depicts a variety of mother-daughter bonds rather than focusing like Kingston on a single primary mother-daughter relationship. As Tan says, "And when you talk to 100 different people to get their stories on a situation, that's what the truth is. So it's really a multiple story" (Tan 1990b, 256). In analyzing the representations of mother-daughter relationships in her stories, it becomes clear that the interactions between mothers and daughters are complicated by broader circumstances within and between China and the United States. The relationships are not to be understood as personal stories or psychological dramas simply to be worked out within and between Chinese immigrant mothers and second-generation Chinese American daughters. Rather, these mothers and daughters are precariously and ambiguously positioned in different geopolitical locations, languages, generations, and histories that seriously affect their ability to interact with each other and with their diverse communities. Out of the ruptures and contradictions resulting from these substantial differences (even within similarities), Tan constructs fictional narratives of self that are deconstructed and reconstructed as each mother and daughter attempts to find spaces to negotiate stronger friendships and alliances as women.

The links between these mothers and daughters in the United States are further complicated by the bonds between the Joy Luck mothers and their mothers (and foremothers) in China. Tan provides access to these past stories by allowing the Joy Luck mothers space in which to tell their own stories. Tan's interest is not in resurrecting imperialist nostalgia or exotica, rather, she amplifies each woman's story and enriches the stories of these mother-daughter pairs by finding their social and emotional resonances in past and present legacies—in the mother-daughter bonds intimately situated in Chinese and Chinese American culture and society. Her multiple pairings suggest the affiliative links between the mother-daughter pairs as well as among a broader community of women. Despite the specificities in the individual stories of the Joy Luck women, Tan's multiple narratives weave this extended community together in terms of an earned and shared history, as does Kingston. The stories of these women provide reinscriptions of the daily making of culture, community, and subjectivity which counter those defined for them in masculinist and imperialist terms.

The Joy Luck Mothers and Their Mothers in China

Mother-daughter bonds in China were represented as embedded in the particular social, economic, and historical realities and fluctuations of a patriarchal Confucian social system.[1] According to Confucian classics, educational handbooks, and women's biographies, women's lives were ideally supposed to revolve around the Three Obediences and Four Virtues: "The Three Obediences enjoined a woman to obey her father before marriage, her husband after marriage and her eldest son after her husband's death. The Four Virtues decreed that she be chaste; her conversation courteous and not gossipy; her deportment graceful but not extravagant; her leisure spent in perfecting needlework and tapestry for beautifying the home" (Ling 1990, 3). Women were perceived as not suited by nature for the intellectual life of a scholar or a statesman. They were denied access to the educational system and examinations which led to the opportunities for political office and public leadership in traditional Chinese society and confined to the private-domestic sphere where their virtue, honor, and chastity could be controlled and preserved. These societal prescriptions permitted the psychic and social abuse of women, an abuse in which women sometimes took part. The Chinese daughters experience their mothers' as well as their own difficult compromises and failures in this culture and society. Some of the Joy Luck mothers develop a critical consciousness or agency derived from their social circumstances and experiences. In Tan's book one becomes sadly aware that the affiliations between Chinese mothers and daughters can often be violently ruptured in that women can become alienated, isolated, and competitive; that they can compromise or betray themselves and other women in trying to survive or gain status in a male-privileged system.

Amy Tan portrays the traumatic social and emotional effects of this socialization on mother-daughter relations in her portrait of An-mei Hsu and her mother. An-mei's beloved mother, like Kingston's No Name Woman, is cast out by her own family for breaking rules and parting with social decorum. The underlying reason for this severe ostracism is the familial and societal perception that she has failed to remain an honorable (faithful), life-long widow, in prostituting herself to a rich man named Wu Tsing. In actuality, she is entrapped and raped by him. She is then asked by Wu Tsing to become his concubine or fourth wife—a relational title and rank in a hierarchy of women. This is a demeaning status for a woman who was the first wife of a scholar. In addition, An-mei's mother does not commit suicide, which was considered an ideal option for a widow in her predicament. Dishonored and discredited, pressured by a sense of her lack of recourse as a woman and her silent shame, she capitulates to his demands.

Sadly, women are complicit in destroying An-Mei's mother through the power arrangements of family and society. Kinswomen refuse to speak of An-mei's mother except in disparaging terms. What is most painful for An-mei is the way in which her own maternal grandmother and aunt fill her head with horrible visions of her mother. Mother is described as a "ghost" among the living and a "stupid goose" (JLC 42).[2] She is a dead woman, "decayed flesh, evil, rotted to the bone" (JLC 216); she is a *ni*, traitor to her husband and ancestors. Her name can never be spoken in the family circle. Like No Name Woman, she is either defined as a forbidden woman, or she is not named or defined at all. She is physically ejected from her home by her family and left without independent means. Even with the father dead, the household of women have internalized patriarchal discourse and learned to "police" themselves. The panoptic gaze of the patriarch-father in the portrait that hangs in the main hall still commands respect from his daughter, who feels his eyes permanently surveying and policing her every word and action:

> The only father I knew was a big painting that hung in the main hall. He was a large, unsmiling man, unhappy to be so still on the wall. His restless eyes followed me around the house. Even from my room at the end of the hall, I could see my father's watching eyes. Popo said he watched me for any sign of disrespect. (JLC 43)

An-mei learns to walk past his portrait with a "know-nothing look" and to hide her private, rebellious face in the corner of her own room (JLC 43).[3]

Wu Tsing's scheming Second Wife also betrays and destroys other women with her tongue. As Kingston says in *The Woman Warrior*, patriarchal society and language appear to "break women with their own tongues!" (*TWW* 56). It is the childless Second Wife, for example, who arranges to entrap An-Mei's mother and who spreads the vicious gossip that she is a "shameless hussy" (JLC 237). As a rich woman, Second Wife uses the borrowed class, wealth, and power of her husband to oppress and manipulate other women. In oppressing other wives, she attempts to guarantee her own tenuous position and status in Wu Tsing's competitive female hierarchy. Since she cannot provide the all important male child for her husband's posterity in a patrilineal society, the Second Wife seeks a slave-concubine who will be able to provide a surrogate son for her. Like Kingston, Tan paints a painfully problematic picture of women's complicity, not only in another woman's oppression, but in their own continuing oppression in, and maintenance of, a patriarchal culture.

It is not hard to understand how An-mei Hsu is confused and traumatized by the stories that tell not only about a bad mother but also about the greedy and naughty girls who come to very bad ends. With her mother's departure, An-mei is portrayed as hungering for, fearing, and resenting her mother. She grows up with stories that continually attempt to disrupt her ability to imaginatively maintain a bond with her outcast-mother. "Now I could imagine my mother, a thoughtless woman who laughed and shook her head, who dipped her chopsticks many times to eat another piece of sweet fruit, happy to be free of Popo, her unhappy husband on the wall, and her two disobedient children. I felt unlucky that she was my mother and unlucky that she had left us. These were the thoughts I had while hiding in the corner of my room where my father could not watch me" (JLC 44). Stories are told by women to break the spirit of strong-willed girls, the disobedient types—like her hidden self. The patriarchal stories are powerful forms of socialization, training her for her proper and public roles in traditional Chinese society as a good daughter, wife, mother, woman.[4] Nevertheless, An-mei finds ways to remain a good subversive daughter to an ostracized mother to whom she still feels deeply bonded. (Likewise, Maxine Hong Kingston identifies in many ways with No Name Woman and some of the "crazy," alienated women that she encountered.) How to re-embody the desire for the feeling and memory of the beloved mother of childhood before and beyond patriarchal language and culture that purport to define her as a bad woman? These are some of the quandaries that Tan's mothers and daughters confront in trying to find their ways back to each other as allies.

Another example of a crippling socialization of girls is found in the story of the Joy Luck mother Ying-ying St. Clair, who charts the alienation and loss of self. At four, Ying-ying is a girl of mischief and motion, darting away from authority figures, ever curious about the world around her. She loves the intoxicating unpredictability of being—"the unsteady feeling of almost falling one way then another" (JLC 74). Ying-ying privately desires a life of continued freedom and adventure. But as a girl, she is brought up to believe that she "can never ask [for what she desires], only listen" (JLC 70). Her mother and amah socialize her into predictability, into the traditional sexual and gendered identities for a well-behaved Chinese woman of her class and times. A mischievous Ying-ying, along with her half-sisters, is warned not to frighten away a red dragonfly. Ying-ying's mother corrects her unacceptable behavior: "A boy can run and chase dragonflies, because that is his nature," she said. "But a girl should stand still. If you are still for a very long time, a dragonfly will no longer see you. Then it will come to you and hide in the comfort of your shadow" (JLC 72). Ying-ying, like her mother and amah, is socialized into a self-negating passivity and masochistic love.

In Tan's telling, Ying-ying is further traumatized by the sad legend of Chang-o, the Moon Lady, who is described as a "selfish" woman who steals and eats her husband's peach of everlasting life. In the traditional shadow play celebrating the lunar festival, she is condemned "to stay lost on the moon, forever seeking her own selfish wishes" (JLC 81). Because she chooses her desires above those of her husband, Hou Yi, she is outcast forever from family and community. This frightening outcome resonates for young Ying-ying and for Chinese women who are brought up within, and dependent upon, strong affiliative familial and communal networks. The lesson of the shadow play ends with a classic dualism between men and women that rationalizes and valorizes the qualities of men over women: "For woman is yin the darkness within, where untempered passions lie. And man is yang, bright truth lighting our minds" (JLC 81). This statement supports the notion that women are emotionally unruly and indulgent and cannot be trusted to make good, rational, or ethical judgments for themselves, families, or society. Ying-ying is bitterly disappointed to discover that the beloved Moon Lady, to whom she hopes to confess her secret desires, is an impostor, a hideous caricature of desire and love. The Moon Lady is exposed as a man with "shrunken cheeks, a broad oily nose, large glaring teeth, and red-stained eyes" (JLC 82). This moment of traumatic disenchantment is a foreshadowing of the harsh and disappointing realities that scar Ying-ying's life as an upper-class woman situated in a patriarchal society. This childhood socialization into the nature of ideal womanhood wears down Ying-ying's adventurous, fiercely independent, and trusting spirit: "And I remember everything that happened that day because it has happened many times in my life. The same innocence, trust, and restlessness, the wonder, fear, and loneliness. How I lost myself" (JLC 83). This growing-up story tracks the conflicted process of socialization into the traumatic loss of an earlier, more empowered agency and subjectivity. The constitution of an other(ed) self is based on an objectified subject positioning within dominant and normative patriarchal feminine formations.

Historical events and natural disasters in China also played a role in shaping women's bonds to each other. Joy Luck mothers and their mothers before them, in one way or another, experience a range of terrible wars, deaths, economic turmoil, revolutionary changes, and famines that seriously impinge on their personal relationships and communications with each other. In the mid 1800s to the mid 1900s, horrendous wars for colonial dominance over China were waged by imperialist powers such as Russia, Germany, France, England, Japan, and the United States. Bloody civil strife resulted from fighting among various factions such as warlords, peasants, the Chinese Communist Party (led by Mao Zedong), and the Guomindang (led by Chiang Kai-shek). Chinese women and their families suffered and, in some cases, survived and surmounted the consequences of these chaotic events. In reading Tan, one does not get a sense that the Joy Luck mothers are so victimized or disabled by the events or disasters in China that they cannot construct a critical sense of personal and social agency in their lives.

Life and necessity, for example, tend to make the Joy Luck mothers clever under oppressive circumstances, tough on themselves in making life-and-death decisions, patient in resistance, duplicitous in word and action, exacting and controlling in their demands for loyalty, obedience, and love. For instance, Suyuan Woo's life, and her fears and ambitions for her daughter June, are clearly influenced by the chaos and brutalities of war, separation from family, death of a husband, and loss of her baby daughters in China. Young Lindo Jong remembers the painful, lonely separation from her beloved mother. Betrothed as a child, she is sent to her spoiled boy-husband's household after disastrous floods, famine, and poverty make it difficult for her family to keep a "useless" daughter. On her wedding day, Lindo promises herself to never forget her own worth. She bides her time as an obedient wife in her husband's household until she can find a clever way to free herself from her unhappy marriage. She convinces her mother-in-law that the marriage is jinxed and that horrible things would happen to Tyan-yu if she remained married to him. Lindo's mother-in-law gives her a rail ticket to Peking and enough money to go to America. Ying-ying St. Clair's concerns for her daughter's safety and her own fears at being sexually harassed on an Oakland street by a stranger could be rooted in her own bitter experiences as a lone married woman migrating from the poor countryside to Shanghai, a city notorious for its foreign decadence and the murder, rape, kidnapping, and prostitution of Chinese women in the early decades of the twentieth century.[5]

But despite the knowledge of their marginality and alienation in China, despite some ugly, angry emotions and memories, despite the trauma of war, the Joy Luck mothers are represented as maintaining a strong attachment to their motherland. The China of their childhood lives in most of these Joy Luck mothers with a vibrant primacy that is a form of profound, constant, and transformative love. A consideration of the social realities of this first world provides valuable access to the Joy Luck mothers' first loves and traumas as well as a world in revolutionary change. These everyday actualities have deeply shaped their broader understanding in the making of memory, subjectivity, family, culture, and society. Insofar as the Joy Luck mothers can maintain their capacity for affiliation, the power of desire that still attracts them toward the world and makes them want to survive within it, their thoughts are always returning to the Chinese motherland—the early site of memory and experience—for the forms of the world by which they construct and enact themselves. For better and worse, their hard-earned mother-daughter legacies in China are what they desire to pass on to their daughters in the United States.

Queen Mothers and Coca-Cola Daughters in the United States

The Joy Luck mothers fiercely nurture and socialize their young daughters into womanhood through the 1950s and into the 1980s.[6] What becomes clear is that all the mothers—whether they directly or indirectly tell their daughters their good intentions—want to protect them from the oppressive circumstances that they and their foremothers endured in China in their personal and social lives. They want their Chinese American daughters to have the best life—not to duplicate the sad, tragic, or restricted lives they and their mothers have known. "In America I will have a daughter just like me. But over there nobody will say her worth is measured by the loudness of her husband's belch. Over there nobody will look down on her, because I will make her speak only perfect American English. And over there she will always be too full to swallow any sorrow! She will know my meaning, because I will give her this swan—a creature that became more than what was hoped for" (*JLC* 17). Tan's mothers want to teach their daughters how to read situations clearly and how to stand up and fight for themselves; hard lessons learned in their lives. They want daughters who will be bolder, more self-assured women; who are independent from their husbands; who will have good jobs, status, and voice; who feel their own merit.

Furthermore, as ambitious but devalued working-class immigrant mothers who speak "broken English," they put their energies into realizing or translating the "daughter/woman of their desires" in a conservative, mainstream middle-class American context as well. That is, they attempt to turn out college educated, yuppie daughters who can acculturate and assimilate into mainstream American society— who can speak perfect English, get a good job, maintain a comfortable, financially secure lifestyle, fit in as they themselves could not. In this effort, they have been successful. Their daughters do achieve a level of economic success and social mobility that their mothers did not have as immigrant women.[7]

Joy Luck mothers all seem to hold on tenaciously to visions of something better, even as they live their lives in compromised and negotiated circumstances as daughters, mothers, and wives in China and later, in the United States. Some of the mothers possess (or think they possess) the sheer power to will their perfect daughters into existence by whatever means. These mothers have *nengkan*—a can-do spirit that seems to steamroll beyond fate, beyond circumstances, beyond daughter. They nurture and educate children, hold their families together, cook, clean, and, if need be, do paid work in and out of the home. Such mothers are willing to sacrifice material goods, family, and a personal life for their daughters to succeed.[8] Suyuan Woo cleans people's houses daily to supplement her husband's income in order to pay for "extras" like piano lessons for her daughter. She dreams up schemes for a perfect daughter. She has a notion of her daughter as a child prodigy, a genius who would excel in her new circumstances in America. Suyuan, An-mei, Lindo and Ying-ying believe their daughters, regardless of their actual abilities, could do and be anything they set their mind to. "You can be best anything" (*JLC* 132).

Furthermore, some of the Joy Luck mothers zealously pressure their daughters to be hard workers and achievers; rules and discipline are signs that they deeply care about their daughters' survival and happiness. Affection is not often displayed in an effusive "touchy-feely" manner; rather, it is dispensed in disciplinary, tough-love doses.[9] The mothers think they have lovingly and ambitiously mapped out their daughters' lives for their own good—even though this may not be the way their Americanized daughters see the game plan. What becomes obvious is the high cost of such survival and love. Emotional bullying can become a form of fierce and frightening love between mothers and daughters.

In part, each daughter becomes a reflection of her mother as she could be anew, a self enacting viable options in new circumstances. The Joy Luck mothers hold up the mirror and see themselves perfected in their daughters, especially as they perceive and dictate perfection. With the birth of her baby girl Waverly, Lindo Jong becomes dissatisfied with the shortcomings in her own life—the years of socialization into submission in her mother-in-law's household and the suppression of her private self. She wants her daughter to turn into a beautiful swan—a perfect, happy, and independent woman. Each mother desires her daughter to demonstrate visibly that she is the most obedient, most respectful, beautiful, and talented swan-daughter. Such a daughter becomes the mother's status symbol or trophy of her success in the United States, achieved after great suffering and disappointment in her own life. In the eyes of a Joy Luck mother, only such a daughter will ameliorate the social and emotional pain of leaving China, mother, and family for life as an outsider in American culture. This is a massive investment and transference of love and ambition that can take a serious toll on mother-daughter relationships.

In return for their maternal work, Tan portrays the longings of the Joy Luck mothers to be loved, understood, obeyed, respected, and memorialized by their daughters. The mothers do not wish to be forgotten. Many maintain few or no links with their families in China; their daughters become the intimate link to past and future: Who will memorialize them and their histories if not their own daughters and granddaughters? The great fear among the mothers is that their daughters do not really know them and do not respect them, their work, advice, or stories. It is with much ambivalence and trepidation then that they look to their daughters to keep their stories and preserve their cultural heritage. What they had hoped for was a daughter with a Chinese mind/character like theirs but in new circumstances— a rather difficult positioning for American-bred Chinese daughters to negotiate gracefully or seamlessly.

Tan's stories continually demonstrate how Joy Luck mothers are frustrated by their daughters' failures. Despite the mothers' efforts to preempt stumbling or errors, their Chinese American daughters fall into traps (often similar to their mothers') in their relationships with each other, with their families and with men. The mothers think their daughters do not know how to select true friends and allies. In part, the mothers blame their daughters' dismal circumstances on their failure to believe or listen carefully to their mothers. In addition, the daughters have no *nengkan* (an ability to accomplish anything one puts their mind to) like their mothers; they have no *shou* (respect) for, or *chuming* (inside knowing) of their mothers. The daughters lack the backbone, self-esteem, perseverance, loyalty, and responsibility to get on with their lives. At times, their daughters seem tired, isolated, and lost, uncertain about what next to do or how to extricate themselves from dead-end relationships and situations. Even when lost, these grown women still have a hard time returning to their mothers for love and advice. The mothers stand by wondering what happened to all their efforts to realize an American version of the ideal Chinese daughter.

The reactions of the Joy Luck mothers to their frustration and anger over these stupid, disobedient, imperfect daughters can be withering. An-mei Hsu wonders whether the cycle of women's oppression can ever be broken: "And even though I taught my daughter the opposite, still she came out the same way! Maybe it is because she was born to me and she was born a girl. And I was born to my mother and I was born a girl. All of us are like stairs, one step after another, going up and down, but all going the same way" (JLC 215). Waverly Jong is a chess champion, nurtured by her mother's support and advice. However when Lindo Jong realizes her daughter's ingratitude for all her efforts, she feels insulted and attacks furiously. Lindo ominously threatens her daughter, "We not concerning this girl. This girl not have concerning for us" (JLC 100). As a result, Waverly Jong has a crippling nightmare about a chessboard and an all-powerful chess queen mother as opponent who wears a triumphant smile and has eyes like "two angry black slits" (JLC 100). Mother Lindo reclaims her ascendancy by checkmating her daughter's presumption to the title of consummate chess queen and strategist. Similarly, for all her best-intentioned efforts to improve her daughter's prospects, Suyuan Woo also thinks her daughter Jing-mei is spiting her efforts. She draws the line when she tells Jing-mei that there are only two kinds of daughters: "Those who are obedient and those who follow their own mind! Only one kind of daughter can live in this house. Obedient daughter!" (JLC 142). In the view of the mothers, only such a daughter can be trained as a woman warrior and ally—according to her mother's rules and desires, of course.

The Joy Luck mothers think that they can transform their ugly-duckling daughters into swans without the daughters having memory of being a goose or duck, that is, without living their lives and making mistakes, without the painful process that the mothers themselves went through. Some mothers try to protect their daughters by force-feeding them the lessons and strategies they have derived from their own bittersweet lives. In this process, these Chinese mothers expect their daughters' strict and unquestioning attention and obedience.[10] Sometimes in their ambitious designs for their daughters, the mothers fail to consider carefully their daughters' dilemmas and what their needs and hopes might be as second-generation Chinese women in America.

Just as mothers love and hate their daughters, so do their daughters love and hate them. The loving dedication to Tan's *The Joy Luck Club* states: "To my mother and the memory of her mother. You asked me once what I would remember. This and much more." And yet, Tan as a rebellious daughter painfully confesses to a time when she "hated [her] life. Wished [her] mother was not [her] mother" (Tan 1991b). On the one hand, mothers can be viewed as nurturing, loving, and protective of their daughters. Suyuan Woo tells her daughter Jing-mei what she wants for her: "Only ask you be your best. For your sake. You think I want you be genius? Hnnh! What for! Who ask you!" (*JLC* 136). On the other hand, a mother can also be perceived as hateful, self-centered, excessively controlling and frightening. The mother's love, ambitions and expectations for her daughter are not always experienced by the daughter in kindly, grateful ways. The definitions and perceptions of mothers and daughters about their roles and responsibilities as women cause a great deal of the miscommunication.

The daughters think that all the constant care, advice, and expectations are intrusive day in and day out; it is a lifelong burden and negotiation between women. It's "don't do this"; "don't shame us"; "don't let your family down"; "don't you know how much we've put up with for you!" This is what the daughters think they hear from their mothers. They internalize the advice from mothers who have protected, sacrificed, and educated them into womanhood; but they also resent this advice. As Jing-mei expresses it to her mother, "You want me to be someone that I'm not!" (*JLC* 142). And as Waverly Jong develops a sense of herself as a preeminent chess queen in her own right, she grows increasingly annoyed and terrorized by her mother: "In her hands, I always became the pawn. I could only run away. And she was the queen, able to move in all directions, relentless in her pursuit, always able to find my weakest spots" (*JLC* 180). To the daughter, it seems that there is no room to be her own person or to individuate in the interstices of her Chinese mother's nurture and ambition.

The daughters don't hear the love or understand the whole context of their mothers' advice. That is, the mothers' advice is rooted in their own lived experience, in past mistakes, which they do not want their own daughters to duplicate; yet these women do not provide clear and full access to the circumstances or rationale for the advice. Tan as a young daughter remembers a similar dilemma with her own mother: "Well, my mother never spoke to me about any of this [her mother's hard life and Chinese context] while I was growing up. She raised me with all her fears and regrets—that I too would lose my innocence and question all my hopes. She hinted at great tragedies that could happen if I didn't see what lay behind smiling faces and sweet words" (Tan 1990a, 5). Tan inherits her mother's multiple social and emotional traumas as well as desires without having full or clear access to their complex frames of reference. The dislocated, fragmented recovery of trauma and desire between mother and daughter affects the formation of subjectivity, identity, and social relations.

The stories that these Joy Luck mothers would tell would make them very vulnerable to their daughters and to mainstream society. The mothers are ashamed of opening up to their Americanized daughters in order to discuss their disappointments in life and in themselves. It is bad enough on a personal level that the stories resurrect tragic and bitter memories, which some mothers wish to suppress. They wish to forget the feelings of regret, shame, guilt, and horror embedded in their experiences. Naive Ying-ying must contend with a husband who abandons her while she is pregnant. She aborts the fetus out of hate toward this man—an act which haunts her life and her daughter's. Suyuan Woo finds it difficult to reveal her guilt over the abandonment of her first children, especially to a daughter who barely cares to know her. Ugly thoughts come out of Jing-mei Woo's mouth as she yells out that she doesn't want to be her mother's daughter. The ultimate emotional stab to her mother's heart is when she says, "Then I wish I'd never been born! I wish I were dead! Like them" (JLC 142). The mother is silenced by these killing words—annihilated by a daughter who does not comprehend the psychosocial and historical roots of tragedy and ambition in her mother's life. "It was as if I had said the magic words. Alakazam!—and her face went blank, her mouth closed, her arms went slack and she backed out of the room, stunned, as if she were blowing away like a small brown leaf, thin, brittle, lifeless" (JLC 142). Jing-mei uses the fragments of her mother's story to hurt her mother. The guilt and pain in Suyuan's loss of her children in China and the loss of this disappointing Chinese American daughter is too much for her; her ability to believe that in America one can do anything is severely moderated by this daughter. This daughter has failed to infer her good intentions. Suyuan is not fully able to tell her daughter the story of her own life and why it is that she has particular hopes for her daughter. Due to such defensive emotional inaccessibility on the part of the mothers, the daughters often fail to understand or appreciate the most important lessons that their mothers wish to pass on to them.

Tan continually portrays this emotional tug-of-war in the daughters between the love and hate, between the awe and the fear they feel for their mothers as they seek to gain a degree of autonomy for themselves. For instance, in the face of rejection by Waverly, Lindo Jong ignores her much adored but ungrateful daughter. She no longer advises or hovers over Waverly; she neither polishes her trophies nor cuts out newspaper articles featuring her daughter. Waverly is worried; mother is silent. It seems that her mother had "erected an invisible wall and [she] was secretly groping each day to see how high and how wide it was" (JLC 172). Waverly begins to lose at chess tournaments and feels she has lost her earlier "magic armor" and "supreme confidence" in her chess skills (JLC 172). She translates these circumstances as her mother's way of destroying her with secret strategies and tricky side attacks to her weakest points.

Rose Hsu Jordan also senses the possible consequences of attempting to go against her mother. In her dream, Rose picks a doll entirely different from the one that her mother knew she would pick. "Stop her! Stop her! cried her mother [An-mei Hsu]. As I [Rose] tried to run away, Old Mr. Chou chased me, shouting, 'See what happens when you don't listen to your mother!' And I became paralyzed, too scared to move in any direction" (JLC 186). The perceived withdrawal of a mother's awesome love, nurture, and inner knowing—*chuming*—of her daughter, is a frightening prospect for a daughter even though she may simultaneously wish to escape or rebel against mother herself. The daughters find it extremely difficult to escape someone who has protected them since childhood. No one seems to know or love them so intimately as their mothers—who were once daughters, too.

Indeed, as Tan demonstrates, there is real psychic danger in a daughter's drive to escape from her mother's control. Jing-mei Woo's story demonstrates how self-destructive a daughter's rejection of her mother can be. In her youth, Jing-mei Woo is very resentful of her mother's ambitious prodding. Suyuan thinks her daughter could be a Chinese version of Shirley Temple, Peter Pan, or classical pianist. These American models of perfection and success grow as Suyuan culls through stories about amazing—not ordinary—children from *Ripley's Believe It or Not*, *Good Housekeeping*, and *Reader's Digest*. There are nightly tests to see what Jing-mei excels at, and the nightly disappointments written like a text on her mother's face as she continually fails the tests. For a while Jing-mei herself is filled with a grandiose sense of herself as a prodigy, of a soon to be perfect daughter, the apple of her adoring and adored mother's eyes. She imagines herself in Western storylines and images—Cinderella, Christ child, a ballerina. To be ordinary for mother or like mother is just not enough.

But her mother's ambitions and expectations are so overwhelming at times that she feels crippled in her ability to think or act on her own behalf. The additional outcome of these pressures is the nagging fear in Jing-mei that she will be nothing. She begins to feel inadequate in her inability to meet her mother's high expectations, expectations often rooted in the mainstream cultural models of American society her mother has appropriated to fulfill her dreams for a better life in America. Jing-mei's feeling of failure grows through her life: she gets no As, is a mediocre pianist and becomes a college dropout. All her life she is frustrated by "raised hopes and failed expectations" (*JLC* 134). She begins to blame her mother for many of her problems in life.

To counteract the power of her mother, she becomes a rebel, a saboteur of her mother's plans. Jing-mei discovers the rebellious side of herself. In a mirror she sees a reflection of her ordinary face as powerful, stubborn, angry.[11] "I had never seen that face before. I looked at my reflection, blinking so I could see more clearly. The girl staring back at me was angry, powerful. This girl and I were the same. I had new thoughts, willful thoughts, or rather thoughts filled with lots of won'ts. I won't let her change me, I promised myself. I won't be what I'm not" (*JLC* 134). She sets up a defensive oppositional stance to her mother; she aggressively *reacts* rather than acts, which does violence to their potential bonding. Both mother and daughter stop honest communication. They withdraw in cold, distant silence:

> And for all those years, we never talked about the disaster at the recital or my terrible accusations afterwards at the piano bench. All that remained unchecked, like a betrayal that was now unspeakable. So I never found a way to ask her why she had hoped for something so large that failure was inevitable.

And even worse, I never asked her what frightened me the most: Why had she given up hope? (JLC 142–3)

It is only in her thirties that Jing-mei realizes that in sabotaging and silencing her frustrated mother, she has sabotaged herself, too. In "Best Quality," she makes some painful realizations after her mother's death: she is a small time copywriter; she can't outsmart Waverly; and she can't choose a good crab: "That was the night, in the kitchen, that I realized I was no better than who I was" (JLC 207). After all these years of trying to be special and resenting her mother for it, what she begins to feel is "tired and foolish, as if I had been running to escape someone chasing me, only to look behind and discover there was no one there" (JLC 207). Like Waverly, Rose, and Lena, she has been so busy fighting off her own overblown image of a powerful, suffocating mother that she has neglected to search into her own inadequacies and motivations. This extreme reaction by a daughter to her mother gets in the way of her ability to love her mother and act on the best choices in her own life.

Dangerous Border Crossings: The American Translation of Immigrant Joy Luck Mothers

The traumatic translation of devalued, ambitious Chinese immigrant mothers to an inhospitable country, and the assimilationist tendencies of their second-generation English-speaking Chinese daughters cause serious ruptures in their relationships and communications with each other. Tan's stories explore these miscommunications and misreadings as the Joy Luck mothers and daughters negotiate the often conflicting positionings they must maintain in order to preserve their families and the fragments of a Chinese culture in an Anglo-American landscape.

The mothers have suffered and forgotten much in their chaotic translation from China to the United States. In Tan's opening vignette to the book, the mothers tell how they had bought a goose/duck that had turned into a swan—"a creature that became more than what was hoped for" (JLC 17). To this swan, they communicate all their hopes and desires, for better circumstances and opportunities not only for themselves but for their daughters and new families in the United States. During immigration, this swan is taken away from the immigrant mother. Under the guise of a fairy-tale-like story, Tan mirrors the painful process and new dilemmas the mothers experience in coming to America in 1949. The story symbolizes their difficulties—the sexism and racism they encountered, the disorientation, loneliness, fear, and anger they confront upon their arrival in the United States. Though coming in a later, more heterogeneous phase in Chinese immigration (1940s–1950s), the Joy Luck mothers are nevertheless socialized into an oppressive silence by American racism and haunted by the history of immigration policies which excluded earlier Chinese and other Asian groups from entry into America.

Given this long history in the United States, it is not difficult to understand the Chinese immigrant mothers' fear of the police, deportation, and backlash from white Americans. In this hopeful new land, these women find themselves again being stripped of self; they must suppress their histories and language in a Eurocentric America that devalues them. It is difficult for these Chinese women to recover and tell their own stories, and even more difficult to recover and translate their stories to their English-speaking daughters. The vital communications between mothers and daughters are fractured by disruptive historical and sociocultural crises and events in the United States.

Despite all her years in the United States, for example, one mother, An-mei Hsu, lives with fears of deportation. Even though she has learned to shout her anger in China, she is silenced in her adopted country. An-mei once considered bringing her brother to the United States, but did not pursue her plans. She has heard through friends that she may bring trouble to her brother in China; that the FBI will give her trouble for the rest of her life; that she will not get a home loan because people will think she is communist (*JLC* 30). An-mei's fears are well grounded, especially if one remembers America's severe anti-communist paranoia in the conservative milieu of the 1940s and 1950s. There were governmental sweeps through the nation and through Chinatowns for communist sympathizers, spies, and "national security threats," and even confessional programs to weed out sympathizers among those who had entered as "paper sons" (see Yung 1995). There were real concerns that the U.S. government would harass, deport, or imprison the Chinese as they had done with the Japanese during World War II. Many Chinese attempted to travel back and forth between China and the U.S. and maintain links with their homeland in an America that was suspicious of their "alien" presence. They sent remittances to their families and communities back home. But the links with Chinese kin abroad were disrupted or went underground; nationalist and leftist political activities stopped: "Conservatism pervaded the community. Many people responded to the red-baiting tactics of this period by assuming a passive stance, coping through evasion rather than confrontation" (ibid., 286). This earlier paranoia is being replayed in the 1990s with media and U.S. governmental reports implying that Chinese Americans are disloyal citizens, spies, and fundraisers for communist China.

In order to survive in the United States, Lindo Jong must again hide her truthful Chinese face. In both China and in the United States, Lindo must make up critical fictions in order to survive threatening situations. She pays an American-raised Chinese girl to advise her on how to negotiate entry into mainstream America: "In America," [the girl] said, "you cannot say you want to live there forever. If you are Chinese, you must say you admire their schools, their ways of thinking. You must say you want to be a scholar and come back to teach Chinese people what you have learned" (*JLC* 258). In order to allay fears of Asian families settling in white America, Lindo is advised to become a trickster. She is advised to say she has no children and does not plan to have any; she is advised to marry an American citizen to ensure her stay in the country (see chap. 3). In another example, Suyuan Woo, arriving in America as an unwanted immigrant, is forced by her husband to hide her shiny

Chinese dresses and to don a plain brown-checked Chinese dress. Her husband does not want to call attention to her as a Chinese woman.[12] In addition, the Woos are pressured to learn English from the Bible and choir practice. They become Christians, not so much from a profound sense of faith or affinity with the white missionaries, but from a need to survive.

Likewise, Ying-ying St. Clair is forced to invent a fictive self that is oriented to her present and future life in the United States, but which does not account for her traumatic past. In the foreign and suffocating spaces that discipline and confine her, Ying-ying is portrayed as numb, off balance, and lost, living in small houses, doing servant's work, wearing American clothes, learning English, accepting American ways without care or comment, and raising a distant daughter. In addition, Ying-ying is not comfortable in Chinatown. Her Mandarin is not fully understood by the more numerous Cantonese speakers in San Francisco; language difference further isolates an already lonely and depressed woman. An automatic sense of loyalty or support cannot simply be assumed because one is "Chinese": there are a multitude of differences and commonalities that exist within racial-ethnic formations not only in the United States but also in China.

Upon her arrival in America, Ying-ying is processed at Angel Island Immigration Station where agents try to fit her into a narrow classification system: war bride, displaced person, student, or wife. She is renamed Betty St. Clair; she loses her Chinese name and identity as Gu Ying-ying and gains a new birthdate. In the Chinese lunar calendar, she is no longer a tiger but a dragon. Her white husband forces her to speak English. He attempts to translate her gestures, moods, silences, and fractured language into optimistic English meanings; however, his translations cannot access the nightmarish world of his wife. It is no wonder that this Joy Luck woman descends into a severe depression, which leaves her silent and inaccessible to her daughter Lena. One is humbly reminded of Sheila Rowbotham's comment about the importance of attuning one's ears to the language of silence, especially the long silence of women through history: "The oppressed without hope are mysteriously quiet. When the conception of change is beyond the limits of the possible, there are no words to articulate discontent so it is sometimes held not to exist. This mistaken belief arises because we can only grasp silence in the moment in which it is breaking. . . . But the fact that we could not hear does not prove that no pain existed" (1973, 30). Lena attempts to articulate the pain and horror of her mother's unspeakable past, a past that has devoured Ying-ying and turned her into a sickly ghost of a woman.

Racist and sexist attitudes and policies in the U.S. accentuate the need of the Joy Luck mothers to be evasive and open to taking on multiple and contradicting stories and positionings in society. It is not inherently genetic or "Chinese" to be "inscrutable"; it is important to be cunning or ambiguous in order to survive difficult circumstances. For such women as An-mei Hsu, Ying-ying St. Clair, Lindo Jong, and Suyuan Woo, it is necessary to maintain a mask of acceptable attitudes and stories in order to legitimize and ensure their stays, and those of their families, permanently in the United States.

Further, if the Joy Luck mothers fear imparting intimate knowledge and stories to the "white ghosts" in mainstream society who may harm them or their families, they also fear imparting this intimate knowledge to their daughters, who ignore and demean them. There is the fear that the "half-barbarian" children may misuse such knowledge against their Chinese parents. In such circumstances, the Joy Luck mothers are often unable or unwilling to tell their stories to their insider-outsider daughters except in sometimes disturbing, frightening, and circuitous fragments. How can these mothers articulate their stories fully if they must hide or deny their past or their language? How can Americanized Chinese daughters begin to understand the fractured and dislocated narratives that surface, made up as they are of so many lies and truths, so many protective layers set up against the outsiders' *chuming*—inner knowing—of them?

Living out the stories necessary to survival in America means risking the loss of one's Chinese faces and Chinese values and culture. On the one hand, to avoid feeling alienated from their adopted country and become "truly American," the Joy Luck mothers sometimes feel they must give up their souls and culture as Chinese women. On the other hand, they find the soul can shrivel from too much alienation and exile from their Chinese motherland. How does one diminish this double alienation? How does a mother pass to her daughter this complex mediation of positionality? This dilemma is confronted by Lindo Jong in the chapter entitled "Double Face." In adapting to a new country, Lindo constantly hides her Chinese face and with her repertoire of trickster faces is uncertain whether she can get back to the more genuine, feisty self that she discovered under her "red marriage scarf" in China. In the United States, Lindo feels more alienated, vacillating between stereotypical Chinese faces constructed for white American consumption (as well as for her yuppie daughter) and her personal, more truthful Chinese face, which she associates in her memory with her mother. Sadly, she has lost the map of her mother's mirroring face as a guide in her life—as her own daughter has, too, in living in the United States.

Lindo discovers that wearing multiple, contradictory faces can be disorienting—sometimes one forgets who one is and what is core. Her daughter is "all American-made," an outsider with no Chinese mind or character (JLC 254). Lindo Jong blames herself for teaching Waverly how to survive in mainstream America (JLC 254); she had hoped to transform their circumstances in America, but she had also hoped to retain the more ideal aspects of Chinese values and culture as part of this process. But Lindo feels she has failed miserably in her attempts to pass on not only a Chinese cultural legacy but also her woman's culture of survival.

The mothers, An-mei, Ying-ying, and Lindo, all speak of the double self that is maintained for survival in oppressive systems. Such strategies can be "survival rich," as María Lugones has suggested, but they also backfire and cause ambiguity and self-alienation. In example after example, Tan demonstrates how mothers are caught in this dilemma. Even as they wish their daughters to grow up with Chinese minds and respect for them, the mothers themselves devalue Chinese culture and language and their own personal histories of survival and resistance as women. The mothers make the painful realization rather late that they may have given up a great deal in encouraging the "Americanization" of their daughters into mainstream middle-class culture and consumption; in the busy work of teaching them how to survive in a dominant culture, they neglected to fully and clearly tell their daughters their own rich stories of struggle and resistance, and their links to the struggles of other Chinese women for empowerment.

As we see frequently in Tan's stories, the specific social context in which a Joy Luck mother is brought up strongly affects the intimate bonding and communication between mother and daughter. In addition, the differences in the social and economic positioning of the immigrant Chinese mother and her second-generation, Americanized daughter also contribute to the rifts between them in the United States.

A Stranger to Myself and to My Mother

In *The Joy Luck Club*, Tan shows how stereotypes of Chinese American women create obstacles in the relationships between mothers and daughters. In particular, she demonstrates how stereotypes of Asian women, embedded in American mainstream discourses and institutions, seriously affect the way Chinese American daughters "read" their immigrant mothers and their own ethnic communities. These stereotypes, especially when internalized, suppress the daughter's desire to deal with an immigrant mother, who is often judged or devalued in terms of an "American mindset," that sees her mother as "other," as "outsider," as "intruder." The mainstream Western culture and society often insinuate that the second-generation Joy Luck daughters would be better off if they forget their "traditional," "repressive," "backwards" Chinese culture, language, and history (see Mohanty 1984, 1991). Yet ironically, the inherited Chinese social, cultural, and historical contexts are still experienced as vital to the daughters' personal and political survival in the United States.

In Euro-American culture, the Americanized daughters are embarrassed by mothers who seem the outcast Other. They fear becoming just like their Chinese mothers. That is, they fear the rejections and ostracism they have seen or heard their mothers suffer as immigrant, working-class women of color who did not fit into the culture, discourse, and values of mainstream, middle-class white America. When Ying-ying and her Amerasian daughter are on the street, people do not readily assume that Ying-ying is Lena's mother. Some mistake Ying-ying for Lena's maid.

As a teenager, Jing-mei vigorously denies that she is Chinese below the skin. Though her face clearly gives her away as Other, she and her Caucasian friends do not see her as Chinese. They recognize those aspects of her which comfortably reproduce their sense of being Anglo-American. And in order to fit in, Jing-mei denies wanting to be Chinese like her mother; she wants to be some type of generic American and fit in with her friends—not an abnormal or inassimilable Chinese Other. Like Maxine in *The Woman Warrior*, the daughters do not want to develop the loud bossy voices of some of their mothers which make them stand out like a sore thumb. They want to assimilate quietly and invisibly into the "American-feminine" mainstream. Jing-mei has nightmares as to what being Chinese may mean: "I saw myself transforming like a werewolf, a mutant tag of DNA suddenly triggered, replicating itself insidiously into a *syndrome*, a cluster of telltale Chinese behaviors, all those things my mother did to embarrass me—haggling with store owners, pecking her mouth with a toothpick in public, being color-blind to the fact that lemon yellow and pale pink are not good combinations for winter clothes" (*JLC* 267). She describes how strange her own mother and Auntie An-mei appear to her Americanized eyes: "She and Auntie An-mei were dressed up in funny Chinese dresses with stiff stand-up collars and blooming branches of embroidered silk sewn over their breasts. These clothes were too fancy for real Chinese people, I thought, and too strange for American parties. In those days, before my mother told me the Kweilin story, I imagined Joy Luck was a shameful Chinese custom, like the secret gathering of the Ku Klux Klan or the tom-tom dances of TV Indians preparing for war" (*JLC* 28). In living in the United States, Jing-mei assimilates certain stereotypical and racist views of the Chinese which alienate her from her own mother and heritage. She turns her mother and the other Joy Luck mothers into foreigners and exotics. These appropriated narratives and images, which reveal her own desires to acculturate and assimilate into white America as a model minority, deny her the opportunity to consider her mother's actual social realities in ways which would bring them closer to each other as women and allies.

Ironically, Jing-mei Woo fails to see that even the Joy Luck mothers, like their daughters, have undergone many changes while living in the United States. "The Joy Luck aunties are all wearing slacks, bright print blouses, and different versions of sturdy walking shoes" (*JLC* 28). In addition, instead of simply winning personal pots from the mah jong games, they invest in stocks and bonds in common. Sometimes the mothers really seem more liberated and more insightful than their hip, yuppie, college-educated, middle-class American daughters. They better adapt to opportunities and ways of doing things. Yet, the daughters have a tendency to stereotype their mothers—to freeze them in space and time as old-fashioned, superstitious Chinese ladies from some mythic time; they do not give their mothers the space to particularize themselves or to cross over into their lives and into history.

For the Joy Luck daughters, their Chinese mothers become disturbingly intimate and embodied reminders of what they do not want to be in America. Tan admits to her own desire to Westernize her Chinese features through plastic surgery: "There was shame and self hate. . . . There is this myth that the United States is a melting pot, but what happens in assimilation is that we end up deliberately choosing the American things—hot dogs and apple pie—and ignore the Chinese offerings" (Wang 1989, 69). Waverly and the other daughters do not want to be identified with their mothers or their stories; with speaking the Chinese language; or with keeping traditional ways and customs. The daughters do not have a profound grasp of their mothers' stories and advice as anchored in pain and tragedy—much less love or politics. When Jing-mei first listens to the fragments of her mother's ever-changing war story, she finds it hard to believe it was "anything but a Chinese fairy tale" (*JLC* 25). Her ways of knowing about mother or China replay the imperialist fantasies, myths, and reveries which seem to set China and women's position in China in nostalgic ahistorical narratives and images, and which do not allow her to access the more complex and rich histories about China and Chinese women. Until the death of her mother, Jing-mei fails to access the history that recounts the revolutionary transformations in a modernizing China, which is also the arena for understanding a major part of her mother's history of trauma and its complicated relation to their interactions in the United States.

The assimilation of the daughters takes many forms besides denial or neglect of mother and her stories and experiences. This denial, as Tan demonstrates, is intertwined with the denial of notions of Chinese culture and identity. The daughters pretend they are becoming white WASPS, and pretend their parents are invisible— or see them as the outcast Other. They desire to learn and speak only the dominant language (English) and they valorize elite Eurocentric perspectives and aesthetics above all others; they participate in the conscious or unconscious appropriation of Orientalist or imperialist views of their own ethnic community (Rich 1986a, 141– 42). For example, Waverly Jong makes up jokes to tell her friends about her mother's arrival in the United States and about her parents' meeting and marriage. She trivializes their stories of struggle and joy. Waverly does not know the true, difficult story of her feisty immigrant mother; or the poignant story of how her parents courted by surmounting ethnic differences and the difficulties of the English language. She does not know the story of how her name was chosen to express her mother's love and hopes for her.

The Joy Luck daughters often fail to read their Chinese mothers and their complex love and intentions in the popular cultural discourses and representations they have grown up within in mainstream America. As a result, the daughters often feel more misunderstood or devalued by their mothers than loved. The daughters in Tan's book become distant and alienated from the contexts of their ambitious, hard-working immigrant Chinese mothers. They do not see their mothers as particularly affectionate or loving from a Westernized point of view, but as demanding taskmasters or exotics from some fantasy distance. They do not fully understand that their mothers are very busy concentrating on the basic survival, both material and cultural, of their families.[13] As working-class women of color in America, many of the Joy Luck mothers do not often have the money, energy, and leisure to spend "quality time" with their young children. Because they speak little or no English and have few marketable skills, a number of the Joy Luck mothers find themselves working in low-paying, dead-end jobs for long hours. Suyuan Woo cleans many people's houses every week to make ends meet and to pay for Jing-mei's piano lessons; An-mei Hsu and Lindo Jong work grueling hours in a fortune cookie factory to survive. Their daughters do not often define the difficult but vital work and nurture of their working-class immigrant Chinese mothers as love.

The Joy Luck daughters, born and raised in the United States, have assimilated and acculturated into the American scene. For example, they talk about love as romantic, Hollywood filmic love; short-termed "fourteen carats" love; "victim to his hero" love; love without "false dependencies" and "obligation"; mild-mannered unconditional love—all very different from forms of Chinese mother love. Tan gives us brief but incisive sketches of the daughters' heterosexual Western definitions of love in their own contemporary American stories, especially in the discussion of their racist notions of Asian men and of their often troubled or misguided relationships with Euro-American men—relationships that do not offer the freedom and nurture they had hoped for.

One daughter, Rose Hsu Jordan, takes great delight in flaunting her new white American boyfriend in front of her disapproving mother An-mei. This is the way Rose describes her attraction to Ted. "I have to admit that what I initially found attractive in Ted were precisely the things that made him different from my brothers and the Chinese boys I had dated: his brashness; the assuredness in which he asked for things and expected to get them; his opinionated manner; his angular face and lanky body; the thickness of his arms; the fact that his parents immigrated from Tarrytown, New York, not Tientsin, China" (JLC 117). By letting the daughters tell their American stories in this way, I believe that Tan exposes their levels of internalized self-hatred. Rose thinks she can escape not only from her Chinese mother but also from Chinese men. From her Euro-American perspective, Chinese men are perceived as passive, effeminate, and weak—they do not meet the mainstream definitions of Western manliness or attractiveness. Robert Ku refers to this way of thinking and behaving as "variations on the Madame Butterfly theme: the idea of an Asian woman who is in Asia or in an Asian American context so oppressed by the maleness or Asian-ness. She becomes free of it through possible assimilation as well as through a process of becoming a Yuppie" (Nguyen 1997, 55). As Gina Marchetti also notes, interracial romance narratives construct "the American Dream of abundance, protection, individual choice, and freedom from the strictures of a traditional society in the paternalistic name of heterosexual romance" (qtd. in Espiritu 1997, 96). Rose's American Dream is anything but perfect. She marries into a rich, racist family who misidentifies her as Vietnamese and bad news for their up-and-coming son. Rose locates herself as a victim to her hero husband Ted. He is put in the position of rescuing her and being responsible for making all the major decisions. He gets tired and disillusioned with always having to take the responsibility for both of them. The marriage heads for divorce and Rose is left feeling *hulihudu* (confused) about what to do with her life.

In Tan's representations the romantic quests to "fall in love" and escape from mother, family, and ethnic community prove to be more painful indicators of a daughter's personal and communal alienation. (In many cases, Joy luck mothers are not portrayed as in a hurry—unlike the stereotype of Chinese mothers crazy to marry their daughters off—to see their own daughters married to any man whether Chinese or Euro-American.) Lena's relationship with her yuppie "equal," Harold, is based on a sense of her inadequacy. Her self-perception is wrapped up in Harold's perception of her—not in her own strengths as a Chinese American woman. "I . . . dredged up my deepest fears: that he would tell me I smelled bad, that I had terrible bathroom habits, that my taste in music and television was appalling. I worried that Harold would someday get a new prescription for his glasses and he'd put them on one morning, look me up and down, and say, 'Why, gosh, you aren't the girl I thought you were, are you?'" (JLC 156). Like a traditional helpmeet to her man, she encourages him in his work, suggests ideas for his work, and yet when it comes to economic and social recognition, it does not appear that they are as equal as Lena thinks. She is stuck in a cold, disappointing marriage, wondering about "this feeling of surrendering everything to him, with abandon, without caring what I got in return" (JLC 162). Lena's dilemma harkens back to her mother's own erasure in a masochistic love relationship to an unfaithful and sadistic first husband. Despite the similar problems in their heterosexual relationships, both mother and daughter find it difficult to communicate with each other.

Waverly Jong and Lena St. Clair are also married to Euro-American men who seem to offer them escape from their "foreign" mothers and seductive entry into mainstream Euro-American middle (and upper) class consumer culture and society—an entry that their mothers did not have either in their own right or in some of their affiliations with Chinese men. Adrienne Rich notes that assimilation sometimes seems to assure people—at least momentarily—an escape from disenfranchisement, from being outcast as Other and sentenced to live by different laws (Rich 1986a, 142). Moreover, the cultural critic Ien Ang has noted, "cultural assimilation is not only and not always an official policy forced and imposed by host countries upon their non-native minorities; there is also among many members of minority groups themselves a certain *desire* to assimilate, a longing for fitting in rather than standing out, even though this desire is often at the same time contradicted by an incapability or refusal to adjust and adapt completely" (Ang 1994, 9). There is a nagging sense that successful as these yuppie daughters appear to be, they are, in their own telling, deeply conflicted within. But the daughters find out, often when it is much too late, that the escape from a difficult mother's love and advice and from a complicated Chinese heritage into the arms of a Euro-American man is often detrimental to both of them.

The daughters begin to realize that their white lovers and husbands cannot cover up for the real tensions that arise in their acceptance of Western notions of love at the expense of the Chinese notions of affiliation they were brought up with. For instance, Waverly sees her lover Rich as a "divine man" and an embarrassing romantic who understands and accepts her thoroughly. But after dinner with her parents, Rich looks pathetic. Instead of acknowledging Rich's faults on her own, she blames her mother for "poisoning" her relationship with him. Lindo questions her daughter's own motives: "Ai-ya, why do you think these bad things about me? ... So you think your mother is bad. You think I have a secret meaning. But it is you who has this meaning" (JLC 181). Waverly finally comes to take responsibility for her own negative reactions to Rich: he bumbles badly through the Chinese dinner with her parents, criticizes her mother's cooking and English, and incorrectly calls her parents Linda and Tim. Lena also finds it difficult to explain her unsatisfactory relationship to her mother. "I think how to explain this, recalling the words Harold and I have used with each other in the past: 'So we can eliminate false dependencies . . . be equals . . . love without obligation . . .'" (JLC 162). From a delimited mainstream notion of autonomy and self-sufficiency, Waverly has a hard time defining *constructive* forms of dependency or need that can articulate her social and emotional desires for affiliation as strengths. The affiliation of the Joy Luck daughters with Euro-American men cannot wholly cover up or solve the profound ruptures within themselves, between the Joy Luck daughters and mothers, or between and within cultures. Furthermore, material consumption and economic success cannot fully substitute for the profound sense of loss and alienation the mothers and daughters feel in their lives.

While interracial romance brings assimilation loudly to the fore in adolescence and adulthood, childhood is the time when the Euro-American sociocultural system quietly makes the case for assimilation. The daughters are taught in a system that often devalues their Chinese values and histories. After a short time in the classroom and in mainstream culture, the daughters are like Maxine in *The Woman Warrior*: half-Chinese and "half-barbarian" to their Chinese parents and communities.

In reading Tan, what becomes obvious is that there are serious advantages and disadvantages in a one-way assimilation-acculturation process into Anglo-American culture and society. On the one hand, the socialization into mainstream culture and values provide access for the daughters into white America. In Tan's book, we are also made aware of the problematic nature of such education and assimilation. For instance, the daughters forget their mother tongue and valorize the English language above all others. As Tan says, the daughters speak only English and swallow "more Coca-Cola than sorrow" (JLC 17). They take their cues from a racist conceptual framework that suggests to them that they are a "better" class of people because they know the "better language" English. The imperative to speak English only, combined with the stereotypes and assumptions of dominant culture about Asian culture (as rigid, conservative, and repressively authoritarian), are internalized by the daughters. Many Chinese American children grow up rebelling against having to go to Chinese school; Cantonese or Mandarin is spoken at home among the family at times, but not in its dealings with the public, where power and value are negotiated. Given this context, it is understandable that the Joy Luck daughters do not want to speak Chinese or the "broken English" that they identify with their mothers or their domestic-familial homeplaces. Tan notes that as the daughter of an immigrant mother she believed that her mother's "broken English" reflected fractured or broken thoughts. Tan began to see her mother as a stupid and inarticulate woman who had nothing of real value to say: "my mother's 'limited' English limited my perception of her. I was ashamed of her English. I believed that her English reflected the quality of what she had to say. That is, because she expressed them imperfectly her thoughts were imperfect. And I had plenty of empirical evidence to support me: the fact that people in department stores, at banks, and at restaurants did not take her seriously, did not give her good service, pretended not to understand her, or even acted as if they did not hear her" (1995, 316). Like Tan, the daughters consciously or unconsciously assimilate destructive and arrogant views in perceiving their own mothers and Chinese families and communities. The English language can become a race and class signifier that divides the daughters from their Chinese immigrant mothers. I believe these self-abusive interactions are politically important issues as they affect our abilities to build more permeable social and political coalitions not only in intimate relationships with one's specific family and community, but also with the broader body politic in the United States and globally.

Sadly, even the Joy Luck mothers yearn to tell their own neglected stories of survival, struggle, and achievement to their loved daughters in "perfect American English." "Now the woman was old. And she had a daughter who grew up speaking only English and swallowing more Coca-Cola than sorrow. For a long time now the woman had wanted to give her daughter the single swan feather and tell her, 'This feather may look worthless, but it comes from afar and carries with it all my good intentions.' And she waited, year after year, for that day she could tell her daughter this in perfect American English" (*JLC* 17). The proud Joy Luck mothers do not want to be put into a subordinate position next to their educated, middle-class, career-oriented, English-speaking daughters. They do not want to sound coarse, uneducated, or alien to daughters who do not understand their Chinese or their native "hillbilly" village or regional dialects.[14] The result is that they produce daughters who seem more like strangers than loving, intimate allies. Jing-mei Woo speaks of the difficulties in mother-daughter communication when both do not have a good grasp of the other's language: "My mother and I never really understood one another. We translated each other's meanings and I seemed to hear less than what was said, while my mother heard more" (*JLC* 37). The inability to fully comprehend each other across translations of geography, cultures, languages, and silences keeps mothers and daughters divided.

In reading Tan, one becomes aware that these Americanized daughters must learn that their mothers' silence or fractured English does not reflect a lack of social, emotional, or intellectual life; it is rather a lack of command of a language to describe the range of experience or do their stories or emotions full justice.

On a broader level, perhaps another obstacle to communication is that there is no language that can fully address the silenced stories and feelings of the Joy Luck women. It may not simply be a question of how to find the English to communicate their social actualities, or how to pass culture and history in Chinese to Americanized daughters, but how to pass their women's standpoints and stories in a language that is not embedded in patriarchal, capitalist, and imperialist discourses and institutions. Are there experiences of these women that cannot be translated or spoken in either English or Chinese? In the long silences before "perfect English," mothers and daughters do not communicate with each other very well. It is easy for both sides to ignore or misread the other, but Tan makes it clear that much that is left unsaid or felt between a mother and daughter is really vital to both women. Each woman's story must be conveyed to the other as a form of potential empowerment. This is a hopeful practice though it has yet to be fully enacted among the Joy Luck women.

Listening to the Mother Talking-Story Next to You

After discussing the many obstacles that can arise in the communications between the Joy Luck mothers and their daughters, it is perhaps difficult to comprehend how or even why mothers and daughters would attempt to bond with each other. I think Amy Tan demonstrates in each of the intertwined stories that the mothers and daughters are alienated and unhappy without the other's love and recognition. There is much that they share as women, even though it is difficult for them to admit it or perceive it amid the differences. One leaves Tan's stories feeling the potential for friendship in many of the relationships. However, the Joy Luck women must *earn* their friendships and alliances through hard work, empathy, and ceaseless effort in countering the numerous obstacles which make their relationships difficult to sustain; even then, there are no guarantees that it will work out among all the mother-daughter pairs. According to Tan, it would be too easy to end her stories in such a fairytale fashion.

With time and distance, the mothers begin to mellow; they realize that their daughters have lives of their own. Suyuan Woo comes to realize that her daughter is not like the others who wanted "best quality," that she was different and wished to be herself and good at whatever ordinary thing she did. She is not at all like tricky, sophisticated Waverly Jong. Suyuan finally believes that her daughter Jing-mei "can make [her] legs go the other way" (JLC 208)—not follow other voices, but her own. The mothers' former ambitions are tempered with the knowledge that their daughters have achieved a certain level of independence and financial success in their assimilation and acculturation into the American mainstream. However, the mothers see below the surface glitter of their daughter's middle-class/yuppie lives: they see the flaws, tensions, the quiet desperation that debilitate their daughters' lives and relationships. They note that their daughters' lives are complicated by their circumstances in the United States—a country filled with other forms of anger, distress, and despair; a confusing, if not paralyzing abundance of choices, identities, cultures, values, politics.

Similarly, the daughters struggle to confront the monstrous images of destructive, all-powerful mothers—whom they view with patriarchal and Western condescension—in order to begin to understand who the mothers are in their own right. They have an "attic" full of racist and matrophobic discourses and images of their mothers which impede a more honest understanding of themselves and their mothers' lives and stories; the daughters must assess these one-dimensional traps, constructed out of their fears of "becoming their mothers."[15] In short, each needs to stop seeing her mother simply as one to be avoided and dismissed. Opportunities for new relationships, growth, as well as social-political practices are sometimes embedded in the prickly space of a perceived "problem" or "crisis" between mothers and daughters, if they are willing to see each other anew. It seems that many of the mothers and daughters in this book are in varying processes of reassessing each other and bridging their differences.

Important strategies for survival and challenge are passed on between the Joy Luck mothers and daughters when they make connections with each other. These empowering practices are often neglected in mainstream and oppositional discussions of Tan's book. In foregrounding the mother's stories, critics tend to reproduce or foreground the timeless fascination with Old China/Orientalist discourses and stereotypes of Chinese women as forever helpless, illiterate, traditional lotus blossoms, tragically oppressed and immobilized by their circumstances in China. In such ahistorical and apolitical discourses, these women's stories are reductively made visible as emotional, private-domestic women's narratives, which, in turn, seem to have little to do with issues of major concern to society. In the fiercely contested discursive terrain for cultural and political power, the women's stories of Tan (as well as Kingston and Ng) can lose their power and visibility as potentially emergent and transgressive narratives in the making of identity. Through her text, I think Tan attempts to construct mother-daughter stories that foreground the status of women as resisting subjects negotiating their varying situations within their specific contexts. In *The Joy Luck Club*, mothers and daughters learn the importance of active agency in their own—and each other's—survival and resistance whether in China or the United States.

Some mothers educate their daughters strictly to survive within the confines of the laws and social customs of a patriarchal system—like An-mei's popo who expels her own daughter and socializes her granddaughter to grow up as a "good daughter" for her own protection and security. Within the strictures of a masculinist and heterosexist society, it can be dangerous for the daughter and the family to do otherwise—remember No Name Woman's story in *The Woman Warrior*. Ying-ying St. Clair's upper-class mother and amah also socialize her into her traditionally ideal feminine roles as a woman. According to Sara Ruddick, some women align with men and internalize the values within a patriarchal system. They reproduce this system by raising girls who are obedient daughters, wives, mothers, women. They do not provide their daughters with a critical apparatus to understand or resist their circumstances because they are not themselves conscious of being powerless or oppressed (Ruddick 1980, 354–55). Women like An-mei's popo or Ying-ying's mother may have a certain level of status. They find rewards, protection, and private and domestic power in their affiliations with men, which ameliorate or compensate for their lack of power in the social arenas reserved for men. Some women may be conscious of inequities but unable or unwilling to come out against the ostracism of their family and society. Tan, like Kingston, complicates the relationships among women, showing us the network of decisions mothers and daughters must negotiate in self-alienating but powerful societal structures.

Other Joy Luck mothers teach their daughters ways to negotiate or circumvent oppressive systems by allying with mothers who love them. An-mei Hsu learns painful, critical lessons for dealing with a variety of people and situations in the world. She identifies with her outcast mother. She recognizes her mother's face as the same face she herself had hidden from her father's portrait—the face that hid itself in the dark corner of female space where she could go to think her own private thoughts beyond the gaze of her authoritarian father or the disciplines of a patriarchal society. The intuitive "secret look"—visual cues—cultivated by each woman and between the two is the key that rekindles and remembers the intimate alliance of flesh before words, before separation by a patriarchal system. It is also her mother's wailing and her touching and rubbing of An-mei's childhood scar—the "skin's memory"— that triggers the love for the lost mother. These resisting visceral subtexts and practices are not fully articulated or represented by dominant or authorized patriarchal institutions. Yet they have a social and emotional power that travels across space and time as it is retold by An-mei to a daughter lost and confused in America.

An-mei's mother returns to Shanghai to visit her sick mother. She shows An-mei how profound and vital mother-daughter love is by returning to the primary source of desire, love, and pain in her life—the dying mother who once denied her and sided with the patriarchy. She literally and figuratively slices off a piece of her own flesh for a soup to heal her dying mother. This act of love and respect makes concrete for An-mei the pain felt between mother and daughter: "Even though I was young, I could see the pain of the flesh and the worth of the pain" (JLC 48). It is powerful, transformative pain, her mother tells her, that can take one back to a remembrance of the original bonding between a mother and daughter, to peel away, strip down to nothing in order to locate what is really at the core, what is in one's bones, what is one's true nature and what are one's true bond and love (JLC 48). In watching her mother nurse her mother, An-mei comes to love her own mother even more. In her mother, she begins to see her "own true nature" (JLC 48). Through this gesture the daughter An-mei has a powerful visual and emotive experience at a young age that enacts and symbolizes the physicality of pain and sorrow in their lives and the inextricable centrality of the bonds between mother and daughter. The mother's gesture, and the interpretation of the gesture by her mother, counters the patriarchal narratives and institutions that specifically attempt to define and alienate the mothers and daughters even beyond death, into the realm of ancestral memory. "This is how a daughter honors her mother. It is *shou* so deep it is in your bones. The pain of the flesh is nothing. The pain you must forget. Because sometimes that is the only way to remember what is in your bones. You must peel off your skin, and that of your mother, and her mother before her. Until there is nothing. No scar, no skin, no flesh" (JLC 48).

After her popo's death, An-mei's mother reclaims her daughter as an ally and takes her back to Shanghai. An-mei's mother searches for ways to pass on useful knowledge to her daughter. Though deeply depressed by her experiences, she struggles not simply to surrender or duplicate servile survival in her social circumstances. She does not want An-mei to be like her own mother nor does she want her daughter to be weak and lacking in options as she was in her own life. However, An-mei is seduced by the luxury and comfort in Wu Tsing's house. She almost betrays her mother and herself for a pearl necklace from the Second Wife. Her mother intervenes to teach An-mei another visual lesson that tells a story about the worthlessness of material goods and false friends. She takes one bead of the pearl necklace and smashes it in front of her shocked daughter, revealing its fakery. The mother recognizes the lies and manipulations of the Second Wife. In another example, An-mei learns to observe her mother's face—when she is sad, dark, and angry in Wu Tsing's household. She develops her ability to intuit the story of the unspeakable suffering of her beloved mother and the moral ambiguity of their lives. The "cocoon of rose silk" is threaded with the daily misery and abuse of the mother. The growing knowledge of her mother's secrets are a particular burden for the daughter who is searching for a way to channel her new-found anger and moral indignation; but it is a necessary burden. As Ruddick observes, it is a movement from the evasiveness and denial of mother and the innocence and obedience of daughter to "wariness, uncertain reflection, at times, anguished confusion" that provides the potential for growth and transformation (Ruddick 1980, 356). This difficult lesson is passed down and registered as a true gift from a true ally by her daughter.

Sadly, An-mei's mother cannot continue to withstand the demeaning nature of her life in Wu Tsing's household. She chooses an extremely self-destructive act to educate her daughter. In a world that has restricted her social and economic options, An-mei's mother sacrifices herself to teach a terrible lesson about agency and freedom. This mother's final desperate gesture is "to kill her own weak spirit so she could give [her daughter] a stronger one" (JLC 240). She literally kills herself. With her mother's death, An-mei loses her ally but gains in material and personal terms. Wu Tsing, fearful of his concubine's vengeful spirit, promises to raise Syaudi and An-mei as his legitimate and honored children. He promises to revere An-mei's mother as his first and only wife. In personal terms, the day of her mother's death is the day that the daughter begins to shout and to act powerfully on her anger, rather than to hold back tears. An-mei finally understands the core truth in her mother's agony and self-sacrifice. And though she is saddened by mother-loss, she is also fiercely empowered as a woman by her mother, both in life and in death.

At the same time that their lives bespeak compromise and tragedy, the Joy Luck mothers do not neglect to pass on empowering interventions to their daughters. These resistances counter the patriarchal and imperialist narratives that they are exposed to in China and America, which have forced them to speak, see, think and act often in disempowering terms. Against the storehouse of stories and experiences that pressure the self-sacrificing mother to give up a daughter—for her daughter's "good" or her own—Tan represents some mothers' desires to keep or reclaim their daughters by fighting fiercely for their hearts and minds, and by responsibly educating them to survive and to subvert the oppressive systems in which they live. In these ways, the Joy Luck mothers are empowered, too.

Lindo Jong attempts to teach her daughter Waverly to believe in herself and endure, to know and act upon a genuine thought, to listen to her mother and to survive as a trickster. As a young woman, Lindo Jong bided her time patiently and cleverly until she could find a creative way to free herself from her unhappy arranged marriage while keeping her promises to be a filial daughter to her mother. As it was in No Name Woman's time, there was no concept of romantic love as in the Hollywood movies, no freedom for most women to choose a lover or husband as her daughter Waverly can. Marriages were often arranged according to the practical needs of the families.[16] A woman was often selected as a wife, mother, and workhorse to her husband's family—"one who would raise proper sons, care for the old people and faithfully sweep the family burial grounds long after the old ladies had gone to their graves" (JLC 51). On her wedding day, Lindo questions and evaluates the circumstances of her life from personal and societal standpoints. At first, she feels victimized and helpless; she even considers suicide in her despair. But Lindo makes an important discovery about herself. She observes the world around her and notes the power of the invisible wind to change the landscape and cause men to "yelp and dance" (JLC 58). As a woman, she cannot go to school, but she has found other ways of learning within the natural world. She is schooled in the details of her daily, practical life.

Like An-mei's mother and Ying-Ying, Lindo looks deep into the mirror of her inner self—not simply the cultural images or identity determined in patriarchal ideologies, discourses, or institutions, but beneath the red wedding scarf. Lindo says she will buy her own 24-carat gold bracelets to celebrate her own worth, which will be judged by a personal ethics of self. She discovers a powerful, invisible, hidden wind force in herself. In a marriage, Lindo fully realizes how easy it is to adapt to social, economic, and cultural pressures, to love being an obedient wife and slave for the Huang household. Many women capitulate under years of domestic drudgery and conformity in patriarchy—to a point of unconscious obedience and submission or desperation. This can make many women forget who they once were. What blocks or restricts individuals from reconceiving the world as other than *inevitable*, according to Raymond Williams, is a "set of identifiable processes of *realpolitik* and *force majeure*, of nameable agencies of power and capital, distraction and disinformation, and all these interlocking with the embedded short-term pressures and the interwoven subordinations of an adaptive commonsense. It is not in staring at these blocks that there is any chance of movement past them. They have been named so often that they are not even, for most people, news. The dynamic moment is elsewhere, in the difficult business of gaining confidence in *our own* energies and capacities" (Williams 1983, 268). Lindo learns to endure and maintain a multiple positioning despite her difficult circumstances in China and the United States. That is, she promises not to lose sight of her feisty hidden self even as she negotiates her outward responsibilities to others.[17] She acts—not through violence and disaffiliation but by cleverness and positioning—in a manner true to herself and to her family and community.

In "Rules of the Game," Lindo Jong seeks to pass to her daughter Waverly the skill of making it in the United States in the subversive ways she has lived. She teaches her daughter the tactical art of the wind—invisible, strong, fluid. She teaches Waverly that crying noisily for something she wanted as a child is not the way to go against the wind. Lindo tells her that "the strongest wind cannot be seen" (JLC 89). Waverly Jong is taught to move like the powerful and invisible wind—just like her mother. It is not a direct force but one which hides its face in a racist, sexist society and bides its time in getting freedom in a clever fashion—through minimal energy and force. She learns the art of guerrilla warfare in enemy territory. She must be swift and decisive under pressure.

In addition, Lindo, the mah jong player, encourages Waverly in chess as a way for her to develop strategic survival skills.[18] When looking at the rules of the chess set the children had gotten at the Christmas party, Lindo tells them: "This American rules," she concluded at last. "Every time people come out from foreign country, must know rules. You not know, judge say, Too bad, go back. They not telling you why so you can use their way go forward. They say, Don't know why, you find out yourself. But they knowing all the time. Better you take it, find out why yourself" (JLC 94). For Waverly, chess becomes a game of secrets "in which one must show and never tell" (JLC 95). She studies the moves and rules avidly and learns, for instance, to "control the center early on; the shortest distance between two points is straight down the middle." She learns the importance of patience and of knowing all possible moves; of knowing how to gauge the strength and weaknesses of an opponent; of formulating the clearest plans for attack and retreat; of gathering invisible strengths and seeing the endgame before the game begins; of knowing why it is important not to reveal "why" to others—as a little knowledge over others is a great advantage to be stored for future use (JLC 94–5). Waverly acknowledges that her mother imparted daily truths so that her children could rise above their circumstances and make something of themselves in America. Tan's stories do not represent passive, suffering women as the ideal form of femininity; rather, the stories portray women who struggle to survive and challenge inequitable and often oppressive relationships and structures in diverse ways and social locations.

Rose Hsu Jordan should also listen to the mother who loves her deeply, according to An-mei. But Rose is "without wood" and listens to too many people. She often chooses "American opinions over Chinese ones." She devalues her Chinese mother's advice. Thirty years later her mother is still trying to make Rose listen to her. "A mother is best. A mother knows what is inside you," she said above the singing voices. "A psyche-atricks will only make you *hulihudu*, make you see *heimongmong*," which means "confused" and "dark fog" (JLC 188). This cacophony of voices in the United States makes it difficult for An-mei to communicate with and understand her daughter.

Rose is weak and confused; she does not hear her mother's advice to stand on her own two feet and act with a capable spirit. She is an emotional cripple, seeking solace and answers in psychotherapeutic discourses that confuse and distract her from acting. An-mei Hsu sees what is wrong in Rose's life and counsels her to speak up and take responsibility for herself: "If she doesn't try, she can lose her chance forever" (JLC 215). An-mei has known what it feels like to "desire nothing, to swallow other people's misery, to eat [her] own bitterness" (JLC 215). She begins to tell Rose about her earlier life and her mother's life, that there was a time when women like her mother swallowed their tears and lost their face. And hiding their faces only brought them greater misery. It takes a while for Rose to understand and apply her mother's counsel to her own situation. Like the other daughters, Rose has to fight off the nightmarish images of mother constructed over a lifetime of miscommunication and neglect.

Rose begins to remember a time when she looked up to her mother and believed everything she told her—when the relationship was clear and unimpeded. Like Maxine Hong Kingston, Rose believed in the "power of her [mother's] words" (JLC 185). She finally gathers enough courage to respond to her bully husband by resonating her mother's words: "You can't just pull me out of your life and throw me away" (JLC 196). The experience is freeing to Rose. In a way, she breaks the sad cycle of her grandmother and great-grandmother by constructively speaking up against her own oppression and enacting her own story. For the first time she is not silenced by her husband or stammering out of fear of him: "I saw what I wanted: his eyes, confused, then scared. He was *hulihudu*. The power of my words was that strong" (JLC 196). Her mother had taught her this and she has enacted the lesson. As I consider these Joy Luck mothers' lives, I am reminded of Adrienne Rich's comment on a mother's care for her daughter:

> What do we mean by the nurture of daughters? The most notable fact that the culture imprints on women is the sense of our limits. The most important thing one woman can do for another is to illuminate and expand her sense of actual possibilities. . . . The quality of the mother's life—however embattled and unprotected—is her primary bequest to her daughter. (Rich 1986b, 246–7)

With the death of Suyuan Woo at the beginning of the book, the mothers grow ever more fearful that they have neglected to pass down the stories of their lives and intentions to their daughters. They worry about how much miscommunication and distance separate them from their daughters—how much continuity and history is lost among women. But, as discussed earlier, mothers sometimes hid their personal stories and "true faces" in order to survive the sexism and racism they encountered in China and the United States. Sometimes they hid their private self so well, they could no longer recover that former self. When they finally desire to pass on their stories, intentions, and strategies to their daughters, they discover that they must first excavate the meanings in these long suppressed experiences. As they look back upon their lives, the mothers also attempt to distill for their daughters fragments of their life stories; but the fragments are ambiguous and difficult to comprehend, riddled with silences, pain, facts and fantasies, defense mechanisms, twists and turns, and contradictions. Yet by talking-story with their daughters, the mothers begin to provide themselves and their daughters—by trial and error—with a consciousness of what features of their social reality were so "intolerable, as to be rejected in behalf of a transforming project for the future" (Bartky qtd. in Ruddick 1980, 356).

All through her life, Suyuan Woo tried to tell her daughter the Kweilin war story. She told it from a variety of different emotional perspectives—sometimes her story would make her daughter see the mythical beauty of Kweilin or would make her laugh; at other times, the story would be very dark and shocking. To Jing-mei, her mother's different renditions of her Kweilin war story seem akin to a Chinese fairy tale about some distant time period—half-baked stories told by her Chinese mother. What triggers the darker shadows of her mother's story is the daughter's constant nagging and sulking over buying a transistor radio. The daughter is set off balance by her mother's remark, "Why do you think you are missing something you never had?" (JLC 25) The difference between the daughter's desire for a radio and the story her mother tells us is very great. Suyuan, in a matter-of-fact tone, tells her about her flight from Kweilin to Chungking during the advance of the Japanese troops. The slaughter is graphically described: "later that day, the streets of Kweilin were strewn with newspapers reporting great Kuomintang [Guomindang] victories and on top of these papers, like fresh fish from a butcher, lay rows of people—men, women and children who had never lost hope, but had lost their lives instead. When I heard this news, I walked faster and faster, asking myself at each step, Were they foolish? Were they brave?" (JLC 26). Suyuan speaks of the struggle to run with two babies and all her treasured material goods until her hands were bloodied by the effort. The road was littered with forsaken treasure—the silver, the carpenter tools, the *hong mu* table, the bolts of silk left by the weary and hopeless or the dying or the dead. She ends her story describing that she had lost all except three fancy silk dresses. The daughter is aghast. What happened to the babies?

Jing-mei's mother attempts to recover the painful horrors of her life: The telling is gradual to accommodate her daughter's ability to understand; at the same time, the remembering is gradual for Suyuan, who must slowly recall the personal and social trauma of her self-punishing silence and guilt. The emotions are so great for the mother that the story cannot be fully revealed and the story is continuous, spilling into her daughter's life unresolved. The mother's stories and reasons are puzzling; her answer, cryptic: "Your father is not my first husband. You are not those babies" (JLC 26). It takes Jing-mei a lifetime to understand how this gradual telling of her mother's story is linked intimately to her own history as a Chinese American woman: "Over the years, she told me the same story, except for the ending, which grew darker, casting long shadows into her life, and eventually into mine" (JLC 21).

Ying-ying St. Clair finally understands why she must tell Lena about her life when she takes a good look at her daughter. Ying-ying's name means "clear reflection" of her mother. Lena is a lost spirit whose eyes do not reflect anything—not even her mother. Ying-ying can intuit the telltale details of emotional turmoil in her daughter's life—an ashtray askew, a checkbook out of balance, a cold house, and an unhappy married life. She has seen it all before in her own life. "I want to tell her this: We are lost, she and I, unseen and not seeing, unheard and not hearing, unknown by others" (JLC 67). She is confident she will win and give her daughter her spirit and love (JLC 252). Her strategy is to cross over the border of pain and to fight for her daughter's lost tiger soul. "I will see a thing that has already happened.

The pain that cut my spirit loose. I will use this sharp pain to penetrate my daughter's tough skin and cut her tiger spirit loose. She will fight me, because this is the nature of two tigers. But I will win and give her my spirit, because this is the way a mother loves her daughter" (JLC 252).

No longer willing to "keep things inside," Ying-ying chooses to resurrect her experiences in order to save her lost daughter and herself. "It is the only way to penetrate her skin and pull her to where she can be saved" (JLC 242). Ying-ying will pass on the tiger spirit—her fierce heart and cunning. She is concerned that her daughter only sees with "outside eyes" and sees her as a "small old lady" (JLC 248). But if her daughter had *chuming*—an inside knowing of things, she would know that her mother was a tiger woman; then she would have "careful fear" of her mother (JLC 248). But Ying-ying's life has been one of such great trauma and self-effacement that she is emotionally imbalanced and depressed. For a long while, she has not been available to her young daughter.

Ying-ying remembers losing herself gradually. "I rubbed out my face over the years washing away my pain, the same way carvings on stone are worn down by water" (JLC 67).[19] Her arranged marriage and its horrific consequences take a toll on Ying-ying physically and emotionally. She describes her attempts to fulfill the self-alienating role of a wife. "I became a stranger to myself. I was pretty for him. If I put slippers on my feet, it was to choose a pair that I knew would please him. I brushed my hair ninety-nine times a night to bring luck to our marital bed, in hopes of conceiving a son" (JLC 247). Later, she is immersed in bitterness, hate and "loathing despair" because of the cruel infidelities of her first husband and aborts their child as a form of revenge. In her second marriage to the Anglo-American St. Clair, she gives up her fierce and cunning tiger spirit to become the passive "daughter of her father's wife" (JLC 251). St. Clair continues the process of erasure of his wife's experiences by changing her identity and appropriating her story. Ying-ying's lifelong erasure of self and the accompanying anger and depression at the injustice of this loss are made evident in the testimony of her body—there are deep lines on her mouth; her feet are swollen, calloused and cracked; her eyes are yellow-stained and clouded. All that she has left to give her daughter in America is a ghostly shadow of her self.

In being silent for so many years in China and America, in suppressing her so called "selfish desires" as well as her tiger spirit, Ying-ying is no longer heard amid the commodified distractions of daily life in the United States—swimming pools, Sony Walkmans, professional husbands, psychotherapists, ritzy houses. Ying-ying is terse and cryptic in her observations and caveats: "When something goes against your nature, you are not in balance. This house was built too steep, and a bad wind from the top blows all your strength back down the hill. So you can never get ahead. You are always rolling backward" or "See how narrow this doorway is, like a neck that has been strangled. And the kitchen faces this toilet room, so all your worth is flushed away" (JLC 109). This is one of the ways Ying-ying attempts to tell her story of roller-coaster emotional states, her sense of her suffocation and alienation as a woman, her sense of being out of balance in environments indifferent to her suffering. Lena thinks her mother is "crazy" and "depressed." She is in the middle, trying to translate the silence and nightmares. Lena does not have all the parts of her mother's story, especially the parts of women's experiences that have been denied, repressed, devalued, and absent in male-privileged discourses and institutions. Lena has developed neither the conceptual frameworks nor the languages to make sense of or to act on these profound stories of distress. In learning to relate through talk-story the sources of her depression, guilt, and rage—not to a woman's natural condition or to fate but to the social injustices of her life—Ying-ying rediscovers a critical form of consciousness and agency, which frees her to reclaim her relationship with her daughter and with herself.

Besides educating daughters to look to their mothers as true allies who can pass on major lessons for daily survival and resistance, the Joy Luck mothers want to transmit their stories and intentions to their daughters as a constructive form of intervention. Many of the mothers want to re-open communications with their grown-up daughters. Tan demonstrates that all the Joy Luck mothers and daughters talk-story about their lives. The problem is that they need to communicate—to talk-story with each other across generations, cultures, classes, languages—fully, directly, and honestly. As we see, women can often use talk-story as a form of "counter-memory" to discount the patriarchal stories and return particularity and significance to oral traditions and to the silenced and neglected stories of women. Talk-story locates itself in the heart of racist, sexist images and narratives as a significant social-political intervention. Four pairs of women speak their first-person points of view and reclaim their stories.[20] Besides strengthening the bonds among women, talk-story "talks back" (see hooks 1989) to those who would deny or lessen the power, beauty, value and pain in women's lives. This is what Kingston spent a lot of time learning in her memoir: "The reporting is the vengeance—not the beheading, not the gutting, but words" (*TWW* 63). It challenges through disjunctures, circular talking, in cryptic messages/caveats, in dreams, in talk-story traditions. It does battle in its narrative structures and in its content. This is talk that challenges the suppression of Chinese American women's voices and identities—suppression that comes not only from a male-dominated culture and society but also from daughters who have become so Americanized that they can barely talk-story with their mothers. These forms of communication are valuable tools in the excavation of these mothers and daughters and of their histories as Chinese Americans. As Leslie Marmon Silko says in the opening of *Ceremony* (1977, 2):

> I will tell you something about stories,
> [he said]
> They aren't just entertainment.
> Don't be fooled.
> They are all we have, you see,
> all we have to fight off
> illness and death.

Time and again, relations between the mothers and daughters are complex and problematic. Under these circumstances, Tan demonstrates that to confront these tensions and to speak forth oneself requires great courage and honesty; the receiver, moreover, must be quick enough to catch the nuances that illuminate the heart of these stories. These women struggle to become highly attentive listeners and witnesses to the quiet alienation and anger, as well as joys and successes, of one another's daily lives. They are the keepers of one anothers' multiple, fragmented stories, concealments, and matrilineal genealogies. The mothers and daughters continually quest for meaning in life. But they often forget that they are units of meaning themselves—not to be dismissed or objectified. They provide collective meaning to each other; despite the fierce struggle, the withering push and pull of the process, Joy Luck mothers and daughters begin to forge a common language at the heart of which is the "freeing word" (Kogawa 1981). Together, they engage in a dynamic, interactive making of culture and history strongly rooted in their shared social and emotional resources. In communicating with each other, they struggle to re-envision themselves, their families, and their communities.

Besides talking-story with their own daughters, the mothers find power and satisfaction in creating broader social and political networks. Pierrette Hondagneu-Sotelo, in her studies of women's experiences of immigration, observes that the social networks of immigrant women within domestic settings can include "visiting kin, neighbors, friends, vendors, co-workers, boarders or houseguests" (Hondagneu-Sotelo 1995, 179). These networks, moreover, give women of color and their families the extended emotional and economic support to carry on with their personal lives and social responsibilities, to find jobs, to facilitate the immigration of kin, to find spouses, and to circumvent or contest domestic patriarchal authority (ibid., 192, see also Kibria 1990). This social networking is also powerfully represented in the narratives of Chinese American daughter-writers.[21]

One of Suyuan Woo's survival strategies was to form the Joy Luck Club in war-torn China. On a wretched day in summer, hot with moths and the sour-stink of the sewer and the rotting dead, amid the screaming of pigs and peasants being beaten, Suyuan Woo thinks up a gathering of women to balance each corner of her mah jong table. This first Joy Luck Club was composed of women who were not kin. Rather, they were from different backgrounds and parts of the country—a woman from a "rich family in Shanghai"; officers' wives from the middle class; and a woman from Nanking who is from the "lower class" who had married an old man. They were united in their harrowing experiences, especially the bombing raids over Kweilin by the Japanese during the 1940s. They were courageous survivors intent on keeping hope alive.

These women with joyful, wishful faces feasted on special *dyansying* foods, which they hoped would bring good fortune. They laughed and talked the night away with stories about the good times in the past and in the future. There was a sense of continuity, strength, shared pain, and resistance in the collective counter-memories of unrelated women bonding and talking-story to each other and talking-back to those who would steal their stories and lives. People thought that they were crazy women, possessed of demons—so unbecomingly "feminine" to be feasting in a city that was starving and eating rats. The general public could not fathom how such women who had lost generations in their families and were separated, husband from wife, brother from sister, daughter from mother, could celebrate in such a manner (JLC 24). But these women provided a means to redirect energies and emotions in more creative, life sustaining ways amid great terror, tragedy and dispersion. They nurtured and preserved each other during the long years of imperial-colonial aggression between nations, civil strife in China (among warlords, Chiang Kai-shek's Guomindang and Mao Zedong's Communist Party), the fragmentation of traditional patriarchal family networks. Amid multiple crises, these women found opportunities to create a women's community or family. It was not that they were blind to the horrific tragedies around them. Suyuan Woo, for example, talks about the period of chaos in the city of Kweilin:

> It's not that we had no heart or eyes for pain. We were all afraid. We all had our miseries. But to despair was to wish back for something already lost. Or to prolong what was already unbearable. How much can you wish for a favorite warm coat that hangs in the closet of a house that burned down with your mother and father inside of it? How long can you see in your mind arms and legs hanging from telephone wires and starving dogs running down the streets with half-chewed hands dangling from their jaws? What was worse, we asked among ourselves, to sit and wait for our own deaths with proper somber faces? Or to choose our own happiness? (JLC 25)

In the United States, Suyuan Woo continues this cultural tradition of the Joy Luck Club with a new extra-familial social network of women. As a woman, she finds solace and like-mindedness among her contemporaries—Chinese immigrant women like herself. "My mother could sense that the women of these families also had unspeakable tragedies they had left behind in China and hopes they couldn't begin to express in their fragile English" (JLC 20). This women's community is a voluntary association of four women starting new lives in the United States. Suyuan is able to form a women's talk-story and mah jong network, creating an extended sense of family among these women. They still speak Chinese dialects and possess the "Chinese mind" even under the assimilative pressures of the new country—unlike their daughters. They intimately understand each other's contexts—the dilemmas and alienation; the isolation from families left behind; the fears, guilt, and satisfactions in their present and future lives in America. The Joy Luck mothers choose to stick together and console each other's spirits in the darkest and in the best of times. Rather than a model of one individual woman sacrificing herself to the needs of her family as a mother and wife, there is a network of women loving, nurturing, learning, and caring for each collectively. Moreover, they help each other to find jobs and husbands, to invest wisely for their families, and to care for each others' husbands and children. In establishing these women's networks, the Joy Luck women construct more permeable and meaningful social and gendered spaces and practices for themselves within their families and communities. If this women's culture, this Joy Luck Club, is to continue, the Joy Luck mothers realize that they must expand their membership to include the next generation of Chinese American women who will take their places at the table—their daughters. They must bring them into a larger circle of dialogue and friendship among women.

Born with Connecting Hope:
How Daughters Can Honor Their Mothers

The mothers' education and protection of their daughters is not a one-way street. The daughters' stories demonstrate that they too have begun the arduous process of empowering themselves and their mothers. It is not always unrelieved war or friction between mother and daughter. In the stories of Chinese American daughter-writers like Tan and Kingston, it is not simply a daughter's rebellion or totalizing search for autonomy or independence from mother, family, or heritage that is the point of focus. Joy Luck daughters begin to see their mothers as women in their own rights. Some attempt to nurture their mothers, like Lena St. Clair, or to fulfill their mothers' unfinished quest and dreams, like Jing-mei Woo. The fact that the daughters tell half the stories in *The Joy Luck Club* must be taken into consideration, though their stories are often neglected in favor of the mothers' "more exotic Old China" stories.

A grown-up Waverly Jong, for example, begins to bridge the gap between her mother and herself. For most of her young life she felt that the walls between her and her mother were impregnable—thick and high. Like some of the other daughters, she thought her mother was out to destroy her at every turn. But Waverly suddenly makes a disarming and radical discovery about the stories she has invented around her relationship to her mother: "I saw what I had been fighting for: It was for me, a scared child, who had run away a long time ago to what I had imagined was a safer place. And hiding in this place, behind my invisible barriers, I knew what lay on the other side: Her side attacks. Her secret weapons. Her uncanny ability to find my weakest spots. But in the brief instant that I had peered over the barriers I could finally see what was really there: an old woman, a wok for her armor, a knitting needle for her sword" (*JLC* 183–84). The walls are fragile, penetrable, human: "With her smooth face, she [Lindo] looked like a young girl, frail, guileless, and innocent. One arm hung limply down the side of the sofa. Her chest was still. All her strength was gone. She had no weapons, no demons surrounding her. She looked powerless. Defeated" (*JLC* 180). Waverly begins to realize that she has projected some of her own personal fears and obsessions on to her mother. She had neglected to risk looking beyond her fears and stereotypes in order to understand Lindo Jong's social realities.

Lena St. Clair, the daughter, seeks ways to empower her sick mother. At first, Lena seems to be a nervous, sad, sensitive, confused girl—never knowing if her now living ghost of a mother will ever get well in their silent, unbalanced house.

There are feelings of horror and fear in the fragments of her mother's stories. But like Maxine in the *Woman Warrior*, Lena refuses to be silent. She refuses to allow unspeakable horrors and mysteries to devour her as they have her mother. Rather, Lena feels the need to confront the deeply embedded subtexts that haunt her mother and their relationship.

One day Lena is distracted by loud fighting voices from the other side of the wall which seem to suggest that a mother is continually arguing with and abusing her daughter. She imagines this daily scenario and feels the "terror of not knowing when it would ever stop" (*JLC* 110). She wonders whose situation is worse—hers or the girl's on the other side of wall—the noisy battles between the neighboring mother and daughter or the "stagnant silence" of her unhappy house? Despite the big fights, everyday the little girl on the other side of wall appears happy and unharmed—not the same girl she had projected from the voice on the other side of wall. In fact, this mother-daughter pair reconciles in a very emotional and demonstrative way; they shout, cry, laugh, and love. Lena is surprised by this outcome: she cries for joy because she had been wrong in her interpretation of the relationship between Mrs. Sorci and her daughter. Lena longs for this expressive, direct relationship between a mother and daughter.

In addition, Lena comes up with new ways of seeing in order to process the chaotic circumstances of her mother's life and her own. In this way, she holds on to a belief in the possibility of change. As Brave Orchid told Maxine in *The Woman Warrior*: "The difference between mad people and sane people is that sane people have variety when they talk-story. Mad people have only one story that they talk over and over" (*TWW* 184). Lena still sees bad things in her mind, but she finds way to transform them, to see how they can be changed. Lena conceives and enacts a new storyline between her mother and herself; they reverse roles, with the daughter nurturing and protecting her unstable mother. They are not exclusive roles. It is the young daughter Lena for now who wants to save her mother by inflicting the death of a thousand cuts. This symbolic slicing will cause her mother to scream and shout, cry out in terror and pain. It will break the deadening silence. This is a way for her to reach the silent mother, who is unable speak the traumas of her life. In this imaginative rescue, the mother's eyes are opened—illuminated; there is no blood, no shredded flesh—but pain that frees to "perfect understanding" (*JLC* 115). Ying-ying has experienced the worst, and there is no worse to be experienced. The hero-daughter pulls the mother out of the wall, rescuing her from a living death and returning her, hopefully, to health.[22]

Tan's last story, "A Pair of Tickets," situated in the mother's section "Queen Mother of the Western Skies," is told by June Jing-mei Woo, the daughter who has taken the place of her deceased mother at the mah jong table with the other Joy Luck mothers. There is a sense of the impending change of guard at the book's end which suggests the continuation and transformation, not closure, of the mother-daughter cycle of stories. *The Joy Luck Club* opens with her mother's death and Jing-mei's assumption of her mother's place in the Joy Luck club; it ends with the daughter in China, reacquainting herself with her sisters and relatives. She literally and symbolically "world travels" (Lugones 1990) to her mother's homeplaces. As Kingston said in the ending of *The Woman Warrior*: "Here is a story my mother told me, not when I was young, but recently, when I told her I also talk-story. The beginning is hers, the ending, mine" (*TWW* 240). In her own talk-story and life, Jing-mei continues her mother's story and her own into the future.

Jing-mei feels awkward and out of place in her mother's home territory. It is one of many homeplaces that must be continually deconstructed and reconstructed if she is to come to some personal understanding of herself in relation to mother and family.[23] Her aunts try to prepare her for the visit. But they seem foreign like her mother; they speak "in their special language, half in broken English, half in their own Chinese dialect" (*JLC* 34). They talk in circles. Just as Jing-mei Woo has little inner *chuming* of who her mother really was, she has no sense of the context or value of this group or its individual members. The group of unrelated aunties, who are also a part of Jing-mei's extended family, provides access to an enlarged sense of self-in-community.

The aunts want Jing-mei to go to Shanghai to find her lost sisters and tell them about their mother. Jing-mei's disappointing response to this: "What will I say? What can I tell them about my mother? I don't know anything. She was my mother" (*JLC* 40). She remembers her mother's indictment—"you don't even know little percent of me! How can you be me?" (*JLC* 27). She could barely understand her mother's language: "I talked to her in English, she answered back in Chinese" (*JLC* 34). The shock of this response sends a shiver down the back of the aunts who are also concerned about their own daughters remembering them. They make her very aware of what is part of her responsibility to her mother and to herself—to tell the story of her mother and her life: "Tell them stories she told you, lessons she taught, what you know about her mind that has become your mind" (*JLC* 40). In a refreshing change of perspective, Jing-mei begins to see their dilemma—not from a daughter's point of view but from a mother's perspective:

> They are frightened. In me, they see their own daughters, just as ignorant, just as unmindful of all the truths and hopes they have brought to America. They see daughters who grow impatient when their mothers talk in Chinese, who think they are stupid when they explain things in fractured English. They see that joy and luck do not mean the same to their daughters, that to these closed American-born minds "joy luck" is not a word, it does not exist. They see daughters who will bear grandchildren born without any connecting hope passed from generation to generation. (*JLC* 40–1)

As a grown-up daughter of thirty-six, she is heading to China in the late 1980s for the first time. She has never given much thought to what it meant to be "Chinese"—except rather superficially and negatively. She slowly realizes the importance of moving beyond the notions of Orientalist exotica that she herself has appropriated and internalized about her "Chineseness." For a long while, she dismissed or neglected an integral part of her familial history and her mother's talk stories. With her mother's death, Jing-mei asked herself questions about her mother to sustain her own grief, to convince herself that she really cared for her mother. With the visit to China, she begins a serious quest to discover the particularities of her mother's life story.

In "A Pair of Tickets," Jing-mei becomes a representative of her Chinese mother and a witness to her life in the United States; and her sisters, too, mirror a facet of her mother left in China. Jing-mei is carrying her mother's dreams back to China, an imaginary homeplace she has never been to before, except through fragments of story shared by her mother. In Guangzhou and Shanghai, she is introduced to relatives whom she has never met or heard about. She is not fluent in Cantonese or Mandarin dialects, nor in the culture and customs of her rural Toishan relatives or urban Shanghai half-sisters. (She does, however, remember a few Chinese phrases and curses.) Jing-mei feels awkward in her appearance. In more ways than one, she worries that she could not pass for "true Chinese," if the authenticating criteria is restricted purely to such things as language, culture, geography, phenotype. She is an outsider-insider, an "overseas Chinese," who is critically beginning to think about what being "Chinese" or "Chinese American" signifies in a more permeable field of possibility. Jing-mei hints of Mongol stock already intermixed in her diverse family bloodlines, which might account for her towering over her "true Chinese" relatives. Her sisters are raised in a Chinese Muslim household. These diverse familial genealogies suggest the hybridity that actually exists in the formations of national (or racial-ethnic) identity, culture, or family, despite hegemonic narratives which attempt to project a fixed, unified homogeneity, whether in Chinese or American contexts.

Moreover, the city of Guangzhou in which the extended family gathers is neither the war-torn China of her parents' experiences nor the frightening "Communist China" represented in the social-political Cold War milieu of the 1950s. Rather, Jing-mei encounters her family in a modern, sophisticated and cosmopolitan city, a financial and cultural center of China. The hotel they stay at is a hodgepodge of shopping/video arcades and restaurants; the rooms are equipped with color TVs, wet bars and marble bathrooms. Jing-mei orders hamburgers, French fries, and apple pie à la mode at the request of her delighted Chinese relatives while she herself fantasizes on a multi-coursed Chinese meal. In this eclectic milieu, Jing-mei's search to understand the vibrant making of "Chinese" identity is, in part, both a precarious and ambiguous transnational, diasporic legacy and project that is constantly negotiated and constructed in multiple, fluid, and intersecting frames of reference in and between China and the United States.

In the hotel room, there is the slow resurrection of familial history, which brings the family together. Her father, Canning Woo, fills in the story of her mother. Jing-mei, in a reversal, asks to hear her mother's story in Chinese—her mother's first language.[24] There is the retelling of her mother's flight from war-torn Kweilin, her near-death situation, the leaving of her daughters to the good will of fate, the discovery of a kind-hearted couple who would care for them, and how she had named the twins—Chwun Yu and Chwun Hwa (Spring Rain and Spring Flower) and Jing-mei. Despite enormous changes in her life and circumstances, Suyuan maintained her social and emotional affiliations to the lost segment of her family and community. She enacted this social bond through her ceaseless and hopeful search for her lost twins till her death. These talk-stories give Jing-mei a more intimate understanding of her mother's suffering, guilt, love, endurance, and courage; they identify boundaries to cross and new social and political sites at which to act.

In the northern cosmopolitan city Shanghai (see Buruma 1996), the final reunion among the sisters is a living reminder of her mother and her long-cherished wish. There are triples of mother anew. Jing-mei makes the realization that the significant part of what is "Chinese" about her is embodied in the lived relational ties and commitments she makes to an eclectic family, and to the collective stories shared despite the substantial differences among them. Family and mother are nothing to be ashamed of, dismissed, or hidden; they are an integral part of who she is. Despite Suyuan's earlier doubts in her daughter's abilities to know her, in the end, the maternal and cultural practices are slowly being reconstructed and lovingly reclaimed by a prodigal Chinese American daughter.

The critic María Lugones, in discussing her own "arrogant perceptions" of her mother, focuses on the dilemmas and obstacles that a daughter confronts in learning to love and identify with her mother. She believes that she was socialized into a destructive perception and enactment of love, which was really a form of abusing and denying her mother as well as herself. Lugones does not want to continue to love or identify with the oppression of her mother; she does not want to be an oppressor of another woman. Such socialization limits the possibilities of the mother and daughter for autonomy and self-definition as women as well as allies. To identify with mother as a woman without "arrogant perception" is to imagine and choose a new definition of love and freedom that is not exploitative or destructive to one or the other.

> I am emphasizing . . . that the failure of love lies in part in the failure to identify [with mother]. Loving my mother also required that I see with her eyes, that I go into my mother's world, that I see both of us as we are constructed in her world, that I witness her own sense of herself from within her world. Only through this traveling to her "world" could I identify with her because only then could I cease to ignore her and to be excluded and separate from her. Only then could I see her as a subject even if one subjected and only then could I see how meaning could arise fully between us. We are fully dependent on each other for the possibility of being understood without which we are not intelligible, we do not make sense, we are not solid, visible, integrated; we are lacking. Traveling to each other's "worlds" enables us to be through loving each other. (Lugones 1990, 394)

I believe that the recognition and reclamation of the social and emotional bonds between a Chinese mother and her daughter, in counterpoint to the images and definitions of women in interlocking patriarchal, capitalist, and imperialist discourses, can be a form of political and historical power and subversion not only for women but for their families and communities. Such a perspective makes visible women's everyday activities and locations in negotiating survival and resistance. To name and define each other—for ourselves, by ourselves, and of ourselves—is a return to the complex dynamics of agency at the multiple social sites we intimately inhabit as women.

Notes

1. For further information on the culture and society of women in China see Belden (1949), Chin (1931), Croll (1978, 1995), Honig (1986), Ko (1997), Mann (1997), Ono (1989), Siu (1981), Stockard (1989), Watson and Ebrey (1991), and Wolf and Witke (1974).

2. See Tan (1989). All references to this edition will appear in the text with abbreviation *JLC*.

3. Lani Guinier refers to her discomfort in returning to Yale to give a speech. She finds herself speaking under the portraits of white male Yale faculty, which remind her of her own former training into becoming a "gentleman":

   > No empowering memories stirred my voice. I had no personal anecdotes for the profound senses of alienation and isolation caught in my throat every time I opened my mouth. Nothing resonated there in that room for a Black woman, even after my ten years as an impassioned civil rights attorney. Instead I promptly began my formal remarks, trying as hard as I could to find my voice in a room in which those portraits spoke louder than I ever could. I spoke slowly and carefully, never once admitting, except by my presence on the podium, that I had ever been a student at that school and in that room before. I summoned as much authority as I could to be heard over the sounds of silence erupting from those giant images of gentlemen hanging on the wall, and from my own ever-present memory of slowly disappearing each morning and becoming a *gentleman*. (1997, 74 and see Wing 1997)

4. In Tan's discussion about an old family photograph of women relatives in China, she notes that the unspoken secrets and tragedies of the women in her family are the reasons that frightening caveats have been passed along in her family like heirlooms. "Each of the women in the photograph suffered a terrible fate, my mother said" (Tan 1991a, 90). Similarly, An-mei's grandmother seeks to recover and protect a precious "good daughter" through her granddaughter by passing on the severe lessons of basic survival she has learned within this culture. She does this even at the expense of destroying her own daughter and their bonds with each other. An-mei is the recipient of the caveats and lessons not practiced by her own disobedient mother; she fills in for the absent presence of her mother—the "bad daughter" according to the laws of the patriarchy. "That is when I began to understand the stories Popo taught me, the lessons I had to learn for my mother. "When you lose your face, An-mei," Popo often said, "it is like dropping your necklace down a well. The only way you can get it back is to fall in after it" (*JLC* 44).

An-mei is forced to take in the stories and language describing a mother as an example of how not to be a woman. She absorbs the lessons her mother had neglected. She absorbs the language used to describe her mother's life and actions in order to survive. This socialization is not easily forgotten, even as she tries to rebel against it. Unfortunately, her Popo does not seem able or willing to teach An-mei or her own daughter how to subvert the injustices against women in such an oppressive system. It is not hard to understand why, after years of compromise, capitulation, drudgery, or coming against the system, women give up.

5. For an extended description of the decadent social milieu of Shanghai in the period between 1918 and 1939, see Sergeant (1990).

6. See Ruddick (1989, 13–27). Ruddick discusses the three demands—for preservation, growth, and social acceptance—that constitute maternal work: "To be a mother is to be committed to meeting these demands by works of preservative love, nurturance, and training" (ibid. 17). See Daly and Reddy (1991), especially "Introduction," (pp. 1–18) for discussion of a non-essentialist definition of mothering that is based on caregiving—a choice that is open to those who give birth and to those who do not. Furthermore, they discuss the work of mothers who

    actively resist the powerful/powerless split, who reach out to other mothers in attempts to subvert patriarchal power through female alliances, who perceive mothering not strictly in biological or in property terms but also in social terms, as a collective responsibility. These mothers find in the practice of mothering a model of social and political action. [They] extend their love of their own children outward, finding in that very intense personal love a less personal but nonetheless powerful love of all children and concern for the future of the human race. (Dale and Reddy 1991, 7)

7. See Yanagisako's critique of Asian American studies' concern for a more working-class orientation to teaching Asian American history and to what constitutes historical consciousness. She asserts that there needs to be recognition of "more than one historical consciousness." Besides privileging the proud history of the working-class Chinatown communities, Asian Americanists must also be open to discussions of the successes, social and economic mobility, and political organizations of various Asians in the U.S., especially in the post-World War II period (Yanagisako 1995, 282–83). She wants to see more work done on third- and later- generations of Asian Americans, and on those who have moved outside their original communities. This is not to fall into the trap of suggesting that every Asian American individual or ethnic group is a total success story (the model minority stereotype) or that other subordinated racial-ethnic groups in the U.S. simply need to emulate Asian Americans to achieve success. It is clear that there is still a great deal of discrimination against Asians in the United States and abroad, and there are still many Asians who have yet to overcome the effects of decades of marginalization.

8. See Yamada's poem "I Learned to Sew" in *Desert Run* (1988). Also see Glenn (1986) on Japanese domestic workers and their reasons for working hard to give their children better opportunities in America.

9. See Collins for her discussion of hardworking African American mothers and their relationship with their daughters in women's fiction. According to Gloria Wade-Gayles, African American mothers are so often busy surviving as workers that they do not have the leisure to display affection though they may be strong and devoted (qtd. in Collins 1990, 127). Furthermore, Gloria Joseph believes that "for far too many Black mothers, the demands of providing for children in interlocking systems of oppression are sometimes so demanding that they have neither the time nor the patience for affection. And yet most Black daughters love and admire their mothers and are convinced that their mothers truly love them" (ibid.).

10. In an interview, Tan describes a Chinese mother-daughter relationship in terms of the
    metaphor of the umbilical cord . . . which gets stretched over time, whether it's the mother or the daughter who severs it or tries to pull it tighter, part of that is individual and part is cultural. In a Chinese family, the mother pulls very tightly on the bond to a point where [the daughter] asks, 'Why can't I know about such and such?' and the [mother answers], 'Because I haven't put it in your mind yet.' The notion that your mother puts everything in your mind—the blank slate theory—is part of Chinese culture. (qtd. in Pearlman and Henderson 1990, 16)

11. Mirror imagery is pervasive in Tan's book. For instance, Lindo Jong looks into the mirror and discovers a core self. Waverly also looks into the hairdresser's mirror. Jing-mei looks into the mirror to discover her secret "prodigy" self. There are also references to mothers as mirrors to their daughters and to the placement of mirrors in rooms.

12. Note the dominant media images in U.S. history and culture of Chinese women as prostitutes or indentured slaves: see Gronewold (1982), Hirata (1979), Hershatter (1991), and Tong (1994). Women, like Lindo Jong, are forced to become invisible for the sake of safety.

13. See, for example, Davis (1983); Dill (1988); Glenn (1985, 1986); Glenn, Chang, and Forcey (1994); Hurtado (1989); Hondagneu-Sotelo (1995); Kibria (1990); Romero, Hondagneu-Sotelo and Ortiz (1997); Zinn (1995); Zinn and Dill (1994); and Yung (1995). They foreground the great difficulties that racial-ethnic women encounter in the social, economic, and cultural maintenance of their families.

14. See Yamada for discussion on the "cult of perfect language" (1990).

15. "Matrophobia" is "the fear not of one's mother or of motherhood but of *becoming one's mother*" (Sukenick qtd. in Rich 1986b, 235). It is a way for a daughter to disavow the condition of her mother as a victimized and compromised Chinese immigrant woman, who constantly reminds her of a woman's subordinate status in culture and society. "Easier by far to hate and reject a mother outright than to see beyond her to the forces acting upon her. But where a mother is hated to the point of matrophobia there may also be a deep underlying pull toward her, a dread that if one relaxes one's guard one will identify with her completely" (ibid. 236).

16. See Watson and Ebrey (1991) and Stockard (1989) on marriage in China.

17. María Lugones explains the importance of a double consciousness and cultural memory for individual and political survival. She discusses the trickster role as a "survival-rich" tactic in this regard:

    > I identify myself as myself through memory and retain myself as different in memory. I can be in a particular "world" [such as the Anglo world] and have a double image of myself. . . . This is a very familiar and recognizable phenomenon to the outsider to the mainstream in some *central cases*: when in one "world" I animate, for example, that "world's" caricature or stereotype of the person I am in the other "world." I can have both images of myself, and to the extent that I can materialize or animate both images at the same time, I become an ambiguous being. This is very much a part of trickery and foolery. It is worth remembering that the trickster and the fool are significant characters in many dominant or outsiders' cultures. (Lugones 1990, 398)

    Also consider native American Indian folktales about the trickster coyote or African American folk tales about Brer Rabbit.

18. The Aunts also induct Jing-mei into the finer points of mah jong which require the "head, very tricky. You must watch what everybody else throws away and keep that in your head as well" (JLC 33). It is a game of strategy—like chess in American gamesmanship. The mothers are training their daughters to be confident and cunning with their minds—not brainless lotus blossoms.

19. The image of Ying-ying's history of erasure as a woman can also be linked to the story about her patrician father's recitation of a poem he is deciphering from ancient stone inscriptions. He notes that certain words were "worn off the slab, its meaning washed away by centuries of rain, almost lost to posterity forever" (JLC 71). But as a male scholar, trained in ancient history and literature, he is given the privilege of solving the missing text. Clifford St. Clair, the Anglo-American male who marries Ying-ying, continues her erasure in the United States.

20. See Andrews' discussion (1986) on African American narrative modes, especially "free storytelling" and the use of first-person point-of-view. Also remember Kingston's reference to the discovery of the English "I" as a form of personal empowerment that allows her to speak in her own voice and from her own experiences and standpoints as a Chinese American woman writer against racist and sexist discourses. In this way, she is able to recover her affiliations with mother, family, and community from a critical distance.

21. See Ko (1997) for a fascinating discussion of the formations of women's culture and communities in seventeenth-century China. She challenges the simplistic and reductive ahistorical notions of women as total victims within Confucian patriarchal formations, thereby returning an active social agency to Chinese women in negotiating the construction of subjectivity, familial-social identity, and gender relations in China. The notion of the Joy Luck Club network may have social-historical links with women's culture in China as well as with in the United States.

22. This reminds one of the women trapped in the wallpaper in Charlotte Gilman's *The Yellow Wallpaper* (Gilman 1980).

23. See Pratt (1984, 9–63) on leaving home to see it anew.

24. See Quan (1990, 212–20).

7

THE HEART NEVER TRAVELS: FATHERS IN THE MOTHER-DAUGHTER STORIES OF MAXINE HONG KINGSTON, AMY TAN, AND FAE MYENNE NG

In honor of my father and five brothers—all beloved and loving men.

> *"Chinaman's do make lousey fathers. I know. I have one," says Tam Lum. [Tam] suggests that he is "a lousey father" himself when he says, "I want my kids to forget me."*
> Frank Chin, Jeffrey Paul Chan, Lawson Fusao Inada and Shawn Hsu Wong
> *"Introduction: Fifty Years of Our Whole Voice"*

> *what we hold in our heart is what matters. The heart never travels.*
> Leon Leong
> Fae Myenne Ng, *Bone*

Extending the Mother–Daughter Heart Work: The Stories of Men and Families

In the 1960s, 1970s, and 1980s, women were vibrantly and fully engaged in critically recovering and examining the stories of women, especially those of mothers and daughters (chap. 1). But for many Asian American women writers it was important to reclaim the stories of Asian men, especially fathers, and of their marginalized families and communities as well. In the "Letter to Ma," Merle Woo (1981) writes about the love, anger, and frustration she feels toward her mother, but turns her personal struggles into a form of social-political activism that embraces a mother, who, as a working class immigrant woman, suffered greatly in the United States. At the same time, Woo's activist writing recognizes the multiple oppressions of racism, sexism, and classism confronted by her father; and the psychic and social violence that humiliates him in front of his family and community, that grinds him down to the bone as well (see also Quan 1990, Kam 1989, and Nunez 1995).[1] Through their stories, Chinese American daughter-writers like Kingston, Tan, and

Ng do not leave their distressed families or communities behind—even when fiercely critical, they return to these traumatic sites of memory. In their temporary, and sometimes necessary, separations and "world travelings" (Lugones 1991), the daughter-narrators—Maxine, June Woo, and Leila Fu—remain deeply affiliated to the primary homeplaces of family and community.

The stories of Chinese (and Asian) American men are still wide-open territory for recovery work. Although Asian American history has represented some important stories of Chinese American men, these stories still often concentrate on the working class "sojourner" or "bachelor society" period of Chinese American history or on men's economic work history (Yanagisako 1995). It is crucial to *continue* the stories of Asian American men and women beyond the early period of a predominantly Chinatown male society and its history of prostitution.[2] For example, it is crucial to reconstruct men's stories from the 1930s through the 1950s, when single and married men were adjusting to the presence of, and reunification with, Chinese women, children, and extended kin immigrating in greater numbers to the United States and establishing new and more permanent communities in Chinatown. The late 1980s and 1990s witnessed growing interest in critical examinations of the constructions of masculinity, but this new wave of masculinity studies has mainly focused on the constructions of white or Black constructions of manhood. Asian American constructions of masculinity should also be a part, and a central part, of this discussion. It is very possible that these marginalized masculinities can suggest more alternative, open-ended, or resisting formations of masculinity than have been previously theorized.[3]

Kingston, Tan, and Ng focus on the struggles of women, especially as they are specifically situated in constantly negotiated domestic and familial spaces. Their daughter-narrators work to tell the frequently silenced, and often traumatic, stories of women who raise families and face daily injustice and humiliation, and attempt to name and work out their own multiple emotional and social tensions and relationships. In excavating this psychosocial site, they begin to re-examine the nature of their relationships to each other and, in this process, to *earn* continuously active and hopeful affiliations and histories together.

It is in first learning to grapple with their mothers that these daughters find critical tools with which to sustain and expand an empathetic understanding, *which is neither arrogant contempt nor patronizing pity*, to Chinese American men, families and communities as well. That is, in doing the intimate heart work within themselves and with their mothers, they construct a complex, nuanced "vocabulary of feeling," as Leila Fu calls it, that can begin to tease out how it feels to live in new familial and cultural sites (B 18). This emergent vocabulary is part of the ongoing struggle for more liberating and imaginative forms of identity and community. Such narratives of self and struggle enrich our exploration into the dynamics of dislocation, adaptation, resistance, and recreation.

In portraying the feelings which are continually negotiated within the daily, practical interactions and sites of Chinese American mothers and daughters in their critical fictions, Kingston, Tan, and Ng attempt to represent the lives and recover the stories of fathers in their families. The daughter-narrators do not represent their fathers as unloved authoritarian patriarchs who are purely oppressive or conservative figures in their lives. These writers understand, for example, that Chinese American immigrant working-class fathers, symbolic patriarchs that they may be in their own families, do not have privilege, power, or status within a historically constructed racial-ethnic hierarchy that privileged white males and their families and communities enjoy. Chinese American men were often forced to find work in domestic occupations devalued as "women's work"; in popular mainstream culture, they have been represented as passive, effeminate, and docile. These modes of racializing, sexualizing, and genderizing subordinated Chinese American men with subordinated Chinese women seriously affected the relationships between them. In certain Asian American masculinist, nationalist, and racial-ethnic discourses (see chap. 4), this constant association of men with feminine disempowerment and with women is seen as a barrier to a reclamation of a specific type of authenticating warrior manhood (and womanhood).

Since Chinese (and Asian) American men have not had the opportunity to fit seamlessly into white notions of masculinity in America, I believe there is a window of opportunity for Asian American men to seriously engage Asian American feminisms and to articulate and enact more transformative, democratizing notions of masculinity. It would also seem more fruitful to seriously engage in the making of practices that have the potential to reconfigure ways of theorizing and articulating social and political affiliations in American society.

But rather than engaging with Asian American feminist perspectives and with women as potential allies—a potentially *radical* form of partnership, considering the racist and sexist oppression suffered by both Asian American women and men—a number of cultural nationalists identify with the socially and emotionally deforming and exclusionary practices of a white racialized patriarchal masculinity that have disempowered them as well as women, families, and communities. They have tried to empower Chinese American men by valorizing certain traditional forms of masculinity as heroic, or by focusing on the tragedy of not being able to be traditional—for example, the regret of not having been "men" enough to protect their women or to be authoritarian patriarchs in control of their women and children.

A number of dominant and oppositional masculinist discourses, for example, do not construct the fatherhood of Chinese American men—men forced to confront terrible humiliation for the sake of the family—as heroic. More importantly, such discourses do not recognize the potentially democratizing and improvisational political formations of Chinese American masculinity that do not duplicate or reify traditional patriarchal-nationalist ideals. That is, some men take gender risks by adjusting to dual or multi-income families, to taking care of children and doing housework, to maintaining a nurturing, stable home environment, and being with independent women. Making acts of transition between ways of life and gender systems, becoming a different sort of man may *seem* like being less of a man from some perspectives, but it can also be seen as heroic work rather than as "dysfunctional," "pathological," "effeminizing," "sell-out," or "model minority."[4]

In attempting to recover more diverse and constructive experiences of Chinese American men, Kingston, Tan, and Ng do not dismiss the sexist practices of fathers—practices that continue to undermine the ways families can supply and nurture empowering social and political energies. The daughters in the stories simultaneously critique their fathers' sexist (as well as racist) practices, and sensitively assess their multiple locations. They tell the stories of fathers at the tangled intersections and distances of love, pain, and anger. These daughters do not have a purely antagonistic relationship with Chinese American fathers or men.

Chinese American (and other Asian American) men as fathers, after all, are crucial to familial and community building processes, especially considering the long legal and political history of denying them access to their families and communities in the United States. Kingston, Tan, and Ng recuperate father stories from women's standpoints, which are attentive to the emotional, social, and physical trauma and negotiations within their families and communities that are variously affected by the inequities of race, ethnicity, class, and gender. They tell the complex stories of their fathers in the intimate social spaces of the domestic and familial as a form of grassroots *realpolitik*. Thomas Laqueur remarks that "the history of men and therefore man-as-father has been subsumed under the history of a pervasive patriarchy—the history of inheritance and legitimate descent, the history of public authority and its transmission over generations. Because men are thought to belong to the 'public sphere of the marketplace and women to the private sphere of the family' (a decidedly nineteenth-century perspective on gender roles), men have not been addressed according to their domestic role as fathers" (Clark 1996, 25). As Raymond Williams reminds us moreover, "social experience, just because it is social, does not have to appear in any ways exclusively in . . . overt public forms. In its very quality and social reality it penetrates, it is already at the roots of relationships of every kind. We need not look only, in a transforming history, for direct or public historical event and response. It can appear as radically and as authentically in what is apparently, what is actually, personal or family experience" (Williams 1970, 65). It is at the merged private/domestic work sites of interaction in subordinated Chinese American families that Kingston, Tan, and Ng foreground and imaginatively explore the dynamic social and emotional formations of politicized and historicized subjectivities and identities.

Part I
Airing out Dirty Laundry: Maxine Engaging the Silent Father

In the second part of her memoir, *China Men*, originally published in 1977, Kingston concentrates on stories of Chinese American forefathers—the hardworking grandfathers who carved out granite mountains, the risk-taking, rebel men who fought back and talked back—who refused to be Crocker's railroad "pets." She reconstructs their gorgeous physicality and sexuality, their longings for the company of Chinese men, women, families, and ethnic communities. She portrays the toll suffered by Chinese men in this country and reclaims their imaginative life and inventive tactics and humor, which helped them to endure and remake this wasteland of a dream called "Gold Mountain." Few critics have substantially focused on this part of Kingston's work. They have focused more attention on condemning or praising her mother-daughter stories rather than on understanding them *in relation* to her stories about Chinese American men. Even Kingston, in referring to her stories about both women and men, dislikes the "overpraising of [her] daughter [*The Woman Warrior*] and the rudeness toward [her] sons [*China Men* and *Tripmaster Monkey*]."[5]

Besides recovering this early Chinese American male history, Kingston also tells the story of the Chinese father, BaBa, in *China Men*. As a daughter, she wants very much to know the father's stories, to hear her father talk-story, to understand his life as well as the nature of his suffering and (psychic and physical) violence. "I want to know what makes you scream and curse, and what you're thinking when you say nothing, and why when you do talk, you talk differently from Mother" (CM 15).[6] BaBa spews out hatred at his daughters: "You scared us. Every day we listened to you swear, 'Dog vomit. Your mother's cunt. Your mother's smelly cunt.' You slammed the iron on the shirt while muttering, 'Stink pig. Mother's cunt.' Obscenities" (CM 12). What is, she wonders, at the buried root of his cruelty, his screams and nightmares, the depression, violence, and silence which affects the life of his young family.

The daughter-narrator Maxine remembers the long, frightening and "articulate silences" of her distant father. "Worse than the swearing and the nightly screams were your silences when you punished us by not talking. You rendered us invisible, gone. MaMa told us to say Good Morning to you whether or not you answered. You kept up a silence for weeks and months. We invented the terrible things you were thinking: That your mother had done you some unspeakable wrong, and so you left China forever. That you hate daughters. That you hate China. . . . " (CM 14). Maxine portrays a difficult, withdrawn, abusive, and self-abusive man, whom she nevertheless loves and seeks to critique and challenge as part of that love.

Maxine acknowledges the difficult struggles of a Chinese father attending to the daily tasks of maintaining the survival of his family: "We knew that is was to feed us you had to endure demons and physical labor. You screamed wordless male screams that jolted the house upright and staring in the middle of the night. 'It's BaBa,' we children told one another" (CM 12–13). She points out, at the same time, how the oppressed father can very quickly turn to victimize, rather than identify with, the oppressed women in the family who toil, bone-tired, beside him. In her talk-story, Maxine responds to her father's sexist behavior with the story of Tang Ao, a story that comes just before the chapter "The Father from China." Tang Ao is a man forced to become a woman in the Land of Women, supposedly in North America.

The literary critic David Leiwei Li observes that forms of oppression suffered by Chinese American women are also suffered by Chinese men in America. That is, "by mythically presenting the emasculation of China Men in America" through the story of Tang Ao, Kingston not only portrays the victimization of men, but also their "previous participation in the cultural subjugation of women so that the victim-victimizer formation merges to reveal that female identity is as much an arbitrary cultural and historical construction as the identity of 'Chinamen.' Her switching of alterity displaces the dominating social group into an imaginative identification with the pain and suffering of being the Other" (Li 1990, 487–88). Cherríe Moraga observes the ways such identifications are lost in minsaming and misrecognizing ourselves in dominant discourses and practices that divide people and communities.

> It is not really difference the oppressor fears so much as similarity. He fears he will discover in himself the same aches, the same longings as those of the people he has shitted on. He fears the immobilization threatened by his own incipient guilt. He fears he will have to change his life once he has seen himself in the bodies of the people he has called different. He fears the hatred, anger and vengeance of those he has hurt. . . . We are afraid to look at how we have failed each other. We are afraid to see how we have taken the values of our oppressor into our hearts and turned them against ourselves and one another. (Moraga 1981, 32)

Moreover, Li notes that the "socially enforced feminization of Chinese manhood [especially in the domestic spaces and occupations they were forced to occupy in this country] leads to another discovery when one begins to perceive the myth and the book in general as a male story envisioned by a female writer . . . who voices her fellow men's valor and anger and redeems them from cultural misconception and historical obscurity" (Li 1990, 487–88).

As part of this recovery of manhood, Maxine indicts her father's sexism in the family, its way of replicating patriarchal violence in physical, emotional, and social terms; she does not dismiss the ugliness in her father's behavior. Strong and tough as her mother Brave Orchid is in her former life in China and in holding the U.S. homeplace together, Maxine tells us in *The Woman Warrior* that she is not interested in purely replicating her mother's life or practices by remaining silent about sexism. For in many ways, this domestic violence is also of a piece with the violence enacted in the larger society, which exploits poor, subordinated, and racialized ethnic families, dividing communities from within and without.

In countering her father's sexism, Maxine tells the story of a paternal sojourner grandfather, Ah Goong. Ah Goong's desire for a daughter was so great that he traded Maxine's BaBa for a little girl. To choose a girl over a boy, especially one with the potential to be a scholar, is an incredibly "crazy idiot" act to everyone in the village community. Ah Goong displays his penis on the dinner table "worrying it, wondering at it, asking why it had given him four sons and no daughter, chastising it, asking it whether it were yet capable of producing the daughter of his dreams" (CM 21). This family history subverts the patriarchal valorization of boys in China and reveals a personal reason for her father's sexist behavior towards women. It also subverts the notion that all Chinese men are sexist and incapable of transgressing patriarchal values and norms.

Maxine also tells the story of Brave Orchid's father who "was an unusual man in that he valued girls: he taught all his daughters how to read and write" (CM 30). Born amid the fluid transnational and transcultural migration and interaction of ideas from all parts of Asia, Europe, and the Americas in the late 1800s and early 1900s, Brave Orchid is the product of a revolutionary roiling of new ideas in China. She is represented as bright, clever, independent-minded, and modern. Maxine retells the story of her parents' wedding day and her mother's unconventional behavior as a bride: "The wedding guests gasped, wanting to reach out and stop the comb; they had also been uneasy at the hairwashing and at hearing the bad words, *death, army, rifle,* and at seeing the woman riding above the men. There was a suspense, a shock to see the bride dressed in funeral white [red is the festive wedding color], to see her feet and butt touch the winnower, which touches food, and to watch the burning of the paper horses like a funeral" (CM 32). On their wedding night, Brave Orchid leaps out of bed and sits facing her new husband "so closely that there was no room for her to kowtow; the kowtowing-to-the-husband part of the ceremony is skipped" (CM 32). Brave Orchid, that is, refuses to kowtow to her husband as part of the wedding ritual that symbolizes her obedience to him. Rather than depicting a fantasy of passive or prostituted women, Maxine represents Brave Orchid in the very process of enacting alternative forms of culture and community in China, which are generated in the social-historical circulation of revolutionary ideas within and among cultures and nations.

As a writer-scholar, Maxine's father, moreover, is revealed as a middling traditional scholar, who does not take top honors in writing for his exams and does not achieve a career in high governmental service. He gets a position in the village teaching mediocre students; not bad for a first-generation scholar. However, he feels his skills as a scholar are wasted on his students; he longs for a more leisurely scholarly life of peace, quiet reflection, and poetry. As a young father, he feels restless and bored, caught in a rut. The stories of village men (including the male family sojourners) upon returning from Gold Mountain capture his imagination with their stories of adventure, wealth, and freedom. He sets his mind on heading to the United States.

Despite the sexism enacted by Chinese American fathers in their families, daughters, like their mothers, keep and tell the stories of their menfolk. But these family stories about fathers enact the power of women in making and remaking culture. They are not complete stories, but fragments of men's stories recovered and retold by women.[7] Maxine acknowledges the great difficulties in accessing the stories of men in her family; the unknowability, for example, of a father who is often silent, withdrawn, who does not tell his stories: "You say with the few words and silences: No stories. No past. No China" (CM 14).[8] But in the inventive space of his silence, she creates the opportunity to tell his story from a daughter's talk-story view.

The story of BaBa's arrival in the U.S.—legal and illegal versions—are imagined and reinvented by the daughter since she cannot ascertain what the true story about his entry is. Even the patriarchal father has his moments of creating a new hybrid identity and of resisting traditional gender notions. Rather than teaching, the Chinese father makes his way to New York and lives a laundryman's existence in New York among his male friends.[9] Life is hard, work in the laundry tedious, but the free time is exhilarating: The Chinese father lives like a married "bachelor," who carouses with his friends, tours New York in a grand fashion, rides planes, goes to the movies and dance halls (he was a ladies' man with the blondes), visits Coney Island and captures this making-of-a-new-man in photographs which he sends home to the village with his remittances. He is becoming a "sophisticated New York gentleman."

BaBa refashions himself as "Ed" (after Thomas Edison, the inventor), a modern man, literally and vainly "well-suited" to be part of the glitter dust of the 1920s Jazz Age in New York, when men lusted after the Gatsbian green light of romantic possibility in the American Dream—just beyond their reach: "On Saturday Ed . . . went to Fifth Avenue to shop for clothes. With his work pants, Ed wore his best dress shirt, a silk tie, gray silk socks, good leather shoes with pointed toes, and a straw hat. At a very good store, he paid two hundred dollars cash for a blue and gray pinstripe suit, the most expensive suit he could find. In the three-way mirror, he looked like Fred Astaire" (CM 63). In the superficial mirroring flash of windows and hubcaps, Ed and his laundryman friends see themselves as "all the same Americans." It is only momentary euphoria—broken by a band of "white demons" who come up behind the new China men and knock their hats off and stomp on them. Ed's flippant response to this troubling incident, "It must be a custom" (CM 63). This "custom" foreshadows a nightmarish side of the Dream that has captivated him.[10]

Ed does not want to go back to China, and toward this goal, he creates a pocket of opportunity for his wife to be educated in preparation for a life in the West as a modern woman. As Linda Ching Sledge notes, the Chinese father is "heroic, too, in his ambitions for himself and for his family. It is he who defies the ancient edict that 'a woman too well educated is apt to create trouble' by encouraging his wife to become a doctor" (Sledge 1980, 9). He works hard to pay for her scientific education as well as her passage to America. He risks the scrutiny of his citizenship in applying for her immigration. Ed wants her to "enter legally and gracefully, no question of asking a lady to ride the sea in a box or to swim to an unwatched shore" (CM 68). This fortunate circumstance reminds me of Pierrette Hondagneu-Sotelo's point that "men participate, albeit sometimes unwittingly, in the dismantling of patriarchy. Migration and settlement introduce new challenges and pressures for change in both women's and men's behavior" (1994, 192).

Having been separated for fifteen years in a split household family, Ed and Brave Orchid are different people. Moreover, she returns to her husband after a glorious and independent period in her life in the school of midwifery and as a doctor, and he has adventured through the American landscape as a "new China man." The reunification of these two people provides an opportunity for rethinking not only a relationship but a culture and community in the United States. The circumstances are, however, very, very different. Brave Orchid, doctor-midwife in her former life in China, must now take on arduous work in the New York laundry. BaBa's Chinese cronies in the New York laundry cheat him out of his share of the business partnership. Husband and wife move cross country to get a fresh start, to Stockton,

California, where he manages an illegal gambling house to support his growing family of six children.

Ed is an expensive and flashy dresser, making his presence felt about Stockton Chinatown by demonstrating his success. This fascinates his daughter: "He [had] the power of going places where nobody else went, and making places belong to him. I could smell his presence. He owned special places the way he owned special things. . . ." (CM 238). But during the 1940s, the gambling house is raided and closed down, and Maxine's father becomes disheartened and suffers a severe depression and withdraws from life and family. Ed has great difficulty managing the various failures in his life; there is growing disillusionment about his ability to maintain a traditional notion of manhood in U.S. society. "He was always home. He sat in his chair and stared, or he sat on the floor and stared. . . . He suddenly turned angry and quiet" (CM 247). He refuses to speak, starts to drink, and is no longer interested in new clothes or his personal hygiene. The literary critic King-Kok Cheung observes Ed's growing disillusionment in America. He remains in the new country, and in doing so, he "loses not only his voice but also his humor. . . . Whereas the other two grandfathers are sojourners who know that they will one day return to China, Baba is here to stay; and staying, as it turns out, entails a brutal self-transformation" (Cheung 1993, 113). The downside of Ed's "heroic dream of achievement [is] the realism of failure in American society" (Sledge 1980, 9). And his failure to achieve the "American Dream" records the brutalizing psychosocial, economic, and political subordination and exploitation practiced in this country against Chinese Americans.

Throughout her husband's major depression, Brave Orchid takes care of him physically and chides him as part of her understanding of her tasks as a responsible wife and a mother: "You're spoiled and won't go looking for a job," or "The only thing you're trained for is writing poems," You're scared," or "You're shy. You're lazy. You never do anything," or "You've lost your sense of emergency" (CM 247, 250). Within the domestic and familial sites, Brave Orchid exercises a level of agency and power as a mother and wife; but she carries the heavy burdens of her family's survival as well. Brave Orchid stands by her debilitated husband's side faithfully, thereby protecting him and their six children. She and the children work as temporary labor in the fields and canneries. The family eats rice and salted fish, "which is what peasants in China eat." And Brave Orchid bemoans her fall in status: "We're slaves of these villagers [the owner of the gambling house and his wife] who were nothing when they were in China. I've turned into the servant of a woman who can't read. Maybe we should go back to China" (CM 245). Nevertheless, Brave Orchid endures her travails. Judy Yung notes that although "family life exacted a heavy toll on [Chinese women's] personal lives, it also served to sustain them. In this sense, family for them was a site of both oppression and resistance. Working hard had meaning for Chinese women because it enabled them to fulfill their filial obligations as well as provide a better future for their children" (Yung 1995, 83).[11]

Being a bold, practical and tough-loving kind of woman, Brave Orchid attempts to revive her husband's spirits but nearly paralyzes him in doing so. "She said she was tired after work but kept moving, busy, banged doors, drawers, pots and cleaver, turned faucets off and on with *kachunks* in the pipes. Her cleaver banged on the chopping block for an hour straight as she minced port and steak into patties. Her energy slammed BaBa back into his chair. She took care of everything: he did not have a reason to get up. He stared at his toes and fingers" (CM 250). She scolds and pampers her husband, medicating him with her concoctions and fattening him on broths to help him recuperate only to have him lose weight, to become, as his daughter notes, a Charles Atlas project—a forty-five year old man weighing 90 pounds. Maxine is critical of her mother's behavior and her failure to understand fully her father's suffering: "She did not understand how some of us run down and stop. Some of us use up all our life force getting out of bed in the morning, and it's a wonder we can get to a chair and sit in it" (CM 248).

The children, like their mother, negotiate the minefield of their father's emotional roller coaster—his ranting and screaming, his nightmares, his sexist abuse and silences. Fortunately, BaBa finally does get out of his chair. His young children, mirroring their mother's behavior, also "goaded him, irked him—*gikked* him—and the gravity suddenly let him go" (CM 253). But, sadly, his first act is to chase down and beat his children—Brave Orchid would be too formidable to challenge. After this outburst, "he did not return to sitting. He shaved, put on some good clothes, and went out" (CM 253). Ed recovers enough to buy a laundry business and puts the whole family to work. He buys a home and plants a backyard full of plants and trees from pits "that take years to fruit" (CM 255). Robert Griswold notes that for men on the margin, "success often meant a steady job and the ownership of their own home. A home, in fact, was a tangible asset and proof of achievement. To own a home meant that a man had gained some success as breadwinner. It was both a hedge against hard times and the caprices of a landlord and a symbol of success that 'could provide a sense of pride in a world where work often denied one feelings of worth'" (Griswold 1993, 40). Despite the ownership of a business and a home, which suggests his manly achievement, BaBa continues his sexist practices toward his wife and daughters at work and in the home. For Maxine, these abusive practices must be critiqued as part of the recovery of more liberating notions of manhood.

In *China Men*, Kingston, the daughter-writer, pays tribute to her complicated and distant father through the honesty of her portrait of him. Part of Kingston's heart work is to "assess the damage," to articulate the emotional and social struggles which seriously strain a family and ethnic community. In this regard, she makes visible the importance of critical self-reflection on not only mother-daughter but also father-daughter relationships. As heroic as one is forced to be in the face of trauma and humiliation for the sake of one's family this is *not* an empowering or heroic *way of life*. If a healing change is to be achieved the social and emotional damage must be honestly engaged. I am speaking of those "ruthless intimacies" which loved ones practice on each other (Gornick 1997), which destroy their ability to make a hopeful future together.

This is an integral part of the rebel-filial daughter's writing, which is, in many ways, a challenge and an honor not only to the mother but also, in this case, to the father. If Maxine both honors and usurps her father's position as a patriarch and scholar-writer, her talk-story form is also interactive and does not assume that one story is correct: "I'll tell you what I suppose from your silences and few words, and you can tell me that I'm mistaken. You'll just have to speak up with the real stories if I've got you wrong" (CM 15). She seeks a talking cure that will challenge her silent father to respond to the anger and love of a daughter. In order to get her scholar-father to answer her, Kingston chooses the challenge of writing a "big novel": "I suppose we're not like ordinary people where you can just have a regular conversation. That is not possible for my father and me. It had to be done on this large level, like on a big stage" (Kingston 1994, P10).

The filial-rebel daughter-writer's challenge is not patronizing contempt or pity for father or family. It is more profound in its heart work: it is an *invitation* to her father to critical reflection and the enactment of more radical social change.

> It's wonderful that he answered in poetry; and he became a feminist, which means that he grew and changed from when he was a young father. His thinking became modern. But at the same time his answering me in poetic form is an ancient tradition. The ancient poets would write poetry back and forth to each other. Also monks or religious people would answer each other in commentary on scripture. They would answer back and forth as they discussed philosophy. I mean, this is the same thing as when there's commentary in the *I Ching*, or poets singing to each other back and forth. And so my father and I communicated the way ancient scholars and poets did. (ibid.)

Maxine Hong Kingston, the daughter-writer, addresses her father as a scholar and poet, honoring his earlier life and aspirations in an American context. In *China Men*, at the birth of BaBa, Ah Po gives him the Four Valuable Things—ink, inkslab, paper, and brush, tools that indicate his promise as a scholar. In coming to America, he hopes to find work as a teacher. Instead, Maxine's father toils a lifetime in Chinatown laundry work. In King-Kok Cheung's discussion of alternative models of masculinity, she mentions the shushen or poet-scholar, who is derived from the traditions of classic Chinese opera and romance.

> The poet-scholar, far from being brutish or asexual, is seductive because of his gentle demeanor, his wit, and his refined sensibility. He prides himself on being indifferent to wealth and political power and seeks women and men who are his equals in intelligence and integrity. . . . This model of the poet-scholar belies the popular perceptions of Asian men as inarticulate, unromantic, and unimaginative, fit only to become computer nerds, engineers, or kung fu fighters. It offers an ideal of masculinity that is at once sexy and nonaggressive and a mode of the conduct that breaks down the putative dichotomy of gay and straight behavior. (Cheung 1998, 190–91)

In recovering this model of masculinity, Kingston addresses the father not as an exploited worker of white patriarchal capitalism but as a scholar-poet in his American transformation. He is a man who knows the brutalizing affects of survival in this country, and the importance of the support of his wife and children. He is a man with a scholar-daughter, who honestly critiques the social and emotional pain in her family in order to recreate space to invite a healing return into community.

Kingston publicly honors their special communication with each other. She put his annotated copy of China Men in a museum exhibition of her work. "The Chinese translation of China Men has wide margins on each page, and my father wrote commentary in his copy. He did it in Woman Warrior, too. . . . A lot of it is so reconciling. I wrote a lot of angry stuff about sexism, especially in Woman Warrior, but everywhere I made those angry feminist accusations, he would add something wonderful like 'Women hold up half the sky'. . . . I wanted his poetry to live somewhere, to be honored somewhere, so I gave his annotated copies to the Bancroft Library at Berkeley, where they had a reception and exhibition of all my work. I took my father there without telling him what he was going to see, and I took him right up to the display case and showed him. A wonderful smile came to his face. He looked around at all the people and he said in English, 'My writing.' So he didn't just live through me. The words came to him" (Moyers 1990, 12).

In her continuing recovery work on men's stories (see 1989a and 1989c), Kingston suggests that Chinese American masculinity must be reconstructed further. Chinese American men, that is, must reject the traditional Eastern/Western models of manhood that link masculinity with violence, racism, and sexism. She calls for new narratives of manhood as well as for womanhood, new ways of writing beyond the conventional endings of stories about identity, masculinity, femininity, community. She was once asked to define a good man: "A good man is one who does not die tragically. Who does not die before he's fulfilled his service to the world. Maybe a good man is a Confucian man, one who comes into a chaotic scene, a chaotic home, or a chaotic country, and finds a way to bring order, community, peace, harmony. He is able to establish peace among people in a family. To set up harmonious relationships between people, between countries, within societies. At the core is the spirit of creation. The humane being evolves" (Moyers 1990, 16). Kingston radically revises the heroic ideal in Three Kingdoms (see Lo 1991), thereby creating more spaces for the enactment of practical and ordinary heroic life other than the one valorized in discourses that envision heroic life in terms of the realities of war, revenge, and death.

Canning Woo: A Joy Luck Father's Healing Talk-Story

In The Joy Luck Club, Amy Tan tells father-daughter stories too. As young women in China, Joy Luck mothers certainly speak of their oppressive relationships with Chinese males like Wu Tsing and Tyan Yu (Lindo's boy-husband). But despite their bad experiences, three of the Joy Luck mothers love and marry Chinese men who can live with clever, practical, and independent-minded women. For example, An-mei Hsu and Lindo meet each other in a fortune cookie factory and become friends. In immigrant women's extended social and political networks, women find support, jobs, and husbands. An-mei and her husband George set Lindo up on a blind date with a telephone man named Tin Jong. Both Tin and Lindo overcome their initial ethnic and linguistic differences (Cantonese and Mandarin) and woo each other through a new language, English. They have a delightful, practical courtship—not the silly story Waverly tells. Rather than enduring an arranged marriage, the feisty, pragmatic Lindo chooses the man she will marry this time around, and this makes a difference in her life. She tells Waverly not only to be proud of her mother's Sun clan but also of her father's Jong clan.

The Joy Luck mothers also toil beside their husbands and teach their children the importance of surviving and maintaining cultural traditions as well as hybrid culture in the minefields of Anglo-American society. The couples travel, play mah jong and socialize together, and learn to pool their resources and invest for their retirement together. This extended social network of husbands and wives extends support to each other's children. The men respect the work of their wives in the care of their children. Resituated in the United States, these couples both enact more hybrid gendered identities in their relationships and continue a social understanding of self-in-community that is, in part, derived from their Chinese world view. Rather than arranged marriages, most of the Joy Luck mothers find more companionate, fluid marriages with Chinese men. Furthermore, the mothers do not tell their daughters never to marry Chinese men; rather, they tell their daughters to be strong and independent first and to affiliate with partners who will love and respect them in their own right.

Though not made central in Tan's recovery of mother-daughter stories, Chinese American fathers are represented in *The Joy Luck Club* as dignified, beloved, and respected presences in the lives of the Joy Luck daughters. Canning Woo, June's father, for example, asks his daughter to take her deceased mother's place in the circle of Joy luck "aunts." June loves the father who takes care of her and who honors his wife's story of struggle. Canning keeps her memory alive in the extended family's archives, as a subversive form of ancestor worship that does honor to his deceased wife as well as to himself. Through his nurture and respect for mother and daughter, he reveals aspects of Suyuan's stories that will bring June to a closer understanding of her mother. He lovingly tells his wife's story to his family in China and to his daughter. And in the telling, he does not skip the *emotional* details—the inner turmoil of her struggle.

Suyuan and Canning meet in a hospital in Chungking during the revolutionary war years in China. She is distraught and suicidal, suffering guilt in abandoning her twin daughters, and is sick with dysentery. She loses her soldier husband in the war. Canning Woo nurses Suyuan back to health through these chaotic and nomadic war years in China. She marries him and they search for her children in Shanghai; and after a long period of wandering together through China and Hong Kong, they both make their way to the United States in 1949. Canning Woo is involved in the nurturing of his wife and family as part of his understanding of meaningful manhood. In the final story, it is he who accompanies June to China in order to reunite her with extended family and with his stepdaughters.

Tan, therefore, honors a father's role in building family, community, and solidarity not just in public or work sites, but also at the homeplace. Canning Woo does not easily fit into Anglo-American or Asian American cultural nationalist notions of male-warrior identities. He does not rampage like a stereotyped heartless Confucian patriarch or a kung-fu fighter through his daughter's life or his family's. He is also not represented as an effeminate or castrated wimp. Instead, Canning Woo models a construction of manhood that is, I believe, emotionally and socially responsible and nurturant. It is a more democratic and permeable notion of Chinese American manhood that does not need to dissociate from women or display a traditional form of masculinity that constantly asserts and re-enacts its repudiation of femininity (see Kimmel 1996, 318).

Furthermore, what needs to be more profoundly healed is not the father wound but the *mother* wound in men (ibid.). That is, the part of the male self that denies or represses emotion, which masks vulnerability, fear, and depression; but which needs to love and be loved, and to nurture and be nurtured, as part of the *human condition*. In privileging and reproducing restrictive and debilitating patriarchal binary systems, it seems that some men have "abandoned precisely those emotional skills that were most needed if women were to achieve equality: nurture, sensitivity, emotional responsiveness" (ibid.). Sheila Ruth makes a good point that "the idea that one who is capable of emotion and sensitivity is incapable of discipline and rational [or intellectual] judgement is absurd. . . . It bespeaks no *undesirable* softness (again, the martial belief that 'softness' is contemptible), no lack of intellect or strength" (Ruth 1990, 215).

Cultural nationalists and critics rarely refer to these men's stories in the work of Tan or Kingston in articulating more expansive, fluid personal and political identities. They do not refer to the tradition of Asian American feminist writing that explores the nature of heroism and the nature of male suffering, anger, and violence in a racist, sexist world, and that acknowledges the contributions of Chinese American men to their families and communities. In making only certain forms of manhood visible or acceptable, masculinist and racialized discourses impose a debilitating *invisibility* to this rich area of men's (and women's) experiences. From their restricted militaristic rhetorical stance, they cannot see these potentially alternative and resisting men's stories as heroic, but only as "emasculating" or "feminizing." As Judith Newton states, more work needs to be done at "the site of investigating masculinity," work that links the "economic and political with the familial and personal, the public with the private" (Newton 1994, 575). Such links are vital to explore if women and men are to build towards more liberating practices in a society.

Part II
Fae Myenne Ng: The Politics of Making a History Together

In *Bone* (1993), Fae Myenne Ng recognizes what is at stake for a Chinatown family and community—psychosocially, culturally, politically, and historically—in her portrayal of the dilemmas and tensions confronted by Dulcie Fu, Leon Leong, and their three daughters Leila, Ona, and Nina. Ng's book is a cultural text situated in the milieu of more recent discussions in ethnic studies as well as feminist and gender (such as masculinity) studies. Ng is a graduate in English at UC, Berkeley with an M.F.A. in writing from Columbia University. She has taught courses in writing and in Asian American literature. Within an Asian American studies cultural context, Ng was familiar with the earlier critiques and debates in the Asian American community surrounding Maxine Hong Kingston and Amy Tan and their mother-daughter writing (see chaps. 2, 4). In her first novel, *Bone*, Ng establishes her own distinct form of women's writing within the contentious and vibrant explorations of Asian American identity and history in the 1990s.

In *Bone*, Leila Fu, the daughter-narrator, explores the interior spaces that an outsider's "Greyhound bus" view of Chinatown cannot access—the "insider's story," which is "something entirely different" and not totally accessible to outsiders and, as we shall see, to insiders. Tourists see the "spidery writing on store signs, the dressed-up street lamps with their pagoda tops, the oddly matched colors" (B 144–45). What the narrator Leila loves about her boyfriend Mason is not only his long and lean good looks, but also how he wears "his face, tough and closed to outsiders, but open to [her]" (B 39). Ng is not interested in reviving the storehouse of Orientalist or mythic fantasies of Chinatown—the lurid or sensationalist tales of tong wars, prostitution, gambling, and opium dens often identified with mainstream Chinatown representations.

Ng firmly situates the Leong family's history, especially its sites of trauma and survival, significantly in the terra firma of San Francisco's Chinatown, U.S.A. The specific map of their history together as a family and social community references Chinatown and its environs (such as street names, parks, buildings, and stores) as the actual lived spaces in the psychosocial and geopolitical formation of Asian American history. One of the earliest historical sites of family and memory in the United States, for example, is the San Fran hotel in Chinatown. Grandpa Leong's bones are left here in the United States. They have failed to make the return home for burial in China as he had wished. His relocated bones are rooted in American soil and history, earned by a lifetime of work, suffering, and death in the United States.[12] His bones are also embodied in the generations of his "paper family" and in their shared stories of survival and recreation. As Leila Fu notes, "Family exists because somebody has a story, and knowing that story connects us to a history" (B 36).

Unlike Amy Tan or even Maxine Hong Kingston, Ng is more vested with recovering the stories of Chinatown life rather than reconstructing or referencing the stories or contexts of earlier lives in China. For example, Ng does not forefront China past or culture as Tan's text does in telling the Joy Luck mothers' stories. Such stories have left Tan more open to critiques and Orientalist appropriations (see Wong 1995). In fact, Ng has been to China only once, leading a tour on a cruise ship on the Yangtze in 1985—not exactly a China expert, as she says. In an interview, she remembers she couldn't speak the dialect and that people on board would ask her: "What's wrong with you?" (Hunnewell 1993, 9). Leila, the narrator, notes that she and her sisters know little about the old country: "We repeat the names of grandfathers and uncles, but they have always been strangers to us" (*B* 36). They are, nevertheless, part of a larger transnational imaginary that refashions story, history, and affiliations from plural geopolitical locations. However, what is central to Ng's narrative is the Leong family history that is being constructed, experienced, and mediated in the continually changing formations of Chinatown community, especially in its engagements with institutions in U.S. society.

The recovery of these Chinatown family stories is *not* about the recovery of traditional or conservative American family romances; of a father as the main provider and mother as the cheerful housewife caring for home and children, of happy endings. Men fail to keep promises and abandon their wives; wives commit adultery; fathers disown daughters; daughters commit suicide, have abortions, abscond to marry. As Leila tells us, to her family "the deformed man is oddly compelling, the forgotten man is a good story, and a beautiful woman suffers" (*B* 36). Leon saves up piles of newspaper clippings full of stories that document the "lost husbands, runaway wives and ungrateful children" (*B* 6). Leila witnesses the daily hardships of her parents and family. She sees how her parents "forced themselves to live through the humiliation in this country so that we could have it better" (*B* 36). For example, Leon, as a merchant seaman, ships out to sea for long stretches of time while Dulcie, a sewing-woman, wife, and mother, anchors the family in Chinatown. She shoulders the major care of home, children, and filial obligations to his extended "paper" kin, duplicating a split-family household formation *within* the United States. Ng testifies to the affect these social deformations have taken on the lives of the three daughters as well.

In her portrayals of a distressed family, Ng counters the superficial and totalizing white mainstream representations of successful or model minority families, which often make invisible the suffering of poor, working class racial-ethnic groups. The representations are the outcome of America's post-civil rights shift to more "positive" stereotypes of Chinese or Asian Americans. In these representations, Asian Americans are constructed as believers in family values, education, tradition, and community. Peter Kwong ascribes this dominant neoconservative ideology to America's concerns over economic and social ills in society: "many Americans have identified the lack of a work ethic and the failure of family values as the central causes of the national malaise. They have turned with envy to the immigrants' attitude toward hard work, disciplined reliance on their own family and ethnic resources, and nondependency on public assistance. The dynamic growth of ethnic Chinese immigrant enclaves seems an ideal alternative to the poverty and deprivation of African American ghettoes" (Kwong 1997, 135). Asian American model minority family representations are used to project and reinforce a sense of hope and security in dominant underlying American beliefs and narratives about the Protestant work-ethic, individualism, meritocracy, family values and multicultural cohesion within the capitalist economy of a white nation-state. They suggest that *some* racial-ethnic groups are moving towards acceptable forms of assimilation and acculturation into the "American Dream."

However, the monolithic representation of a Chinese American model minority marginalizes the long, repressed history of xenophobia, racism, and violence against the Chinese in the United States. This historical legacy coupled with social-economic exploitation still affects the lives and options of those working-class immigrants who live in Chinatowns (Kwong 1997, Lin 1998). As Bonnie Honig has noted, "It is by now commonplace to hear the capitalist success of (a small minority of) immigrant and ethnic groups explained in terms of their immigrant drive (often said to be lacking in domestic minorities) and in terms of their large extended families and communities (which provide cheap labor and pool their resources). What is valued here are the resources available to be sacrificed for financial success, not the *affective family or community relations* or their potential to serve as sites of *associational political power*" [italics mine] (Honig 1998, 4). Ng situates the Leong family's lives at the localized sites of their daily desperation, domestic violence, suffering, and anger; as well as their endurance, love, and courage. In this way, she makes visible the social-emotional "heart-hollerings" which are erased within hegemonic U.S. discourses. At the same time, without romanticizing these social locations, she reconstructs them as vibrant social and political sites of cultural memory, agency, resistance, and recreation. This is an insider's story-in-process to contest the obliterating model minority one.

Ng's stories do not fit comfortably in any one place. That is, her representations of a Chinese American family and its various members do not invisibly melt into standard Anglo-American cultural or social representations or stereotypes. They are distinctly not "failed versions of their white, male-headed nuclear counterparts" (Iglesias 1998, 509). They cannot simply be inserted into mainstream feminist critiques of the nuclear family as a purely oppressive privatized or politically neutral site. Despite attempts in mainstream U.S. media to appropriate immigrant family relations as a national narrative that projects a nostalgic desire for the restoration of traditional patriarchal gender and social formations (the good old days syndrome), the Leon family constructs its own provisional social formations and understandings out of their daily experiences.

The stories in *Bone* are not *Chinese* stories played out in the United States in some continuous, seamless fashion, but *Chinese American* and *Asian American* stories, which are in the process of being lived, contested, and constructed in the flux of U.S. culture and society. If anything Ng's stories annoy, disturb, and frighten by making visible what the larger culture would prefer not to acknowledge. She registers the pains and struggles in familial relations as the affect of hegemonic and *hypocritical* discourses and practices that seek to silence their voices and discipline their bodies and hopeful spirits. Such writing cannot help but be *political* in its very act of recuperating these personal experiences and alternative ways for surviving and transgressing dehumanizing circumstances and dominant institutions.

It is, I believe, vital to see Ng's as well as Kingston's and Tan's diverse talk-stories as serious transgressive institutional critiques of the nature of the inequities in American society. These Chinese American daughter-writers articulate that which deforms or suppresses the constructive relations, and the narration of these relations, within subordinated Chinatown families as a *political* matter, not as purely personal or psychological therapy work. Thus, the talk-stories engage the oppressive practices that deny subordinated families their visiblity, dignity, and search for accountability and justice in the voicing of their psychosocial realities at the (exterior and interior) sites at which they are experienced and theorized. David Goldberg suggests the potential of poor, racialized city spaces—slums, ghettoes, housing projects—to be "sites of affirmative resistance." "It is . . . only on and *from* these sites, the social margins, that the battles of resistance will be waged, the fights for full recognition of freedoms, interests, claims and powers, for the autonomy of registered voices, and the insistence upon full incorporated social institutions, resources, *spaces*. After all, . . . to change one's geography—not only to move from but equally to transform one's spaces and its representation—may well be to change one's world" (Goldberg 1993, 205).

With the burden of this family history and responsibility, Ng portrays parents and three daughters struggling to resolve the dilemmas of the diverse familial homeplaces they are carving out for themselves in the United States. She charts the personal and spiritual cost of leaving one life in order to make or remake another: "An old world is being broken down and a new world is to be created" (Ng 1994, 87). *Bone* revisits Chinatown as a dynamic, diversified, mediated, and contentious community for Chinese immigrant families. In this specific location, Ng explores how each familial member contends with their relationships within and without this site—how they deal with the desire to stay together and to escape or leave.

In an interview, Ng stated that the outsider may construct a perception of Chinatown as insular or stereotypically tribal, conservative, and backwards. "But within Chinatown, for the inhabitants looking out, it's like living in a glass globe. You want to fly, you want to go, because this is our instinct. We came from a generation of travelers, of pioneers, so we want to break out . . . but something holds us back" (Lu 1993, 4). Ng explores the inward *and* outward tendencies (psyhosocial and physical) of these immigrant Chinese parents and American-born daughters as they move like travelers and pioneers trailing multiple, and often painful, histories. Leila's family is not composed of stereotypical old-fashioned Chinese parents; they are rebels and trail-blazers. They chart new border crossings, attempting to forge out new lives for themselves and their children in transnational and transcultural frontiers.

Their American-born daughters, following in their footsteps, continue to chart their own social interactions within and without the Chinatown family and community. Leila as well as her sisters do not and cannot live in their mother's (or father's) "world" though it affects their own lives. Leila Fu, the oldest, works in Chinatown as a student-parent mediator at the Edith Eaton school while she negotiates a life in transit between her boyfriend Mason in the Mission and

Tenderloin districts and her Chinatown family home. Her personal "world" also includes auto repair shops, fast cars, love marriages, recreational drugs and sex, trendy restaurants, as well as hip, talky, and tough working-class Chinese American male friends and lovers from the "hood," who will fight if they hear "fucken Chinese jokes" (B 46). Sleek and temperamental Nina moves out of Chinatown and heads to New York, where she remains in contact with her family from a protective distance. She conducts tours to China and has an array of Chinese lovers. Ona works at the tacky Polynesian Traders restaurant and struggles desperately and unsuccessfully to balance her loyalties to her Peruvian-Chinese boyfriend Osvaldo and to her beloved father. Her death exposes the secret failings within the family as each member contends with private failures and regrets that haunt their lives. In their individual and social border crossings, Ng reveals the insider's experiences of these complicated families who live in such multiple contexts.

Dulcie Fu: A Life Stitched to the Stamping Needle

Dulcie Fu is a woman working to support her family. She is a seamstress who tracks her lost youth and hopes in the ruthless stamping of the sewing needle. When abruptly abandoned by her first husband, the playboy-gambler Lyman Fu, Dulcie must find work and she takes a job in Tommie Hom's garment factory.[13] Dulcie and Lyman Fu lived in a one-bedroom apartment. The sewing factory where Dulcie works is just down the stairs, the domestic site is merged intimately with the economic one, reflecting the merged spaces of their lives. Dulcie has dinner rice in her mouth even as she sews. Leila's bedroom is also the sewing room. While she sleeps, her mother sews. In her sewing factory "homework," the immigrant mother cannot escape exploitation even in her home, where children assist in the making of garments.[14] Ng recalls her own memories of her mother's garment sweatshop life in San Francisco Chinatown: "I got a penny for each buckle. . . . Many women had cradles next to their machines. The shops were open all night, and the women went home and sewed some more" (Hunnewell 1993, 9). "One of my duties was to write the little code number of my mother's sewing machine onto the laundering tabs. I used to sneak out on weekends and go to the department stores, and look for the dresses she'd sewn. I never found her dresses, but somehow, finding my book in the bookstore was like that—finally finding something that belonged to me" (Tannenbaum 1993, 26). One reviewer interestingly related Ng's writing to the sewing world of Dulcie Fu, noting that she "assembles her characters' varied histories much the way Mah pieces together culottes and party dresses at her sewing machine, one seam, one story at a time" (Garcia 1993, 8).

While visiting with a Chinese immigrant family in Chinatown, Leila Fu recalls her own familial locations in the constricted emotional and physical spaces, spaces in which identity, family, and community are constantly and painfully practical. Ng sought to find a language that could capture the bare honesty of these spaces, the frugality of "hard-working classes of people who have very little but don't waste anything" (Stetson 1993, 3). Leila Fu critically observes the Chinatown world she is attempting to leave behind even as she mediates among students and Chinatown families in her work. As an insider-outsider, she sometimes sees herself as "doing a bit of a missionary number" (B 16).

> Both parents work. Swing shift. Graveyard. Seamstress. Dishwasher. Janitor. Waiter. One job bleeds into another. . . .Being inside their cramped apartments depresses me. . . . The sewing machine next to the television, the rice bowls stacked on the table, the rolled-up blankets pushed to one side of the sofa. Cardboard boxes everywhere, rearranged and used as stools or tables or home-work desks. The money talk at dinnertime, the list of things they don't know or can't figure out. Cluttered rooms. Bare lives. Everyday I'm reminded nothing's changed about making a life or raising kids. Everything is hard. (B 17)

It is a domestic and familial space, like her own Salmon Alley site, that is never free of exploited labor or the disciplining of subordinated people's lives.[15] The cultural critic Lisa Lowe states the case for rethinking various historical Chinatown sites where "the buildings and streets, the relations between spaces, and the relations between human individuals and work, to leisure, to life and death are all material testimonies to the means through which U.S. society has organized Chinatown space to enhance production and to reproduce the necessary relations of production" (Lowe 1996a, 120). More specifically, she notes that the "the family relations in *Bone* allegorize the conditions of immigrant life within contradictions of the liberal nation-state as capitalism extends globally: the immigrant's lack of civil rights promised to citizens of the nation permit the 'private' space of the immigrant home to become a workplace that prioritizes the relations of production over Chinese family relation" (Lowe 1996a, 169; see Dill 1988). Ng recovers the physical and psychosocial sites of trauma, of entrapped immigrant workers exploited by co-ethnic bosses within the Chinatown garment sweatshops and homes. She charts as well their exploitation by wealthy multinational American companies who benefit from the cheap wages and substandard conditions cultivated in a competitive, profit- and time-driven capitalist labor economy. Within the allegedly private spaces of domestic-familial life and within marriage relationships, there are nagging reminders of the larger public world—goods and services, employment, social welfare, legal forms, finances, lack of time, immigration, and green cards. The private world is hardly private as the nation-state intervenes in the deformation of this family's life.

Leila, as her mother's confidant, witnesses her mother's suffering, tracked on the crumpled map of her body and spirit: "She said she was ready to quit the sewing shops. I was glad to hear it. I'd watched the years of working in the sweatshops change her body. Her neck softened. Her shoulders grew heavy. Work was her whole life, and every forward stitch marked time passing. She wanted to get out before her whole life passed under the stamping needle" (B 163). Dulcie feels her body fast fading before her living and loving can be done. In her loneliness and desperate fears, the exhausted mother turns not only to an adulterous affair with her sweatshop boss, Tommie Hom, but also to her daughters, wanting them all home, especially the oldest, Leila, who is her intimate social and emotional confidant and witness. "I'd seen Mah suffer. I'd seen her break. Now more than anything, I wanted to see her happy" (*B* 19). Leila is afraid to tell Dulcie about her marriage to Mason because it may resurrect painful memories and the "refeeling of mistakes" for her mother (*B* 12).

Finding talk-stories that can articulate these complex feelings and experiences is difficult but vital work for Leila: "I have a whole different vocabulary of feeling in English than in Chinese, and not everything can be translated" (*B* 19). As a daughter, Leila, for example, must develop vocabularies to understand her mother (as well as her father), vocabularies that cannot be encompassed in words alone. Leila learns to recognize Mah's impatient "sewing-factory voice," which continually reminds her how Dulcie's work crosses over into the emotional relations between mother and daughter. Like the Joy Luck daughters and Maxine, Leila feels her mother's power to elicit guilt and frustration by a gesture, a sigh, a word or two. She translates her mother's shorthand for disgust, blame, and anger—almost like the sound of a stamping needle on a sewing machine:

> Just like that.
> Did it [Leila's quickie marriage to Mason] and didn't tell.
> Mother Who Raised You.
> Years of work, years of worry.
> Didn't! Even! Tell! (*B* 22)

Furthermore, Leila deals with Dulcie's raw "endless laments," "one-track moaning" and grunts, "a huumph sound that came out like a curse," and registers the maternal gestures as part of this vocabulary—Dulcie's poking at things and how her wrists whipped back and forth which reminds Leila of "how she used to butcher birds on Salmon Alley" (*B* 22). There are, at such times, no words for the anger or despair Dulcie feels about her life, failed relationships, work, uncomfortable compromises and lost options. No words to fully make these feelings acceptable or safe for expression to herself and to others. Despite her multiple failings, Dulcie is still concerned about the issues of maintaining a proper face as a good wife, mother and woman within her Chinatown community. Sounds and gestures deceptively coded and read by intimate confidantes like her daughter Leila or the sewing woman circle chart the emotional eruptions *and* suppressions that reveal the depressing affects of maintaining a multiple, often conflicting positionality, as an immigrant, working-class Chinese American woman.

The confidante-daughter Leila is a primary witness to the anger, the suicidal depression, and guilt jags of her mother. The daughter suffers guilt and resentment in dealing with her, yet she loves her distressed mother even as she longs for escape. It is difficult for Leila (as it was for the Joy Luck daughters and Maxine) to translate and attend to her mother's complex personal "vocabulary of feeling," which shapes their lives and histories as well as their decisions for the future.

Dulcie's sewing women friends, like Brave Orchid's school colleagues and the Joy Luck Club women, are also a part of her social and emotional support network.

They know the cooing words of consolation that call her back from her sadness, worries, fears, and loneliness, that draw out the poisons in her life. They are women who talk-story among themselves about the intimate details of private struggles, the "long-stitched versions of [a] story, from beginning to end" (B 23). They bring the healing foods, village advice, and necessary rituals; they "use Mah's personal name, and the intimate sound of it made [Leila] think about Mah as a young girl. Before Leon. Even before [her] father" (B 105). Watching and learning from this consoling circle of cooing women, Leila wonders if "true comfort came only from the arms of other women" (B 81).

The San Fran—The Family's Oldest Place in America

Ng tells the difficult mother-daughter story but she wonderfully recuperates the father-daughter stories of Chinese American men, who are in the process of remaking themselves as part of a hybrid world. The father-daughter stories are situated within the familial and communal dynamics of Chinatown society. In an interview, Ng remembered her childhood in San Francisco Chinatown in the 1950s: "We were young children, so unusual in Chinatown, so we were treasured. We had many grandfathers. . . . I witnessed how hard they worked, how alone they were at the end of their lives without the comfort of family. I thought someone should tell their story" (Hunnewell 1993, 9). Unlike the Chinatown community that considers a family of girls an unlucky or "failed family," Leon attributes people's remarks to jealousy and subverts their sexist clichés with a new saying "Five sons don't make one good daughter" (B 1). In the beginning of her story, Ng makes an emphatic point to not privilege totalizing ahistorical accounts about sexist patriarchal Chinese men and their passive, victimized women, as Tan and Kingston have often been severely, and unfairly, accused of doing in their stories.[16]

Leila, the daughter-narrator, learns to read the "noisy loneliness," the "heart howlings," of her stepfather Leon Leong (B 24). Leon is an integral part of that crucial social history of the transitional formations of family, community, and culture in San Francisco's Chinatown and it is important to recover his story. In this way, Ng significantly expands the emancipatory potential in women's stories, which foreground the painful conflicts at complex social-familial sites while exploring their roots in economic, cultural, and political institutions.

Leila recovers the story of Leon Leong in the earlier male milieu of Chinatown. Leon arrives through immigration at Angel Island in the late 1930s as a 15-year-old with false papers—a "paper son" to a "paper father" with a "paper history" that he must memorize down to the last detail if he wishes entry into the United States.[17] It is this paper history which haunts him through his life—in fulfilling his filial duties as a son, in determining his legal status, and in applying for social security and disability benefits. On paper, he is reinvented as the "fourth son of a farm worker in the Sacramento valley, his mother had bound feet, her family was from Hoiping" (B 9). Leon promises his paper father Leong that he will return his bones back to

China, an unkept promise that haunts his life. In this country, paper becomes "more precious than blood" (B 9). Paper creates an opportunity to re-fashion himself as a new man in a "new China" in the Gold Mountain country. At the same time, the traumatic trail of paper documents his lies, failures, and rejections by this country.

Leong associates with his male friends in Chinatown locales. Leila talks of the "Chinatown drift-abouts. Spitters. Flea men in the Square. [Like] Jimmy Lowe the Mo-yeah-do-Bak (Mr. Have-Nothing-to Do)" (B 13). The "time-wasters" socialize at the local cafes and dream up schemes, play cards or chess at Portsmouth Square and/or solicit Leila at the park for a date in their room. To Leila, they look like "dark remnant fabric;" she notes the details of their worn and patched yet still feisty lives—the "tattered collars, missing buttons, safety-pinned seams, patch pockets full of fists" (B 8).

In *Bone*, Ng portrays diverse familial and social formations that are not limited to loyalties based on blood or biology. Within this male social community or fictive family, You Thin Toy and Leon, for example, have a long intimate history together, coaching each other on their paper histories for immigration officials on Angel Island, laboring together, and nurturing each other. They both define themselves as brothers. They are a fraternal family formation created, in part, out of social, emotional and material needs. With no wife, children, or kin to grieve for them, the elderly Chinatown men respectfully attend to each other's "poor man's funeral":

> We watched the old men file slowly up to the coffin. Each old man approached the coffin alone, bowing to both ends of the box. The Newspaper Man from the Grant and Washington corner tucked something inside the coffin. The man from Grandview Theatre bowed from the waist like a movie star. I recognized a chess player, the herbalist, a butcher from Hop Sing's, a waiter from the Universal. They all went straight up to the coffin, bowed and then came to tell Mah they had to leave and go back to work. (B 83)

These old men memorialize the deceased as best they can in telling the fragments of stories that have been passed down from other men. As Leon notes, "it's time that makes a family, not just blood" (B 3). Those who intimately share and know each other's experiences and stories are part of the continual making of community together in this country.

From this standpoint, Leila names the San Fran, an "old man hotel on Clay Street," as one of the "*family's* oldest place," their "*beginning place* and *new* China" where her bachelor "paper" Grandpa Leong lived out his days and to which Leon returns to work out his traumas in life [italics mine] (B 4).[18] At the San Fran hotel, "there's a toilet and bath on each floor and the lobby's used as a common room. No kitchen" (ibid.). These historical sites are not traditionally remembered as sites conducive to the privileged formation and protection of standard nuclear or extended families; they are lonely homeplaces long devoid of women, children, and stable communities. Nevertheless, Ng includes this as a primary and originary site for the social domestic-familial history of the Chinese in the United States.

"High Fire": Marriage of Toil

Leon marries later in life and starts a family with Dulcie Fu, a single mother abandoned by her first husband. Dulcie, burned by a first marriage to a fancy man, is in search of a practical, tempered love match which will help her and her daughter Leila survive economically and save her from disgrace in the tight-knit and gossipy Chinatown community. Leon also has the coveted green card which will ensure her stay in the United States. And with Leon at sea, Dulcie hopes to protect her heart from further hurt. But with his long periods away, she is unable to withstand the daily stress and fears of her own constricted life and begins an affair with her employer Tommie Hom. This nearly destroys her new family.

Leila is witness to horrendous fights and recriminations, the "ruthless intimacies" between her father and mother, which cause great tensions in the family. Leila comes to recognize that her parent's lives were "always on high fire. They both worked too hard; it was as if their marriage was a marriage of toil—of toiling together. . . . Matches were made, strangers were wedded, and that was fate. Marriage was for survival. . . . Their lives weren't easy. So is their discontent without reason?" (B 34–5). She remembers the domestic violence (physical and psychic) in the family, children trying to separate fighting parents: "The flat *ting!* sound as the blade slapped onto the linoleum floor, the wooden handle of the knife slamming into the corner. Which one of us screamed, repeating all their ugliest words? Who shook them? Who made them stop?" (B 35). After the death of Ona, the fights get worse, spilling out of the home—into the alley, the Baby Store, the bank, the butcher shop; they "were fighting at both ends [of the marriage bed] and the middle" (B 90). These family quarrels are generated by their daily toiling together in a country that cares little for their social and emotional well-being.

Leon, as a Chinese American working-class immigrant father and man, in his constant search for stable, family-wage work, confronts racism and overt discrimination in society, the stressful daily micro-reminders of rejection in his interactions with white majority culture. He tries to explain to Dulcie what it is to go out and earn a living: "You don't know. You're inside Chinatown; it's safe. You don't know. Outside, it's different" (B 181). Leon is a man trying to be a responsible father by providing economically for his family.[19] He works as a merchant seaman, shipped out for months away from family. On land, the work he finds is unstable, temporary, low-paying and low-status: fry cook, busboy, dishwasher, janitor, night porter, and factory worker. As an older man, he confronts the daily humiliations of applying for menial, entry-level work to support his family. It is honest, hard work, but degrading to his traditional notions of manhood.

Like some of his male friends, Leon wants a more stable land-based job in order to tend to his family. But behind closed doors, Dulcie and Leon realize that they are always short on money and time to make ends meet, even with both of them working. Dulcie reminds him he must go back to sea. Leon also takes on multiple jobs on land, but is deeply frustrated by the constant toil and small returns (see Griswold

1993, 34–67). In the face of rejection, humiliation, and injustice, Leon struggles nevertheless to endure and maintain the survival of his young family, and in this regard, his work should be recognized as heroic.

Despite the low wages, Leon takes a great deal of pride bringing home his earnings to his family. He is also loaded with presents, which symbolize his care for his family. But Leila makes a shocking discovery in Leon's suitcase of papers that brings her closer to a compassionate understanding of her father's suffering. As a "stepdaughter of a paper son . . . I've inherited [a] whole suitcase of lies. All of it mine. All I have is those memories, and I want to remember them all" (B 61). Leila recovers this eclectic suitcase-archive of her father's nomadic life and documents it as part of their family history: applications, check stubs, IOUs, aerograms, remittance to China receipts, pawn tickets, a diary of overtime pay, maps, photos, newspapers, coins, dinner menus and cookbooks (B 59). Unlike other paper sons who "confessed" their illegal entry to the U.S. government during the communist scare of the 1950s and received their naturalization papers, Leon, distrustful of the government and believing his stay in the U.S. to be temporary, refuses to "confess." However in doing so, he is held captive to lifetime of constructing a history of legitimate and illegitimate genealogies, aliases, and birthdates, which puts him in trouble with the law and governmental policies.[20]

Furthermore, in seeking Leon's paper documentation for social security and disability benefits, Leila discovers in the suitcase piles of papers that document Leon's history of daily degradation and rejection in a country that basically says "We Don't Want You." Leon's lack of English leads to rejection by the army, and when applying for jobs and apartments. These rejections track fifty years of life in a racist nation-state that perceives him as an outsider, and an illegal.

To help his family comfortably account for these rejections, Leon makes up a lifetime of humorous or flippant stories. But the formal written words on paper shock Leila—"the stories came back, without the humor, without hope. On paper Leon was not the hero" (B 57). Yet, Leila begins to understand that this paper blood trail is also Leon's fierce claim to this country. His life speaks to the claims of the Chinese American men before him, claims to being in this place and to rooting a family, culture, community, and history. In this country, "for a paper son, paper is blood" and "Leon had paid; Leon had earned his rights. American dollars. American time. These letters marked his time and they marked his endurance" (B 61, 58).

Leon, the dreamer, feels he just needs one big chance, a perfect business scheme that will somehow reward the hard work and hopes he has vested in this country, in the American notion of meritocracy. Leon's life is littered with the detritus of broken dreams—humiliating work and temporary get-rich enterprises (the noodle-making equipment and the coffee buying experiments, for example); he thinks of owning his own business. Leon goes into partnership with Luciano Ong. He admires the swaggering confidence of Luciano, the man about town who seems to have it all. For a while, the family laundry business supports his family and gives Leon a sense of ownership and pride. He feels like his American dream is finally coming true. He is a co-owner in command of his own laundry machines; his labor and mechanical expertise is used to further his family business.

Thus, the family laundry is another site that is symbolic of the long interlocked history of Chinese American labor and domestic-familial life. This site tracks the history of "forced withdrawal of the Chinese into a segregated ethnic-labor market. . . . In fact, in 1870 of the 46,274 Chinese in all occupations, only 3,653, or 8 percent were laundry workers. By 1920, of 45,614 gainfully employed Chinese, 12,559, or 28 percent (nearly one out of three) were laundry workers. The number of Chinese laundries soared in the first half of the twentieth century. In Chicago for example, there were 209 of them in 1903, and 704 twenty-five years later. In New York City by 1940, 38 percent of all gainfully employed Chinese were engaged in laundry work" (Takaki 1989, 240). When Leon loses his laundry to his scam-artist business partner, he is enraged and humiliated. He loses the family's life savings. His hard work fails again to achieve the comfort, security, and recognition he has sought all his life. Leon feels he cannot protect his family and children from long exhausting hours of work. He can not command or control the love, respect, and loyalty of his wife and children as a traditional man should do.

To add salt to the wound, Dulcie Fu becomes an entrepreneur who opens up a baby goods store in Chinatown, suggesting the changing dynamics of Chinatown communities from male communities to familial ones. However, this is a site of family fights and marital discord. "She [Dulcie] called him a useless thing, a stinking corpse. . . . Well, he swore to jump from the Golden Gate, told her not to bother with burying him because even when dead he wouldn't be far enough away. And then he used that stupid thousand-year-old curse of his . . . something about damning the good will that blinded him into taking her as his wife" (B 31). All his previous work identities and ventures become constant reminders of a lifetime of failures as a more traditional man, father, and husband. As Dulcie realizes, "something always went wrong for Leon" (B 52).

"One Mile Forward and Eight Miles Back"

In matters of the heart, Leila tells us, Leon prefers the simple. He doesn't like fanfare and ceremony. At his funeral, he prefers the understated—no flowers, no bugle and drums. He does not feel comfortable in the complications of emotions that shake up his home and his heart. When emotionally cornered or angered and frustrated by life, Leon copes by disappearing; he escapes by shipping out to sea. At other times, he withdraws into silences or explodes in emotional outbursts of anger, frustration, self-pity—his "heart hollerings" (or perhaps, in Chin's terms, his "aiiieeeee!").

Besides dealing with his own sense of failure at work and the racism of a larger society, Leon feels great anger over the adultery of his wife. It shames him within his family and Chinatown community. Leon moves out to the San Fran in a rage. Dulcie repents her behavior, she gives up Tommie, as well as her job at his sewing factory. After a long separation, they agree to stay a family but things are never the same again. As a father, Leon is further humiliated by his daughters' dismissive treatment of him. For example, Leila publicly humiliates him by yelling and swearing at him in the social security office. This is hard for Leon as swearing is a "license in language," which is often perceived, "as a masculine prerogative" (Schwenger 1984, 24). When he is not forced to ingratiate himself to survive the racism of his daily interactions, Leon is angrily defensive in trying to explain himself in a fractured English which constantly signifies his difference and which hampers his ability to make himself understood among his children and the larger society: "I be in this country long time! . . . People be the tell me. I never talk English good. Them tell me" (B 56). And when there are no words to clearly or reasonably explain himself, Leon swears as a signal of his anger and frustration. Leila tells us that Leon rants and curses because he has "nothing but his anger" with which to endure and resist the injustice: "Iiiinamahnagahgoddammcocksucksonnahvabitch!" "I know Leon, how ugly his words could become. I've heard him. I've listened. And I've always wished for the street noises, as if in the traffic of sound I could escape. I know the hard color of his eyes and the tightness in his jaw. I can almost hear his teeth grind. I know this. Years of it" (B 34).

The Loss of the "Forward-Looking One"

Even more painful for Leon is Ona's rejection and alleged suicide. When stripped of his laundry business by Osvaldo's father, Leon turns on the world, and most viciously, he turns on his beloved daughter, Ona, as a scapegoat for his failures. In assuming the traditional patriarchal role of father, of absolute authoritarian, he attempts to control, compete for, and, all else failing, to command his daughter's love and loyalty by threatening to disown her. In this effort, he fails: In a violent Salmon alley night conflict between father and daughter, Ona disobeys her father and runs off with Osvaldo, the son of his former partner Luciano Ong. Worse yet, twenty-year old Ona, on downers and living with secrets and emotionally alienated from her family, may have commited suicide.

By falling or jumping off the M floor of Ping Yuen public housing project in Chinatown, Ona locates another Leong family site that records the difficult and painful making of family and community. Ona situates the family within the struggles of working-class Chinatown immigrant families who were building multiple homeplaces in the United States. "Nam Ping Yuen, the last of the four housing projects built in Chinatown. *Nam* means south and *ping yuen*—if you want to get into it—is something like 'peaceful gardens.' We call it the Nam. . . . For us, the Nam is a bad-luck place, a spooked spot" (B 14). "Nam" recalls the Vietnam War, but this time, the war zone is the urban ghetto of Chinatown in the heart of San Francisco within the white supremacist history of California.[21]

The first three Ping Yuen projects, built between 1951 and 1961, housed new families of Chinese immigrant paper sons, who brought their wives over in the 1950s (Nee and Nee 1972, 320–324). Most of these families eked out a living with the men working as janitors, waiters, store clerks, or cooks; and wives working in garment factory sweatshops in Chinatown (ibid., 320). With both parents working, there was little time for the children or for leisure: "Fatigue [six days of work, ten hour days, for example] of the two parents when they return from work, and the fact that they themselves have shared no common activity during the day and may have little to talk about, further weakens the attraction of the nuclear family unit. . . . one older Ping Yuen adolescent described [dinner at home] . . . no one would think of talking about what they did that day. My mother washes the dishes and then, she's tired, so she goes right to bed. It's like a bunch of strangers sitting at the same table" (ibid., 321). With the bone-weariness of their parents' social and economic struggles, and without extended kin structures, both American born and immigrant parents find a lack in communication as well as a widening cultural gap: "When children reach adolescence, a sharpened sense of the barrenness and functionality of communication at home often emerges in the form of intolerant criticism. . . . Teenagers, too, then become increasingly withdrawn at home" (ibid., 322). Though love struggles to exist, relations are strained; and for daughter-writers, this domestic-familial site is a very important arena in which to examine the crucial making (and deforming) of identity and sociality.

Everyone in the family—not just Leon—is guilt-ridden over Ona's death, a death that becomes a catalyst for a deeper interior meditation on their individual and communal failures. The narrative winds its ways into the past, sorting out and reorganizing the interlocking fragments of memory and experience that defined their relations with each other. It is as if the narrative cannot go forward, but stumbles backwards into traumatic emotional time. They want to forget time, freeze time, and go back into time. Ona, the heart of the family, the forward-looking one who counted future time and living with anticipation, is lost.

In trying to find reasons for Ona's death, Dulcie dredges up the guilt of her first bad marriage and her indiscreet adultery with Tommie in her "endless laments." She is haunted by her failures not only as a woman but as a mother and wife: twenty-five years of sweatshop labor, a Gold Mountain prince turned into a toad, and three daughters: "one unmarried, another who-cares-where, one dead" (B 24). Likewise, Leila speculates on Ona's disappointment in her as a Big Sister and in her parents—Leon's possessiveness and Dulcie's lack of support. Leila wants a new life to escape the guilt and memories. Nina thinks it's Chinatown itself and its suffocating hold on Ona and the rest of her family. Ona's problem, she thinks, is also her inability to separate from her family. In doing this necessary heart work, the family gets lost in their private grief and lashes out at themselves and each other, hoping to figure out the ultimately unknowable reasons for Ona's untimely death.

Ona is her father's daughter most of all and Leon must confront his inner demons to deal with this immense loss of hopes for the future. He blames everyone and everything for this tragedy. In his more self-critical moments, he blames himself for the broken promise to take Grandpa Leong's bones back to China or even his own inadequacies as a father. He asks himself why couldn't Ona turn to him and talk to him—wasn't he after all her father? After Ona's death, the dreamer father who could talk up new ideas and projects constantly, hardly started anything, "he told Mason that his concentration was gone, that something disconnected between his mind and his heart" (B 49). He leaves the family home and ships out to sea— out to the big bowl of salt tears to find his bearings and to draw out the poisons that fester within.

This is not just a private psychological or emotional struggle for healing but a communal and political enactment of an intense effort towards more life-affirming change. In *The Joy Luck Club*, An-mei's mother searches for what is essential to a mother-daughter alliance despite the disownment of her mother. She returns to the site of her pain and sorrow in order to rethink what was central. Maxine does this also in her mother-daughter and father-daughter stories. As daughter-narrators meditate on the structuring of familial dynamics, they also expose the deep roots of private suffering and emotional trauma in their relationship to social, economic, and political injustices suffered in this country. But even more importantly, they recover the deep roots of love as a form of resistance, those acts not only of resolution and forgiveness but also of fierce moral accountability and struggle against human deformation and violence. Such love honors the dead by refusing to despair or to violate.

"The Heart Never Travels": Coming to Terms

The lives of the Leong family have not been easy and I do not wish to minimize this or to suggest that the relationship between Dulcie and Leon or with their daughters suddenly ends happily. Rather I suggest that they make a life together, take social and gender risks, and struggle to adapt to the changing realities of their family. For Leon, "'to get long' meant to make do, to make well of whatever we had; it was about having a long view, which was endurance, and a long heart, which was hope" (B 176). Family members negotiate the various obstacles in their lives, survive some difficult traumas and come to provisional understandings of each other they can live with as a family.

Like other daughter-narrators I have discussed, Leila recovers not only the sorrows but also the joyful memories of her father Leon Leong. The sewing women counsel, "Talk. Talk good things and urge the sadness away" (B 132). Leila begins to remember the comforting sounds of the Salmon Alley homeplace and the world of feeling in the four thin walls of home—not just the silences, angry cursing, and lamenting (B 129). She remembers her mother's initial attraction to Leon's eternally optimistic talk and "heady compliments." For a long time Dulcie held on to a belief in his dreams and his stamina to enact them: "She told us for a man with so many failures, Leon had a heart full of hope. Each new scheme, each voyage was his way of showing us his heart" (B 163). Leon works hard to make his dreams come true, to secure the future of his family of daughters. "He said life was work and death the dream" (B 181). Upon his return from sea, Dulcie cooks fabulous meals in his honor and it is her love and excitement that keeps alive the presence of this seaman father for their daughters: "We remembered how good Mah was to him. How else would we have known him all those years he worked on the ships? Mah always gave him majestic welcomes home, and it was her excitement that made us remember him" (B 34). In return, Leon, the "bachelor man," like other men who had been denied access to Chinese women, families, and permanent communities in U.S. society, is appreciative of Dulcie's companionate-sexual presence in his life, her stable care for their children, and her economic contributions to the family unit.

When they are not fighting, Leon and Dulcie work to maintain each other and their family. Even in their long fights and separations, Dulcie sends food, herbal brews, and money to Leon at the San Fran. He comes home to repair fixtures and clean the house. They understand they have a "marriage of toil," which is meant to ensure the well-being of their daughters. These are not model minority marriages, which represent happy family units supported in social-economic terms by the "family values" discourses and institutions in mainstream culture. Their marriage of toil reflects the *lack* of social-economic and political options for subordinated racial-ethnic families in U.S. society.

Both share similar cultural world views and values. Dulcie and Leon sometimes gang up on their children for their lack of traditional "good home education." At the same time, both parents are eclectic, flexible, and practical in their parenting practices—not completely conformists to the "old world" ways as cultural stereo-types suggest.

> They made up rules as they needed them, and changed them all on a whim. Mah had her ways when Leon was out at sea, but when he came home all her rules relaxed. Nina called their parenting chop suey, a little of everything. There were nights we had to speak Chinese . . . and there were other nights we could laugh and talk English all we wanted and even take our bowls out to the front room and eat while watching *I Love Lucy*. One day we could run wild in the alley until way after dark and stay up all night eating candy and watching television. The next day we had to sew culottes until our eyes crossed. (B 117)

They also share and maintain transnational interests in China and affiliations with relatives back home. For example, they have their "Hong Kong talk" about family and relatives: "It didn't matter who these people were, Mah and Leon seemed to enjoy talking about their problems almost as if realizing that other people had problems cheered them up. Strange medicine" (B 100). In their "long gossip ritual about the relations," I think they maintain their affective and affiliative links to a larger community of suffering and resistance not only in Chinatowns but also in China, Hong Kong, Australia, and other diasporic sites.

For all his ugly words and behavior, Leon Leong is also remembered as a loving and beloved father to his daughters. Leila remembers Leon's kindness in Reno, his gracious gift-giving as he intuits her awkwardness in having a new stepfather in her life. It is Leon that Leila wishes to tell about her marriage to Mason. "He's not my real father, but he's the one who's been there for me. Like he always told me, it's time that makes a family, not just blood" (B 1). Fae Myenne Ng, in her representations of Leon as well as Chinatown elders, reclaims men who enact fatherhood (biological and non-biological) as a form of nurturing manhood. This representation counters the stereotypes of men as single or married loners and wanderers—uncaring and indifferent to the formation of families and communities.

The first child of Leon and Dulcie's union is Ona, who represents their hopes for the future and their anticipation of having a better life for themselves and their children. "Leon/Ona. *On* was part of Leon's Chinese name, too. It means "peace" in our dialect. Mah said it seemed respectful and hopeful. Leon was her new man and Ona was their new baby" (B 131). Ona is infinitely hopeful about life. It is she who counts down the days to her father's return, and "every night that Leon was gone, she'd count out ninety-nine kisses to keep him safe, to bring him back" (B 88). Ona's ritual of counting time and anticipating the future gave meaning to those around her. Leon adores her and is adored by Ona. She is her father's daughter, the one who seems most like him in her adventurous, rebellious spirit and stamina. She is the one who wants to ship out to see the world, "to see everything Leon saw" (ibid.). It is Ona who follows him to the "old-man hotel," gently and patiently attending to his anger. She hangs out with her father and his friends at cafes. She waits with him at bus stops and employment agency lines and rummages through the Goodwill Stores as he does. She is the one that accompanies him to the "old-style movies," the "love stories about the butterfly lovers, fox spirits, snake goddesses, and the four great beauties" (B 158). And finally, it is she who works hardest to bring her beloved father back home, back to his family of women.

It is this love between father and daughter that calls Leon back to life. After Ona's death, the family searches for private and communal rituals that heal and return them to the hopeful business of life and family. "Completion. Luday kept saying the word, as if repetition was a way of plucking the pain out. 'Completion. Completely. All of it.' I don't know how to explain the effect the word had on me. Something about the way Luday said it was calming, her mouth rounding to mean 'full,' her lips meeting in a thin line to mean 'still.' That was completion: change" (B 105).

The "Underneath Thread" of His Heart

To complete his circuit of sorrow, Leila describes the various ways that Leon copes with his multiple losses and sorrows. He is a restless man with a need, as Dulcie knows, "to be lost in new places, new things" (B 162). She tells Leila that "staying on land too long made Leon feel like he was turning to stone. The ocean was his whole world: complete. A rush of wind and water. The salt taste like endless crying" (B 150). At sea, Leon can put his sorrow, anger, and restless energy into hard work as well as healing heart work. ". . . Leon told us that sorrow moves through the heart the way a ship moves through the ocean. Ships are massive, but the ocean has simple superiority. Leon described the power: One mile forward and eight miles back. *Forward and forward and then back, back.* Inside all of us, Ona's heart still moves forward. Ona's heart is still counting, true and truer to every tomorrow" (B 145).

And Leon, for all his wanderings, returns to his family one way or another. It is Leon who tells his daughter that what they hold in their heart is what matters—*the heart never travels* (B 193). Unlike Dulcie's first husband or even Tommie Hom, Leon is a man with the stamina to continue hoping and loving without the final certainty of success.

Leon, the dreamer father, is constantly reinventing his world in his big dreams and in his small-scale projects. What Leila comes to realize is that what her father enjoys most is "making old things work" (*BP* 13). Leila thinks her father haunts junk shops for *lop sop* or garbage, but this is another way Leon focuses his creative energy to renew himself and re-envision the world. He buys up the broken and used junk of a modern material culture and invents new curiosities. Far from being a man of the past, an alien to modernity, Leon, like the other fathers I have discussed, is a trailblazer in his own right. In an American mainstream culture fascinated by the new, Americans throw out old, obsolete things (and people). In many ways, Ng reclaims Frank Chin's character Tampax Lum in the play *The Chickencoop Chinaman* (Chin 1991). Tampax is described as the "comic embodiment of Asian American manhood" in that he is "forced to invent a past, mythology, and traditions from the antiques and curios of his immediate experience. In an effort to link himself with the first known Chinese Americans, [Tampax] states, 'Chinamen are made, not born, my dear. Out of junk-imports, lies, railroad scrap iron, dirty jokes, broken bottles, cigar smoke, Cosquilla Indian blood, wino spit, and lots of milk of amnesia'" (Chin et al. 1991c, 36). Leon's recreated hodge-podge of cookie tin clocks, clock lamps, rice cookers, radios, and an intercom/cash-register/alarm system—his *lop sop*—are symbolic of his own "odd beginnings" and self-inventions, for example, as a "paper son" in this country. His packrat collection of takeout containers, aluminum tins, plastic bags of ketchup and sugar, government issue cans of vegetables, towers of Styrofoam cups, restaurant napkins, red string, rubber bands, and newspaper piles also reflect the nomadic and eclectic life of the Chinatown old-timer in the debris of the American landscape.

Unlike Tampax Lum, Leon is a *bricoleur* who creatively invents new forms out of the used and broken things of a taken-for-granted mainstream American culture, excavating and collecting the fragments of obsolescence to be made anew. This improvisational activity provides Leon a level of control and power over his life, and displays his mechanical expertise as well. He tinkers and fixes things, even if he cannot always fix the bigger broken things of life or people—those that are damaged or dead. Moreover, Leon fixes in new ways what other people throw away, and in his inventive spirit we see the making of a syncretic American identity, culture, and community as well. It is symbolic of Leon's ways of dealing with his own feelings of rejection and exploitation in society.

Moreover, the recovery of this father story also speaks of the poor, subordinated and racialized individuals and communities (the San Fran or the Ping Yuen projects) that are neglected, thrown out, by American society. Leon returns and mends at the San Fran among the elderly men, those neglected invisible "rejects" from his former domestic-familial homeplace. This reminds me of a passage from *The Great Gatsby*, in which Nick Carraway talks about the rich and privileged lives of "careless people" who "smashed up things and creatures and then retreated back into their money or their vast carelessness, or whatever it was that kept them together, and let other people clean up the mess they had made" (Fitzgerald 1925, 180). Leila's recovery of Leon's life as well as his healing rituals demonstrate this father-man's great stamina to keep coping, hoping, and loving. He works towards a provisional completion and resolution that will free him to move forward again. In this regard, he mends himself to return to family and community. It is a patched and battered-up heart he fixes, and like most of his hybrid projects, it is a lifelong process and unfinished. He invents new rituals and sites to constructively address the sorrows and failures of his life and his family's as well. Leila recovers the "terrible beauty" of this heroic life of a father and a man making and remaking himself in social and emotional terms, accounting for and bridging multiple, and often conflicting and distressed, homeplaces.

Leon seeks out his paper father's bones after the death of Ona. He had promised to return the ashes to China, but he never did complete this promise to his "paper father" who sponsored his arrival in America. He believes that this failure is related to Ona's suicide and to his own failures in life. "This wasn't all about Grandpa Leong. Leon was looking for a part of his own lost life, but more than that, he was looking for Ona" (B 88). He pays his final respects to these forgotten and neglected bones of Grandpa Leong and is consoled that Grandpa Leong is buried among his Gold Mountain friends. "Remembering the past gives power to the present. Memories do add up. Our memories can't bring Grandpa Leong or Ona back, but they count to keep them from becoming strangers. Leon had it all turned around . . . about there being more dead than living. If Ona was here, she would count the living; Ona would tell us that there are more living than dead" (B 89).

While Dulcie is on vacation with Nina in China, Leon returns to the family home to make his peace with Ona. He spreads out his men's things in the domestic-familial site; he takes apart Ma's sewing machine in order to repair it. Leila is angry that Leon will only leave a clutter and worries whether he can ever finish this task. Leon fixes the sewing machine and he cleans up the house for Dulcie's return. *"Finish one thing before beginning another"*(B 109).

Leila thinks that Leon has finally forgotten about Ona's death. This is not true and is touchingly portrayed by the improvisational sacred shrine that he quietly creates to honor his beloved *daughter's* bone ashes. Leon centers the urn at the intersection of work and family: He sets up a card table shrine next to Dulcie's sewing machine, symbolic of their life of toil as a family. She is remembered in the heart of her family, that is, in the extended family of the living and dead. Besides, "Ona had always been the forward-looking one. She was always excited about the next day, the tomorrow. She wanted to grow very old, as old as Grandpa Leong; Ona wanted to be a smart old goddess" (B 88). Such a subversive politics of cultural memory, which is continuously mediated in the present, roots the experience of profound loss and grief into the future life of the family and community that refuses to abandon or forget their beloved dead.

According to the daughter-narrator Maxine in *The Woman Warrior*, people who have only one story to tell will go insane; those who can improvise and tell more than one story can survive the fluctuations of loss, dislocation, and re-situation. Daughter-writers like Kingston, Tan, and Ng are attentive to their mothers' stories but they are also attentive to their fathers' stories. They capture as well the complex silences and vocabularies of feeling which are part of these new localities and experiences. For dislocated and distressed families-in-transition and recreation, often carrying very little from one place to another, home or family is transported *as a feeling*. As Ng notes, it's something she learned from the old-timers. "They made home wherever they were. Traveling a lot the last few years really gave me a sense of how to live—taking everything with you that you needed" (Tannenbaum 1993, 26). Those who make an identity, a history, family, or community work together toward a shared and earned legacy of solidarity; and those who do not will be appropriated or lost. Emotional and social ties are crucial to building a genuine community. Making and earning a life together is about nurturance, love, stamina, flexibility, courage, and commitment to building a more emancipatory and ethical environment in the daily activities of life. Such oppositional practices are the root of our critical ability to re-envision the world and to act.

Through the talk-stories of daughters, fathers are represented as men struggling to deal with the pain, rejection, and dislocation of the past, the continuous pressures of the present, and the real fears of the future that may bring more of the same violence and humiliation. Yet, at the same time, these daughters are able, from a woman's standpoint, to reveal the heroic aspects of their fathers' lives—their rebellious, risk-taking spirit and indomitable faith, hope, creativity, and love—never forgetting the realities of hard labor and injustice their fathers have faced and resisted as Chinese men. I am reminded of a point made by William James, which is applicable to the filial-rebel daughters and fathers (and mothers) in these stories, especially in their negotiations with each other:

> Faith means belief in something concerning which doubt is still theoretically possible; and as the test of belief is willingness to act, one may say that faith is the readiness to act in a cause the prosperous issue of which is not certified in advance. It is in fact the same moral quality which we call courage in practical affairs; and there will be a very widespread tendency in men [and women] of vigorous nature to enjoy a certain amount of uncertainty in their philosophic creed, just as risk lends a zest to worldly activity.[22]

Notes

1. Ng uses the word "bone" for the title of her novel. It is resonant of a variety of meanings which signify the experiences of many working-class immigrant families in America—to the bone; bone marrow; bone tired, bone raw; bone dry; bone ash, bone dust; bone meal; bone bed; bone picker; bone spirit; bone yard; make no bones about it; have a bone to pick; feel in one's bones; bone of contention; bone china.

2. For recovery work on early Chinatown histories of male society see Chu (1961), Nee and Nee (1972), and Siu (1987). See Asian Women United (1989), S. Chan (1991a, 1991b, 1998), Chu (1976, 1986), Dong (1992), Hirata (1979, 1982), Yung (1986, 1990, and 1995), and Zhao (1996) for some examples of the recovery work on Chinese women's history in the U.S.

3. Besides examining hybrid formations of heterosexual masculinities, there is, for example, much work to be done in examining Chinese (Asian) American gay men's formations of masculinity and sexuality as well. Such work has begun in earnest. See for instance, work in Chua (1998), Eng and Hom (1998), Fung (1991), Hinsch (1990), Hwang (1988), Manalansan (1995), Leong (1996), Limark (1995), and N. Wong (1994).

4. The term "model minority" may need to be re-examined as Sylvia Yanagisako (1995) suggests. She believes it too simplistic and dismissive to account for the real successes of Asian Americans in this way.

   Furthermore, if one looks carefully, the daughter-writers' explorations of Chinese American families do not advocate that parents or daughters seek total acculturation or assimilation into dominant white society. They actually create more hybrid spaces for families and communities in their stories. What I am saying is that some Chinese American immigrant parents endure humiliation and hard work in order to give their children a better chance at social and economic opportunities and security in life that they themselves did not have after a life of toil. But they do not all become model minority types in the process (Chin's "honorary whites"). Many hybrid Chinese American families do not forget cultural traditions, or the nature of survival, suffering, racism, and resistance in their own experiences.

5. "Kingston always envisioned her two memoirs as having equal weight; in fact she originally conceived them as one book. Now she worries that *China Men* is being neglected in comparison *The Woman Warrior*" (Talbot 1990, 12). However, this situation has a lot to do with mainstream white male publishing decisions as well as the reading tastes cultivated by the various audiences of her work. See also Kingston's *Tripmaster Monkey* (1989a), which is the story of a 1960s male protagonist named Whitman Ah Sing, told from a woman's standpoint.

6. See Kingston (1989c). All references to this edition of *China Men* will appear in the text with abbreviation CM.

7. Even Frank Chin acknowledges the grandmothers and mothers who keep the stories of men (see 1979–80 and 1988).

8. Sigrid Nunez in *A Feather on the Breath of God* (1995) also recalls the profound silences of her father, Chang, in the family home and his refusal to share his past history with his children, who were like cruel strangers to him, asking him to resurrect the traumatic past which was at times unspeakable. See also Lee (1995).

9. See Siu (1987) for laundrymen's life in Chicago in the 1930s, and for New York laundrymen's history see Yu (1992); for New York Chinatown life see Chu (1961).

10. There are some Great Gatsbian resonances in this identification of beautiful, expensive clothes, which symbolized the wealth, excitement, and romantic possibility in the 1920s.

11. Judy Yung talks about the hard lives of her immigrant parents. Her mother was a sewing woman and her father a janitor. She describes their marriage as

    an interdependent partnership, with priority always going to the well-being of the family. They shared decisions about our welfare, and Father was never ashamed to don an apron and help with the cooking, washing, and ironing. Mother ruled at home, controlling the pursestrings, disciplining us, and signing our report cards, but Father was always the head of the household in public, the spokesperson for the family in clan matters. Although the separation of public and private spheres had weakened over time, it remained in effect to a consistent degree: Mother always stayed home at night with us while Father went out to his tong to smoke the bamboo water pipe with his fraternal brothers" (Yung 1995, 285).

12. See Shawn Wong's *Homebase* (1991) which is a book about Rainsford Chan's search and reclamation of a great-grandfather's roots and legacies in America.

13. In this fractured family tale, the Fa-Fa prince Lyman Fu turns into a toad: he abandons wife and daughter Leila to sojourn in Australia where he hopes to make it rich. He ends up a very lonely man who, in later life, loses his links with Dulcie and his daughter. His years of sojourning in Australia have netted him very little.

14. Lisa Lowe notes that "the marriage of Leon and Mah mediates the changes in the Chinatown community . . . as sweatshops first made use of Chinese male labor during the garment industry's growth from the 1920s through the 1940s and then turned increasingly to female labor after the 1946 modification of the Magnuson Act permitted Chinese wives and children to enter as non-quota immigrants and the Immigration Act of 1965 abolished Asian national origin quotas" (Lowe 1996a, 169).

15. See chapter 1 for discussions on the various ordinances enacted against the Chinese through the 1800s and 1900s, which attempted to govern not only the economic arena but also their personal lives.

16. Besides the father-daughter stories, Leila, Ona, and Nina are also affiliated with Chinese and Chinese American males as boyfriends, husbands, and lovers. Moreover, Ng portrays the sexual love-making between Leila and Mason, which opens up new territory for exploring the construction of Asian American sexualities. She describes Ona's passionate love for Osvaldo, which leads to a painful separation from her father.

17. During the San Francisco earthquake and fire in 1906, legal documents such as birth records and immigration files were lost, creating an opportunity for Chinese in this country to claim citizenship. As U.S. citizens, Chinese men claimed the children (by name, sex, and addresses) by their Chinese wives as American citizens. This circumstance allowed these children the opportunity to come to this country. Peter Kwong notes that this "paper son" system of entry evolved into a "lucrative racket in

which illegal immigrants paid fees to become 'sons' of Chinese Americans. . . . A purchaser would appear at a port of entry with fictitious name, based upon earlier statements of the returning citizen, and would claim United States citizenship through the purported relationship to the citizen" (Kwong 1997, 94). Upon arrival paper sons were questioned on all the painstaking details of their "family" history. Judy Yung reminds us that this "paper son" history should also include the often neglected history of "paper daughters" whose arrival contributed to the gradual development of a second generation in the United States (see Yung 1995, 106–7).

18. When Grandpa Leong is too old to work in the alfalfa farms of Marysville, he gets on a Greyhound bus and returns to the "elephant graveyard" of Chinatown to die. As Leila notes, he left behind a paper family to mourn him along with a few elderly bachelor men to eulogize him. In his room, he left behind a "snake in a jar and a tame pigeon tied to his windowsill" (B 78).

19. Yearly national surveys, according to Susan Faludi, still report that a good provider is a primary criteria for manhood (1991, 65).

20. As Judy Yung (1986) notes, there was the U.S. government's concern about fraudulent or illegal entry of early Chinese immigrants, such as the "paper sons," especially during the Red Scare of the 1950s and 1960s. People were concerned about communist spies and sympathizers lurking among the Chinese American population. A confessional program was set up by the government in collusion with the Chinese Six Companies. Paper sons were given an opportunity to "confess" their true identities without deportation. Yung further recounts the story of Laura Lai whose uncle was tricked by the government into "confessing" his paper son status. As a result, Lai and her family lost their citizenship rights; she could not apply and receive permanent resident status for seven years and she could not change her employment and was fearful of being deported. A number of Chinese Americans in this period stopped their political activities and were less enthusiastic and public about their interest in China (ibid., 82–83).

21. See Almaguer (1994), Omi and Winant (1986), and Takaki (1989, 1993).

22. Quoted in West (1993), epigraph

8

Coda:
The Political Heart of the Matter

At the end of exploring
Will be to arrive where we started
And know the place for the first time
T.S. Eliot, from "Little Gidding,"
The Four Quartets

I will remove from your body the heart of stone
and give you a heart of flesh.
Ezekiel 36:26

In *The Joy Luck Club*, June Woo's mother gives her an heirloom jade pendant by which she will know her mother's meaning. But June notes that she and other jade pendant wearers were "all sworn to the same secret covenant, so secret we don't even know what we belong to" (*JLC* 198). The jade pendant is an emblem of the experiences and stories of Chinese American mothers and daughters that have often been erased, distorted, or devalued in society. This pendant, in the final story of the book, speaks also to the value of reclaiming a living covenant between a deceased mother and an adult daughter. June begins the difficult process of coming to know a woman and a legacy she has long neglected and misunderstood.

In Ng's *Bone*, the daughter-narrator Leila Fu struggles to find a "vocabulary of feeling" in which she can compassionately engage the memories and experiences of her extended San Francisco Chinatown family and community. She tells us that this vocabulary often translates differently in Chinese and English, and sometimes no translations of these feelings are possible. She vacillates between the desire to

233

forget and the need to remember a history that burdens her with its daily reminders of what has been endured by her family.

Cherríe Moraga reminds us that the oppression within ourselves as well as in our communities must be critically assessed. But, she also warns us that "danger lies in attempting to deal with oppression purely from a theoretical base. Without an emotional, heartfelt grappling with the source of our own oppression, without naming the enemy within ourselves and outside of us, no authentic, non-hierarchical connection among oppressed groups can take place" (Moraga 1981, 29). Leila confronts this oppression within her family and community. She can forget neither the sound of the relentless stamping needle that registers her sewing mother's rage and fears, nor the brick-colored suitcase filled with the papers that mark her stepfather's humiliating sweat-and-blood passage in this country. "I never forget. I'm the stepdaughter of a paper son and I've inherited this whole suitcase of lies. All of it is mine. All I have is those memories, and I want to remember them all" (*B* 61). Such histories of injustice and sorrow cannot be superficially mourned or quietly buried; they cannot be released by the living or the dead, who intimately know and preserve the unofficial histories of this country. Though she furiously seeks escape—any buffering zone or forgiving distance away from her Salmon Alley home—Leila comes to realize that a sociality coheres in the dailiness of what they create and share together. An intricate, multilayered web of relationships roots individuals in a dynamic community.

As the traumatized narrative of *Bone* indicates, it is difficult but crucial to examine not only the painful memories and experiences but also the celebratory ones that embody the excitement, value, dignity, hope, and love within the Leong family and community (*B* 194). In such conflicted spaces of memory and experience, Leila exposes the "underneath thread" of the heart, which powerfully sutures her distressed family and community, and continues to help them survive and resist dehumanizing conditions. This is not to naively suggest that such difficult, compromised social and emotional recoveries can easily or quickly overturn the inequities that circulate in their world. It is also not to say that such recoveries cannot fall prey to purely privatized medical or psychotherapeutic discourses and practices which manage "illness," "disease," "depression," "dysfunction," or "pathology" and restore an "adjusted" individual to the same dehumanizing conditions in society. An individual who suffers from racism and sexism may also be redirected to solve her social-economic exclusion and deprivation by renouncing or blaming her marginalized racial-ethnic upbringing, community, or culture. The forms of individual and communal distress that Kingston, Tan, and Ng portray have *institutional* roots that must be critiqued and challenged by individual and collective action and resistance.

The writers represent the different and powerful ways women reclaim and assert social agency in their recovery of memory, feeling, and experience. The writers articulate understandings of the difficult yet vital work of marginalized mothers in juggling daily material survival, as well as in negotiating the fluctuating terrain of self and family in community. They tell of women, displaying both strengths and weaknesses, in their complicated quest to break stereotypes and rigid definitions that continually attempt to name or exploit them. For example, in Kingston's *The Woman Warrior*, Maxine states that it is important to "report a crime." That is, in the social act of witnessing and narrating the events and crises that affect her "real" life and human potential, she comes to a critical consciousness of her conflicted and ambiguous roles within culture and society. She labels the injustices and develops a transgressive voice that constructs story lines that help her to make sense of the world. Maxine configures a complex, permeable self in response to the diverse communities (real and imaginary) she inhabits. Such an act fractures and contests the notion of a monolithic, self-contained, linear, and unitary self. It counters the long history of stereotypical representations and one-dimensional narratives about Chinese American women, and re-envisions the world; resignifying affiliations, responsibilities, and priorities; and acting in newly empowered ways.

The Chinese American mothers and daughters do not want to remain decentrified objects whose stories are continually co-opted by those who devalue their hopes and realities, and refuse them their own voice. Rather, there is a strong desire on the part of the mother-daughter pairs to reclaim one another's repressed stories and voices—to break, in acts of memory and language, the disciplining injunctions to silence and set the records straight about their realities. By attending to these women's talk-story practices, a reader explores more nuanced understandings about the diverse ways women perceive and access the world they inhabit; that is, how they pursue, acquire, and express knowledge derived from their specific positionings. These practices also suggest ways for valuing and strengthening the diverse relational networks of individuals and coalitions who work together against injustice and violence.

The critical work of theorizing the diverse nature of Asian American women's identities and experiences is an ongoing process. There are Korean American, Japanese American, Filipina, South and Southeast Asian American women writers, for example, who have rich women's stories to tell and share. Within Asian American groups, within families and communities, within women's relationships, there are many distinctions and variations: we aren't all the Same. The mothers and daughters in *The Woman Warrior*, *The Joy Luck Club*, and *Bone* cannot be easily stereotyped in simplistic binary paradigms as "old-fashioned" or "modern" women, or "Eastern" or "Western." Lisa Lowe, for example, notes the complex locations that must be negotiated not only by Asian immigrant women but also by immigrant groups. "As with other diasporas in the United States, the Asian immigrant collectivity is unstable and changeable, with its cohesion complicated by intergenerationality, by various degrees of identification and relation to a 'homeland' and by different extents of assimilation to and distinction from 'majority culture' in the United States" (Lowe 1991, 27). Asian and Asian American culture are much more heterogeneous, more fluid than phallocentric, monolithic, binary divisions would suggest.

The stories of Chinese immigrant mothers and their American-born daughters must be engaged in ways that situate the fluctuating realities within their particular psychosocial, economic, cultural, political, and historical formations. This task requires a search for more innovative, multiply positioned knowledges and practices, which may not often be centrally located or valorized in traditional and ahistorical Western-based institutions. Such work needs to be done in earnest before one can speak comprehensively about the formations of Asian American mother-daughter writing or women's experiences.

One primary and often neglected political site at which to begin this important re-examination is in the overlapping spaces of family, work, and community life. In the stories, Chinese American mothers and daughters often work under the heavy burdens and constraints of racism, classism, and sexism, which profoundly affect their personal lives. Nevertheless, at these less than perfect homeplaces, Kingston, Tan, and Ng portray how women build social, emotional, and cultural networks in their families and communities. They confront, for example, the daily damage and violence done at multiple and often unpredictable sites of crises—locations not fully accessible or accounted for in abstract, objective scientific theorizings and methodologies. Chinatown families and communities in Ng's stories, for example, inhabit peripheral environments; many people are poor and working-class, living in cramped and impoverished material conditions, and jobs are often labor-intensive, menial, low paying, exhausting. There is a lack of access to decent job options, to education and health, to financial resources, and decent housing. Addressing concerns and issues that would ensure the well-being of such families and communities would be the task of an ethically responsible and accountable society, but they are not often or substantially visible or heard in their own voices in the dominant arenas that regulate their lives and environment.

According to Kay Anderson, such contained sites are the "function of that set of historical categories constituting the idea of the project: idealized racial typifications tied to notions of slumliness, physical and ideological pollution of the body politic, sanitation and health syndromes, lawlessness, addiction, and prostitution" (qtd. in Goldberg 1993, 198). These sites sharply contrast with the mainstream American perception of the home as "a place of peace, of shelter from terror, doubt, and division, a geography of relative self-determination and sanctity" (Goldberg 1993, 199). The writers represent how Chinese American women are situated within a society that valorizes individual freedom and achievement, profit, efficiency, and commodity exchange as forms of progress and virtue. However, this "progress" and "virtue" have obscenely profited from a bloody history of suffering and exploitation of poor, working-class, and racial-ethnic groups. It would appear that such a foundationally stratified (raced, gendered, sexed, and classed) system is profoundly compromised and restricted in trying to understand or resolve the poverty, crime, violence, suffering, and other social ills at the marginalized sites and communities it oversees and exploits.

The families and communities in these writers' texts are not portrayed as stereotypically model minority or pathological. The writers do not advocate a rugged "bootstraps" individualism or levels of achievement or competition lauded in traditional white American culture and society. They do not advocate a simplistic one-way assimilation into white middle-class lifestyles or consumption. The social and emotional work is not purely privatized work or a reconfiguration of the conservative "family values" rhetoric of the capitalist nation-state. That is, the writers' notions of "family values" do not refer back to nostalgic or idealized models of a tight-knit, happy, white middle-class nuclear family structure, featuring a benevolent patriarchal father bringing home a family wage to an ever affectionate and self-sacrificing wife-mother, who, in turn, tends solely to the education of responsible and virtuous citizen-workers for the white capitalist economy. The cheerful housewife in this narrative works for free and is fueled by love in the privatized and domesticated security of her familial domain. This is not the scenario for the women and families portrayed in many of the stories discussed here: Domestic-familial sites are not portrayed as apolitical or neutral; they are also not purely sites of abundant love and care. Brave Orchid, Dulcie Fu, and the Joy Luck women are definitely not simple, passive custodians of traditional culture, history, or genealogies but are makers of culture and practices in their imperfect lives and fluctuating circumstances.

Ng embraces a notion of family that values the elderly Chinese immigrant men in San Francisco's Chinatown, who were affected by the exclusionary laws, the anti-miscegenation laws, and the revolutions in China. These created circumstances in which Chinese immigrant men "lived out their lives in this country, many dying without the comfort of family" (*B* 87). In Ng's stories, these men are not dismissed or stereotyped as "dirty old men," lonely strangers, or lost individuals; they are incorporated into memory, into the expansive familial and communal network so that they will not become estranged.

Thus, the personal recovery by Maxine, June Woo, and Leila Fu of their stories is intimately linked to the recovery of the history of Chinese Americans in the U.S. In the exposure of the prejudices hidden behind official legal and governmental paper and their impact on personal and social life, they are subversive on behalf of the community as a whole. They represent what abstract legal doctrines, governmental policies and statistics, and techno-bureaucratic practices *felt* like as they imposed on the lives of Chinese American women, immigrants, poor and working-class people, non-English speakers or the illiterate, and racialized communities in this country. Adrienne Rich recounts how she is continually "pursued by questions of historical process, of historical responsibility, questions of historical consciousness, and ignorance and what these have to do with power" (Rich 1986a, 137). It is essential to counter the violent, heartless discourses and practices of imperialist-capitalist nostalgia and power that would bury or negate the brutalizing experiences of slavery, exclusionary laws, violence, and genocide and "that [see] only certain kinds of human lives as valuable, as deserving of history at all" (ibid.). To question the multiple oppressions—racial, gender, sexual, and economic—that have appropriated the experiences and history of Chinese Americans is to begin to *ethically* expose spaces to engage the communities and histories that have been unjustly subjugated and delegitimated by dominant groups and institutions.

Kingston, Tan, and Ng each foreground the right of oppressed individuals and collectivities to speak and enact critical experiential understandings for themselves. Thus, recovering each other's stories is a form of personal and communal struggle and agency. In giving voice to these stories, these writers continue to extend the exploration of representing Chinese American families in their pain and complicities, and, most importantly, in their inventive and eclectic strategies for survival. Necessity—not privilege—requires the reformation of identity, family, culture, and community in their daily lives. For example, I am reminded of Audre Lorde's assertion that "the master's tools will never dismantle the master's house" (Lorde 1984, 110). Lorde seeks to craft new tools to radically deconstruct and reconstruct the master's world because the "fruits of patriarchy" cannot be substantially critiqued by the very tools derived from the same racist, sexist patriarchy. "It means that only the most narrow perimeters of change are possible and allowable" (ibid.). We must try harder.

The mother-daughter stories indicate a more nuanced and complex understanding of a social-political imaginary that has valuable implications for rethinking notions of identity and sociality. The hard work of talking to each other, for example, can lead toward more compassionate understandings of our differences as well as similarities as women. In her essay "Age, Race, Class, and Sex: Women Redefining Difference," Audre Lorde reminds us often of how differences among people have been misnamed, misused, or ignored in order to keep us divided and confused (Lorde 1984, 115). Differences, as she says, have not often been used as a *starting point* for bonding and power. The fact that mothers and daughters are attempting to talk to each other, to tell their stories, to emotionally and socially access each others' experiences speaks to their commitment to the very difficult yet practical work of constructing and earning reciprocal relationships and friendships. The stories do not essentialize or naturalize a seamless mother-daughter bond among the various sets of mothers and daughters in these cultural texts; they memorialize the fruits of their efforts to understand one another.

Conversing, especially when one would rather mutter, whine or posture, according to David Shipler, is a "rare and heavy accomplishment" (1997, 473). In learning to talk-story with each other and in struggling to come to the intimate knowledge of, and respect for, the struggles in their families, the Chinese American mothers and daughters in these stories come to realize what sews their families and racial-ethnic communites together—"*knowing* the story [that connects them] to a history" [italics mine] (B 36). Such social, dialogical practices of talk-story can enable women and men to fruitfully negotiate alliances, and create opportunities for the development of strong, supportive interactive communities. Developing social talk-story practices among diverse individuals and groups can make visible the counterfeit discourses and practices that detract from the actual development and empowerment of communities.

Attentive listening and interaction can begin to engage the cruel, angry emotions that are the result of too much repressed pain, silence, and injustice, too much raging and fighting, too much assuming, inferring, and miscommunicating. Psychosocial violence and numbness deter people and communities from interacting actively and responsibly; and such "socially deforming" (Williams) and obscenely "pornographic" (Lorde) practices are a *political* issue as well. The Chinese American mothers and daughters try, with varying degrees of success and failure, to critically engage the varying struggles in each other's lives as part of a practice that seeks to free them to act and relate in potentially more constructive, liberating ways. In the story "Scar," An-mei's mother realizes the importance of returning to the root of her pain, the betrayal by her mother, in order to remember and reclaim what was valuable, satisfying, and central to their relationship. Building social and emotional relations that acknowledge the similarities and differences of people, that seek to unravel and make visible the tangled roots of suffering, anger, violence and their relationship to injustice, is a crucial form of political and ethical accountability and activism. The daughters learn how important it is to do this quality heart work in order to reconnect with their mothers as well as with their fathers, families, and communities.

From this standpoint, to speak up as women against silencing and invisibility, an "unnatural disaster" as Mitsuye Yamada (1981) names it, is to begin to imagine the voices that have been left out. Reclaiming women's voices and processes is a significant part of a community's political survival and resistance. If mothers and daughters do not articulate their stories, they and their families and communities will lack the rich legacies of women who have contributed to the collaborative and continual making of culture and community. They would be, as Adrienne Rich reminds women, "unable to imagine a future because [they] are deprived of the precious resource of knowing where [they] come from: the valor and the waverings, the visions and defeats of those mothers and foremothers who went before [them]" (Rich 1986, 141). The recovery and reconstruction of the narratives of self and the struggles between mothers and daughters can provide vital entry into complex individual lives as well as into an ongoing, collective history of women and social communities; a history that criss-crosses and stitches together diverse generations, cultures, languages, classes, nations, and peoples. These stories represent a facet of the history of the Chinese diaspora—the traumatic displacements, as well as the terrifying beauty and power, of naming and enacting new formations of identity and sociality in other locations.

Building more fluid collaborative alliances requires rethinking a *grassroots* politics inclusive of our often uncritical habits of being. It is on the level of our personal and social engagements, of how we socialize with one another—not just on the level of what is ordinarily recognized as "the political" or the abstracted public dispensation or spectacle of political empowerment rhetoric—that we begin to demonstrate what "guts" it takes to realize a more just and liberating vision of a society yet-to-be. Likewise, the dissembling or bravado discourses of empowerment can only go so far—the hard heart work needs to be done. William James reminds us that a test of our faith [in this case, in the possibility of justice, human dignity, and collaborative alliances] is in our "readiness to act in a cause the prosperous issue of which is not certified in advance" (see chap. 7, n22). It is the daily, embodied praxis that articulates and enacts the building and earning of a sense of community, that works to forge more complex and fulfilling relationships among various individuals and social constituencies in society.

The women's stories and standpoints that Kingston, Tan, and Ng construct are inclusive of the stories of Chinese American men: Canning Woo, Ed Hong, and Leon Leong represent the richness of Chinese American formations of masculinity that are forged in transnational and transcultural contexts. When Leon, for example, is angry, he can curse, scream, brood, fight violently with his wife, and demand patriarchal allegiance from Ona. And when the homeplace and emotions are too much for him to handle, he escapes to the sea or to the San Fran. Leon displays a patriarchal form of manhood that is part of his familiar repertoire. Yet, in many of these stories, fathers also gradually come to recognize the importance of domestic-familial work as part of a conception of responsible and meaningful manhood. Michael Kimmel encourages men's re-entrance into the domestic-familial sphere in parenting as well as in educating their sons [and daughters] into an emotionally responsible and nurturant manhood [and womanhood] as a part of adult behavior (Kimmel 1996, 318). With great care, Ng shows how Leon struggles to do this work with his daughters.

In Ng's text, Leon Leong is portrayed with a level of complexity and compassion that includes the uglier aspects of his character. Leon wrestles to modify or re-invent himself against the more dominant patriarchal notions of masculinity circulating in culture and society; Leon has the capacity to destroy and fix things. After Ona's death, he returns home, displaying another kind of masculine presence in his home while Dulcie is in Hong Kong. He repairs her broken sewing machine—the site of the relentless stamping needle that signifies her rage and disappointments in life. The machine represents her exhausting sweatshop labor in an exploitative global-capitalist marketplace, and is also a reminder of her adultery and Leon's rage and retreat from the homeplace. Leon scrubs down the old floors in the kitchen and bathroom, and upon Dulcie's return, he is clean, freshly shaved and wearing "self-ironed" dress slacks (B 100). In this reflective interim of peace and quiet, he returns his daughter Ona to the world of the living by enshrining her ashes next to her mother's sewing machine, a central site of their family life and survival. He memorializes a beloved and hopeful daughter who longed one day to be a goddess; he makes their shared sorrows an integral part of their present and future life together. It is his powerful and graceful forgiving practices that speak louder than words, which *show* his heart and "long view" of life, and which excite Dulcie's respect and love for Leon. Mah brings him a gift of a watch that works, and they begin the comforting "long gossip ritual about the relations" (ibid.). These intimate and dignified social gestures reflect the nuances of their private codes of conciliation and love as a couple. Like Dulcie, who stitches together the bone structure of dresses, and his daughter Leila, who struggles to make sense of the fragments of trauma through the stitchery of her narrative, Leon also finds ways to patch up his vulnerable family, and to complete a cycle of their sorrow in order to move forward, to make a life together in the social wastelands of the United States.

There needs, I think, to be more theorizing of the complex formations of Chinese American (and Asian American) masculinities. If we take Gary Okihiro's (1994) earlier question about rethinking Chinese American women's making of culture, and expand the question to include men as well, we could begin to analyze how Chinese American men, while passing on a culture encrusted with patriarchy and men's oppression, may also pass on a culture that resisted European American racism and colonization. We could also begin to situate men's practices in the making of domestic-familial and social community dynamics. Furthermore, we can begin to analyze why oftentimes more radically resisting and democratizing constructions of subordinated masculinities are so under-theorized in dominant white patriarchal-capitalist discourses as well as certain oppositional discourses— a complex psychosocial, economic, and political question in its own right.

Judith Newton (1998) discusses the processes practiced by those who are helping to build new, more eclectic social, cultural, and political communities. She reminds us that building a diverse community should never be the work of one gender, class, or race alone. In this regard, she calls for the reinvention of a progressive masculinity that works to build social-political communities; that is, a masculinity that is not restricted solely to working on individual adjustment or personal relations. She has observed repeatedly that "it is women, and a very, very few men, who shoulder the work of building community. Mainly it is women . . . juggling their scholarship, teaching, administration, committee work, housework and children, while also organizing their colleagues, building bridges, resolving conflict, and inviting people in. In the dawning age of alliance politics, women and a very few men cannot do this work alone" (ibid., 593). She warns that such democratizing identity practices, whether in the academic setting or elsewhere, will not be easy for those men "whose identities were not formed as nurturers, for men who are immersed in a capitalist culture that requires competition, rationality, and suppression of emotion; for men who inherit and perpetuate political discourse that emphasizes analysis, lack of compromise, and fierceness of debate while scorning self-criticism and attention to community and personal relation" (ibid., 594). She encourages feminists to contribute to these efforts of transformation by creating and supporting social sites which do not "continue, ambivalently, to assume that men can't change or that, if they do it's into 'something totally unacceptable'" (ibid.).

Cornel West speaks of a new community built with *all* our protean identities and energies and answering to the "intellectual rigor, existential dignity, moral vision, political courage and soulful style" of our human condition (West 1993, 32). In her story "Report from the Bahamas," June Jordan reminds us that the "ultimate connection cannot be the enemy" (Jordan 1990, 124). What happens, she asks, when we get the monsters off our back and run in different directions? Jordan does not assume that people who organize alliances based on misery will necessarily encourage or envision a partnership for radical or transformative change. More significantly, she asserts that the "ultimate connection must be the need that we find between us. It is not only who you are, in other words, but what *we can do for each other that will determine the connection*" [italics mine] (ibid.). Gloria Anzaldúa reminds us that it may not be "enough to stand on the opposite river bank, shouting questions, challenging patriarchal, white conventions," which locks the oppressor and oppressed in mortal combat and debilitating violence (1990a, 378). In Anzaldúa's assessment, such a defiant counter-stance which refutes and reacts against authority is necessary, but it is not a complete or fulfilling way of life. She points out one path beyond this state: "At some point, on our way to a new consciousness, we will have to leave the opposite bank, the split between the two mortal combatants somehow healed so that we are on both shores at once and, at once, see through serpent and eagle's eyes" (ibid.). And Cherríe Moraga circles back to the scars of self-hatred and self-abuse, of the enemy within that needs to be confronted: "If we are interested in building a movement that will not be constantly subverted from the inside at every turn, then we build from the inside out, not the other way around. Coming to terms with the suffering of others has never meant looking away from our own" (Moraga and Anzaldúa 1981). All these writers are aware of the real systemic injustices they have encountered in their own hard-fought battles, and they recognize the need for struggle and vigilance over human rights, accountability, and justice. They do not deny or make light of the multiple difficulties, tensions, and compromises of the legacies or projects they envision.

However, in their fierce and passionate contestation against forms of injustice and violence, they adamantly desire the "long view" practices of a life-oriented, rather than a death-oriented, society. Audre Lorde asserts a radical and expansive notion of an *erotics of life* rather than of death. This erotic life is intimately connected to the sensual, spiritual (psychic, intellectual, and emotional), and the political: "The dichotomy between the spiritual and the political is also [like the dichotomy between the erotic and the spiritual] false, resulting from an incomplete attention to our erotic knowledge. For the bridge which connects them is formed by the erotic—the sensual—those physical, emotional, and psychic expressions of what is deepest and strongest and richest within each of us, being shared: the passions of love, in its deepest meanings." For Lorde, the "principal horror of any system which defines the good in terms of profit rather than in terms of human need, or which defines human need to the exclusion of the psychic and emotional components of that need—the principal horror of such a system is that it robs our work of its erotic value, its erotic power and life appeal and fulfillment" (Lorde 1984, 55, 56). Envisioning and enacting discourses, social practices, and political structures that would realize such a vision would challenge the destructive discourses and institutions prevalent in American society.

Daughters like Maxine, June Woo, and Leila Fu witness the suffering of their families and communities; heroically resistant but exhausted and exploited. Through their talk-story narratives, Kingston, Tan, and Ng critically define and challenge forces that so often attempt to suppress the affective character of social relations and agency. The daughters in these stories learn how important it is to do the difficult heart work in order to earn relationships and alliances even as they continue to explore new places to work, live, love, and contest.

It is important to study the intimate relationships between competing hegemonic and subordinated discursive communities in U.S. society. As Stuart Hall (1996) asserts, competing discourses, after all, are part of the way "reality" and power are configured, sustained, and challenged in culture and society. Discourses are not static; they interact and relate to each other in complex ways—not in simple binary oppositions. One cannot forget that discourses, especially dominant or privileged ones, have very real and serious effects—ideological, social, economic, and political— in the lives of people subjected to them. At the same time, discourses situated at the margins do not, as Gerald Torres reminds us, necessarily guarantee resistance, radical thinking, or transformative change (qtd. in Goldberg 1993, 216). Both hegemonic and oppositional discourses and their communities must be examined and critiqued. In situating my mother-daughter narratives within such contested terrain, it becomes possible not only to engage more fully with Kingston's, Tan's, and Ng's mother-daughter texts but to examine how power interests and relations are constituted, justified, and practiced in unequal relationship to each other. This broader analysis may give us a sense of the dynamic, complex, interactive border crossings—inside-outside, complicit-resisting, regressive-liberatory—of dominant and subordinated discursive communities as they struggle to articulate and enact their power and political strategies in society.

In writing this book, I hope to facilitate critical "talk-story" practices within the multiple communities and environments I inhabit. My own practices are passionately rooted and nurtured in living legacies and commitments inherited outside traditional western-based academic institutions and affiliated with my Popo and mother, and a very rich primary homeplace and hybrid culture in Honolulu, O'ahu. I believe such practices can engage the differences that separate individuals and competing communities, and can initiate more progressive ways to name and express these differences without reproducing debilitating hierarchies or exclusionary institutional structures. Furthermore, I hope that such practices encourage the formation of diverse social and political networks that build strong, permeable, and genuine communities. As an activist scholar and teacher "engaged in daily acts of cultural translation and negotiation" (Giroux 1988, 15), I believe it crucial to be conscious of how we are *all* complexly and diversely situated in this struggle for social, economic, cultural, and political power and how we may form more collaborative, open-ended, fulfilling, and just alliances with one another.

References

Abel, Elizabeth. 1981. (E)merging identities: The dynamics of female friendship in contemporary fiction by women. *Signs: Journal of Women in Culture and Society* 6, no. 3: 413–44.

———, Barbara Christian, and Helene Moglen, eds. 1997. *Female subjects in black and white: Race, psychoanalysis, feminism.* Berkeley: University of California Press.

Adams, Alice. 1995. Maternal bonds: Recent literature on mothering. *Signs: Journal of Women in Culture and Society* 20, no. 2: 414–27.

Alcoff, Linda. 1988. Cultural feminism versus post-structuralism: The identity crisis in feminist theory. *Signs: Journal of Women in Culture and Society* 13, no. 3: 405–36.

Alexander, M. Jacqui, and Chandra Mohanty, eds. 1997. *Feminist genealogies, colonial legacies, democratic futures.* New York: Routledge.

Allen, Paula Gunn. 1986. *The sacred hoop: Recovering the feminine in American Indian traditions.* Boston: Beacon Press.

Almaguer, Tomás. 1994. *Racial fault lines: The historical origins of White supremacy in California.* Berkeley, Los Angeles, Oxford: University of California Press.

Amott, Teresa L., and Julia A. Matthaei. 1991. *Race, gender and work: A multicultural economic history of women in the United States.* Boston: South End Press.

Andersen, Margaret. 1988. Moving our minds: Studying women of color and reconstructing sociology. *Teaching Sociology* 16 (April): 123–32.

Andrews, William L. 1986. *To tell a free story: The first century of Afro-American autobiography, 1760–1865.* Urbana: University of Illinois Press.

Ang, Ien. 1985. *Watching Dallas: Soap opera and the melodramatic imagination.* Translated by Della Couling. London: Methuen.

———. 1994. On not speaking Chinese: Postmodern ethnicity and the politics of diaspora. *New Formations* 24 (winter): 1–18.

———. 1995. I'm a feminist but . . . "other" women and postnational feminism. In *Transitions: New Australian feminisms*, edited by Barbara Caine and Rosemary Pringle. New York: St. Martin's Press, 57–73.

———. 1996. The curse of the smile: Ambivalence and the "Asian" woman in Australian multiculturalism. *Feminist Review* 52 (spring): 36–49.

Anzaldúa, Gloria. 1987. *Borderlands/La frontera: The new mestiza*. San Francisco: Aunt Lute Books.

———. 1990a. La conciencia de la mestiza: Towards a new consciousness. In *Making face, making soul: Haciendo caras*, edited by G. Anzaldúa. San Francisco: Aunt Lute Books, 377–89.

———, ed. 1990b. *Making face, making soul: Haciendo caras*. San Francisco: Aunt Lute Books.

Applebaum, Richard P. 1996. Multiculturalism and flexibility: Some new directions in global capitalism. In *Mapping multiculturalism*, edited by Avery Gordon and Christopher Newfield. Minneapolis: University of Minnesota Press, 297–316.

———, and Gregg Scott. 1996. Travelogue: The garment industry in Los Angeles and East Asia. In *Mapping multiculturalism*, edited by Avery Gordon and Christopher Newfield. Minneapolis: University of Minnesota Press, 330–45.

Aptheker, Bettina. 1989. *Tapestries of life: Women's work, women's consciousness, and the meaning of daily experience*. Amherst: University of Massachusetts Press.

Armstrong David. 1993. Filming Luck joyously. *San Francisco Examiner*, 22 August, sec. D, p.1 ff.

Ashley, Kathleen, Leigh Gilmore, and Gerald Peters, eds. 1994. *Autobiography and postmodernism*. Amherst: University of Massachusetts Press.

Asian Women United of California, eds. 1989. *Making waves: An anthology of writings by and about Asian American women*. Boston: Beacon Press.

Aubrey, James R. 1989. "Going toward war" in the writings of Maxine Hong Kingston. *Vietnam Generation* 1, no. 3–4: 99–101.

Avins, Mimi. 1993. How to tell the players in *The joy luck club*. *New York Times*, 5 September, sec. H, p. 14.

Badinter, Elizabeth. 1995. *On masculine identity*. Translated by Lydia Davis. European Perspectives: A Series in Social Thought and Cultural Criticism. New York: Columbia University Press.

Bambara, Toni Cade. 1980. *The salt eaters*. New York: Vintage Contemporaries.

Bannan, Helen. 1979. Warrior women: Immigrant mothers in the works of their daughters. *Women's Studies* 6: 165–77.

Barker-Nunn, Jeanne. 1987. Telling the mother's story: History and connection in the autobiographies of Maxine Hong Kingston and Kim Chernin. *Women's Studies* 14: 55–63.

Basch, Linda, Nina G. Schiller, and Christine S. Blanc. 1994. *Nations unbound: Transnational projects, postcolonial predicaments, and deterritorialized nation-state*. Australia: Gordon and Breach Science Publishers.

Bassin, Donna, Margaret Honey, and Meryle Mahrer Kaplan. 1994. Introduction. In *Representations of motherhood*, edited by Donna Bassin, Margaret Honey, and Meryle Mahrer Kaplan. New Haven and London: Yale University Press, 1–25.

Bates, Judy Fong. 1997. *China dog and other tales from a Chinese laundry*. Toronto: Sister Vision, Black and Women of Color Press.

Bederman, Gail. 1995. *Manliness and civilization: A cultural history of gender and race in the United States, 1880–1917*. Chicago: University of Chicago Press.

Belden, Jack. 1949. *China shakes the world*. New York: Harper and Brothers.

Benstock, Shari. 1988. Authorizing the autobiographical. In *The private self: Theory and practice of women's autobiographical writings*, edited by Shari Benstock. Chapel Hill and London: University of North Carolina Press, 10–33.

Bhabha, Homi K. 1994. *The location of culture*. New York and London: Routledge.

Bobo, Jacqueline. 1995. *Black women as cultural readers*. New York: Columbia University Press.

Boelhower, William. 1982. The brave new world of immigrant autobiography. *MELUS* 9, no. 2: 5–23.

Bonacich, Edna. 1996. The class question in global capitalism: The case of the Los Angeles garment industry. In *Mapping multiculturalism*, edited by Avery Gordon and Christopher Newfield. Minneapolis: University of Minnesota Press, 317–29.

Bourdieu, Pierre. 1984. *Distinction: A social critique of the judgment of taste*. Translated by Richard Nice. Cambridge: Harvard University Press.

———. 1993. *The field of cultural production*. New York: Columbia University Press.

Brodzki, Bella. 1988a. Mothers, displacement, and language in the autobiographies of Nathalie Sarraute and Christa Wolf. In *Life/Lines: Theorizing women's autobiography*, edited by Bella Brodzki and Celeste Schenck. Ithaca and London: Cornell University Press, 243–59.

———, and Celeste Schenck, eds. 1988. *Life/Lines: Theorizing women's autobiography*. Ithaca and London: Cornell University Press.

Bromley, Hank. 1989. Identity politics and critical pedagogy. *Educational Theory* 39, no. 3: 207–23.

Buena Vista Pictures Distribution, Inc.. 1993. *The joy luck club* production information (Hollywood Pictures film). Distributed by Buena Vista Pictures Distribution, Inc.

Buhle, Mari Jo. 1998. *Feminism and its discontents: A century of struggle with psychoanalysis*. Cambridge: Harvard University Press.

Bulkin, Elly, Minnie Bruce Pratt, and Barbara Smith, eds. 1984. *Yours in struggle: Three feminist perspectives on anti-Semitism and racism*. Brooklyn: Long Haul Press.

Buruma, Ian. 1996. The twenty-first century starts here. *New York Times Magazine*, 18 February.

Cade, Toni, ed. 1970. *The Black woman: An anthology.* New York: Mentor Books.

Cao, Lan. 1997. *Monkey bridge.* New York: Viking Press.

Caraway, Nancie. 1991. *Segregated sisterhood: Racism and the politics of American feminism.* Knoxville: University of Tennessee Press.

Carr, Helen. 1988. In other words: Native American women's autobiography. In *Life/Lines: Theorizing women's autobiography,* edited by Bella Brodzki and Celeste Schenck. Ithaca and London: Cornell University Press, 131–53.

Chambers, Veronica. 1993. Surprised by Joy. Review of *The joy luck club* (Hollywood Pictures film). *Premier* 7 (October): 80–84.

Chan, Jeffery Paul. 1977. Jeff Chan, Chairman of SF State Asian American studies, attacks review. *San Francisco Journal,* 4 May, 6.

———, Frank Chin, Lawson Fusao Inada, and Shawn Wong, eds. 1991. *The big aiiieeeee!: An anthology of Chinese American and Japanese American literature.* New York: Meridian.

Chan, Sucheng. 1986. *This bittersweet soil: The Chinese in California agriculture, 1860–1910.* Berkeley: University of California Press.

———. 1989. *Social and gender boundaries in the U.S.* Mellen Studies in Sociology, vol. 1. New York: Edward Mellen Press, 155–86.

———. 1991a. *Asian Americans: An interpretive history.* Twayne's Immigrant Heritage of America Series. Boston: Twayne Publishers.

———. 1991b. The exclusion of Chinese women, 1870–1943. In *Entry denied: Exclusion and the Chinese community in America, 1882–1943,* edited by Sucheng Chan. Philadelphia: Temple University Press, 91-146.

———. 1998. Race, ethnic culture, and gender in the construction of identities among second-generation Chinese Americans, 1880s to 1930s. In *Claiming America: constructing Chinese American identities during the exclusion era,* edited by K. Scott Wong and Sucheng Chan. Philadelphia: Temple University Press, 3–40.

Chang, Lan Samantha. 1998. *Hunger: A novella and stories.* New York: W.W. Norton and Company.

Chen, Kuan-Hsing. 1998. *Trajectories: Inter-Asia cultural studies.* New York: Routledge.

Chen, May Ying. 1976. Teaching a course on Asian American women. In *Counterpoint: perspectives on Asian America,* edited by Emma Gee. Los Angeles: Asian American Studies Center, UCLA.

Chen, Ying. 1998. *Ingratitude.* Translated by Carol Volk. New York: Farrar, Straus and Giroux.

Cheung, King-Kok. 1988. "Don't tell": Imposed silences in *The color purple* and *The woman warrior.* PMLA 103: 162–74.

———. 1990. *The woman warrior* versus *The Chinaman pacific*: Must a Chinese American critic choose between feminism and heroism? In *Conflicts in feminism,* edited by Marianne Hirsch and Evelyn Fox Keller. New York: Routledge, 234–51.

———. 1993. *Articulate silences: Hisaye Yamamoto, Maxine Hong Kingston, Joy Kogawa.* Ithaca: Cornell University Press.

———. 1998. Of men and men: Reconstructing Chinese American masculinity. In *Other sisterhoods: Literary theory and U.S. women of color,* edited by Sandra Kumamoto Stanley. Urbana and Chicago: University of Illinois Press, 173–99.

Cheyfitz, Eric. 1991. *The poetics of imperialism: The translation and colonization from The tempest to Tarzan.* New York: Oxford University Press.

Chin, Frank. 1972. Confessions of a Chinatown cowboy. *Bulletin of concerned Asian scholars* 4, no. 3: 58–70.

———. 1979–1980. How to watch a Chinese movie with the right "I." *Bamboo Ridge: The Hawaii Writers Quarterly* 5: 57–65.

———. 1981. *The chickencoop Chinaman; and The year of the dragon: two plays.* Seattle: University of Washington Press.

———. 1984. The most popular book in China. *Quilt* 4: 6–12.

———. 1985. This is not an autobiography. *Genre* 18 (summer): 109–30.

———. 1988. *The Chinaman Pacific & Frisco R.R. Co.: Short stories.* Minneapolis: Coffee House Press.

———. 1991a. *Donald Duk.* Minneapolis: Coffee House Press.

———. 1991b. Come all ye Asian American writers of the real and the fake. In *The big aiiieeeee!: An anthology of Chinese American and Japanese American literature,* edited by Jeffrey Paul Chan et al. New York: Meridian, 1–92.

———. 1994. *Gunga din highway.* Minneapolis: Coffee House Press.

———. 1997. Rashomon road: On the tao to San Diego. In *MultiAmerica: Essays on cultural wars and cultural peace,* edited by Ishmael Reed. New York: Viking Penguin, 286–308.

———, and Jeffery Paul Chan. 1972. Racist love. In *Seeing through shuck,* edited by Richard Kostelanetz. New York: Ballantine, 65–79.

———, Jeffrey Paul Chan, Lawson Fusao Inada, and Shawn Wong. 1991a. Preface. In *Aiiieeeee!: An anthology of Asian American writers,* edited by Frank Chin et al. New York: Mentor Books, xi–xxii. Originally published in 1974 by Howard University Press.

———, Jeffrey Paul Chan, Lawson Fusao Inada, and Shawn Wong. 1991b. Aiiieeeee! revisited: Preface to the Mentor edition. In *Aiiieeeee!: An anthology of Asian American writers,* edited by Frank Chin et al. New York: Mentor Books, xxiii–xli.

———, Jeffrey Paul Chan, Lawson Fusao Inada, and Shawn Wong. 1991c. Introduction: Fifty years of our whole voice. In *Aiiieeeee!: An anthology of Asian American writers,* edited by Frank Chin et al. New York: Mentor Books, 1–58.

————, Jeffrey Paul Chan, Lawson Fusao Inada, and Shawn Wong, eds. 1991d. *Aiiieeeee!: An anthology of Asian American writers*. New York: Mentor Books. Originally published in 1974 by Howard University Press.

Chin, Pa. 1931. *The family*. Boston: Cheng and Tsui.

Chin, Sara. 1997. *Below the line*. San Francisco: City Lights.

Chiu, Vivian. 1992. China's secret texts. *World Press Review* 39, no. 6: 50.

Chodorow, Nancy. 1978. *The reproduction of mothering: Psychoanalysis and the sociology of gender*. Berkeley: University of California Press.

Chong, Denise. 1994. *The concubine's children*. New York: Viking Press.

Chow, Crystal. 1988. Sixty years on the silver screen. *Rice* September, 10–22, 47.

Chow, Esther. 1989. "The Feminist Movement: Where are all the Asian American Women?" In *Making waves: An anthology of writings by and about Asian American women*, edited by Asian Women United of California. Boston: Beacon Press, 362–76.

Chow, Rey. 1991a. Violence in the other country: China as crisis, spectacle, and woman. In *Third world women and the politics of feminism*, edited by Chandra Talpade Mohanty, Ann Russo, and Lourdes Torres. Bloomington: Indiana University Press, 81–100.

————. 1991b. *Woman and Chinese modernity: The politics of reading between West and East*. Theory and History of Literature Series, vol. 75. Minnesota: University of Minnesota Press.

————. 1993. *Writing diaspora: Tactics of intervention in contemporary cultural studies*. Bloomington: Indiana University Press.

Choy, Philip P., Lorraine Dong, and Marlon K. Hom, eds. 1994. *The coming man: Nineteenth century American perceptions of the Chinese*. Seattle: University of Washington Press.

Chu, Judy. 1976. Anna May Wong. In *Counterpoint: Perspectives on Asian America*, edited by Emma Gee. Los Angeles: Asian American Studies, UCLA, 284–88.

————. 1986. Asian American women's studies courses: A look back at our beginnings. *Frontiers* 8, no. 3: 96–101.

Chu, Louis. 1961. *Eat a bowl of tea*. Secaucus, NJ: Lyle Stuart.

Chua, Lawrence. 1998. *Gold by the inch*. New York: Grove Press.

Chuang, Hua [pseud.]. 1986. *Crossings*. Boston: Northeastern University Press. Originally published 1968.

Chun, Gloria H. 1998. "Go West . . . to China": Chinese American identity in the 1930s. In *Claiming America: Constructing Chinese American identities during the exclusion era*, edited by K. Scott Wong and Sucheng Chan. Philadelphia: Temple University Press, 165–90.

————. 1991. The high note of the barbarian reed pipe: Maxine Hong Kingston. *The Journal of Ethnic Studies* 19, no. 3: 85–95.

Chung, L. A. 1991. Chinese American literary war. *San Francisco Chronicle*, 26 August, sec. D, p. 3 ff.

Cixous, Hélène. 1981. Sorties. Translated by Ann Liddle. In *New French feminisms: An anthology*, edited by Elaine Marks and Isabelle de Courtivron. New York: Schocken Books, 90–98.

Clark, Danae. 1996. Father figure. In *Boys: Masculinities in contemporary culture*, edited by Paul Smith. New York: Westview Press, 23–37.

Cloutier, Candace. 1984. Maxine Hong Kingston. *Contemporary Authors*, Gale, Vol. 13. New Revision series, 281–94.

Collins, Patricia Hill. 1987. The meaning of motherhood in Black culture and Black mother/daughter relationships. *Sage* 4, no. 2: 3–10.

———. 1990. *Black feminist thought: Knowledge, consciousness, and the politics of empowerment*. Perspectives in Gender, vol. 2. Boston: Unwin Hyman.

———. 1994. Shifting the center: Race, class, and feminist theorizing about motherhood. In *Representations of motherhood*, edited by Donna Bassin, Margaret Honey, and Meryle Mahrer Kaplan. New Haven and London: Yale University Press, 56–74.

Combahee River Collective. 1981. A Black feminist statement. In *This bridge called my back: Writings by radical women of color*, edited by Cherríe Moraga and Gloria Anzaldúa. New York: Kitchen Table, Women of Color Press.

Confucius. 1979. *The analects*. Translated by D.C. Lau. London: Penguin Books.

Constable, Nicole. 1997. *Maid to order in Hong Kong: Stories of Filipina workers*. Ithaca: Cornell University Press.

Croll, Elisabeth. 1978. *Feminism and socialism in China*. London: Routledge and Kegan Paul.

———. 1995. *Changing identities of Chinese women: Rhetoric, experience and self-perception in twentieth-century China*. London: Zed Books.

Culley, Margo, ed. 1992. *American women's autobiography: Fea(s)ts of memory*. Madison: University of Wisconsin Press.

Daly, Brenda O., and Maureen T. Reddy, eds. 1991. *Narrating mothers: Theorizing maternal subjectivities*. Knoxville: University of Tennessee Press.

Daniels, Roger. 1988. *Asian America: Chinese and Japanese in the United States since 1850*. Seattle: University of Washington Press.

Dasenbrock, Reed Way. 1987. Intelligibility and meaningfulness in multicultural literature in English. *PMLA* 102: 10–19.

Dasgupta, Shamita Das, ed. 1998. *A patchwork shawl: Chronicles of South Asian women in America*. New Brunswick, NJ: Rutgers University Press.

Davidson, Cathy, and E.M. Boner, eds. 1980. *The lost tradition: Mothers and daughters in literature*. New York: Frederick Ungar Publishing Co.

Davis, Angela. 1983. *Women, race and class*. New York: Vintage. Originally published in 1981.

de Lauretis, Teresa. 1984. *Alice doesn't: Feminism, semiotics, cinema*. Bloomington: Indiana University Press.

————. 1986. Feminist studies/critical studies: Issues, terms, and contexts. In *Feminist studies/critical studies*, edited by Teresa de Lauretis. Theories of Contemporary Culture, vol. 8. Bloomington: Indiana University Press, 1–19.

Delgado, Richard, and Jean Stefancic. 1998. Racial depiction in American law and culture. In *The Latino/a condition: A critical reader*, edited by Richard Delgado and Jean Stefancic. New York: New York University Press. 209–14.

Demetrakopoulos, Stephanie A. 1980. The metaphysics of matrilinearism in women's autobiography: Studies of Mead's *Blackberry winter*, Hellman's *Pentimento*, Angelou's *I know why the caged bird sings*, and Kingston's *The woman warrior*. In *Women's autobiography: Essays in criticism*, edited by Estelle C. Jelinek. Bloomington: Indiana University Press, 180–205.

Dill, Bonnie Thornton. 1988. Our mothers' grief: Racial ethnic women and the maintenance of families. *Journal of Family History* 13, no. 4: 415–31.

Dinnerstein, Dorothy. 1976. *The mermaid and the minotaur: Sexual arrangements and the human malaise*. New York: Harper and Row Books.

Divakaruni, Chitra Banerjee. 1995. *Arranged marriage: Stories*. New York: Anchor Books.

Dong, Lorraine. 1992. The forbidden city legacy and its Chinese American women. *Chinese America: History and Perspectives*. 125–48.

Donnelly, Nancy. 1994. *Changing lives of refugee Hmong women*. Seattle: University of Washington Press.

du Plessis, Rachel Blau. 1985. *Writing beyond the ending: Narrative strategies of twentieth-century women writers*. Bloomington: Indiana University Press.

duCille, Ann. 1994. The occult of true Black womanhood: Critical demeanor and Black feminist studies. *Signs: Journal of Women in Culture and Society* 19, no. 3: 591–629.

Easley, Brian. 1987. Patriarchy, scientists, and nuclear warriors. In *Beyond patriarchy: Essays by men on pleasure, power, and change*, edited by Michael Kaufman. Toronto: Oxford University Press, 195–215.

Ebrey, Patricia Buckley. 1991. Introduction. In *Marriage and inequality in Chinese society*, edited by Rubie S. Watson and Patricia Buckley Ebrey. Berkeley, Los Angeles, Oxford: University of California Press, 1–24.

Ehrenreich, Barbara. 1983. *The hearts of men: American dreams and the flight from commitment*. New York: Anchor Books.

Eliot, T.S. 1971. *Four quartets*. New York: Harcourt Brace and Company. Originally published in 1943.

Eng, David L., and Alice Y. Hom, eds. 1998. *Q & A: Queer in Asian America.* Philadelphia: Temple University Press.

Enloe, Cynthia. 1989. *Bananas, beaches and bases: Making feminist sense of international politics.* Berkeley: University of California Press.

Espiritu, Yen Le. 1997. *Asian American women and men: Labor, laws and love.* The Gender Lens Series, vol. 1. Thousand Oaks, CA: Sage Publications, Inc.

Faludi, Susan. 1991. *Backlash: The undeclared war against American women.* New York: Crown Publishers.

Feldman, Gayle. 1989. *The joy luck club*: Chinese magic, American blessings, and a publishing fairy tale. *Publishers Weekly,* 7 July 24–26.

Fernández, Roberta. 1990. *Intaglio: A novel in six stories.* Houston: Arte Publico Press.

Fischer, Michael M. J. 1986. Ethnicity and the post-modern arts of memory. In *Writing culture: The poetics and politics of ethnography*, edited by James Clifford and George E. Marcus. Berkeley: University of California Press, 194–233.

Fitzgerald, F. Scott. 1925. *The great gatsby.* New York: Charles Scribner's Sons.

Flax, Jane. 1978. The conflict between nurturance and autonomy in mother-daughter relationships and within feminism. *Feminist Studies* 4, no. 2: 171–189.

Fong, Katheryn M. 1977. To Maxine Hong Kingston, a letter from Katheryn M. Fong. *Bulletin of Concerned Asian Scholars* 9, no. 4: 67–69.

Fong, Yem Siu. 1990. Review of *The joy luck club. Frontiers* 6, no. 2–3: 122–23.

Fox-Genovese, Elizabeth. 1988. My statue, my self: Autobiographical writings of Afro-American women. In *The private self: Theory and practice of women's autobiographical writings*, edited by Shari Benstock. Chapel Hill and London: University of North Carolina Press, 63–89.

Fraser, Nancy. 1990. The uses and abuses of French discourse theories for feminist politics. *Boundary 2* 17, no. 2: 83–101.

Fregoso, Rosa Linda, and Angie Chabram. 1990. Introduction: Chicana/o cultural representations: Reframing alternative critical discourses. *Cultural Studies* 4, no.3: 203–16.

Frenier, Mariam Darce. 1984. The effects of the Chinese revolution of women and their families. In *Women and the structure of society: Selected research from the Fifth Berkshire Conference on the History of Women*, edited by Barbara J. Harris and JoAnn K. McNamara. Durham: Duke Press Policy Studies, 232–52.

Friday, Nancy. 1977. *My mother/my self: The daughter's search for identity.* New York: Delacorte Press.

Friedan, Betty. 1963. *The feminine mystique.* New York: Dell Press.

Friedman, Susan Stanford. 1988. Women's autobiographical selves: Theory and practice. In *The private self: Theory and practice of women's autobiographical writings*, edited by Shari Benstock. Chapel Hill and London: University of North Carolina Press, 34–62.

Fung, Richard. 1991. Looking for my penis: The eroticized Asian in gay porn. In *How do I look? Queer film and video*, edited by Bad Object-Choices. Seattle: Bay Press, 145–68.

Galang, M. Evelina. 1996. *Her wild American self*. Minneapolis: Coffee House Press.

Gandhi, Leela. 1998. *Postcolonial theory: A critical introduction*. New York: Columbia University Press.

Garcia, Cristina. 1993. Reading Chinese fortunes. Review of *Bone*, by Fae Myenne Ng. *Washington Post*, 10 January, 8.

Gardiner, Judith Kegan. 1985. Mind mother: Psychoanalysis and feminism. In *Making a difference: feminist literary criticism*, edited by Gayle Greene and Coppélia Kahn. London and New York: Methuen, 113–45.

Gee, John. 1976. Life in a Chinese laundry: Interview with John Gee. By Buck Wong. In *Counterpoint: Perspectives on Asian America*, edited by Emma Gee. Los Angeles: Asian American Studies Center, University of California, 338–44.

Giddings, Paula. 1984. *When and where I enter: The impact of Black women on race and sex in America*. New York: Bantam Books.

Gilman, Charlotte Perkins. 1980. The yellow wallpaper. In *The Charlotte Perkins Gilman reader*, edited by Ann J. Lane. New York: Pantheon Books, 3–20.

Gilroy, Paul. 1991. It ain't where you're from, it's where you're at . . . : The dialectics of diasporic identification. *Third Text: Third World Perspectives on Contemporary Art and Culture* 13 (winter): 3–16.

Giroux, Henry. 1988. Border pedagogy in the age of postmodernism. *Journal of Education* 170, no. 3: 162–81.

Glenn, Evelyn Nakano. 1985. Racial ethnic women's labor: The intersection of race, gender and class oppression. *Review of Radical Political Economics* 17, no. 3: 86–208.

———. 1986. *Issei, Nisei, war bride: Three generations of Japanese American women in domestic service*. Philadelphia: Temple University Press.

———. 1987. Gender and the family. In *Analyzing gender*, edited by Beth Hess and Myra Marx. Newbury Park, CA: Sage, 348–80.

———. 1990. The dialectics of wage work: Japanese-American women and domestic service, 1905–1940. In *Unequal sisters: A multicultural reader in U.S. women's history*, edited by Ellen Carol DuBois and Vicki L. Ruiz. New York: Routledge, 345–72.

———. 1994. Social constructions of mothering: A thematic overview. In *Mothering: Ideology, experience, and agency*, edited by Evelyn Nakano Glenn, Grace Chang, and Linda Rennie Forcey. New York and London: Routledge, 1–29.

————, and Stacy G. H. Yap. 1998. Chinese American families. In *Minority families in the United States: A multicultural perspective.* 2d edition. Edited by Ronald L. Taylor. Upper Saddle River, NJ: Prentice Hall, 128–58. Originally published in 1994.

————, Grace Chang, and Linda Rennie Forcey, eds. 1994. *Mothering: Ideology, experience, and agency.* New York and London: Routledge.

Goldberg, David Theo. 1993. *Racist culture: Philosophy and the politics of meaning.* Oxford: Blackwell.

————, ed. 1994. *Multiculturalism: A critical reader.* Oxford. Blackwell.

Gordon, Avery, and Christopher Newfield, eds. 1996. *Mapping multiculturalism.* Minneapolis: University of Minnesota Press.

Gornick, Vivian. 1997. *The End of the Novel of Love.* Boston: Beacon Press.

Grewal, Inderpal. 1994. Autobiographic subjects and diasporic locations: *Meatless days* and *Borderlands.* In *Scattered hegemonies: Postmodernity and transnational feminist practices,* edited by Inderpal Grewal and Caren Kaplan. Minneapolis: University of Minnesota Press, 231–54.

————, and Caren Kaplan. 1994. Introduction: Transnational feminist practices and questions of postmodernity. In *Scattered hegemonies: Postmodernity and transnational feminist practices,* edited by Inderpal Grewal and Caren Kaplan. Minneapolis: University of Minnesota Press, 1–33.

Griswold, Robert L. 1993. *Fatherhood in America: A history.* New York: Basic Books.

Gronewold, Sue. 1982. Beautiful merchandise: Prostitution in China 1860–1935. *Women and History* 1, (spring): 1–114.

Guinier, Lani. 1997. Of gentlemen and role models. In *Critical race feminism: A reader,* edited by Adrien Katherine Wing. New York: New York University Press, 73–80.

Guy-Sheftall, Beverly. 1995. *Words of fire: An anthology of African-American feminist thought.* New York: The New Press.

Hage, Ghassan. 1993. Republicanism, multiculturalism, zoology. *Communal/Plural* 2: 113–38.

Hall, Stuart. 1989. Cultural identity and cinematic representation. *Frame Works* 36: 68–81.

————. 1996. The questions of cultural identity. In *Modernity: An introduction to modern societies,* edited by Stuart Hall, David Held, Don Hubert, and Kenneth Thompson. Cambridge: Blackwell Publishers, 595–634.

Hamamoto, Darrell Y. 1994. *Monitored peril: Asian Americans and the politics of TV representation.* Minneapolis: University of Minnesota Press.

Hattori, Tomo. 1998. Psycholinguistic Orientalism in criticism of *The woman warrior* and *Obasan.* In *Other sisterhoods: Literary theory and U.S. women of color,* edited by Sandra Kumamoto Stanley. Urbana and Chicago: University of Illinois Press.

Henderson, Mae G. 1995. Introduction. In *Borders, boundaries, and frames: essays in cultural criticism and cultural studies*, edited by Mae G. Henderson. New York: Routledge, 1–30.

Hershatter, Gail. 1991. Prostitution and the market in women in early twentieth-century Shanghai. In *Marriage and inequality in Chinese society*, edited by Rubie S. Watson and Patricia Buckley Ebrey. Berkeley, Los Angeles, Oxford: University of California Press.

Heung, Marina. 1993. Daughter-text/mother-text: Matrilineage in Amy Tan's *The joy luck club*. *Feminist Studies* 19, no. 3: 597–613.

Hinsch, Bret. 1990. *Passions of the cut sleeve: The male homosexual tradition in China*. Berkeley: University of California Press.

Hirata, Lucie Cheng. 1979. Free, indentured, enslaved: Chinese prostitutes in nineteenth-century America. *Signs: Journal of Women in Culture and Society* 5, no. 1: 3–29.

———. 1982. Chinese immigrant women in nineteenth-century California. In *Asian and Pacific American experiences: Women's perspectives*, edited by Nobuya Tsuchida. Minneapolis: Asian/Pacific American Learning Resource Center and General College, University of Minnesota, 38–55.

Hirsch, Marianne. 1981a. Mothers and daughters. *Signs: Journal of Women in Culture and Society* 7, no. 1: 200–22.

———. 1981b. Incorporation and repetition in *La princesse de Clèves*. *Yale French Studies* 62: 67–87.

———. 1989. *The mother/daughter plot: Narrative, psychoanalysis, feminism*. Bloomington: Indiana University Press.

———. 1990. Maternal narratives: "Cruel enough to stop the blood." In *Reading Black, Reading feminist: A critical anthology*, edited by Henry Louis Gates, Jr. New York: Meridian, 415–430.

———, and Evelyn Fox Keller. 1990. *Conflicts in feminism*. New York: Routledge.

Ho, Wendy. 1991. Mother/daughter writing and the politics of race and sex in Maxine Hong Kingston's *The woman warrior*. In *Asian Americans: Comparative and global perspectives*, edited by Shirley Hune, Hyung-Chan Dim, Stephen Fugita, and Amy Ling. Pullman: Washington State University Press, 225–37.

———. 1996. Swan-feather mothers and coca-cola daughters: Teaching Amy Tan's *The joy luck club*. In *Teaching American ethnic literatures*, edited by John R. Maitino and David R. Peck. Albuquerque: University of New Mexico Press, 327–45.

Hoffman, Eva. 1989. *Lost in translation: A life in a new language*. New York: Penguin Books.

Holte, James Craig. 1982. The representative voice: Autobiography and the ethnic experience. *MELUS* 9, no. 2: 25–46.

Homsher, Deborah. 1979. *The woman warrior* by Maxine Hong Kingston: A bridging of autobiography and fiction. *Iowa Review* 10, no. 4: 93–98.

Hondagneu-Sotelo, Pierrette. 1994. *Gendered transitions: Mexican experiences of immigration.* Berkeley, University of California.

Hong, Terry. 1994. The woman warrior wars. A. *Magazine*, Special Woman's Issue, 54–57.

Honig, Bonnie. 1998. Immigrant America? How foreignness "solves" democracy's problems. *Social Text* 56, no. 3: 1–27.

Honig, Emily. 1986. *Sisters and strangers: Women in the Shanghai cotton mills, 1919–1949.* Stanford: Stanford University Press.

hooks, bell. 1989. *Talking back.* Boston: South End Press.

———. 1990. *Yearning: Race, gender, and cultural politics.* Boston: South End Press.

———. 1991. Narratives of struggle. In *Critical Fictions: The politics of imaginative writing*, edited by Philmena Mariani. Seattle: Bay Press, 53–61.

———. 1992. *Black looks: Race and representation.* Boston: South End Press.

———. 1994. Black is a woman's color. In *The woman that I am: The literature and culture of contemporary women of color*, edited by D. Soyini Madison. New York: St. Martin's Press, 206–13.

———. 1996. *Reel to real: Race, sex, and class at the movies.* New York: Routledge.

Hossfeld, Karen J. 1994. Hiring immigrant women: Silicon Valley's "simple formula." In *Women of color in U.S. society*, edited by Maxine Baca Zinn and Bonnie Thornton Dill. Philadelphia: Temple University Press, 65-93.

Hsu, Vivian. 1983. Maxine Hong Kingston as psycho-autobiographer and ethnographer. *International Journal of Women's Studies* 6, no. 5: 429–42.

Hull, Gloria, Patricia Bell Scott, and Barbara Smith, eds. 1982. *All the women are white, all the Blacks are men, but some of us are brave: Black women's studies.* New York: The Feminist Press.

Hunnewell, Susannah. 1993. When the old began to die. *New York Times Book Review*, 7 February, p. 9.

Hunt, Linda. 1985. "I could not figure out what was my village": Gender versus ethnicity in Maxine Hong Kingston's The woman warrior. *MELUS* 12, no. 3: 5–12.

Hurtado, Aida. 1989. Reflections on White feminism: A perspective from a woman of color. In *Social and gender boundaries in the U.S.*, edited by Sucheng Chan. Mellen Studies in Sociology, vol. 1. New York: Edward Mellen Press, 155–86.

Hwang, David Henry. 1988. *M butterfly.* New York: Plume Books.

Iglesias, Elizabeth M. 1998. Maternal power and the deconstruction of male supremacy. In *The Latino/a condition: A critical reader*, edited by Richard Delgado and Jean Stefancic. New York: New York University Press, 508–15.

Jaschok, Maria, and Suzanne Miers. 1994. Women in the Chinese patriarchal system: Submission, servitude, escape and collusion. In *Women and Chinese patriarchy: Submission, servitude and escape*, edited by Maria Jaschok and Suzanne Miers. London: Zed Books, Ltd., 1–24.

Jayawardena, Kumari. 1986. *Feminism and nationalism in the third world*. London: Zed Books Ltd.

Jelinek, Estelle C. 1980. Introduction: Women's autobiography and the male tradition. In *Women's autobiography: Essays in criticism*, edited by Estelle C. Jelinek. Bloomington: Indiana University Press, 1–20.

Jen, Gish. 1996. *Mona in the promised land*. New York: Vintage Contemporaries.

———. 1991. Typical American. New York: Houghton Mifflin/Seymour Lawrence.

Jones, Gayl. 1991. *Liberating voices: Oral tradition in African American literature*. New York: Penguin Books.

Jones, Louis. 1993. Dying to be an American. *New York Times Book Review*, 7 February.

Jordan, June. 1990. Report from the Bahamas. In *Women's voices: Visions and perspectives*, edited by Pat Hoy II, Esther Schor and Robert Di Yanni. New York: McGraw-Hill Publishing Co., 119–26. Originally published in 1984.

———. 1994. War and memory. In *The woman that I am: The literature and culture of contemporary women of color*, edited by D. Soyini Madison. New York: St. Martin's Press, 85–91.Originally published in 1989.

Juhasz, Suzanne. 1980. Towards a theory of form in feminist autobiography: Kate Millett's *Flying* and *Sita*; Maxine Hong Kingston's *The woman warrior*. In *Women's autobiography: Essays in criticism*, edited by Estelle C. Jelinek. Bloomington: Indiana University Press, 221–37.

———. 1985. Maxine Hong Kingston: Narrative technique and female identity. In *Contemporary American women writers: Narrative strategies*, edited by Catherine Rainwater and William J. Scheick. Lexington: University of Kentucky Press, 173–189.

Kadohata, Cynthia. 1989. *The floating world*. New York: Viking Press.

Kam, K. 1989. The hopeland. In *Making waves: An anthology of writings by and about Asian American women*, edited by Asian Women United of California. Boston: Beacon Press, 92–98.

Kamani, Ginu. 1995. *Junglee girl*. San Francisco: Aunt Lute Books.

Kaplan, E. Ann. 1987. Mothering, feminism, and representation: The maternal in melodrama and the woman's film, 1910–40. In *Home is where the heart is: Studies in melodrama and the woman's film*, edited by Christine Gledhill. London: British Film Institute, 113–37.

———. 1992. *Motherhood and representation: The mother in popular culture and melodrama*. New York and London: Routledge.

Keller, Nora Okja. 1995. *Comfort woman*. New York: Viking Press.

Kibria, Nazli. 1990. Power, patriarchy, and gender conflict in the Vietnamese immigrant community. *Gender and Society* 4, no. 1: 9–24.

———. 1998. Vietnamese families. Chinese American families. In *Minority families in the United States: A multicultural perspective*. 2d edition. Edited by Ronald L. Taylor. Upper Saddle River, NJ: Prentice Hall, 128–58. Originally published in 1994.

Kim, Daniel Y. 1998. The strange love of Frank Chin. In *Q & A: Queer in Asian America*, edited by David L. Eng and Alice Y. Hom. Philadelphia: Temple University Press, (270-303).

Kim, Elaine H. 1981. Visions and fierce dreams: A commentary on the works of Maxine Hong Kingston. *Amerasia* 8, no. 2: 145–161.

———. 1982. *Asian American literature: An introduction to the writings and their social context*. Philadelphia: Temple University Press.

———. 1986. Asian Americans and American popular literature. In *Dictionary of Asian American history*, edited by Hyung-Chan Kim. New York: Greenwood Press, 99–113.

———. 1990. "Such opposite creatures": Men and women in Asian American literature. *Michigan Quarterly Review* 29, no. 1: 68–93.

Kim, Patti. 1997. *A cab called reliable*. New York: Wyatt Books/St. Martin's Press.

Kim, Ronyoung. 1987. *Clay walls*. Seattle: University of Washington Press.

Kimmel, Michael. 1996. *Manhood in America: A cultural history*. New York: Free Press.

King, Deborah K. 1988. Multiple jeopardy, multiple consciousness: The context of a Black feminist ideology. *Signs: Journal of Women in Culture and Society* 14, no. 11: 42–72.

Kingston, Maxine Hong. 1977. *The woman warrior: Memoirs of a girlhood among ghosts*. New York: Vintage. Originally published in 1976.

———. 1982. Cultural mis-readings by American reviews. In *Asian and Western writers in dialogue: New cultural identities*, edited by Guy Amirthanayagam. London: Macmillan, 55–65.

———. 1989a. *Tripmaster monkey: His fake book*. New York: Alfred A. Knopf.

———. 1989b. The novel's next step. *Mother Jones*, December, 37–41.

———. 1989c. *China men*. New York: Vintage International. Originally published in 1977.

———. 1991. Interview by Shelley Fisher Fishkin. *American Literary History* 3, no. 4: 782–791.

———. 1997. Interview by Karen Amano. *Performing Arts*, May, 8–12.

————. 1998. Honolulu interview: Maxine Hong Kingston. Interview by Karen Horton. In *Conversations with Maxine Hong Kingston*, edited by Paul Skenazy and Tera Martin. Jackson: University Press of Mississippi, 5–13.

Ko, Dorothy. 1997. *Teachers of the inner chambers: Women and culture in seventeenth-century China*. Stanford: Stanford University Press.

Koenig, Rhoda. 1989. Heirloom China. *New York Magazine*, 20 March, 82–83.

Kogawa, Joy. 1981. *Obasan*. Boston: Godine.

Kosasa-Terry, Geraldine E. 1991. Localizing discourse. In *New visions in Asian American studies: Diversity, community, power*, edited by Franklin Ng, Judy Yung, Stephen Fugita, and Elaine Kim. Pullman: Washington State University Press, 211–21.

Kwong, Peter. 1997. *Forbidden workers: Illegal Chinese immigrants and American labor*. New York: The New Press.

Lau, Evelyn. 1995. *Runaway: Diary of a street kid*. Toronto, Canada: Coach House Press.

Lavie, Smadar, and Ted Swedenburg. 1996. *Displacement, diaspora, and geographies of identity*. Durham: Duke University Press.

Lee, Li-Young. 1995. *The winged seed: A remembrance*. New York: Simon and Schuster.

Lee, Sky. 1990. *Disappearing moon cafe*. Seattle: Seal Press.

Leonard, Karen. 1992. *Making ethnic choices: California's Punjabi Mexican Americans*. Philadelphia: Temple University Press.

Leong, Russell, ed. 1996. *Asian American sexualities: Dimensions of the gay and lesbian experience*. New York: Routledge.

Li, David Leiwei. 1988. The naming of a Chinese American "I": Cross-cultural sign/ificators in *The woman warrior*. *Criticism* 30, no. 4: 497–515.

————. 1990. *China men*: Maxine Hong Kingston and the American canon. *American Literary History* 2, no. 3: 482–502.

Lim, Shirley Geok-Lin. 1990. Japanese American women's life stories: Maternality in Monica Sone's *Nisei daughter* and Joy Kogawa's *Obasan*. *Feminist Studies* 16, no. 2: 188–312.

————. 1992. The tradition of Chinese American women's life stories: Thematics of race and gender in Jade Snow Wong's *Fifth Chinese daughter* and Maxine Hong Kingston's *The woman warrior*. In *Fea(s)ts of Memory*, edited by Margo Culley. Madison: University of Wisconsin Press, 252–67.

————. 1996. Growing with stories: Chinese American identities, textual identities. In *Teaching American ethnic literatures*, edited by John R. Maitino and David R. Peck. Albuquerque: University of New Mexico Press, 273–92.

————, ed. 1991. *Approaches to teaching Kingston's* The woman warrior. New York: The Modern Language Association of America.

————, Mayumi Tsutakawa, and Margarita Donnelly, eds. 1989. *The forbidden stitch: An Asian American women's anthology.* Corvallis, OR: Calyx.

Lin, Jan. 1998. *Reconstructing Chinatown: Ethnic enclave, global change.* Minneapolis: Minnesota University Press.

Ling, Amy. 1990. *Between worlds: Women writers of Chinese ancestry.* The Athene Series. New York: Pergamon Press, Inc.

Ling, Susie. 1989. The mountain movers: Asian American women's movement in Los Angeles. *Amerasia* 15, no. 1: 51–67.

Linmark, R .Zamora. 1995. *Rolling the r's.* New York: Kaya Production.

Lionnet, Francoise. 1990. Autoethnography: The an-archic style of *Dust tracks on a road. Reading Black, reading feminist: A critical anthology,* edited by Henry Louis Gates, Jr. New York: Meridian, 382–414.

Lipsitz, George. 1998. The possessive investment in whiteness: How white people profit from identity politics. Philadelphia: Temple University Press.

Lo, Kuan-chung. 1991. *Three kingdoms: China's epic drama.* Translated by Moss Roberts. Berkeley: University of California Press.

Loke, Margarett. 1989. 'The tao is up'. *New York Times Magazine,* 30 April.

Lorde, Audre. 1982. *Zami: A new spelling of my name.* Freedom, CA: Crossing Press.

————. 1984. *Sister outsider: Essays and speeches.* New York: Crossing Press.

Lott, Juanita Tamayo. 1989. Growing up, 1968–1985. In *Making waves: An anthology of writings by and about Asian American women,* edited by Asian Women United of California. Boston: Beacon Press, 353–61.

Louie, Miriam Ching. 1992. Immigrant Asian women in Bay Area garment sweatshops: "After sewing, laundry, cleaning and cooking, I have no breath left to sing." *Amerasia* 18, no. 1: 1–26.

Lowe, Lisa. 1991. Homogeneity, hybridity, multiplicity: Marking Asian American differences. *Diaspora* 1, no. 1: 24–44.

————. 1996a. *Immigrant acts: On Asian American cultural politics.* Durham: Duke University Press.

————. 1996b. Imagining Los Angeles in the production of multiculturalism. In *Mapping multiculturalism,* edited by Avery Gordon and Christopher Newfield. Minneapolis: University of Minnesota Press, 413–423.

Lu, Alvin. 1993. *Bone* machine. *San Francisco Bay Guardian.* Literary Supplement. vol. 27, no. 21: 1 ff.

Lugones, Maria. 1990. Playfulness, "world"-travelling, and loving perception. In *Making face, making soul: Haciendo caras,* edited by Gloria Anzaldúa. San Francisco: Aunt Lute Books, 390–402.

Luluquisen, Esminia, Kristin Groessl, and Nancy Puttkammer. 1995. *The health and well-being of Asian and Pacific Islander American women.* Oakland, CA: Asians and Pacific Islanders for Reproductive Health.

Manalansan, Martin F., IV. 1995. In the shadows of Stonewall: Examining gay transnational politics and the diasporic dilemma. *GLQ: A Journal of Lesbian and Gay Studies* 2, no. 4: 425–38.

Manganyi, Noel Chabani. 1983. Psychobiography and the truth of the subject. *Biography* 6, no. 1: 34–52.

Mani, Lata. 1992. Multiple mediations: Feminist scholarship in the age of multinational reception. In *Knowing women: Feminism and knowledge*, edited by Helen Crowley and Susan Himmelweit. Cambridge, UK: Polity Press, 306–22.

Mann, Susan. 1997. *Precious records: Women in China's long eighteenth century.* Stanford: Stanford University Press.

Mar, Laureen. 1993. Book review of *Bone. Amerasia* 20, no.1: 184–186.

Mar, M. Elaine. 1999. Paper daughter: A Memoir. New York. HarperCollins.

Marchetti, Gina. 1993. *Romance and the "yellow peril": Race, sex and discursive strategies in Hollywood fiction.* Berkeley: University of California Press.

Marshall, Paule. 1981. *Brown girls, brownstones.* New York: The Feminist Press. Originally published in 1959.

———. 1990. Poets in the kitchen. In *Women's voices: Visions and perspectives*, edited by Pat Hoy II, Esther Schor, and Robert DiYanni. New York: McGraw-Hill Publishing Company.

Martin, Biddy, and Chandra Mohanty. 1986. Feminist politics: What's home got to do with it? In *Feminist studies/critical studies*, edited by Teresa de Lauretis. Theories of Contemporary Culture, vol. 8. Bloomington: Indiana University Press, 191–212.

Mason, Sarah Refo. 1994. Social Christianity, American feminism and Chinese prostitutes: The history of the Presbyterian mission home, San Francisco, 1874–1935. In *Women and Chinese patriarchy: Submission, servitude and escape*, edited by Maria Jaschok and Suzanne Miers. London: Zed Books, Ltd., 198–220.

Matsui, Yayori. 1987. *Women's Asia.* London: Zed Books, Ltd.

Matsumoto, Valerie. 1990. Japanese American women during world war II. In *Unequal sisters: A multicultural reader in U.S. women's history*, edited by Ellen Carol DuBois and Vicki L. Ruiz. New York: Routledge, 373–86.

———. 1991. Desperately seeking "Deirdre": Gender roles, multicultural relations, and Nisei women writers of the 1930s. *Frontiers: A Journal of Women Studies* 12, no. 1: 19–32.

McClain, Charles T. 1994. *In search of equality: The Chinese struggle against discrimination in nineteenth-century America.* Berkeley: University of California Press.

McDonald, Dorothy Ritsuko. 1981. Introduction to *The chickencoop Chinaman; and The year of the dragon: two plays*, by Frank Chin. Seattle: University of Washington Press.

McKay, Nellie Y. 1988. Race, gender and cultural context in Zora Neale Hurston's *Dust tracks on a road*. In *Life/lines: Theorizing women's autobiography*, edited by Bella Brodzki and Celeste Schenck. Ithaca and London: Cornell University Press, 175–188.

Miller, Margaret. 1983. Threads of identity in Maxine Hong Kingston's *The woman warrior*. *Biography* 6, no. 1: 13–32.

Miller, Stuart Creighton. 1969. *The unwelcome immigrant: The American image of the Chinese, 1785–1882*. Berkeley, Los Angeles, Oxford: University of California Press.

Milvy, Erika. 1994. *Woman warrior* conquers the stage. *San Francisco Chronicle*, 15 May, Datebook: 38–39.

Mohanty, Chandra Talpade. 1984. Under Western eyes: Feminist scholarship and colonial discourses. *Boundary 2* 12–13, nos. 2–3: 333–58.

———. 1991. Cartographies of struggle: Third world women and the politics of feminism. In *Third world women and the politics of feminism*, edited by Chandra Talpade Mohanty, Ann Russo, and Lourdes Torres. Bloomington: Indiana University Press, 1–47.

———, Ann Russo, and Lourdes Torres, eds. 1991. *Third world women and the politics of feminism*. Bloomington: Indiana University Press.

Mohr, Nicholasa. 1985. *Rituals of survival: A woman's portfolio*. Houston: Arte Publico Press.

Moore, Nancy. 1995. Janet Yang. In *Notable Asian Americans*, edited by Helen Zia and Susan B. Gall. New York: Gale Research Inc., 430–31.

Moraga, Cherríe. 1981. La Güera. In *This bridge called my back: Writings by radical women of color*, edited by Cherríe Moraga and Gloria Anzaldúa. New York: Kitchen Table, Women of Color Press, 27–34.

———. 1983. *Loving in the war years*. Boston: South End Press.

———, and Gloria Anzaldúa, eds. 1981. *This bridge called my back: Writings by radical women of color*. New York: Kitchen Table, Women of Color Press.

Mori, Kiyoko. 1993. *Shizuko's daughter*. New York: Henry Holt and Co.

———. 1995. *The dream of water: A memoir*. New York: Henry Holt and Co.

Morrison, Toni. 1973. *Sula*. New York: Bantam.

———. 1987. *Beloved*. New York: Knopf.

Moy, James S. 1993. *Marginal sights: Staging the Chinese in America*. Studies in Theatre History and Culture. Iowa City: University of Iowa Press.

Moyers, Bill. 1990. Maxine Hong Kingston: Writer. *A world of ideas 2: Public opinions from private citizens*, edited by Andie Tucher. New York: Doubleday, 11–18.

Myers, Victoria. 1986. The significant fictivity of Maxine Hong Kingston's *The woman warrior*. *Biography* 9, no. 2: 112–25.

Nee, Victor G., and Brett de Bary Nee. 1972. *Longtime californ': A documentary study of an American Chinatown.* Stanford. Stanford University Press.

Neubauer, Carol E. 1983. Developing ties to the past: Photography and other sources of information in Maxine Hong Kingston's *China men. MELUS* 10, no. 4: 17–36.

Newton, Judith. 1994. Family/value: Reflections on a long revolution. *Victorian Studies* 37, no. 4: 567–81.

———. 1998. "White guys." (review essay) *Feminist Studies* 24 no 3: 572–98.

Ng, Fae Myenne. 1993. *Bone.* New York: Hyperion.

———. 1994. Interview by Jennifer Brostrom. *Contemporary Literary Criticism Yearbook* 81, 87–88.

Ng, Mei. 1998. *Eating Chinese Food Naked.* New York: Scribner.

Nga, Tiana Thi Thahn. 1995. The long march. From Wong to Woo: Asians in Hollywood. *Cineaste* 21, no. 4: 38–40.

Nguyen, Lan N. 1997. The next Amy Tan. A. *Magazine*, February/March, 46–51, 55.

Nunez, Sigrid. 1995. *A feather on the breath of god.* New York: HarperCollins.

Okihiro, Gary Y. 1994. *Margins and mainstreams: Asians in American history and culture.* Seattle: University of Washington Press.

Omatsu, Glenn. 1994. The "four prisons" and the movements of liberation: Asian American activism from the 1960s to the 1990s. In *The state of Asian America: Activism and resistance in the 1990s,* edited by Karin Aguilar-San Juan. Boston: South End Press, 19–69.

Omi, Michael, and Howard Winant. 1986. *Racial formation in the United States: From the 1960s to the 1980s.* New York: Routledge.

Ono, Kazuko. 1989. *Chinese women in a century of revolution: 1850–1950.* Edited by Joshua A. Fogel. Stanford: Stanford University Press.

Ono, Kent. 1995. Re/signing "Asian-America": Rhetorical problematics of nation. *Amerasia Journal* 21, nos. 1–2: 67–78.

Osajima, Keith. 1993. The Hidden Injuries of Race. In *Bearing dreams, shaping visions: Asian Pacific American perspectives,* edited by Linda Revilla, Gail Nomura, Shawn Wong and Shirley Hune. Pullman: Washington State University Press, 81–91.

Pascoe, Peggy. 1990. Gender systems in conflict: The marriages of mission-educated Chinese American women, 1847–1939. In *Unequal sisters: A multicultural reader in U.S. women's history,* edited by Ellen Carol DuBois and Vicki L. Ruiz. New York: Routledge, 123–40.

Payne, James Robert, ed. 1992. *Multicultural autobiography: American lives.* Knoxville: University of Tennessee Press.

Pearlman, Mickey, and Katherine Usher Henderson. 1990. Amy Tan. *Inter/view: Talks with America's writing women*. Lexington: University Press of Kentucky, 15–22.

Pérez-Torres, Rafael. 1995. *Movements in Chicano poetry: Against myths, against margins*. Cambridge: Cambridge University Press.

Pesquera, Beatriz M., and Denise M. Segura. 1993. There is no going back: Chicanas and feminism. In *Chicana critical issues*, edited by Norma Alarcón, Rafaela Castro, Emma Pérez, Beatriz Pesquera, Adaljiza Sosa Riddell, and Patricia Zavella. Berkeley: Third Woman Press, 95–115.

Powell, Linda C. 1983. Black macho and Black feminism. In *Home girls: A Black feminist anthology*, edited by Barbara Smith. Kitchen Table, Women of Color Press, 283–292.

Pratt, Minnie Bruce. 1984. Identity: Skin blood heart. In *Yours in struggle: Three feminist perspectives on anti-semitism and racism*, edited by Elly Bulkin, Minnie Bruce Pratt and Barbara Smith. New York: Firebrand Books, 9–63.

Quan, Kit Yuen. 1990. The girl who wouldn't sing. In *Making face, making soul: Haciendo caras*, edited by Gloria Anzaldúa. San Francisco: Aunt Lute Books, 212–20.

Quintana, Alvina. 1990. Politics, representation and the emergence of a Chicana aesthetic. *Cultural Studies* 4, no. 3: 257–63.

Rabine, Leslie W. 1987. No lost paradise: Social gender and symbolic gender in the writings of Maxine Hong Kingston. *Signs: Journal of Women in Culture and Society* 12, no. 3: 47–92.

Rampersad, Arnold. 1983. Biography, autobiography, and Afro-American culture. *Yale Review* 73, no. 1: 1–16.

Rayson, Ann. 1987. Beneath the mask: Autobiographies of Japanese-American women. *MELUS* 14, no. 1: 43–84.

Reagon, Bernice Johnson. 1982. My black mothers and sisters or on beginning a cultural autobiography. *Feminist Studies* 8, no. 1: 81–96.

Rebolledo, Tey Diana, and Eliana S. Rivero, eds. 1993. *Infinite divisions: An anthology of Chicana literature*. Tuscon: University of Arizona Press.

Reed, Ishmael, ed. 1997. *MultiAmerica: Essays on cultural wars and cultural peace*. New York: Viking Press.

Reid, Mark A. 1997. *Postnegritude visual and literary culture*. Albany: State University of New York Press.

Rich, Adrienne. 1986a. *Blood, bread, and poetry: Selected prose 1979–1985*. New York: W. W. Norton and Co.

————. 1986b. *Of woman born*. 10th ed. New York: W. W. Norton and Co.

Robnett, Belinda. 1997. *How long? how long? African American women in the struggle for Civil Rights*. New York: Oxford University Press.

Romero, Mary, Pierrette Hondagneu-Sotelo, and Vilma Ortiz, eds. 1997. *Challenging fronteras: Structuring Latina and Latino lives in the U.S.* New York: Routledge.

Rooks, Curtiss J., Jr., and Jon Panish. 1993. The dilemma of the ethnic writer: A case study of Maxine Hong Kingston. In *Bearing dreams, shaping visions: Asian Pacific American perspectives*, edited by Linda Revilla, Gail Nomura, Shawn Wong, and Shirley Hune. Pullman: Washington State University Press, 129–39.

Root, Deborah. 1996. *Cannibal culture: Art, appropriation, and the commodification of difference.* Boulder, CO: Westview Press.

Rose, Shirley K. 1987. Metaphors and myths of cross-cultural literary: Autobiographical narratives by Maxine Hong Kingston, Richard Rodriguez, and Malcolm X. *MELUS* 14, no. 1: 3–15.

Rowbotham, Sheila. 1973. *Women's consciousness, man's world.* London: Penguin.

Ruddick, Sara. 1980. Maternal thinking. *Feminist Studies* 6, no. 2: 342–367.

———. 1989. *Maternal thinking: Towards a politics of peace.* New York: Ballantine Books.

Ruth, Sheila. 1990. *Issues in feminism: An introduction to women's studies.* Mountain View, CA: Mayfield Publishing Co.

Rutherford, Jonathan. 1997. *Forever England: Reflections on masculinity and empire.* London: Lawrence and Wishart.

Said, Edward. 1978. *Orientalism.* New York: Pantheon.

Sakade, Florence, ed. 1958. *Peach boy and other Japanese children's favorite stories.* Tokyo: Charles E. Tuttle Company.

Saldívar, Ramon. 1990. *Chicano narrative: The dialectics of difference.* Madison: University of Wisconsin.

Sandmeyer, Elmer C. 1973. *The anti-Chinese movement in California.* Chicago: University of Chicago Press.

Sandoval, Chela. 1991. U.S. third world feminism: The theory and method of oppositional consciousness in the postmodern world. *Genders* 10 (spring): 1–24.

Sartre, Jean-Paul. 1969. *Being and nothingness: An essay on phenomenological ontology.* Translated by Hazel E. Barnes. London: Methuen.

Sasaki, R.A. 1991. *The loom and other stories.* St. Paul: Graywolf Press.

Sato, Gayle K. Fujita. 1991. Ghosts as Chinese-American constructs in Maxine Hong Kingston's *The woman warrior.* In *Haunting the house of fiction: Feminist perspectives on ghost stories by American women*, edited by Lynette Carpenter and Wendy K. Kolmar. Knoxville: University of Tennessee Press, 193–214.

Sayler, Lucy. 1995. *Laws harsh as tigers: Chinese immigrants and the shaping of modern immigration law.* Chapel Hill: University of North Carolina Press.

Schenck, Celeste. 1988. All of a piece: Women's poetry and autobiography. In *Life/lines: Theorizing women's autobiography*, edited by Bella Brodzki and Celeste Schenck. Ithaca and London: Cornell University Press, 281–305.

Schueller, Malini Johar. 1992. Theorizing ethnicity and subjectivity: Maxine Hong Kingston's *Tripmaster monkey* and Amy Tan's *The joy luck club*. *Genders* 15 (winter): 72–85.

Schwenger, Peter. 1984. *Phallic critiques: Masculinity and twentieth-century literature*. London: Routledge and Kegan Paul.

Scott, Daryl Michael. 1997. *Contempt and pity: Social policy and the image of the damaged Black psyche, 1880–1996*. Chapel Hill: University of North Carolina Press.

Scott, Joan W. 1989. Gender: A useful category of historical analysis. In *Coming to terms: feminism, theory, politics*, edited by Elizabeth Weed. New York: Routledge, 81–100.

Sergeant, Harriet. 1990. *Shanghai: Collision point of cultures 1918/1939*. New York: Crown Publishers, Inc.

Shigekuni, Julie. 1995. *A bridge between us*. New York: Anchor Books.

Shih, Nai-An. 1972. *Water margin*. Translated by J. H. Jackson. Two volumes in one. Cambridge, MA: C and T Co.

Shipler, David. 1997. *A Country of Strangers: Black and Whites in America*. New York: Alfred Knopf.

Showalter, Elaine. 1985. Feminist criticism in the wilderness. In *Feminist criticism: Essays on women, literature, theory*, edited by Elaine Showalter. New York: Pantheon Books, 243–70.

Silko, Leslie Marmon. 1981. *Storyteller*. New York: Seaver Books.

———. 1986. *Ceremony*. New York: Penguin Books. Originally published in 1977.

Siu, Bobby. 1981. *Woman of China: Imperialism and women's resistance 1900–1949*. London: Zed Press.

Siu, Paul C. P. 1987. *The Chinese laundryman*. Edited by John Kuo Wei Tchen. New York: New York University Press.

Skenazy, Paul, and Tera Martin, eds. 1998. *Conversations with Maxine Hong Kingston*. Jackson: University Press of Mississippi.

Sledge, Linda Ching. 1980. Maxine Hong Kingston's *China men*: The family historian as epic poet. *MELUS* 7, no. 4: 3–22.

Smith, Barbara, ed. 1983. *Home girls: A Black feminist anthology*. Kitchen Table, Women of Color Press.

Smith, Craig S. 1992. A rare shot at screen stardom for Asians. *Wall Street Journal*, 1 September, sec. A, p. 12.

Smith, Dorothy E. 1990. *The conceptual practices of power: A feminist sociology in knowledge*. Northeastern Series in Feminist Theory. Boston: Northeastern University Press.

Smith, Paul. 1993. *Clint Eastwood: A cultural production*. Minneapolis: University of Minnesota Press.

Smith, Sidonie. 1987. *A poetics of women's autobiography: Marginality and the fictions of self-representation*. Bloomington: Indiana University Press.

Sone, Monica. 1953. *Nisei daughter*. Seattle: University of Washington Press.

Spelman, Elizabeth. 1988. *Inessential woman: Problems of exclusion in feminist thought*. Boston: Beacon Press.

Spivak, Gayatri Chakravorty. 1988. "Can the subaltern speak?" In *Marxism and the Interpretation of Culture*, edited by Cary Nelson and Lawrence Grossberg. Urbana: University of Illinois Press, 271–313.

Ssu-ma, Ch'ien. 1961. *Records of the grand historian of China*. Translated by Burton Watson. 2 vols. New York: Columbia University Press.

Stetson, Nancy. 1993. Honoring her forebears. Review of *Bone*, by Fae Myenne Ng. *Chicago Tribune*, 4 April, 3.

Stockard, Janice E. 1989. *Daughters of the Canton delta: Marriage patterns and economic strategies in South China, 1860–1930*. Stanford: Stanford University Press.

Streitfeld, David. 1993. The "luck" of Amy Tan. *Washington Post*, 8 October, sec. F, p. 1 ff.

Sturdevant, Saundra Pollock, and Brenda Stoltzfus. 1992. *Let the good times roll: Prostitution and the U.S. military in Asia*. New York: The New Press.

Sumida, Stephen H. 1991. *And the view from the shore: Literary traditions of Hawai'i*. Seattle: University of Washington Press.

———. 1992. Protest and accommodation, self-satire, and self-effacement, and Monica Sone's *Nisei daughter*. In *Multicultural autobiography: American lives*, edited by James Robert Payne. Knoxville: University of Tennessee Press, 207–247.

Sun, Tzu. 1963. *The art of war*. Translated by Samuel B. Griffith. London: Oxford University Press.

Tachiki, Amy, Eddie Wong, Franklin Odo, and Buck Wong, eds. 1971. *Roots: An Asian American reader*. Los Angeles: UCLA Asian American Studies Center.

Tajima, Renee. 1989. Lotus blossoms don't bleed: Images of Asian women. In *Making waves: An anthology of writings by and about Asian American women*, edited by Asian Women United of California. Boston: Beacon Press, 308–317.

———. 1991. Moving the image: Asian American independent filmmaking, 1970–1990. In *Moving the image: Independent Asian Pacific American media arts*, edited by Russell Leong. Los Angeles: UCLA Asian American Studies Center and Visual Communications, 10–33.

Takaki, Ronald. 1983. *Pau hana: plantation life and labor in Hawaii, 1835–1920*. Honolulu: University of Hawai'i Press.

———. 1989. *Strangers from a different shore: A history of Asian Americans*. Boston: Little, Brown and Co.

———. 1993. *A different mirror: A history of multicultural America.* Boston: Little, Brown and Co.

Takeda, Izumo, Miyoshi Shoraku, and Naomi Shoraku. 1971. *Kanadehon Chushingura/The treasury of royal retainers.* Translated by Donald Keene. New York: Columbia University Press.

Talbot, Stephen. 1990. Talking story: Maxine Hong Kingston rewrites the American dream. *Image*, 24 June, 6 ff.

Tan, Amy. 1989. *The joy luck club.* New York: G. P. Putnam's Sons.

———. 1990a. Amy Tan on Amy Tan and *The joy luck club. California State Library Foundation Bulletin* 31 April: 1–10.

———. 1990b. The *Booklist* interview: Amy Tan. By Donna Seaman. *Booklist*, 1 October, 256–57.

———. 1991a. Lost lives of women. *Life*, 1 April, 90–91.

———. 1991b. Lecture for Asian American Student Union, Van Hise Hall. Madison, Wisconsin, 11 April.

———. 1991c. *The kitchen god's wife.* New York: G. P. Putnam's Sons.

———. 1991d. Amy Tan: An interview. By Barbara Somogyi and David Stanton. *Poets and Writers* 19, no. 5: 24–32.

———. 1995. *The hundred secret senses.* New York: G.P. Putnam's Sons.

———. 1997. Required reading and other dangerous subjects. In *Out of the mold: Independent voices breaking out of the mold*, edited by Jill Perstein. Tarrytown, NY: American Booksellers Association, 133–48.

Tannenbaum, Abby. 1993. Getting to the Marrow. *New York*, 25 January, 26.

Thompson, Becky, and Sangeeta Tyagi, eds. 1996. *Names we call home: Autobiography on racial identity.* New York: Routledge.

Thompson, Phyllis Hoge. 1983. This is the story I heard: A conversation with Maxine Hong Kingston and Earll Kingston. *Biography* 6, no. 1: 1–12.

Thurer, Shari L. 1994. *The myths of motherhood: How culture reinvents the good mother.* New York: Penguin Books.

Tong, Benjamin. 1977. Critic of admirer sees dumb racist. *San Francisco Journal*, 11 May, 6–7.

Tong, Benson. 1994. *Unsubmissive women: Chinese prostitutes in nineteenth-century San Francisco.* Norman, Oklahoma: University of Oklahoma Press.

Umansky, Lauri. 1996. *Motherhood reconceived: Feminism and the legacies of the sixties.* New York and London: New York University Press.

Van Deburg, William L. 1992. *New day in Babylon: The Black power movement and American culture.* Chicago: University of Chicago Press.

Wade-Gayles, Gloria. 1984. The truths of our mothers' lives: Mother-daughter relationships in Black women's fiction. *Sage* 1 no. 2: 8–12.

Walker, Alice. 1983. *In Search of our mothers' gardens*. New York: Harvest/HBJ.

Wallace, Michele. 1990. *Black macho and the myth of the superwoman*. London: Verso Press. Originally published in 1979

Walters, Suzanna D. 1992. *Lives together/worlds apart: Mothers and daughters in popular culture*. Berkeley: University of California Press.

Wang, Alfred S. 1988. Maxine Hong Kingston's reclaiming of America: The birthright of the Chinese American male. *South Dakota Review* 26, no. 1: 18–29.

Watson, Rubie S., and Patricia Buckley Ebrey, eds. 1991. *Marriage and inequality in Chinese society*. Berkeley, Los Angeles, Oxford: University of California Press.

Wei, William. 1993. *The Asian American movement*. Asian American and Culture Series, vol. 1. Philadelphia: Temple University Press.

West, Cornel. 1993. *Keeping faith: Philosophy and race in America*. New York: Routledge.

White, E. Frances. 1995. Africa on my mind: Gender, counterdiscourse, and African American nationalism. In *Words of fire: An anthology of African-American feminist thought*, edited by Beverly Guy-Sheftall. New York: The New Press, 504–24.

Williams, Raymond. 1970. *The English novel: From Dickens to Lawrence*. New York: Oxford University Press.

———. 1983. *Towards 2000*. London: Chatto and Windus/Hogarth Press.

Wing, Adrien Katherine, ed. 1997. *Critical race feminism: A reader*. New York: New York University Press.

Wolf, Margery, and Roxane Witke. 1975. *Women in Chinese society*. Stanford: Stanford University Press.

———. 1974. Chinese women: Old skills in a new context. In *Woman, culture, and society*, edited by Michele Zimbalist Rosaldo and Louise Lamphere. Stanford: Stanford University Press, 157–72.

Wong, Diane Yen-Mai. 1993. Survival. Review of *Bone*, by Fae Myenne Ng. *Belles Lettres: A Review of Books by Women* 8, no. 3: 21.

———, and Dennis Hayashi. 1989. Behind unmarked doors: Developments in the garment industry. In *Making waves: An anthology of writings by and about Asian American women*, edited by Asian Women United of California. Boston: Beacon Press, 148–158.

Wong, Eugene Franklin. 1978. *On visual media racism: Asians in the American motion pictures*. New York: Arno Press.

Wong, Hertha D. 1994. Plains Indian names and "the autobiographical act." In *Autobiography and Postmodernism*, edited by Kathleen Ashley, Leigh Gilmore and Gerald Peters. Amherst: The University of Massachusetts Press.

Wong, Jade Snow. 1989. *Fifth Chinese daughter*. Seattle: University of Washington Press. Originally published in 1945.

Wong, K. Scott. 1998. Cultural defenders and brokers: Chinese responses to the Anti-Chinese Movement. In *Claiming America: Constructing Chinese American identities during the Exclusion Era*, edited by K. Scott Wong and Sucheng Chan. Philadelphia: Temple University Press, 127–64.

Wong, Norman. 1994. *Cultural revolution.* New York: Persea Books.

Wong, Sau-ling Cynthia. 1988. Necessity and extravagance in Maxine Hong Kingston's *The woman warrior*: Art and the ethnic experience. *MELUS* 15, no. 1: 3–26.

———. 1992. Autobiography as guided Chinatown tour? Maxine Hong Kingston's *The woman warrior* and the Chinese-American autobiographical controversy. In *Multicultural autobiography: American lives*, edited by James Robert Payne. Knoxville: University of Tennessee Press, 248–79.

———. 1993. *Reading Asian-American literature: From necessity to extravagance.* Princeton: Princeton University Press.

———. 1995. "Sugar sisterhood": Situating the Amy Tan phenomenon. In *The ethnic canon: Histories, institutions, and interventions*, edited by David Palumbo-Liu. Minneapolis: University of Minnesota Press, 174–210.

Wong, Shawn. 1991. *Homebase.* New York: Plume/Penguin. Originally published in 1979.

Wong, Su-ling [pseud.], and Earl Herbert Cressy. 1952. *Daughter of Confucius: A personal history.* New York: Farrar, Straus and Giroux.

Wong, Suzi. 1977. Maxine Hong Kingston's *The Woman Warrior. Amerasia* 4, no. 1: 165–67.

Woo, Deborah. 1989. The gap between striving and achieving: The case of Asian American women. In *Making waves: An anthology of writings by and about Asian American women*, edited by Asian Women United of California. Boston: Beacon Press, 185–96.

Woo, Merle. 1981. Letter to Ma. In *This bridge called my back: Writings by radical women of color*, edited by Cherríe Moraga and Gloria Anzaldúa. New York: Kitchen Table, Women of Color Press, 140–47.

Wood, Julia T. 1999. *Gendered lives: Communication, gender, and culture.* 3rd edition. Belmont, CA: Wadsworth Publishing Company.

Wu, Cheng-en. 1977–1983. *The journey to the West.* 4 vols. Translated by Anthony C. Yu. Chicago: University of Chicago Press.

Wu, Cheng-Tsu, ed. 1972. *"Chink!" A documentary history of Anti-Chinese prejudice in America.* New York: World Publishing Company.

Wu, Pei-Yu. 1990. *The confucian's progress: Autobiographical writings in traditional China.* Princeton: Princeton University Press.

Xu, Ben. 1994. Memory and the ethnic self: Reading Amy Tan's *The joy luck club. MELUS* 19, no. 1: 3–19.

Yamada, Mitsuye. 1981. Invisibility is an unnatural disaster: Reflections of an Asian American woman. In *This bridge called my back: Writings by radical women of color*, edited by Cherrie Moraga and Gloria Anzaldúa. New York: Kitchen Table, Women of Color Press, 35–40.

———. 1988. *Desert run: Poems and stories*. Kitchen Table, Women of Color Press.

———. 1990. The cult of the "perfect" language: Censorship by class, gender, and race. In *Sowing ti leaves: Writings by multi-cultural women*. Irvine: Multi-Cultural Women Writers of Orange County.

Yamamoto, Hisaye. 1988. *Seventeen syllables and other stories*. New York: Kitchen Table, Women of Color Press.

Yamamoto, Traise. 1998. *Masking selves, making subjects: Japanese American women, identity, and the body*. Berkeley: University of California Press.

Yamanaka, Lois-Ann. 1996. *Wild meat and the bully burgers*. New York: Harvest Books.

———. 1997. *Blu's hanging*. New York: Farrar, Straus and Giroux.

Yamauchi, Wakako. 1994. *Songs my mother taught me: Stories, plays, and memoir*. New York: Feminist Press at CUNY.

Yanagisako, Sylvia. 1995. Transforming orientalism: Gender, nationality, and class in Asian American studies. In *Naturalizing power: Essays in feminist cultural analysis*, edited by Sylvia Yanagisako and Carol Delaney. New York: Routledge, 275–98.

Yang, Belle. 1994. *Baba: A return to China upon my father's shoulders*. New York: Harcourt Brace and Co.

Yang, June Unjoo. 1996. Reading between the lines. A. *Magazine*, February/March, 34–39.

Yoshikawa, Yoko. 1994. The heat is on Miss Saigon coalition: Organizing across race and sexuality. In *The state of Asian America: Activism and resistance in the 1990s*, edited by Karin Aguilar-San Juan. Boston: South End Press, 275–94.

Younger, Joseph D. 1993. The joy luck writer. *Amtrak Express*. July/August, 33–36.

Yu, Connie Young. 1989. The world of our grandmothers. In *Making waves: An anthology of writings by and about Asian American women*, edited by Asian Women United of California. Boston: Beacon Press, 33–41.

Yu, Renqiu. 1992. *To save China, to save ourselves: The Chinese Hand Laundry Alliance of New York*. Philadelphia, Temple University Press.

Yung, Judy. 1986. *Chinese women of America: A pictorial history*. Seattle: University of Washington Press.

———. 1989. Appendix: A chronology of Asian American history. In *Making waves: An anthology of writings by and about Asian American women*, edited by Asian Women United of California. Boston: Beacon Press, 423–32.

————. 1990. The social awakening of Chinese American women as reported in *Chung Sai Yat Po*, 1900–1911. In *Unequal sisters: A multicultural reader in U.S. women's history*, edited by Ellen Carol DuBois and Vicki L. Ruiz. New York: Routledge, 195–207.

————. 1995. *Unbound feet: a social history of Chinese women in San Francisco.* Berkeley: University of California Press.

Zhao, Xiaojian. 1996. Chinese American women defense workers in World War II. *California History* 75, no. 2: 138–53.

Zinn, Maxine Baca. 1995. Chicano men and masculinity. In *Men's lives*, edited by Michael S. Kimmel and Michael A. Messner. Boston: Allyn and Bacon, 33–41.

————, and Bonnie Thornton Dill. 1996. Theorizing difference from multiracial feminism. *Feminist Studies* 22, no. 2: 321–31.

————, eds. 1994. *Women of color in U.S. society.* Philadelphia: Temple University Press.

INDEX

A

abuse
  fathers and 200, 204
  mothers and 175
  of self 131, 242
  sexual 82
  speaking against 34
  women and 100, 151, 204
academic institutions 25–26, 55, 241
academic "training" 25, 189
acculturation 165. *See also* assimilation
  American Dream and 211
  concerns and critiques of 51, 94, 99, 110, 170
  gender roles and 75
  of Chinese in America 15, 120
activism 32, 85–86, 239
  cultural 86–87. *See also* Asian American Movement
  social-political 34, 41, 97, 104
  women and 97
  writing and 195
Adams, Alice 36
addiction 68, 236
African Americans. *See* Blacks
agency
  formation of 111, 144, 145, 151, 153, 173
  learning 50, 135, 138, 175, 181
  loss of 154
  narratives of 243

women and 35, 82, 126, 134, 189, 203, 234
agricultural work 73
Aiiieeeee! (book) 24, 87–88
alienation. *See also* identity: loss of
  in *The Joy Luck Club* 154, 164, 168–170, 181, 183–184
  of marginalized people 106–107, 164
  women and 104, 152, 182
Allen, Paula Gunn 132
Almaguer, Tomás 69
American Dream 78, 168, 202–203, 211, 219
Americanization 15, 112, 164–166, 171. *See also* acculturation
Anderson, Kay 236
Ang, Ien 51, 55, 115, 122, 169
Angel Island 72, 97, 163
Anzaldúa, Gloria 26, 39, 242
Arendt, Hannah 138
Asian American Movement
  Asian women and 32, 95, 96
  Berkeley and 41
  capitalism and 33, 86
  historical context of 85
  sexism in 96
Asian American women
  activism and 32, 34. *See also* Asian American Movement
  collective consciousness 23, 27